APOCALYPSE IN CRISIS

Liverpool Science Fiction Texts and Studies, 72

Liverpool Science Fiction Texts and Studies

Editors
David Seed, *University of Liverpool*
Sherryl Vint, *University of California Riverside*

Editorial Board
Stacey Abbott, *University of Roehampton*
Mark Bould, *University of the West of England*
Veronica Hollinger, *Trent University*
Roger Luckhurst, *Birkbeck College, University of London*
Andrew Milner, *Monash University*
Andy Sawyer, *University of Liverpool*

Recent titles in the series

55. Chris Pak, *Terraforming: Ecopolitical Transformations and Environmentalism in Science Fiction*
56. Lars Schmeink, *Biopunk Dystopias: Genetic Engineering, Society, and Science Fiction*
57. Shawn Malley, *Excavating the Future: Archaeology and Geopolitics in Contemporary North American Science Fiction Film and Television*
58. Derek J. Thiess, *Sport and Monstrosity in Science Fiction*
59. Glyn Morgan and Charul Palmer-Patel, *Sideways in Time: Critical Essays on Alternate History Fiction*
60. Curtis D. Carbonell, *Dread Trident: Tabletop Role-Playing Games and the Modern Fantastic*
61. Upamanyu Pablo Mukherjee, *Final Frontiers: Science Fiction and Techno-Science in Non-Aligned India*
62. Gavin Miller, *Science Fiction and Psychology*
63. Andrew Milner and J.R. Burgmann, *Science Fiction and Climate Change: A Sociological Approach*
64. Regina Yung Lee and Una McCormack (eds), *Biology and Manners: Essays on the Worlds and Works of Lois McMaster Bujold*
65. Joseph Norman, *The Culture of "The Culture": Utopian Processes in Iain M. Banks's Space Opera Series*
66. Jeremy Withers, *Futuristic Cars and Space Bicycles: Contesting the Road in American Science Fiction*
67. Sabrina Mittermeier and Mareike Spychala, *Fighting for the Future: Essays on Star Trek: Discovery*
68. Richard Howard, *Space for Peace: Fragments of the Irish Troubles in the Science Fiction of Bob Shaw and James White*
69. Thomas Connolly, *After Human: A Critical History of the Human in Science Fiction from Shelley to Le Guin*
70. John Rieder, *Speculative Epistemologies: An Eccentric Account of SF from the 1960s to the Present*
71. Sarah Annes Brown, *Shakespeare and Science Fiction*

APOCALYPSE IN CRISIS

Fiction from *The War of the Worlds*
to *Dead Astronauts*

CHRISTOPHER PALMER

LIVERPOOL UNIVERSITY PRESS

First published 2021 by
Liverpool University Press
4 Cambridge Street
Liverpool
L69 7ZU

Copyright © 2021 Christopher Palmer

Christopher Palmer has asserted the right to be identified as
the author of this book in accordance with the Copyright, Designs and
Patents Act 1988.

All rights reserved. No part of this book may be reproduced, stored in a
retrieval system, or transmitted, in any form or by any means, electronic,
mechanical, photocopying, recording, or otherwise, without the prior
written permission of the publisher.

British Library Cataloguing-in-Publication data
A British Library CIP record is available

ISBN 978-1-80085-604-2 cased

Typeset by Carnegie Book Production, Lancaster
Printed and bound by CPI Group (UK) Ltd, Croydon CR0 4YY

Thanks for advice and encouragement to
Laura Booth, Ewan Coffey, Steve Moline,
Kim Stanley Robinson, Christabel Scaife, Iain Topliss
and, especially, Marisa Palmer.

Contents

Introduction: Apocalypse Now and Then   1

Part 1: The Nineteenth Century to the Postwar Disaster Novels

1. Modern Apocalypses and Modernism: Enter Science Fiction   57
2. The Postwar Disaster Novels: Apocalypse Contained   83

Part 2: Post-Imperial Subjects

3. Style and Immolation: J. G. Ballard   127
4. Apocalypse in 1969: Brian Aldiss and Angela Carter   157
5. Darker Imaginations, Harder Lessons: Anna Kavan and Doris Lessing   173

Part 3: Resistance and Revision

6. Apocalypse, Comedy, Multiplicity: Arno Schmidt, Anthony Burgess and Ursula K. Le Guin   209
7. Apocalypse and Everyday Life: Tom Perrotta and Douglas Coupland   239
8. Apocalypse in the Contemporary World City: Don DeLillo and China Miéville   265
9. Beyond Apocalypse – Two Paths: Jeff VanderMeer and Kim Stanley Robinson   295

Works Cited   325

Index   337

Introduction
Apocalypse Now and Then

> The apocalypse is part of our ideological baggage. It is an aphrodisiac. It is a nightmare. It is a commodity like any other. ... It is ever-present, but never 'actual': a second reality, an image that we construct for ourselves, an incessant product of our fantasy, a catastrophe of the mind.
>
> (Hans Magnus Enzensberger)

> We have to understand it, of course, this catastrophe; to understand it, we have to imagine it, so we need the imaginative arts. But we also need to justify it and forgive it, this catastrophe, however minimally. Why did it happen, this mad act of Nature, this crazed human moment? Well, at least it produced art. Perhaps, in the end, that is what catastrophe is *for*.
>
> (Julian Barnes)

The present is a good time and a difficult time – good because difficult – to survey and assess the recent history of apocalyptic fiction. This book begins with a prelude on the nineteenth century, and then follows the story from 1945 to now. It is a story that is intertwined with conditions and confusions of modernity – the relations of secular and religious; the unrelenting pressure of crisis; the vicissitudes of revolution and revolutionary hope for transformation; the contrary paths of the individual subject towards more emphatic assertion, and towards absence and loss; the gulf between everyday life and the global abstractions of system.

Apocalypse is so hard to define, nowadays, as to be itself in crisis as a concept and an imaginative resource. The epithet 'apocalyptic' is widely and sometimes wildly used to signify a worrying disaster or threat. The definition of apocalypse to be offered here will be tentative and selective. (Most definitions of apocalypse are in fact selective, though frequently not tentative enough.) We have to deal with an orientation of the mind, a 'set' towards apocalypse as Frank Kermode (1985) put it, long-lasting, therefore deep-seated, and often murky in its motivations and impulses; but, fortunately, we are also dealing with a form of narrative, and the latter, at least, can be defined in its traditional form. We can begin from there. The varied shapes, the recourses and experiments of modern fictions of apocalypse are usefully seen in the light of traditional apocalypse. Modern apocalyptic fictions can neither reproduce the traditional form of the narrative nor escape from its cultural shadow. The attempt to escape from the traditional form prompts new inventions and insights and expresses new, often shifting attitudes, but also reveals blockages and contradictions, and sometimes pursues unholy agendas.

Apocalypse threatens but it can be emotionally and imaginatively attractive, for reasons that are perennial as well as topical. Sudden, unexpected transformation is part of our recent historical experience – the fall of communism, 9/11 and its aftermaths, the Covid-19 virus lockdown. Its forms are redolent of traditional apocalypse: the first transformation altered the direction of history and appeared to usher in a New Jerusalem of freedom and independence, the second launched indiscriminate death and destruction, the third an emphatically global threat and experience. Apocalypse is, arguably, in crisis because it is so hard to distinguish from – as it happens – crisis, crisis being the concept we use to try to understand the threats and emergencies that bring about change in the contemporary world: crisis as the vehicle and vector of modernity. Contemporary modernity lives in crises and thinks in terms of crises. To define our condition and our prospects at a given moment is to define the smorgasbord of crises, emergencies and global threats on offer, some enticing, most of them unappetising. Preoccupation with crises can decline into what Alain Peyrefitte called 'spasmophilia'.[1] Apocalypse, on the other hand, aspires to be – to be imagined as – total and unrepeatable: The End. It is threatened by this competition among possible endings or at least (how can we tell, without knowing the future?) of likely really bad outcomes. The figure of apocalypse, an imagined, palpable global disaster, is itself undermined by this condition of multiple crises. Crisis is not apocalypse, but the condition of fearing and anticipating apocalypse and the condition of

---

[1] Cited in Hazareesingh 2015, 240.

habituation to its possibility are both shaped by thinking in terms of crisis. Contemporary apocalyptic fiction has increasingly adjusted to this condition, by way of irony and comedy, and by subjecting an apocalyptic narrative to the competition of other narratives when it occurs in a text stranded of different stories.

Then again, apocalypse in its wholesale decisiveness can serve as a welcome relief from the frustration and anxiety of prolonged crisis. Equally, because apocalypse is habitual, a reflex and a long tradition of narrative, this acts as a spur to inventiveness, so as to distinguish any given new imagination of wholesale disaster from the others that have been imagined, and to respond to the urgency of new threats. Apocalypse is available for the release of ambivalent or aggressive feelings; a provocation to scepticism, satire and critique, because of the paradox that the ultimate and final end is imagined so often; a field of fiction that is open to invention of the wildest kind, but often haunted by historical fact and threat, since apocalypse encroaches on the real and actual.

Apocalypse in Crisis is centred on a discussion of apocalyptic fiction since the 1950s. It's easy to exaggerate the stresses and complications of the contemporary, since they are happening all around and inside one, but it does seem clear that the feeling, the imagination and the possible fact of apocalypse are all of them more intense in the present age. It's not possible to define 'the contemporary' precisely; in *Apocalypse in Crisis*, the contemporary is taken to stretch back to the 1980s, when the cultural revolution of the 1960s had begun to lose impetus or settle, and the conditions of the postmodern had begun to strengthen and to infiltrate consciousness. As regards fiction, the differences between the most recent decade and that of the 1980s seem to me to be less marked than the continuities. 'Modern' is taken to refer to the era from the nineteenth century to the present. Contemporary apocalyptic fiction is subject to the anxieties and habits that prompt us to reach for 'apocalyptic' very frequently – whenever an emergency is seen as a crisis ready to tip towards disaster. Apocalyptic fiction also traces a narrative arc, however, and this arc can be sketched by looking at traditional apocalypse, even though modern and contemporary apocalyptic fiction have diverged from traditional apocalypse in many ways. By looking at traditional apocalypse and by tracing the narrative arc of apocalyptic fiction, we can clarify the complexities and confusions of our habituation to the apocalyptic.

Given that disaster is a constant in human history, it is understandable that humans try to imagine how it might have meaning and even bring about a better state of affairs.[2] Apocalypse is inescapable to think with, in modern times, yet in modern times it has become more difficult to think with. It has been secularised, and thereby deprived of some of the features that organised and delimited it, and limitation is important just because apocalypse is so global if not limitless as a prospect. Its sequential narrative structure – catastrophe, aftermath, transcendence – is jeopardised by those contemporary conditions that make linear narrative seem inadequate. (Jeff VanderMeer's *Dead Astronauts* (2019),[3] one of the last novels to be discussed in *Apocalypse in Crisis*, dispenses with sequential narrative, and takes us beyond apocalypse: the catastrophe it treats is apocalyptic in the broad sense, but has destroyed linear temporality.) The imagination of wholesale destruction, even of an end to human life, visits us often enough, encouraged by our own fears and desires and stimulated by the possibility of nuclear war and the grim progress of climate change, but it is now harder to see the wholesale destruction as succeeded by a New Jerusalem – a heavenly city, a perfect society of the just – as in the traditional narrative. The traditional structure of apocalypse, with its reassuring, delimiting and determined features, stemming from the fact that someone (indeed, Someone) was in control of its unfolding, has lost its power. Versions of the New Jerusalem are ambiguous and hesitant, or associate transcendence with self-immolation. There is a split between the fundamentalist revival of 'traditional' apocalyptic thinking in America, and in the Islamic world, and the scepticism and metafictional awareness of many of the most inventive apocalyptic fictions of recent times. There is a split between fictions that reiterate with increased emphasis that the apocalyptic catastrophe involves a contest between good and evil and leads to a New Jerusalem, or at least to the salvation of the elect, and fictions that imagine catastrophes in which good and evil are irrelevant, and the disaster is so complete as to make mere survival of at least some humans and some relics of civilisation the best that can be expected. Narratives involving a clash of good and evil ask for a certainty about the individual hero or anti-hero (or superhero) about which the novel as a form of fiction has often been uneasy, and that is thrown into uncertainty by contemporary investigations of the depths or the slipperiness of the

---

[2] And it does bring about an improvement, according to Walter Scheidel, in the ironic sense that only disaster ever brings about a significant levelling of inequality: *The Great Leveller: Violence and the History of Inequality from the Stone Age to the 21st Century* (2017); see Runciman 2018, 78. Hence apocalyptic and millenarian movements and narratives, by no means confined to the Christian world.

[3] Dates given in parentheses in the text are those of first publication.

subject. There is heightened awareness both of the historical possibility – even likelihood – of apocalypse, and of the contrasting fact that apocalypse is something that we imagine, repeatedly and, even, with a certain enthusiasm. And the transcendental aspects of apocalypse persist; secularisation is incomplete.[4]

Since H. G. Wells, the enterprise of apocalyptic fiction has mainly been carried forward by science fiction, and this enterprise has largely involved the invention of images and story types that answer to the challenge of secularising apocalypse. The science-fictional treatments of apocalypse that followed Wells, notably in the aftermath of the Second World War, for example in the novels of John Wyndham, Nevil Shute and George R. Stewart,[5] explored the rationally predictable consequences of imagined catastrophe. At first, the reaction against, and beyond, the postwar fictions of disaster happened within science fiction, in novels by J. G. Ballard and Brian Aldiss; then its scope expanded and deepened, as part of a general counter-cultural reaction against prevailing codes and assumptions. The counter-cultural still exerts its power in more recent fictions, but many also resort to an enhanced realism, one that embraced some of the innovations of modernism. This enhanced realism, often sceptical or in the vein of comedy, is accompanied in recent fictions of apocalypse by more radical departures. Rather than encountering reasoned extrapolations and depictions of the sober struggle to survive or rebuild, we tend to encounter shifting visions – versions of what A. S. Byatt in *Ragnarök* (2011, 44) terms the 'inordinate', some of them brutal, some of them comic or whimsical. *Apocalypse in Crisis* explores the likelihood that these fictional inventions and complexities are responses to a general crisis of apocalypse. Contemporary science-fiction apocalypses have often partaken of the extremism and scepticism that mark contemporary apocalyptic fiction outside science fiction. Contemporary culture provokes the imagination of apocalypse but makes it harder to shape into fiction. Structures (for instance, those of traditional apocalypse) and boundaries are less distinct; apocalypse threatens to blur into crisis, or crises; something like the narrative form

---

[4] Koerner 2008, 61–62 discusses the shifting meanings of the term. A religious object is secularised when it is appropriated by the state, for instance, losing its ecclesiastical context and religious aura; but then it ends up in a gallery, grouped with other masterpieces, and gains a different kind of aura ('the gallery picture as secularized cult image, the museum as secularized church' (62)). The secular transforms rather than abolishes the sacred: see also Chadwick 1975 whose theme is that the secular and the religious each define the other in a continuing boundary dispute.

[5] Further discussed in chapter 2.

is still available, but it has to be reinvented: a complicated and even hazardous process. Tim Park: 'Whenever a magical world crumbles and its demons are put to flight, you can be sure they will turn up again elsewhere, and without the reassuring distance old boundaries guaranteed.'[6]

Sensational disaster and destruction are exciting, and the desolation or dystopia that is brought about by many an imagined catastrophe is tempting, too, since it frees one from democracy, mundane social negotiation, the pressure of population, the stress of city living and much more. Contemporary apocalyptic fiction is the field of ironic critiques of apocalypse and its place in our culture, and of relentless imaginations of its limitless power, but also the field of easy dystopian formulas and conventions, and of the expression of fascinating but questionable agendas and impulses.

The sheer volume of imaginations of apocalypse is a kind of embarrassment for the self-conscious creator of yet another version, of yet another imagination of what is after all meant to be a unique event in its finality. Apocalypse is simultaneously shop-soiled and imminent (and immanent, too). This doesn't mean we should give up on the term as applied to contemporary imaginings, and confine it to traditional apocalypse with its recognisable list of features. It means that contemporary apocalyptic fiction is the scene of a series of critiques of our habituation to apocalypse, *and* a series of recourses that set out to reimagine features of traditional apocalypse, such as the arrival of the New Jerusalem, and the transcendence (not merely the end) of History, which the arrival of the New Jerusalem traditionally entailed.

As was noted earlier, the contemporary world has seen a revival of *traditional* apocalyptic thinking, and acting, in certain quarters both in the Western and in the Islamic world, and one that has arguably been stimulated by the apparent hegemony of secularism.[7] The perennial attraction of apocalypse to the underdog is understandable, since those who are put upon and oppressed are scheduled to replace their

---

[6] Park 2015, 22. Later discussion will note changes in the depiction of monsters in apocalyptic fiction from Wells to Miéville and VanderMeer, and also how magic (to call it that in shorthand) re-enters apocalyptic fiction (in Le Guin, Miéville, and Coupland).

[7] Lundberg 2009 details the popularity of *Left Behind* (60 million copies sold) among many Christians in the United States; Manne 2016 discusses Dabiq (the online voice of the Islamic State of Iraq and Syria (ISIS)) and shows the centrality of apocalypse to the world-view of the movement; Banville 2019 discusses Roberto Calasso's argument that Islamic and other terrorisms are founded on a hatred of secular society.

oppressors. As regards the contemporary attraction of 'The Rapture' to those who believe they will survive it, it does seem that there has been a hardening and narrowing, that an ethical poverty has taken hold, a desire more for revenge than for justice.[8] It is arguable that in their cruelty and narrowness these revivals also exhibit the crisis of contemporary apocalypse.

Apocalypse has been both a very broad and persistent field of narration and interpretation, and also something controversial, hard to control, driven to the periphery. This tension has existed in varying ways since Augustine established the orthodox Christian position, that no cataclysm was to be expected any time soon. It has persisted up to modern times, when apocalypse attracted restive and unorthodox spirits such as Blake and Lawrence, not to mention a variety of cultists short on rationality and knowledgeable about a select range of texts and prophecies but about little else. Apocalyptic and, more broadly, millenarian thinking has been strong in English and American culture since the seventeenth century, yet even when this thinking is central in the sense of being very widely accepted, it is also subversive and disruptive. Apocalyptic and millenarian thinking tends to flare up as a challenge to the normality of the ongoing. When the modern world – the world of scientific rationality, capitalism and democracy – is born and matures, so, accompanying this complex transformation of life on Earth, there is born a series of dissents and critiques, which are, paradoxically, part of modernity as well as against it: socialism, romanticism, the modern movement in art and literature. This interchange affects the imagination of apocalypse, at the same time reasserting and secularising the religious view of end time, sweeping away ordinary middle-class or urban life, or labouring to re-establish it.[9]

---

[8] Tom Perrotta's *The Leftovers*, discussed in chapter 7, offers a more humane take on 'The Rapture'.

[9] The attempt to secularise apocalypse has a long history and only its later phases are discussed here. Delumeau 1995 discusses 'novels of the flood' from the late seventeenth century, for instance: Thomas Burnet, *Sacred Theory of the Earth* (1691), or William Whiston, *A New Theory of the Earth* (1696) in which the Flood is caused by a comet, a standby of more recent apocalyptic fictions.

Crisis and Apocalypse

> I can only see one emergency following upon another as wave follows upon wave.
>
> (H. A. L. Fisher)

> 'New Yorkers,' Willett puffed sadly. 'They will not be told. Everything left to the last moment. [...] Too much individuality. Too much incredulity. New Yorkers have seen everything and live in a perpetual state of apprehension. There is nothing new to make them feel new fear. Millions dead, I have no doubt.'
>
> (Anthony Burgess, *The End of the World News*)

Since the great political revolutions, with their mixed effects, the modern imagination of apocalypse is less likely to deliver a better and more just society in this world, after the cataclysm, than did the imagination of traditional Christian millenarianism, in which society was to be perfected in order to be ready for the Last Days, and the subsequent rule of the Saints.[10] Apocalypse in the modern imagination is frequently brought about by alien invasion or impersonal forces of nature; it is neither the work of an ultimately benevolent god nor the achievement of revolutionaries. This impersonal, non-human figure of catastrophe expresses the feeling that history is something that happens to us, as if no human agent were involved, a feeling that is plausible enough given the conditions of contemporary history and the contemporary economy. Hence the possibility that imagination of a catastrophic End blocks other kinds of thinking about the future, exerting the authority, and the attraction, of the single and unqualified. Apocalypse, involving not merely catastrophe but transformation and the prospect of a new beginning or new state of being, begins to be overshadowed by Doom. A kind of nihilism threatens. Narrative of unqualified doom takes us

---

[10] See the discussions of the anticipation of the Last Days during the Reformation in MacCulloch 2004, for instance at 152–155, 550–555. Perfecting society might involve burning witches (568), but MacCulloch emphasises the tension and excitement that prevailed in the early years of disruption, and fuelled activism of many kinds ('It was wonderfully exciting' (155): more or less what Wordsworth and many others felt in the early phases of the French Revolution). This excitement and activism as the End approaches is rare in twentieth-century fictions of apocalypse; the exception is the attitude of some American believers in the coming End, who think that the worse the situation brought about by global warming, the sooner the Last Days will arrive; see, for instance, MacCulloch 2017, 6.

beyond apocalypse. It is significant that two novels, *The Scar* and *Kraken*, that qualify this picture and deal with the possibility of apocalypse in an energetic this-worldly way are by China Miéville, a Marxist, author also of *October: The Story of the Russian Revolution* (2017). Revolution that really occurs replaces apocalypse that might have occurred in *The Scar*, and the other novels in Miéville's Bas-Lag trilogy, *Perdido Street Station* and *Iron Council*, also dramatise popular revolt and find ingenious images for its continuing potential in the face of its defeat. In *From Utopia to Apocalypse* (2010), Peter Y. Paik investigates a variety of recent apocalyptic films, comics and mangas with the need for revolution, as well as its tragic violence, always in view. His discussion is examined later in this introduction.

Yet the notion of revolution – violent rupture that changes history and ushers in the reign of justice: a form of secular apocalypse – has now lost much of its force in the general culture.[11] So, arguably, has the broader assumption attributed by Tony Judt (2005, 198) to radicals of right and left that 'genuine change *necessarily* led through root-and-branch destruction'. Revolutionary will took possession of apocalypse: as Colin Jones (2003, 421–422) puts it, the French revolutionaries attempted 'a major transformation of all aspects of life – and [this] was in the process of volitional actualization'. Revolution gained authority from the argument that it was the product of long-term factors gathering strength so that the actual outbreak was the expression of a deep-seated inevitability. Revolution was inevitable, and it would be made, by revolutionaries. Contemporary revisionist historians such as Conrad Russell on the English Civil War (*not* 'the English Revolution') and François Furet on the French Revolution emphasise instead contingencies, and forces released by the events of the revolution itself. The deep roots of revolution, which gave it an aspect of inevitability, are severed by the revisionists.[12] Crises are now less likely to be interpreted, or to be

---

[11] According to Reinhart Koselleck (1988, 127 and 167–168, n.31), crisis enters political and moral thinking during the Enlightenment as a way of naturalising and expecting revolution; this is surely no longer the case, but Koselleck is himself tracing mutations in the concept of crisis, which, as he notes, originated in medicine. Janet Roitman ('Crisis and Contradiction') argues that crisis is the blind spot that we need to produce knowledge in a groundless world.

[12] Conrad Russell, *The Origins of the English Civil War* (1973) – as against Christopher Hill, for instance *Intellectual Origins of the English Revolution* (1965); François Furet, *Interpreting the French Revolution* (1981, first published, 1978); and see Doyle 1999, especially 'Revisionism' and 'Post-Revisionism' (10–41). Grand, sweeping historical interpretations and historical sociologies

actively seized on, as harbingers of revolution or as events that can be forced towards revolution. The candidates for revolution of recent times have tended to be renamed 'springs' (Prague Spring, Arab Spring), and activism from the left is now given the more modest term 'resistance'. Andrew Tate (*Apocalyptic Fiction*, 96) comments on the 'shared act of walking as resistance' with reference to the final pages of Cormac McCarthy's *The Road* (2006): walking as resistance is not going to usher in a revolution.

We have the crisis or emergency as a permanent condition, immanent rather than, or as well as, imminent. We retain neither the consoling belief that the immanence signifies progress nor the consoling belief that the crisis will blossom into revolution.[13] It is best to be careful here: that habit of crisis that I am discussing tends to encourage sweeping statements, such as 'we have lost faith in Progress', or that History, Man and so forth have ended. These statements of mine with regard to crisis and revolution may themselves be symptoms or tics of the habit, their validity a lot more limited than might appear. It is worth recalling Dickens's aside at the beginning of *A Tale of Two Cities* regarding excited assertions about the present: 'some of its noisiest authorities insisted on its being received, for good or for evil, in the superlative degree of comparison only'.[14] Further, most people most of the time in the West live lives of prosperous security, with boredom or irritation the most pressing daily threat. The regime of crisis manifests itself in the media; it's in the head: 'The things we only know about second hand are the things we tend to fear the most' (Runciman 2018, 76). It's a matter of how we interpret events or how they are presented to us, how we sense we are linked to them, how we imagine possibilities.

Complexity itself seems to threaten: forms of global interconnection themselves have apocalyptic potential – system crashes, fast-spreading

---

are, however, still being produced: see, for instance, the essays in Anderson 1992.

[13] Evidence of the very high casualties suffered by the North Vietnamese army in some of their offensives, and of how their leaders nonetheless pressed on in the faith of final victory, dramatised in the recent Ken Burns documentary on the Vietnam War, might remind us that faith in Revolution as secularised apocalypse still lived, at least for the rulers of North Vietnam in the 1960s and 1970s: a revolutionary New Jerusalem would follow the suffering and sacrifice. For Americans, in contrast, the war came to mean indiscriminate violence, massacres and waste: catastrophe without reward, bolted into an archetypal modern story of evil and degeneration when *Apocalypse Now* (1979) was modelled on *Heart of Darkness* (1899).

[14] *A Tale of Two Cities* 1985 (1859), 11.

epidemics. Thence, arguably, the tendency of contemporary apocalyptic fictions to crank up the volume or to see apocalypse as a concatenation of multiple crises or as having brought about a situation in which we cannot quite define what hit us. We live in the world that systems analysis and chaos theory were developed to understand, or to cope with. The sequence of event and effect, convenient in narrative, and emphatically underlying the sequence from catastrophe to transcendence in traditional apocalypse, struggles to meet the case.

Furthermore, both history and fiction suggest that crisis can come from anywhere – epidemic; nuclear; antibiotic ('antibiotic apocalypse', stemming from the growing inefficacy of antibiotics); ecological; financial;[15] as mass sterility (Brian Aldiss's *Greybeard*, P. D. James's *The Children of Men*; Amin Maalouf's *The First Century After Beatrice*) – not to mention zombies, invasions of aliens, collisions with asteroids and so on, with their varied suggestions as metaphors and embodied fears. We are *habituated* to apocalypse, and more recent apocalyptic fiction (discussed here in part 3) has increasingly adjusted to this condition, by way of irony and comedy, and by subjecting an apocalyptic narrative to the competition of other narratives when it occurs in a text stranded of different stories.

A quick survey such as this one makes it all seem almost ludicrous; it seems odd that a single threat should have to fight to make itself heard, over the crowd of competitors, as apocalyptic, as laying claim to Finality. Such claims are frequently politicised: any important alleged threat in this near cacophony of alleged threats is treated as an extension of politics, and involves a contest over language and perception; or one threat is inflated so as to induce us not to think about another. Iain Sinclair (2010, 260) on the swine flu epidemic panic: 'Hit them with a worst-case scenario, a flash-frame from the *Revelation of St John*, and whatever actually comes along won't look so bad.' The terminology can itself mislead: 'global warming' is too cosy, 'the sixth extinction event' at once too grim and too obscure, 'climate change' smuggles in the contemporary necessity and acceptance of change (as with

---

[15] See Don DeLillo's *Cosmopolis* (2003) for a fictional treatment, or Lionel Shriver's *The Mandibles* (2016). Financial apocalypse is not a new fear. John Martin was the nineteenth-century painter who specialised in Apocalypse. Boyd Hilton (2006, 114) associates Martin's painting of the Deluge with the financial crash of 1825: 'The previous year's financial crash had prompted many capitalists to suppose that cosmic events were "visibly marching forward to a great visible era of doom and triumph".' Martin did several paintings of the Deluge; that of 1826 has been lost; see Johnstone 1974, 74.

'change management', a phrase employed when lots of redundancies are planned):

> 'The stakes just keep getting higher.'
> 'Yes. That's why they call it climate change.'
> 'What do you mean?'
> 'I mean they're trying to pretend it's only about climate! When really it's about everything – it's *everything change.*'
> (Kim Stanley Robinson, *Green Earth*, 644)

Or perhaps it should be termed ecocide.

History and Invention

The makers of apocalyptic fiction have to be aware of the very many apocalyptic fictions and myths already in existence, and have to establish their new fiction in relation to all these existing fictions, but they also have to be aware that horrendous disaster has often happened in history. To put a horrendous disaster into a fiction you have to imagine it, but the force and pressure of the actual, of the extraordinary and painful things that actually happen and are then narrated, can have a chastening effect. Here is a mother trying to clean the recovered body of her daughter, recounted by Richard Lloyd Parry in his *Ghosts of the Tsunami*, a non-fictional account of the 2011 tsunami in Japan:

> 'I had nothing else, so I used my clothes to wipe off the mud. Her eyes were half open – and that was the way she used to sleep, the way she was when she was in a very deep sleep. But there was muck in her eyes, and there were no towels and no water, and so I licked Chisato's eyes with my tongue to wipe off the muck, but I couldn't get them clean, and the muck kept coming out.'
> (Parry 2017, 42)

Here is an encounter in Don DeLillo's novel about 9/11:

> A man was dangling there, above the street, upside down. He wore a business suit, one leg bent up, arms at his sides. A safety harness was barely visible, emerging from his trousers at the straightened leg and fastened to the decorative rail of the viaduct.
> She'd heard of him, a performance artist known as Falling Man.
> (*Falling Man*, 2007, 33)

If you make a fiction of apocalypse, then your imagination brings freedom, but that imagination is also making a space apart from the actual, and one that can be seen as a necessary space apart, though the actual in this case is probably present to most readers, in the form of film of bodies falling from the burning skyscrapers. Imagination of apocalypse can involve aestheticising it, or simply highlighting the pleasure and power of words and images, as will be discussed later with J. G. Ballard and Brian Aldiss: an emphasis, broadly speaking, on literariness. How novelists of apocalypse come to terms with death will be discussed later; many avoid depicting mass death altogether, though catastrophe usually involves mass death.

The push and pull of history and invention sets the scene for interplay between the sober recording of reality and the experimental or fantastic embrace of new possibilities and transformations. A writer might be drawn to grapple with the prospect of nuclear war or of climate change, and find to hand a mass of sober and sobering fact, and of reasoned and alarming prediction. Frank Kermode (2000, 182–183) reminds us that people in most periods have tended to feel uniquely threatened by some imminent apocalypse,[16] but as Martin Amis says (2003, 22), 'Our time is different. All times are different, but our time is *different*. A new fall, an infinite fall, underlies the usual – indeed traditional – presentiments of decline.' So, some especially harsh historical possibilities may press on the maker of apocalyptic fictions, with behind them the authority of Science and the evidence of huge historical catastrophes such as the World Wars. Amis had nuclear catastrophe in mind; very many commentaries on the threat – or the inevitability – of disastrous climate change also assume that 'our time is different'.[17] Yet an author might be drawn to apocalypse by the prospect – by the natural but dubious pleasures – of wholesale destruction, release from mundane pressures and socialities, release into freedom, transcendence, enjoyment of evocative ruins, deserted penthouse suites full of expensive brandies and perfumes, even enjoyment of the imperatives, as they seem, of tribal violence in a newly primitive world. The sheer quantity of fictions of disaster and the aftermath of disaster, whether that aftermath be dystopia or utopia or some condition that is fluidly open, provokes writers to new inventions of forms of disaster, as well as permitting repetitions of conventional formulas. At the same time as he was publishing four early apocalyptic novels, J. G. Ballard

---

[16] In Umberto Eco's *The Name of the Rose* Pope Benedict XI is a nomination for Anti-Christ: not a name on many subsequent lists (1984, 62).

[17] See, for instance, Tate 2017, 5.

was prolific in short stories, many of them imagining the aftermath or process of some catastrophe or other: Ballard must have been destroying civilisation as we know it every couple of weeks during this period. The list of ways in which the world has been devastated in the fiction of the twentieth century and later is, if nothing else, a tribute to the imaginative ingenuity of (especially) science-fiction writers.[18] Further, the tradition of apocalypse, together with cognate stories of catastrophe and radical overthrow, is so ramified and, often, formulaic, as to have reached the point where it demands reflective examination, experimental variation, critique: the condition characteristic of belatedness in a cultural form.

Yet history presses, whether in the form of fact and prospect, or in the form of terrifying inruptions into peaceful normality that prompt us to reach for the word apocalyptic when they figure in the media. Further, history realises catastrophe, repeatedly. The makers of these real catastrophes sometimes see them in apocalyptic terms, or imagine them in terms of plots and fantasies. In *The Bombers and the Bombed*, discussing the Second World War, Richard Overy (2013, 96–98, 136) notes how operations were named Millennium I and II (Cologne and Bremen, 1942) or Gomorrah (Hamburg, 1943: one of the most terrifyingly – or successfully – destructive of all bombing raids). In *Bloodlands: Europe Between Hitler and Stalin* (2010), Timothy Snyder details the reality of massacre, deportation and atrocity in which the German and Soviet antagonists collaborated, imitating and goading one another, in Eastern Europe from the Ukrainian famine to the end of the Second World War. The events he narrates are grimly material (for instance, in the many ways the bodies of the dead are abused) but are also the product of fantasy on the part of the perpetrators: vast conspiracies imagined, elaborated, made 'real' by the finding or rather the fabrication of threats and conspirators who are then eliminated.[19]

---

[18] *The Wind from Nowhere, The Drought, The Drowned World* and *The Crystal World* were originally published 1962–6; see also *The End of the World*, edited by Eric S. Rabkin, Martin H. Greenberg and Joseph D. Olander, 1983, and the entry on the end of the world in *The Science Fiction Encyclopedia*, edited by John Clute and Peter Nicholls, 1993.

[19] See, for instance, Snyder 2011, 26, 41, 81–86, 387–388.

Traditional Apocalypse[20]

How closely should a given narrative conform to earlier models to qualify as an apocalypse? Bernard McGinn (1984, 21) reports, 'There have been those who have doubted whether John's Apocalypse [that is, *The Revelation to John*] is really an apocalypse, because it lacks some of the features of Jewish apocalypses.' Frank Kermode (1985, 103, n.1) quotes John J. Collins: 'Apocalypse is a genre of revelatory literature within a narrative framework, in which a revelation is mediated by an otherworldly being to a human recipient, disclosing a transcendental reality which is both temporal, insofar as it envisages eschatological salvation, and spatial insofar as it involves another, supernatural world.' This manages to overlook the element of destruction and disaster that is very fully present in *The Revelation to John*, and dominant in many later apocalyptic fictions. Amos Funkenstein (1985, 57) similarly asserts that true apocalypticism lasted among the Jews and early Christians for 200 years and that what came later can be dismissed as too general, only vaguely dependent on apocalypticism proper.

So much for the scholarly debate; meanwhile, in the contemporary world, almost any crisis, emergency or disaster can be labelled apocalyptic. This reflex needs to be analysed, but for the discussion of narrative it is best to begin by noting the commonly recurring features of traditional apocalypse, and they can be found in the version most influential in the Christian West, the Apocalypse of John, the Book of Revelation.

Traditional, biblical apocalypse as a narrative form involves all or most of the items on the following list. There is supervision by God (and angels and so on); the participation of the heroic Messiah (the Son of Man, the Lamb):[21] the outcome is determined, and nothing is meaningless or accidental; and there is a witness/prophet. There is wholesale death and devastation, in particular of cities, and often an

---

[20] A suggestive account of the origins of apocalypse in Middle Eastern and then Jewish religious thinking is given by Norman Cohn in *Cosmos, Chaos and the World to Come* (1993). Cohn discusses the apocalypses and allusions to last judgement in the Hebrew Bible and the Gospels; but there is much disagreement among scholars.

[21] Jean-Claude Carrière (1999, 107) notes that it is common in many traditions to imagine the coming of 'some providential figure whose arrival, in the majority of cases, will precede the completion of the ages'; that is, many features of the pattern traced here can be found in a variety of cultures. Aeneas is given a horrifying glimpse of the gods themselves destroying Troy in book 2 of the *Aeneid*; E. L. Harrison (1990, 48) terms this 'the great apocalypse that forms the unforgettable climax of the book'.

epic final battle, Armageddon. There is differentiation between the good and the bad, or the faithful and the worldly, so that the death and devastation is meaningful; at least in theory, destruction and death are not indiscriminate. There is participation of monsters, such as the beast with seven heads, clearly evil; participation of Anti-Christ, who is a false prophet. There is an opening to a New Jerusalem after the wholesale death and destruction; 'without apocalypse no paradise'; apocalypse converts 'the tragedy of human history into cosmic comedy'.[22] With the New Jerusalem, time stops. History is finished, whereas post-apocalyptic episodes figure largely in contemporary versions of apocalypse, so that history resumes. In traditional apocalypse we shift from time to eternity, and this is a human-centred eternity, in that everyone is either enjoying bliss or suffering punishment. Science since the late eighteenth century has required us to recognise that Earth and the universe would survive the end of humanity. There is, finally, a Last Judgement, whereby individual death is surpassed by mass resurrection and judgement.

These features confer a clarity on traditional apocalypse: the good and the bad are clearly differentiated, or are defined as the faithful and the infidel or apostate; the hero is unambiguous; the catastrophe is determined and directed; the rule of the Saints and the New Jerusalem will come. The Last Judgement will put an end to death and fix the meaning of the lives of the saved and the damned for all eternity. Traditional apocalypse tends to definiteness in the details, for all that the story it tells is one of wholesale destruction and judgement: in Daniel, the writing on the wall tells Belshazzar that his days are 'numbered, weighed, divided' (Daniel, V, 26–28); in John, we have 144,000 of the faithful, seven seals to be opened, four horsemen. These figures have about them a certain mythical authority – seven seals, as with seven days of the week, seven sleepers of Ephesus and so on – and they constitute an invitation to detailed interpretation, one that has frequently been enthusiastically accepted, most notably in the case of 666 as the number of the Beast.[23] Frank Kermode discusses the processes of reinterpretation and elaboration that apocalypse has undergone in *The Sense of an Ending*. It seems that as these processes have become less attractive to the general culture, while the prospect of apocalypse reasserts itself in history, the burden, or opportunity, is taken up by fictional re-imaginings, rather than by interpreting the number of the Beast, or identity of Anti-Christ.

---

[22] The quotations are from Hans Magnus Enzensberger 1982, 233, and from M. H. Abrams 1984, 344.
[23] In some of the earliest manuscripts the number is 616: a further challenge. Beal 2018, 7.

Secular and Sacred

Traditional apocalypse is supervised by God, has a clear moral structure (sheep and goats) and ushers in a New Jerusalem. These features are reassuring as well as terrifying. Their absence or attenuation points to the problems faced by modern apocalyptic fictions. It can seem that the modern enterprise of secularising apocalypse is doomed: the religious force and scope of the idea and the sublimity of the image of the ultimate end, of global disaster, disrupt attempts to explain and detail in terms of science and reason. Apocalyptic catastrophe is often evidence of the failure of science and reason as they were practised until things went catastrophically wrong. The catastrophe is not brought about by the intervention of the deity, but by the failure of science and reason. The apocalypse is secular but points towards the failure of the secular. The impulse to spiritualise the secular is as strong as the urge to imagine a substitute for a religious narrative that is no longer credible or no longer relevant to the causes of catastrophe. Not all modern makers of apocalyptic fictions want to, or can, eradicate the religious aspects; they are often freely adopted, or explored, or accompany imagination of the sublime dimensions of apocalypse, or simply persist;[24] for instance, there are a surprising number of false prophets in post-apocalyptic fiction, and they might be taken to relate to one aspect of the Anti-Christ of traditional apocalypse.[25]

Apocalypse almost always involves the ultimate and the sublime, and the religious waits in the wings and sometimes comes on stage in modern apocalyptic fictions. An explicitly Christian rendition of post-apocalyptic dystopia and redemption is P. D. James's *The Children of Men* (1992), in which the miraculous birth of a baby after decades in which it seemed certain that humanity was doomed by a plague of sterility is given the shape of a fable. The birth happens in a wood-shed; equivalents to Mary, Joseph and Herod are not hard to find. The main witness to the birth is Theo Faron, disillusioned rationalist; he had in an earlier life accidentally killed his young daughter, so the wonderful birth of a child is posed against this death of a child. J. G. Ballard's *The Drowned World*, enacts, and in many ways celebrates, the triumph of the Sun as god, while suggesting a transcendence – the protagonist as a new Adam – that is also a submission to oblivion. A kind of deity presides over other

---

[24] Andrew Tate (2017) returns often to the 'spiritual' aspects of contemporary apocalyptic fictions; see his chapters 2, 3, 4 and 5.
[25] Further discussion below (49), where it is pointed out that these prophets and gurus are usually failures.

recent apocalyptic fictions, and sometimes imports into the text an aura of the sacred: the omnipotent and creative process of crystallisation in Ballard's *The Crystal World*, the Overmind in Arthur C. Clarke's *Childhood's End*, which brings Earth to an end while absorbing Earth's children into itself; less sublime, the unseen power that has wreaked catastrophe in Tom Perrotta's *The Leftovers* and Douglas Coupland's *Girlfriend in a Coma*. The power of Ballard's and Clarke's deities is, however, more apparent than their benevolence or even their possession of purpose. In general, the powerful superheroes in the texts discussed by Peter Paik in *From Utopia to Apocalypse* are absent from the texts discussed in *Apocalypse in Crisis*, where power is usually ascribed to alien or impersonal forces rather than human agents.

Science Fiction and Fictions of Apocalypse

'Science Fiction is just beginning to catch up with the Old Testament.'

(Zapalac in Don DeLillo, *End Zone*)

Science fiction has carried much of the weight and scope of apocalyptic fiction since H. G. Wells's *The War of the Worlds* (1898). With its Martian invasion and its complex bearing on European imperialism and on the possible future of modern civilisation, *The War of the Worlds* intervened dramatically in the popular genre that imagined coming wars with the Germans, or the French or Asian hordes, and this intervention can stand for the potential of apocalyptic science fiction to stimulate and provoke. Both the broader culture and the formal qualities of science fiction assist in this. Science fiction in its allegiance to science and reason is equipped to secularise apocalypse, yet the possibility that science and reason have given rise to apocalypse troubles and stimulates science fiction, which can then be provoked into examining or exceeding the terms of its own ethos. Science fiction, often celebrated for its sense of wonder, invites the sublime, a quality of apocalypse. Science fiction has had limited relations, and sometimes no relations, with modernist scepticism about plot and re-examination of the nature and fixity of the subject, though, as we will see, this changes in the 1960s, and the change transforms and rejuvenates science-fiction apocalypses. Science fiction is sympathetic to the ordinary person as protagonist, so that he or she is likely to be fitted for the role of witness that traditional apocalypse invites. On the other hand, science fiction has sometimes been attracted to the utopia of Mind, as if the body were best transcended or discarded, and also attracted towards over-valuation of an elite of scientists or experts, as against the ignorant and panicky masses. Science fiction is accustomed to sub-genres – time travel stories, first contact stories and so on – to their conventions, their innovations, the possibilities of variation, subversion and parody. There is thus space in science fiction to vary or rethink the traditional narrative of apocalypse, which is among many other things a genre of narrative, and space also to parody or subvert the standard tropes and persons of science fiction itself.

While science-fiction narratives are often formulaic and sensational, science fiction is also often open to the discursive, to discussing or expounding broader issues: characters in science fiction discuss issues and offer explanations. This openness to the discursive is not an unequivocally good thing: info-dumps can drop clunkily into the text; editorialising can expose the limits of the author's wisdom or sophistication. The divergence between what the author knows and what the witness to apocalypse experiences can be troubling in any apocalyptic fiction, and it can be obtrusive when the author claims to know and explain a lot; but the gain in realism and the invitation to the reader to think broadly are positives. Kim Stanley Robinson's *Green Earth* (2015), an anti-apocalyptic novel about climate change, is a good example: the characters discourse, read, discuss, as people, including scientists, do in actual social life. By contrast, in Lionel Shriver's *The Mandibles* (2016), a novel about a financial apocalypse, discussion struggles to find space amid notations of the characters' self-absorption and helplessness.

Science fiction is usually committed to the delineation of a world so different from our own as to be a new thing, a novum, and this involves a conspectus of interlocking details, an impression, at least, of comprehensiveness. Apocalyptic fiction seeks to find relations among aspects of a world transformed by destruction: not an easy task if what prevails is disorder and fragmentation. One recourse is to focus on a small group of survivors in a confined locality, as the British postwar novelists of disaster did. Another is to broaden and deepen the scope of relations by a richness of imagery and allusion, and this is what many apocalyptic fictions of the 1960s did. Contemporary novelists of apocalypse increasingly face the fact that social reality is becoming harder to depict, putting a strain on reportorial realism, demanding a density of depiction and notation that perhaps goes beyond any realism. This density, with its risk of overload, is to be found in DeLillo, Miéville and Coupland – by which point we are outside science fiction as a tradition.

All science fiction is apocalyptic, as David Ketterer (1976) has argued: its worlds are the products of radical transformation. Yet the apocalyptic is challenging to science fiction, especially earlier science fiction, with its appetite for 'wonder', its belief in progress and technology, its belief in the ingenious individual and in practical expedients to solve problems or simply to survive. J. G. Ballard's apocalyptic fictions are science fiction as anti-science fiction in the way they deny the practicality and the commitment to moral common sense that has been an important part of the ethos of science fiction. Catastrophe frees Ballard's protagonist from practicality and prompts him to choose oblivion and the aesthetic.

In general – not only in science fiction – apocalypse or apocalyptic emergency can make the world available to the individual who has been lost or hampered in the vastness of the modern city and globalised society. In the aftermath of catastrophe all sorts of local details and factors offer themselves as clear needs or opportunities – or catastrophe can narrow the perspective, forcing everyone and everything into the one plot, one reality. Contemporary apocalyptic novels often exploit the first possibility and often, especially recently, resist the second. Apocalyptic catastrophe transforms or destroys both the inhabited and the natural worlds; apocalyptic fiction confronts in varying ways the opposition between the country and the city that has perennially shaped the literary imagination, especially in England. Survivors of the science fiction disasters of the 1940s and 1950s often leave the city without regret, and retreat to the pastoral; later apocalyptic fictions often take a contrary stand, seeing apocalypse as arising from the – otherwise positive – energies of the city. Many apocalyptic fictions of the 1960s and 1970s turn aside from pastoral images of nature and find in nature a new, sometimes threatening, power and richness. In some recent apocalyptic fictions, human nature is put into question as part of nature in general; humans are examined as a species of primate, for instance, in Kim Stanley Robinson's *Green Earth* and Audrey Schulman's *Theory of Bastards* (2018). These investigations draw on recent science to reapproach the nature and boundaries of the human. *Green Earth* refers to climate science, genetics and animal behaviour; *Theory of Bastards* to primatology and other kinds of work on animal and human mating behavior.

Science fiction has had a strong commitment to the Future considered not merely as what is going to happen next, but as the time of progress, advance, venturing outwards and upwards. Apocalypse, with its sublime transformations – limitless, leaving us gasping and feeling puny – accommodates this drive, but it does so in a grim and dreadful fashion. Apocalypse is therefore frequently a challenge to the utopian or progressive side of science fiction, and to the side that revels in an expansive sense of wonder. The post-apocalyptic future can be modest and small-scale, as in George R. Stewart's *Earth Abides*, or blank, as in Nevil Shute's *On the Beach*, a novel that refuses the sublime at every point. Belief that apocalypse leads to positive transformation persists; for instance, among the contributors to a collection of essays on the end of the world (Rabkin, Greenberg and Olander 1983), Eric S. Rabkin writes of destroying the world in order to renew it, Gary K. Wolfe of 'the promise of a better world to come' (3) and W. Warren Wagar of 'ends that lead to fresh beginnings' (73).[26] These critics are all American; Brian Stableford, the representative of Britain in the collection, argues differently.

In recent times there has been a convergence between science fiction and the broader streams of fiction – so-called 'literary fiction', and also fantasy and 'weird fiction'. This book aims to test the hypothesis that works of genre science fiction that imagine apocalypse, and fictions of apocalypse from outside genre science fiction are illuminatingly read together. Apocalypse invites everyone who makes a narrative of it into the reasoned or intuitive or fantastic imagination of future transformation – transformation in the form of massive catastrophe, but catastrophe that ushers in a new state of affairs, perhaps even a new state of being, and certainly one from which our contemporary condition falls into new patterns and significances. It's true that the author of an apocalyptic fiction can easily avoid this challenge by resorting to available formulas. If almost everyone who imagines the situation after catastrophe thinks that society will fall into tribal violence and dictatorship of the ruthless (often supposed to be the fittest), who am I (an author might think) to disagree? Thence, he or she gives us another formulaic dystopia of regression to an imagined violent tribalism. The frightening toughness and shockingness of, for instance, *Lord of the Flies*, fades into a series of clichés. But the challenge of reimagining apocalypse is often taken up, and then a great deal is revealed about views of society and the individual, views of what in society, or indeed in civilisation, might survive, and what might mutate, and what might disappear, under extreme stress. A great deal is revealed also about an author's and an age's impulses and compulsions, fears and desires.

Apocalypse in Crisis concentrates on apocalypse as narrative. Apocalypse is an event; indeed, in its traditional form, it is a set sequence of events. Apocalypse invites narrative, even as it challenges or threatens narrative because the events it involves are massive and unqualified and final, and also global, exceeding the perspective of an individual or a small group, the perspective on which most fictions are based.

The texts selected for discussion in *Apocalypse in Crisis* present an apocalyptic narrative, a narrative arc shaped by catastrophe and its

---

[26] For a wide-ranging discussion of the tendency for disaster in America to be taken positively, see Rozario 2007.

aftermath, as distinct from apocalyptic episodes or images. The burning of Paris at the end of Zola's *The Debacle* (1892) is an example of an apocalyptic episode, and a very grim and powerful one, but it is not productive to consider the novel's overarching account of the French defeat in the war of 1870 as an apocalyptic narrative. On the other hand, W. G. Sebald's *The Rings of Saturn* (1995) collects a whole series of apocalyptic incidents and images (the annihilation of the herrings, the holocaust of silkworms, the hurricane of 1987),[27] making these shadow the Holocaust, and avoiding a single apocalyptic narrative in the interest of a more open, meditative investigation of extreme destruction as an element in history. *The Rings of Saturn* is a response to the proliferation of catastrophes, and it is both haunted and fascinated by the time and climate in which they can make themselves present to memory and perception. Sebald's book, however, falls outside this present book's project, which is to focus on narratives with an apocalyptic arc, novels that set themselves to depict a world transformed by catastrophe, and then to explore whether there can be a recovery, or the foundation of a new world, or a transcendence (a version of the traditional New Jerusalem).

Apocalypse in Crisis concentrates on British and American texts, arguing that a coherent history of apocalyptic fiction can be drawn from some commonalities in the experiences of these two societies in the period from 1945 to the present. British and American science fiction shares a tradition, though it is one that sometimes clarifies and sharpens differences in approach. The postwar disaster novels to be discussed in chapter 2 tended to use the Second World War as a model for reaction to apocalypse in a relatively confident way. This changed drastically in apocalyptic novels of the 1960s and beyond. Attitudes to the state, attitudes to truth and fiction and attitudes to the individual all shifted, and British and American authors grew particularly aware of the burdens and complications of their imperial and post-imperial situations. The process is a complicated one, involving delays (in the immediate postwar period) and sudden spurts (in the 1960s: part two of *Apocalypse in Crisis* is 'Post-imperial Subjects'). It is harder to trace a history in more recent apocalyptic fictions, and part 3 is structured less in terms of sequence and more in terms of genres and locations (the comic and satirical; the city; everyday life), with the final chapter emphasising the open situation of the fiction of apocalypse by discussing two recent texts that are in very strong contrast.

[27] Herrings, 53–59; silkworms, 292–294; hurricane, 265–268 (Harvill Press edition of 1999, translated by Michael Hulse).

The texts discussed in *Apocalypse in Crisis* are various in form and genre. There are science-fiction novels, some of them from genre science fiction, some of them mocking or breaking the conventions of science fiction. There are novels not easily classifiable as science fiction and that can be classified in diverse ways – comic, satirical, suburban, cosmopolitan, satirical. This mixture reflects the merging of science fiction with other forms of fiction that has intensified since the 1980s, and the stress apocalyptic fiction has been subject to as it has become both more necessary and more self-conscious. Most of the novels selected are discussed in depth and in comparison, at the rate of two or three in each chapter, and this further brings out the various approaches to imagining apocalypse taken by authors in this shifting Anglo-American tradition. For instance, chapter 8 looks at two novels set respectively in New York and London as contemporary world cities, Don DeLillo's *Cosmopolis* and China Mieville's *Kraken*. The first might be classified as advanced contemporary fiction; the second its author would probably term 'weird fiction'; they are very different, hard to contain in a chapter of comparison, and that, arguably, is the point: apocalypse has become both a cliché and an urgent threat, and recent fictions of apocalypse have been cast into strange shapes in response to this condition; yet these novels can usefully be cast into contrast with the postwar novels of disaster whose orientation is pastoral.

Many of the texts selected are by authors who can be termed canonical, though this is a shifting and controverted term, and this means that they are very often by white males (themselves a far from uniform bunch). This has the advantage that many readers are likely to know them and have their opinions about them already. J. G. Ballard, discussed in chapter 3, is surely inescapable in any account of the changing history of fictions of apocalypse. Brian Aldiss is a canonical science-fiction author, but the novel selected here, *Barefoot in the Head*, is often overlooked. Doris Lessing is a canonical author, but also a very prolific one; the radical and rebarbative quality of two of her fictions of apocalypse can usefully be exhibited when they are taken from the rest of her oeuvre and set in a discussion of apocalyptic fiction of the 1960s and 1970s; something similar can be said of Don DeLillo's *Cosmopolis*, a text that has not been regarded with much enthusiasm by readers: again its interest is enhanced by its being discussed as a recent apocalyptic fiction set in the city. Arno Schmidt is German, but *Nobodaddy's Children* earns its place by illuminating the argument of chapter 6, and perhaps discussing it here will make it better known. In general, I would consider *Apocalypse in Crisis* a success if all the differing texts which it treats became 'canonical' in the sense that they were more often read and argued about.

An Outline of *Apocalypse in Crisis*

Part 1: The Nineteenth Century to the Postwar Disaster Novels

Chapter 1 sketches the varieties of apocalyptic thinking and apocalyptic fiction in the cultures of nineteenth-century Britain and America. It looks at a series of canonical fictions that were grouped in an essay by Saul Friedländer, and argues that they deal with a complicity between the apocalypse-threatening non-human monster or invader and its human antagonists. This takes us to H. G. Wells's *The War of the Worlds*, a crucial text for science-fictional apocalypses in the twentieth century. *The War of the Worlds* uses alien invasion to question the human, and introduces many of the challenges of making modern apocalyptic fiction: relating the individual experience and the mass experience; valuation of the country and the city; relations of reason and anxiety.

Chapter 2 considers a series of disaster fictions of the 1940s and 1950s: British (John Wyndham, *The Day of the Triffids*; Nevil Shute, *On the Beach*; Arthur C. Clarke, *Childhood's End*) and American (George R. Stewart, *Earth Abides*). H. G. Wells sets the scene for these novels, in varying ways. There is a tendency to retreat from the ruined city to the countryside with its prospect of pastoral harmony, in contrast to some later fictions that explore the complex possibility that apocalypse originates in the dynamic energies of the city. Catastrophic mass death is passed over or sketched; the source and embodiment of catastrophe is clear, and it comes from outside the characters' daily experience; the narrative ends with focus on individual death, and sometimes killing. With the exception of *Childhood's End*, the tendency is to expect that civilised, often middle-class, decency will survive the catastrophe, or re-emerge in its aftermath. There is still trust in authority, either figures of authority (as in *Childhood's End*, where these figures are alien invaders) or the manners and structures of authority. The prose usually eschews the personal and figurative for the clarity and directness of the reporter. There is no radical questioning of human nature in its middle-class form, and this restraint brings advantages, as well as a certain narrowness of view. *Childhood's End* is more radical in its imagination both of a utopia – after the first apocalyptic transformation that the novel stages – and of the end of the Earth and translation to a new state of being – after the second apocalyptic transformation. Clarke's novel also illuminates many of the problems of the science-fictional belief in One World and in an upwards evolution of humanity: a belief that is abandoned and critiqued in later science-fictional apocalypses. *On the Beach* seems to give the clearest of endorsements to middle-class decency and domesticity, yet ends with the suicides of all the characters and the end of humanity.

Part 2: Post-Imperial Subjects

After the 1950s there was a reaction against the reportorial realism that had prevailed in science-fiction apocalypses. Science fiction embraced some of modernism's stylistic innovation and verve, and its interest in the vagaries of subjectivity. Chapters 3, 4 and 5 engage with the transformation that overcomes apocalyptic fiction in Britain in the 1960s and 1970s: a radical re-examination of the pleasures and the pains of apocalypse; new and threatening imaginations of transformation and transcendence; a new awareness of the literary and the aesthetic – allusion, symbol, play with language. Catastrophe now transforms the scene so that return to or re-foundation of previous ways and values cannot even be thought of. The new world suggests or embodies new kinds of being. This vision of apocalypse expresses a restless, post-imperial sense of Britain, whose imperial decline most of the authors of these novels had experienced directly, and one ready to rethink values and also pleasures in the spirit of the 1960s. There is an awareness of the subjective, of the agendas – sexual, death-obsessed, aesthetic – that the individual can pursue as catastrophe unfolds.

Chapter 3 looks at J. G. Ballard (*The Drought*, *The Drowned World*, *The Crystal World*). Ballard's protagonists embrace the end of civilised order, and refuse to engage with the project of rebuilding society after catastrophe. These texts play with modernist – and decadent – images and personalities. Apocalypse is in varying ways aestheticised.

Chapter 4 looks at a pair of novels from 1969 that reflect the emerging spirit of 1960s counter-culture in more exuberant ways; Brian Aldiss's *Barefoot in the Head* and Angela Carter's *Heroes and Villains*. Like Ballard, they offer the pleasures of language – images, rich description, allusion, and in Aldiss's case puns, portmanteaus and poems. In neither case does the protagonist do more than toy with any project of remaking the world. Aldiss's Charteris leads a madcap procession of drivers across a drug-addled Europe, and then abandons it; Carter's Marianne enjoys sex with Jewel, but sees him as threat, object of art, and enigma, and is freed by his death. In both novels present experience, enjoyable, crazy, disturbing or perverse, is of much more account than where it might be heading.

Chapter 5 groups two novels by Doris Lessing, *The Memoirs of a Survivor* and *The Making of the Representative for Planet 8*, with one by Anna Kavan, *Ice*. These novels are much darker. *Ice* centres on the blocked sado-masochistic relationship of the three central characters, whose selves tend to blend; the oppressive landscape of apocalypse (recurrent wars, and an advancing Ice Age) serves mostly as backdrop to the depiction of the tortured central trio. In *Memoirs* and *Planet 8* Lessing reacts against the pleasures of style that were so evident in the texts discussed in chapters 3 and 4, problematises the questing subjectivity of the characters in the texts discussed in chapters 3 and 4 and works towards endings that express a hard-won, and hardly won, transcendence.

Part 3: Resistance and Revision

The final section of *Apocalypse in Crisis* looks at recent apocalyptic fictions as revising the depiction of apocalypse, or as resisting apocalypse itself. Apocalypse is imagined more as condition, in which characters are immersed, than as event to be figured in the text and responded to by the characters. Subjectivity is more precarious. The tendency of apocalypse to dominate the text and the story is resisted or mocked; and the paradox that apocalypse is both a real threat and a habitual way of thinking and narrating is addressed by comedy, parody, and manipulation of prevailing conventions and tropes.

Chapter 6, 'Apocalypse, Comedy, Multiplicity', looks at a set of novels that utilise the forms of comedy to take a sceptical look at apocalypse and to resist its power to embrace everything and everybody in the same predicament. Multiplicity of circumstance and incident, together with human waywardness, dissolves the totalising power of apocalypse in these texts. In fact, the trilogy by Arno Schmidt, *Nobodaddy's Children*, sets the aftermath of nuclear catastrophe in a sceptical context by centring the third novel on this disaster after those of the Second World War occupied the first two, and by seeing the whole sequence through the eyes and attitudes of an eccentric, self-centred protagonist. This protagonist is scornful of most of his contemporaries, happy when disaster removes them from the scene, and devoted to Germany's literary past. Anthony Burgess gives one of the three narrative strands of *The End of the World News* to the coming apocalypse, which takes the traditional science-fictional form of the collision of a huge asteroid with Earth. This narrative centres on two thoroughly irresponsible protagonists, and culminates in farcical confusion at the gates of the station in Kansas whence a starship carrying a selection of the scientific elite is to be launched before Earth is destroyed. The novel's other narrative strands offer us a vivid account of Freud's career and movement and a facetious take on Trotsky's time in New York. The coming of apocalypse does not monopolise the novel, and apocalyptic fiction is offered as one of several genres and ways of playing with truth. The third novel considered in this chapter, Ursula K. Le Guin's *The Lathe of Heaven*, stages a series of apocalyptic transformations, which are both real and imagined, brought about by the combined efforts of Orr and Haber, the first a good man who has the power of 'effective' dreaming, the second an ambitious and hollow scientist who controls and attempts to direct Orr's dreams. The unstable combination of the two characters enacts problems of truth and authority that had not figured in earlier apocalyptic fictions, and produces unexpected and inept global 'improvements', one of which leads to an alien invasion of Earth (another science-fiction staple). This outcome introduces a third term – benign aliens – that breaks the blockage of the Orr–Haber relationship and brings about a resolution, in the form of a return of everyday muddle.

Apocalypse has to justify its power in the face of everyday life, with its local concerns and realities. This need is present in the texts discussed in chapter 6, and it recurs in the two novels considered in chapter 7. Tom Perrotta's *The Leftovers* treats the aftermath of a catastrophe ('the Disappearance') that is without sublimity, drama or even apparent point, and shows the struggles of those left behind after the apparently random snatching from their lives of many of their community. Its setting is American small-town ordinariness and it sympathetically revisits banal places, practices and conflicts (the mall; buying Christmas presents; adolescent stroppiness). Meanwhile, 'the Disappearance' casts a dark, violent shadow. The plot issues in both murder and new life, and the series of departures from the town with which the novel ends can be seen as a sort of normalising of the catastrophic disappearances that threw everything into doubt before the novel began. Douglas Coupland's *Girfriend in a Coma* presents a very different and much edgier take on everyday life – the life of drifting and media-enmeshed young people in the suburbs of Vancouver. The end of the world happens, and is dramatised with great vim; everybody dies except the group of friends who are at the centre of the novel; but this happens in a context of weirdness in which the boundaries between life, the media, the simulacral, death, death-in-life (the girlfriend of the title) and afterlife as a ghost are all blurred. And it happens in a context in which the everyday materiality of life is mediated, brand-named, at once familiar and tired. The road to recovery and perhaps to a new purpose is very much twistier than was the case in *The Leftovers*. The ending of Coupland's novel acknowledges the fictionality of fictions of apocalypse in a risky way.

Chapter 8 moves to the contemporary city, indeed the contemporary world city. The British disaster fictions of the 1940s and 1950s that are considered in chapter 2 tended to abandon the ruined city, without regret, for practical struggle in the countryside. The revolt against the pastoral that was part of the reorientation of apocalyptic fiction in the 1960s and 1970s involved a very different imagination of Nature, powerful and inexorable in Ballard, rich but dangerous in Carter. In the novels considered in chapter 8, Don DeLillo's *Cosmopolis* and China Miéville's *Kraken*, the scene is the city, with its energies, violent instability, traditions and unexpected encounters. Apocalyptic disaster is threatened and in progress: these are not novels of aftermath. This is so because it is the energy of the city that produces apocalypse – and also foments alternatives and resistances to its on-rush. In both novels, however, this energy also manifests as something like insanity, a rush of events and personalities and distortions of time and space that can be seen as the marks of apocalypse as it begins to shift prevailing reality (such as it is) off its axis. The protagonist of *Cosmopolis* serves as caricature of the quest for subjective self-realisation and the drive towards death that had figured in many of the novels discussed in chapters 3 and 4, as well as an up-dating of the figure of Anti-Christ. The city through which Eric Packer passes on his way towards death offers, out of its communal energy, a series of moments of transcendence that he witnesses but hardly experiences. The action of *Kraken* sets a trio of ordinary Londoners against several weird and vicious abhuman villains who are trying to bring about the abolition of reality itself, yet reality is already unstable in both productive and horrifying ways, and the usual boundaries between animate and inanimate, alive and dead, do not apply.

Apocalypse – the sequence of catastrophe, aftermath and perhaps recovery, or transcendence – has always had its rivals where social fear and gloom are concerned: the normality of crisis and emergency in modern society; the imagination or the fear of unqualified doom, an end to everything, without aftermath (as happens in Shute's *On the Beach*, and impends in Ballard's *The Crystal World*); notions of Decline and Fall, or the coming of a new Dark Age, such as are felt to threaten to recur with civilisations and empires; the heat death of the universe. There is a general – not to say cluttered – contemporary imaginary of bad events and conditions, of which apocalypse is only one. What is more, the real history of violence and destruction (the World Wars, the Holocaust, other genocides) presses hard on the element of hope that figures in traditional apocalypse and recurs in many contemporary apocalyptic fictions. Perhaps apocalyptic fiction fails to go far enough, given the history of the twentieth century; or perhaps, alternatively, apocalypse and its dark cousins are balefully blocking the possibilities of constructive resistance to threatened doom, and need to be thought past. In chapter

9 two very different novels are contrasted. First, Jeff VanderMeer's *Dead Astronauts*. *Dead Astronauts* is set in the aftermath of catastrophe, and in this wrecked and fragmented world varied personages best categorised as abhuman struggle with painful pasts they can remember and face only in images or in stalled, remorseless repetitions. The text adapts to this extreme situation by abandoning a single narrative, delving into the feeling-worlds of each of its inhabitants in turn, and making use of a range of variations of syntax and typography. Second, Kim Stanley Robinson's *Green Earth*. *Green Earth* tells of the coming of seriously dangerous climate change – it's not merely impending, it is happening – but imagines how humans might draw on civilisational resources, not merely of science and of democratic politics, but also of sociability and curiosity, to lessen destruction and make society more just. Modern humans such as ourselves make only a feeble appearance in *Dead Astronauts*, and one not commensurate with the harm they have done; it's from the anger, disgust and dismissiveness of the writing that we infer ourselves and how we are endangering nature. In each of these novels, we are taken in a radically contrary direction beyond apocalyptic narrative.

Apocalyptic Narratives and Contemporary Temporality

> The power of an event can flow from its unresolvable heart, all the cruel and elusive elements that don't add up, and it makes you do odd things, and tell stories to yourself, and build believable worlds.
>
> (Don DeLillo, *Underworld*)

Modernity begins by organising time and making it uniform. Raymond Williams (1985, 295) catches the shape the day falls into once this has been brought about: 'the morning newspaper, the early radio programme, the evening television'. A totalitarian regime might take this much further: there is a ten-hour clock in *Metropolis*; or it might come to signify the imprisonment of routine, as with the clock that strikes 'with a dead sound on the final stroke of nine' in *The Waste Land* (line 68). In more recent culture this inescapable order and clarity shifts and erodes. The clocks stop at 1:17 at the moment of catastrophe in *The Road*, and in this the novel follows history (at Hiroshima; in the 2011 tsunami in Japan).[28] Eric Packer in *Cosmopolis*, who lives by the

---

[28] McCarthy 2007, 54; Boyer 1996, 159; Parry 2017, 209; and there is the shifting minute hand in the clock of the Bulletin of Atomic Scientists. And

instantaneous information the data screens convey, finds that his watch – which is also a camera – jumps ahead to show him his own corpse in the morgue. In J. G. Ballard's *The Drowned World*, Kerans explores the partly submerged city, abandoned in the catastrophic heating of Earth:

> One of the clock-faces was without its hands; the other, by coincidence, had stopped at almost exactly the right time – 11-35. Kerans wondered whether the clock was in fact working, tended by some mad recluse clinging to a last meaningless register of sanity [...] (*The Drowned World*, 57)

In George R. Stewart's *Earth Abides*, the post-apocalyptic passage from the remnants of modern civilisation to tribalism is blended with the central character's passage from youth to age and death, and this gives the whole narrative a quiet inevitability and naturalness. In more recent apocalyptic fiction, stable temporality is often modified in uncanny ways, or seen as collapsing altogether. The apocalyptic mythos always allowed for this – history, and time as we have known it, come to a stop in traditional apocalypse. In science-fiction apocalypses, the catastrophe that destroys the present state of humanity often comes out of the blue, as an invasion from outside the prevailing scheme of things (a comet approaching Earth, a hitherto unknown and also incurable disease). Contemporary apocalyptic fictions often press these conditions to extremes. Moreover, temporality has developed new intensities and densities in contemporary culture. Contemporary apocalyptic fictions give form to these intensities and densities.

Apocalyptic narrative often conforms to the modern emphasis on the immanent, on process: events accumulate, grimly; characters wait and witness. Sometimes they tour a series of significant sites, but in more recent fictions this movement tends to become a wandering. (Stewart's Ish makes the tour; Ballard's and Kavan's characters wander, or drift; in *Dead Astronauts* there are significant sites, but no topography, no sense that you might travel from one to another.) The reader experiences an alternation of, or sometimes a conflict between, dramatic, even sensational happenings, and repetition or stasis. There is an emphasis on the sudden, the overwhelming, the explosive happening, with an eliciting of the sensual desires that it can satisfy (orgasm, vertigo, expansion as of an explosion caught in slo-mo); there is also a tendency

---

there is the shattered clock of Big Ben in Ballard's *The Wind from Nowhere* (1967, 123). See also Margaret Atwood (2008, 167) on the tradition of the clock stopping at the moment of death.

to a plethora of violent, sudden, dramatic events that tend to cancel one another out or lead to a kind of drunkenness. We find this effect in Don DeLillo's *Cosmopolis*, and in Iain M. Banks's Culture novels, for instance, *Consider Phlebas* (1987), in which horrendous acts of violence or huge destruction are piled on top of one another until the novel ends in exhaustion with most of the characters either dead or unable to do more than babble. Recent apocalyptic fictions tend to feature an overload of events, indeed, of disasters (Ursula K. Le Guin, *The Lathe of Heaven*); fragmented, multi-stranded plots (Anthony Burgess, *The End of the World News*); post-apocalyptic conditions in which memory and temporality are haywire (Jeff Noon, *Falling out of Cars*; Jeff VanderMeer, *Dead Astronauts*). Catastrophe and its aftermaths in Margaret Atwood's *MaddAddam* trilogy are narrated in flashbacks and with abrupt jumps in time.[29] In Coupland's *Girlfriend in a Coma* a very thorough catastrophe enters into a world that is full of simulacra and is already subject to alternate states, not merely of consciousness but of being, and events in individual lives and for humanity as a whole are subject to abrupt stalls and recoveries.

This complexity – extreme events, but many of them – may reflect contemporary uncertainty about disaster, which is at the same time singular and frequent. Repeated disaster or atrocity can overwhelm the apocalyptic narrative structure altogether – in which case we are left with Hell, in which succession gives way to repetition. This happens in Jeff VanderMeer's *Dead Astronauts*, in which the characters are imprisoned by past torture or abuse so that their present is a repetition of memories, or are entrapped in scenarios that are versions of previous scenarios, and in Cormac McCarthy's *Blood Meridian*, in which the repetition of massacre and murder is distributed evenly across time and space.

Again, apocalyptic fictions will often slow into scenes, pageant-like tableaus, refusing the forward momentum of the plot. The clearest examples of this repetition are to be found in J. G. Ballard's apocalyptic fictions of the 1960s and later: time stalled or reversing, characters not journeying so much as wandering among certain sites (*The Drought, Hello America, The Day of Creation*): one thing next to another rather than one thing after another, to borrow from Stephen Daedalus in *Ulysses*.[30] In Don DeLillo's *Zero K*, apocalypse is present only as a series of installations – videos of harrowing war and disaster displayed on giant screens.

Helga Nowotny observes a pervasive element in contemporary life that leads her to posit that we are living in an 'extended present' that

---

[29] *Oryx and Crake* (2003), *The Year of the Flood* (2009), *MaddAddam* (2013).
[30] Joyce 1960, 45 (first page of the Proteus section).

has absorbed the future: the future, in health, technology and ecology, consists of a series of coming problems that need to be solved now. Relevant here is the contemporary imperative of total availability: in an earlier period only the emergency services had to be on call 24/7, but this obligation now extends to shopping hours, global finance, attention to one's text messages and so on (Nowotny 1994, 96–99). This prevailing public time encroaches on private time. In *Cosmopolis*, Eric Packer shifts between the screens and messages that tell of the fate of the yen (his bet on the yen is causing his and the world's financial meltdown) and the screens that, as he watches, convey the condition of his internal organs: moment to moment, in both realms; meanwhile, rioters are actually shaking and defacing his limo, in an intrusion of the unscreened. Kim Stanley Robinson's *Green Earth* celebrates the richness of data and experience that is now available, and its potential to generate ideas and solutions, but also dramatises the dangers of intimate surveillance, the aspirations of some dark agencies for 'Total Information Awareness'. The intensified realism and satire of *Cosmopolis* and the more traditional science-fiction realism of *Green Earth* are pointing to similar phenomena.

The more recent concept of the 'post-histoire', 'a perpetual present, structures reproducing themselves in a void without hope' goes further, and has been usefully applied to J. G. Ballard.[31] Nowotny sets out her analysis in terms of an intensifying modernity; more recent discussions fall under the heading of postmodernity, globalisation or 'liquid modernity'. It is something like this all-embracing present, without anchor in a narrative of the past and without apparent consequences and repercussions that is crammed into a single day in *Cosmopolis*, so that the text seems to have assembled the materials for apocalypse without an apocalyptic narrative taking hold. In Douglas Coupland's *Girlfriend in a Coma*, apocalypse enters daily life in the suburbs, crammed with images and commodities; the central characters have no place in history beyond the vague one that is given by their membership of a generation, and at first the catastrophe makes little change in their way of life. Purpose only comes into their lives after it is revealed that the end of the world was faked, laid on for their edification, a sort of mega-media event based on special effects.

There are recent apocalyptic fictions in which time and everyday reality succumb to uncanny shifts, for instance *Cosmopolis*, in which

---

[31] Gasiorek 2005, 20. The formulation also fits Ernst Jünger's *On the Marble Cliffs* (1939), a novel that very definitely aestheticises apocalypse. Jünger is one of the disillusioned would-be aristocratic thinkers discussed in Neithammer and van Laak in relation to the post-histoire.

time is apt to jump ahead of itself and happenings appear on film before they 'actually' happen – and this in a narrative set on a single day, but one so crammed with events as to parody the notion of setting a novel on a single day (as in *Ulysses*). Meanwhile, the notion of apocalypse is itself parodied because the financial collapse is set going by the novel's main character, who cannot be bothered to explain why he is doing this, though (being a character in a novel by Don DeLillo) he is in other respects dazzlingly intelligent. Time runs backwards in *Time's Arrow* (Martin Amis, 1991), from the present to the Holocaust, at which point, in this reversal, Jews are removed from the ovens and restored to life; it's a fantasy of restoration and resurrection that depends disturbingly on the dazzling ingenuity of the text; the way in which effect usually follows cause is so thoroughly revised that we are left with the poignant impossibility of the wish that the Holocaust should never have happened, which the novel has ingeniously managed to make into a narrative.

In other apocalypses, alternative realities coincide or compete with or succeed one another (Ursula Le Guin, *The Lathe of Heaven*; Jonathan Leithem, *Amnesia Moon*; Doris Lessing, *The Memoirs of a Survivor*): there is no single ground to reality and time. In *The Lathe of Heaven* this succession of realities, each fundamentally changed from those that preceded it, is what constitutes the apocalypse, though it is a condition of the wholesale reality shifts that only one person is aware of them, and everyone else is blank to the preceding realities and accepts each new one as if it had always been in existence. In *Amnesia Moon* (1995) we have at first alternative societies, dystopian enclaves, in the aftermath of a more general collapse, toured by the novel's protagonist in a fashion that is common in apocalyptic fictions, and then reality is gradually unhinged and shown to be malleable. In *The Memoirs of a Survivor* the ongoing social collapse is narrated by the survivor, who, however, cannot be bothered to analyse or explain it, and emphasis gradually shifts to other realities, sometimes visionary, sometimes domestic, that open up for her when she crosses a threshold in her apartment. One of these other realities figures a past that is closely tied to the present of its characters, whose behaviour it seems to explain, but the other figures a future that is transcendentally free of the present of the novel. In Anna Kavan's *Ice*, the characters wander a world subject both to the onset of an Ice Age and to disastrous, formless modern wars, but occasionally find themselves in a past of primitive barbarism, in which the young woman at the centre of the modern story seems to have a double. In Howard Jacobson's *J* (2014), catastrophe has left individuals in a kind of blank aftermath in which they move and speak uncertainly, largely because the catastrophe cannot be named – and is forbidden to be named – and hence is so pervasively present as not to be in the past at all.

Apocalypse Reimagined: Patterns and Shifts

The maker of a modern apocalypse fiction can be seen as facing a series of choices, which can be put in the form of questions. The pressure of these choices varies, depending on how much of traditional apocalypse he or she wants to hew to. Traditional apocalypse offers a sequence, and a series of figures, and by selecting and varying the author of a modern apocalypse expresses in recognisable forms overlapping imaginations of global conditions, global transformations, the prospects of the individual, the terrors and attractions of transformation, the absence or presence of powers greater than the human or out of human control, the options of escape from or submission to these powers or, alternatively, from the situation that prevailed before catastrophe. *Apocalypse in Crisis* traces how these choices have shifted over time, in particular, after a prelude on the nineteenth century, over the period from 1945 to the present, in the changing circumstances of (mostly) Anglo-American society and culture. Its subject is the changing poetics of the fiction of apocalypse, and the political and social implications of these changes.

Apocalypse begins with catastrophe: how is this imaged, what form does it take? Catastrophe involves mass death and destruction: how is destruction imaged, and how is death depicted, or not depicted? Death and dying is a culturally uncertain matter for the contemporary individual, not to speak of the narrative and emotional challenges of depicting mass death, or finding a substitute expression of it in an apocalyptic fiction.[32] Endings are questionable in modernist fiction, inescapable in fiction of the End (Kermode 1967/2000, especially chapter IV). Traditional apocalypse is directed by God and involves the triumph of the Messiah over the Anti-Christ: how do modern apocalyptic fictions depict power, whether that of invading aliens, benevolent or destroying, that of figures equivalent to the Anti-Christs and false prophets of traditional apocalypses, or simply that of leaders? In traditional apocalypse, catastrophe is followed, after an interval, by the arrival of a New Jerusalem: do modern apocalyptic fictions find an equivalent to this, in a secular or largely secular age? The answers

---

[32] The clearest example of this difficulty is the Holocaust, seldom represented and mainly unmentioned for years after 1945. See Judt 2005, 808–809.

to this last question turn out to be bound up with the answers to the question about death: the issue that embraces both questions is, how do apocalyptic fictions, which are about catastrophic endings, organise their own endings?

The Image of Catastrophe

In the earlier fictions among those discussed in *Apocalypse in Crisis*, catastrophe is imaged as something separate from the humans who witness it, cope with it, submit to it or rebuild after it. It takes the form of an intrusion into the world as it existed (often, in domestic peacefulness) before catastrophe happened – often, an invasion or epidemic. Because it takes this form, with a clear beginning as it arrives, it has the quality of an event rather than a situation or condition. It is witnessed – the narrator of *The War of the Worlds* sees and describes for us the emergence from its spacecraft of the first of the Martian invaders. It is something given, and indicated by clear signs (the epidemic in *Earth Abides*); its approach can be predicted and measured (the death of grass in John Christopher's novel of that name), or its nature and causes can be puzzled out (as in *The Day of the Triffids* and *The Kraken Wakes* by John Wyndham). Its agents are revealed, as the Overlords and then the Overmind are revealed in *Childhood's End*. All this might seem in the nature of any apocalyptic fiction, given that the point of an apocalyptic fiction is to assemble fears and possibilities into an image, an imagined phenomenon that exerts the unmistakeable power of the given and active. In fact, however, this quality of apocalyptic fictions will change, at first fading, and then being replaced by something different, more elusive or more immersive, either hard to grasp or hard to see as separate and intrusive: more in the nature of a situation or condition. The history of apocalyptic fiction can be seen as the history of a coming to terms with generality, abstractness and invisibility in the source of apocalyptic catastrophe. Catastrophe is somewhere between a distinct problem (whether a menacing asteroid or nuclear war or climate change) and a general condition that is a threat and an oppression because it is hard to define and all-encompassing. In the latter case, the catastrophe is something like System or History, conceived as determinant and hard to escape. So, the fictions vary between clear-cut images of what is destroying or transforming the world (a monster, an event) and more abstract suggestions. It is the latter that comes to prevail, though even recent apocalyptic fictions, such as China Miéville's *Kraken* and Jeff VanderMeer's *Dead Astronauts*, set themselves to redefine the monster.

Before following this shift, however, it is worth glancing at an issue raised by the intruding, invading kind of catastrophe. In its separateness it might seem to image our powerlessness and our lack of responsibility: it comes from elsewhere, it is alien, it is a freak of nature such as an epidemic, it is irresistible. In its clarity and solidity, it might also serve as compensation: what is felt as elsewhere, above us, diffused in global conditions, is now palpable and visible.

Perhaps the catastrophe has a human origin, in the tensions and aggressions of great power rivalries that led to nuclear war (in *On the Beach*) or the release of rogue weapons from space (in *The Day of the Triffids*), or its power is increased by human misuse of pesticides and fertilisers (in *The Death of Grass*). As the post-catastrophic narrative unfolds we find ourselves with a group of ordinary people who had no control over these global abuses. Indeed, an apocalyptic fiction in which the catastrophe is imaged as invader or intruder is very often local and domestic in its narrative, something that asks for our sympathy with a struggling group of survivors who are not much different from ourselves. (This focus on the struggling group of ordinary survivors will change in later fictions, together with a change in the image of the catastrophe itself.) So, the invading or intruding source of disaster, often monstrous in form, can serve as image of our powerlessness, or a means of exculpating us from the folly that led to disaster. Freed from responsibility for a world now destroyed, we can become agents again, rebuilding some form of society, or learning to face death (in *On the Beach*).

The apocalyptic catastrophe may begin as a chance event (in *The End of the World News*, for instance, the bad luck of an asteroid that is on a collision course with Earth), but it comes to stand for ineluctable necessity: no one on Earth is outside its power. Paradoxically, however, the transformation it wreaks may release the survivor into free action, even capricious action. This may take the form of resistance to the all-encompassing nature of the catastrophe, or of submission to it. In any case, apocalyptic catastrophe has the effect of unsettling, or shaking up, relations between necessity and contingency, relations that, before the catastrophe, had been felt to have frozen into stagnation (the regime of conformity) or merely settled into the modern condition of continual, confusing crisis. Global catastrophe releases the survivors into clear tasks or into subjective choices (in Ballard, for instance).

The tendency in the earlier part of the history traced here is for the figure of apocalyptic threat or disaster to change from the gothic to something more impersonal and abstract, even, unseen and therefore bodiless. The nineteenth-century apocalypses briefly discussed in chapter l embody the threat in a monster, often uncannily arousing both awe and horror, at first single (Dracula, Moby Dick), later, in *The War of the Worlds*, collective (the invading Martians). In later fictions of the 1940s, the catastrophe is different: an epidemic almost without observed symptoms in *Earth Abides*; an invisible process happening elsewhere and showing its spread only in the absence of life in *On the Beach* (radioactive fallout: the investigating submarine sees only deserted but intact cities), and in later texts the spread of ice in *Ice* and *Planet 8*. Monsters figure in *Childhood's End*, cleverly varied – the Overlords resemble the traditional image of Satan but are actually benign; but the aspect of apocalyptic transformation that probably most grips the reader in this novel is again impalpable and general, the mutation of Earth's children that at once bestows vast powers on them and separates them utterly from the rest of humanity.

Because the catastrophe has a clear origin and can be clearly figured, the narration can focus on a witness who reports. The clearest example of the witness is the narrator of *The War of the Worlds*, at times granted a panoramic view, at times imprisoned and restricted to a peephole, while the narrative of *Earth Abides* is shaped by Ish's life history as much as by the affairs of his 'tribe'. Often there is a tour of the devastated world, a kind of survey, before the characters settle in one locality as in *Earth Abides* (a tour by car) and *On the Beach* (by submarine). In later fictions, in keeping with changes in the nature of the catastrophe and in the individual subject's agendas, and as the protagonist ceases to act as witness, the tour becomes a wandering, for instance in Ballard's apocalypses and in Carter's *Heroes and Villains*; a later example is Cormac McCarthy's *The Road*. An extreme rendition of this wandering is the impeded journey of Eric Packer's limousine in *Cosmopolis*: he is slowly going nowhere in his huge vehicle that is more like a room than a car, while scenes of apocalyptic disorder come to him.[33]

The source of catastrophe can often be interpreted as an image of technology in its advanced, impersonal and incomprehensible form, as is plausible with the Martians in *The War of the Worlds* and the triffids in Wyndham's novel (the triffids originate as plants bred and altered for human use and pleasure); if so, once this aspect of technology is loaded onto the alien and invasive, we can freely use our own technology – guns and warships unsuccessfully in *The War of the Worlds*, rifles and flamethrowers effectively in *The Day of the Triffids*, a submarine as seeker in vain for signs of life in *On the Beach*.

---

[33] Gary K. Wolfe (1983, especially 8–16) discusses the journey through the wasteland as a phase in the narrative of catastrophe and its aftermath.

That catastrophe is something with an explicable cause that can be summed up is still the case in the novels by Ballard and Aldiss that are discussed in part 2 of *Apocalypse in Crisis*, but the explanation in each of these novels is brisk, summary and of little weight in the text as a whole. The emphasis in the text as a whole is on how the catastrophe is ongoing, and still transformative, so that the protagonists are living inside it, in the regime of transformation and all that it has released. The small group on whom the narrative centres in the apocalyptic fictions of the 1940s and 1950s lives in a locality, domestic, and very often perennial, in that they have taken refuge in the countryside, which, more than the city, is where they can be felt to belong anyway. The protagonists of, for instance, J. G. Ballard's apocalyptic fictions of the 1960s make their way through a shifting and transformed landscape. If the characters in the postwar disaster novels are returned to the countryside where they naturally belong, the central characters in Ballard's novels, and also in Carter's *Heroes and Villains* and Aldiss's *Barefoot in the Head*, are released into a new world. This transformed world has come to reflect dreams and impulses as well as allowing them. What it is that it has released the protagonist to seek will appear when we discuss the depiction of death in some apocalyptic novels of the 1960s and 1970s; certainly, it is no longer the re-foundation of ordinary social and family life.

The erosion of the clear-cut image of catastrophe is taken a step further in *The Memoirs of a Survivor*, where the central characters are living in conditions of social breakdown with which they cope from time to time but that they cannot explain and, eventually, decide not to try to explain; after which they turn inwards, away from the disorder in the streets of the city, and depart for another state of being altogether. In this case it is part of the condition of disaster that those living through it cannot really define it.

The shift is fully emplaced by the time we reach *Cosmopolis* and *Kraken*. Here the catastrophe, manifest as ongoing chaos, and threat with multiple symptoms, is a condition in the midst of which the protagonists live. They cannot witness or describe it as if it were something separate; they are immersed. There is a thickening of detail and imagery in response to the fact that apocalypse is not now intruding or invading, but pervasive. The central character of *Cosmopolis*, the mega-rich financier Eric Packer, is as monstrous as Haber in *The Lathe of Heaven* or Crake in Margaret Atwood's *Oryx and Crake*, but his destructiveness is merely a part of the disorder and cannot be seen as its centre and source. In *Kraken* the notion that the apocalyptic threat might be identified, tracked down and averted helps to shape the rather frantic plot, but never really reaches a centre. The monster in the case, though it is decorated with the traditional apocalyptic associations of the Kraken, is in fact a victim needing to be rescued. *Kraken* can be seen as a parody of problem-solving apocalyptic fictions such as Wyndham's *The Kraken Wakes* (where the task that occupies the protagonists is to piece together evidence as to the nature of the unseen aliens who emerge from under the sea), or of those based on sensational revelations as more and more is made plain and the fate of humanity comes into clearer view, such as *Childhood's End*. Neither with *Cosmopolis* nor with *Kraken* can we see apocalyptic catastrophe as embodying the power of technology when imagined as something over against humans. Eric Packer's power can be represented in ones and zeroes, but proves to be immaterial and elusive; technology in *Kraken* is subsumed in the controllable but magical interactions of matter and spirit, animate and inanimate.

In *The Leftovers* and *Girlfriend in a Coma*. we can identify yet a further stage in the slipping from view of the image of catastrophe, and, paradoxically, it occurs in apocalyptic fictions that return to the local and domestic, the narrative of ordinary people coping with transformation, this time not in England (as was the case with many of the postwar disaster novels) but in the small towns and suburbs of North America. The paradox is that the disaster actually involves, or it points towards, a deity, as in traditional apocalypse, but it also involves the imposition by the deity of a sort of blankness, an emptiness, in *The Leftovers*, and the imposition by the deity of an elaborate fake in *Girlfriend*. In *The Leftovers* the catastrophe is that huge numbers of people have disappeared, vanished from life. What but a deity could bring this about – a kind of negative miracle – yet there seems neither pattern nor point to the disappearances, nor is there concrete and visible devastation (ruins, say). It is this blankness and absence that the survivors must deal with in their grief, and the novel examines its reverberations through their ordinary small-town relationships. In *Girlfriend* the central characters live in unhappiness at their lives' lack of meaning and indeed of content apart from commodities and bits of pop culture, while the boundaries of life and death are blurred in multiple ways. Into this condition of anomie and confusion there comes the end of the world, organised, we have to assume, by some superpower or deity (there's nothing that would get us closer to a definition, let alone a theology, than these guesses) whose angelic messenger is the callow ghost of a teenager. Then there is the revelation that the end of the world was faked, and when life resumes as if after sleep (or coma), the central characters are invited to venture into it with a sense of mission. They have been rescued, and meaning has supposedly been restored to their lives, by a kind of trick, a mega-simulation in a world of simulations.

In the most recent of the fictions discussed in *Apocalypse in Crisis*, *Dead Astronauts* (2019), a condition of post-apocalyptic wreckage and fragmentation prevails. The novel offers a diagnosis of the causes of the calamity, but the personages who inhabit its world, victims or monsters or a combination of both, are mostly contending with the conditions of aftermath, in which identities merge and split, death is postponed or repeated and reproduction is compromised. The past causes and nature of the catastrophe are suggested, but they are emphatically past, and figure often as hauntings or as memories that cannot be faced.

Death and the Individual

Apocalyptic catastrophe very commonly involves mass death as well as vast destruction, but none of the diverse texts discussed in *Apocalypse in Crisis* really depicts mass death, piles of rotting corpses or vast vistas of ruin. Peter Paik's *From Utopia to Apocalypse* makes a different selection of texts, which do depict mass death, and pursues a different argument about apocalypse.

If mass death is assumed but not confronted, then the death that does happen, and very often at the conclusion of the text, and thus by way of conclusion, is individualised. Individual death, witnessed or explained, is a staple of fiction; apocalyptic fiction would seem to be turning away from mass death towards this more familiar topic. It would be mistaken to attach a set significance to a death (or, as will be noticed later, a birth) when it occurs at the end of an apocalyptic fiction. Individuality itself tends over the course of the history traced here to be blurred or blended, or exaggerated. The treatment of death, usually occurring towards the end of the apocalyptic fiction, serves as a way of expressing the text's attitude to the individual, and this suggests that investigating – even, dismantling – the individual subject is central to modern apocalyptic fiction.

In many cases, the effect is an attempt to re-balance normal social life, in which, in peacetime, death is inevitable but individual. An example is the death of Joey in *Earth Abides*. Joey is the promising son of Ish and Em who are the novel's equivalent to Adam and Eve. He dies of disease. His death is painful, but it can be mourned and accepted. The mass death that began the novel was only vaguely observed, not really shown. Eventually, however, Ish comes to see that Joey's promising abilities were not what the new world needed anyway. Again, in *On the Beach* the attempt to imagine death as inevitable but chosen, in the context of domestic life (children, pets) falters in the face of the characters' tendency blankly to deny what is happening. Death is at once domestic and absent (in the image of the cities viewed from a submarine – empty and lifeless, with no signs of corpses).

In other cases, the death is a killing, justified because it is the act of an agent or agents, and in that way a recovery of meaning in the face of mass catastrophe. In *Earth Abides* it is the collective of elders of the tribe that decides on the execution of Charlie, a diseased and dissolute stranger. In *The War of the Worlds* the narrator kills the curate, with whom he has shared refuge in a cellar, because the curate has been unhinged by fear and threatens to give away their presence to the Martians busy close outside. This death can be compared to the death of the Martian whose uncanny wailing the narrator hears in the deserted London at the end of the novel – a death that signals rescue for the defeated human race, but that has a poignancy in contrast to the hole-in-corner killing of the curate. There is nothing quite like the death of the Martian in later texts. We see the first Martian born from the pit its landing has made, and the last wailing (it seems) as it dies; the first Martian is utterly alien, the last can (almost) be mourned.[34] In contrast, steady and pragmatic, is John Christopher's *The Death of Grass*, which follows a band of survivors, fighting their way from London to a refuge in the north of England, the family farm of the Custances. The only way to survive the mass death brought about by the death of grass is to inflict death on opponents as they are encountered, and the text accepts this. There are plenty of killings, each worried over and eventually justified by the leaders of the band, John Custance in particular. The exception to this conscientiousness is the ruthless and rational Pirrie, who often takes the lead in the violence, and eventually dies by accident just as they fight their way into safety – a convenient death that underlines the ruthless rationality of the text itself: Pirrie is disposed of, having served his purpose in the narrative.[35]

If a death – in these cases, individual, comprehensible, caused, and in those ways normal – seals the end of an apocalyptic story that began

---

[34] Wells's later *The World Set Free* (1914) ends with 'The Last Days of Marcus Karenin', one of the author's enlightened mouthpieces. Wells's choice to end his confident and optimistic novel with a death is a striking one, even if in his last days Karenin holds forth to a group of respectful young people and we are mainly given more opinions, having had many already.

[35] Yet, at this point, as the band are finally attaining entrance to their refuge and Pirrie is eliminated, John's brother David who had founded the refuge is (accidentally) killed: an echo of the killing that seals the foundation of the city (Romulus kills Remus): not so simply a matter of the rationality of the text, then.

with mass death, then birth can signal a new beginning, and with birth can be grouped the appearance of new life when it had seemed that there was no prospect of this. There are plenty of examples of this, and they will be sketched below, but it is worth entering a preliminary qualification. Apocalypse presents an extreme image of the crisis of change in modern society, change that tends to divide parents and children, and different generations. Apocalyptic catastrophe often opens a distance between the old and the young; the young become alien, or simply hard to understand. In *Childhood's End*, this gap is sensational, and central to the catastrophe: the young cease to be human. In *The Memoirs of A Survivor* the behaviour of the young is the subject of puzzled observation, hard to fit into any pattern – sometimes feral, sometimes rational. Don De Lillo's *Falling Man* offers at one point a vignette of the separate universe of the young, in which Bin Laden figures as a mythical figure, a mysterious 'Bill Lawton'.[36] In *The Leftovers*, a more securely domestic novel, the uneasy relations between Kevin, his daughter Jill and her lively friend Aimee pull the novel out of the apocalyptic and back into the contemporary normal – it is Jill's mother who has become incomprehensible because of her jarringly different responses to the catastrophe.

Yet the motif of birth or new life is recurrent. Sometimes this new life simply appears. This is the case with the wonderful survival of the narrator's wife in *The War of the Worlds*, which seems like pure contingency; with Brian Aldiss's *Greybeard*, where it had appeared that humans, become sterile, were slowly dying out, only for a hint, a glimpse, of pregnancy to occur; and with Cormac McCarthy's *The Road*, where after unremitting struggle, gloom and violence (cannibalism), it appears that new people have appeared from across the sea who are human in being neither cannibals nor degraded nor crazy prophets. In *Dead Astronauts*, a novel in which human reproduction is seen as poisoned by the abuse of children, there are several moments in which new life appears by spawning, magical, joyful, involving the dissolution of the creature that spawned, and unrelated to human birth or death. In Kim Stanley Robinson's *Green Earth*, catastrophe is averted by intelligent, co-operative action, and a seal is put on this – anti-apocalyptic – outcome when the novel ends with pregnancy and marriage. To complete the picture of mortal life, there is also a death, from old age, that of the protagonist's Tibetan friend and counsellor, Rudra.

In other instances the pairing of new life and killing would seem to elaborate rather than alter the recurrent pattern of normalising death by

---

[36] DeLillo 2007, 73–74; see also 16–17, 37–39.

giving it individual quality and/or an agent. P. D. James's *The Children of Men* is set in a future in which humans have become sterile and Britain has fallen into the rule of a dictatorship that organises mass killings of the aged. (One of these killings is dramatised in the novel (108–111), an exception to the observation that depiction of mass killing is usually absent from the texts discussed in *Apocalypse in Crisis*.) *The Children of Men* ends with a miraculous birth in a woodshed, clearly a recurrence of the birth of Christ in a stable, though at almost the same time the narrator of the story (hitherto sceptical and disillusioned, now brought to belief) kills the dictator, who figures in the fable as a Herod. Margaret Atwood's *Oryx and Crake*, in which as far as we know humans have been eliminated except for Snowman, ends with the appearance from across the seas of human strangers, and the way is presumably prepared for the rebuilding of a more organic, less corrupt society in the following two novels, *The Year of the Flood* and *MaddAddam*. *Oryx and Crake* has involved mass death, though also a single killing, the murder of Oryx by Snowman, an enigmatic event in which, however, motive is hard to define.

These more recent cases, in which an apocalyptic fiction ends with a killing (if, also, with the prospect of a birth), seem to extend the pattern that was observed of the postwar disaster novels such as *Earth Abides*. Another recent novel can be added to the list, *The Leftovers*, which concludes with the acceptance of a newborn baby into the community that has been trying to recover from mass disappearance, but also with a death perpetrated at the orders of a sect, the Guilty Remnant, whose members have responded to the Disappearance in a more violent and perverse fashion, though still one that involves planning and a kind of logic. Does this mean that the kind of shift that was observed above in the discussion of the image of apocalypse does not happen with the treatment of death? Is modern apocalyptic fiction, on the evidence of the novels selected for discussion in *Apocalypse in Crisis*, stubbornly centred on the individual? Does it continue to reimagine death as occurring to a single person in particular circumstances, not lost among millions in a welter of extermination, and, when the death is a killing, as it often is, seeing it as something motivated and intended, not (again) the result of vast impersonal process, as, for instance, killing in war is? The implications of the different texts discussed by Peter Paik will need to be discussed, because they divide their interest between superheroes and the vast mass of the dead, but, first, a very important variation in the depiction of individual death needs to be examined. This will demonstrate a shift parallel to those observed with the image of apocalypse itself.

The treatment of death that has been summarised so far tends to reassert ordinary life, and death – even 'ordinary' killing – in the face of vast apocalyptic disaster. In this respect, apocalyptic novels of the 1940s resist apocalypse, reasserting the ordinary and domestic in the shadow of the vast catastrophe of the Second World War itself, in which masses had been deprived of autonomy, if not dehumanised, in global conflict. The transcendent is absent, or expresses itself painfully by a lack. Yet apocalypse traditionally ends with the appearance of a New Jerusalem, a transcendental outcome in which History, and mundane worldly life, come to an end.

In many later apocalyptic fictions, the death that closes the story is a suicide, a kind of oblivion, and one that is chosen. It resembles an immolation, perversely or ambiguously transcendental. This effect links otherwise diverse texts in the 1960s and 1970s: all three of those by J. G. Ballard that are discussed in part 2, *Ice* by Anna Kavan and arguably Angela Carter's *Heroes and Villains* (which ends with a death and a prospective birth that are both ambiguous). In a much more complicated way, in the form of a departure from the scene of disaster towards a state of being that is beyond death, it occurs in the endings of *Planet 8* and *The Memoirs of a Survivor* by Doris Lessing.

The case is clearest in Ballard's apocalyptic novels of the 1960s, where the protagonist's drift towards death is a form of self-immolation, and comes as he answers to the message of the landscape that has been transformed by the catastrophe itself, releasing new and powerful natural forces (in *The Drowned World* and *The Crystal World*). The transformed landscape becomes the scene of enacted impulses and performances. Catastrophe has swept away not merely the banality and tedium of ordinary life but the dominance of reason. The regime of necessity – the catastrophe as global and all-encompassing – releases individual will and impulse, in the form of drift away from engagement with others and towards death in the protagonist, in the form of violent caprice in others whom he encounters, such as Lomax in *The Drought* and Strangman in *The Drowned World*. The protagonist already experiences transcendence, in the form of the landscape that expresses his dreams and drives. He experiences 'the promise of a lyric intensity outside the measure of normal experience', in Don DeLillo's phrase.[37] Suicide comes as final submission to this new condition. As regards *Ice* it is not appropriate to talk of transcendence in this way, but the drive of the three central characters, locked in a sado-masochistic relationship that at times blurs

---

[37] DeLillo, *Zero K*, 2017, 48. Contrast 'the inexpressibly dense experience of a man or woman alive on the earth' (*Zero K*, 142).

their identities, is towards pain and stultification, and the landscape of war and encroaching ice through which they travel is as much an emanation of their condition as it is an objective state.

In *Planet 8* and *Memoirs* the protagonists pass through death to a state beyond death and beyond material life, so here we have another form of transcendence at the end of a novel that stages, in *Planet 8*, the elimination of human and animal life on the planet by inexorable climate change, and in *Memoirs*, a prevailing disorder whose causes and even whose nature remain unclear. The two novels contrast in many ways. In *Planet 8* the catastrophe, the spreading of the ice, is a natural disaster that could not have been prevented and cannot be coped with or managed; transcendence is approached by experience of inexorable loss, a stripping away of comfort and hope, and by education at the hands of Johor, the representative of the supposedly wiser planet Canopus. The protagonists contemplate and deconstruct the notion of individuality, then, in passing beyond life, they shed individuality and become one ('the Representative'). In *Memoirs* the catastrophe is social, people – the young people whom the Survivor contemplates – try to cope with it, and it is not explained. Transcendence comes through another, uncanny place in which the Survivor has experienced (among other things) painful vignettes of how the young are formed and oppressed by their parents. This time, there is no teacher on hand, and the meditations of the Survivor shy away from conclusions. The eventual passage into another realm, with a rescuing female 'Presence', is scarcely preluded: it comes about, but this time it is not really learnt. *Planet 8* and *Memoirs*, otherwise so different, have in common their elimination of individual separateness and will and, in association with this, their concluding suggestion of a state beyond death. In this respect the embrace of transcendence, which marks the novels that follow after the postwar disaster science fictions and precedes the more sceptical later fictions, reaches a climax in *Planet 8* and *Memoirs*.

There are exceptions to this drive towards death and transcendence in apocalyptic fictions of the 1960s to the 1980s. Chapter 6 discusses some texts that resist the power of apocalypse to bring everything to one point (death, for instance). The protagonist of Arno Schmidt's *Nobodaddy's Children* finds the removal of almost all other humans a satisfactory confirmation of his feeling, or pose, that they are not worth much anyway. In Ursula Le Guin's *The Lathe of Heaven* the stakes in the relationship of Haber and Orr are not death and life but sanity and madness: Orr's unusual strength as a person means that he will neither murder Haber nor kill himself, though either action would have brought a stop to the repeated apocalyptic transformations that he and

Haber are causing. In Anthony Burgess's *The End of the World News* the strand of the text concerned with apocalypse ends by posing two very different suicides, that of the US President (very eloquent) and that of one of the main characters, the rambunctious Willett, largely motivated by the prospect that the ship that is to escape the annihilation of Earth will lack liquor.

Cosmopolis can be grouped with the 1960s novels of self-immolation, but only in a way that brings out its difference. The central character Eric Packer proceeds with very few hesitations towards his death. By this point he has stripped himself of his vast wealth, and his wife's, of any purposes and pleasures he has exhibited beyond the momentary and passing, of his limo, his clothes and his identity. So far, the protagonist's passage towards death is as undeviating as anything in Ballard and as grim as anything in Kavan, but the overall effect is very different. Transcendence passes from Eric Packer to what he witnesses in the later stages of his journey towards death – the quiet conversation of his driver and his barber, the naked mass photograph in which he participates, the funeral of the rap star Brutha Fez – this last the most striking example, but of course one that follows on from a death. These are incidents that depend on the vitality of the city that is (also) in apocalyptic chaos, yet incidents that so to speak leap out of its ordinary routine and texture. So, in *Cosmopolis* the self-immolation of the protagonist is more determined than it was even in the earlier Ballardian examples, but is stripped of its aspects of transcendence; the ordinary life – in this case, of the great city – is valued again, but, this time, in moments and flashes only. This fits with the imagination of apocalypse in *Cosmopolis* as something that both stems from the vitality of the city and is resisted by the vitality of the city.

A similar case can be made of *Kraken*, very much a novel of (threatened) apocalypse – in fact, apocalypses – in London, but there is now no steady approach towards death. There are killings in the novel, mostly bizarre in their modes, but they cannot be seen as marking a trajectory towards 'normal' death. The conditions of existence in the novel's world rule this out; the distinction between alive and dead is blurred, and it is possible to pass back and forth between the two, or to exist liminally in between the two; life in the form of purpose and animation is distributed across the whole spectrum of matter – the sea, London, scraps of detritus, various golems and puppets, as well as vermin, birds and humans. This transformed state of affairs and conditions of life is both the source of apocalyptic threat and what has to be managed and used by those who set out to avert it. *Dead Astronauts* elaborates a similar but much bleaker picture: violence and killing are rife, but death is sought as a possible end and release in a world where repetition and entrapment prevail. The novel does end when a death is accomplished, and the person dying is comforted as might be hoped for in a good death, but death is very often empty, merely the prelude to being revived and tortured and killed again, or withheld from a character whose existence is that of a wraith, or succeeded by another version of a mission that ended in death but that cannot be renounced. We have reached a point of extreme distance from what is found in most of the postwar disaster novels and in *The War of the Worlds*, in which recognisable, predictable normal life subsisted before the catastrophe and can be re-established or returned to after it.

Even in more recent apocalyptic novels that return to everyday realism, the distinction between life and death is blurred, complicated or to be desired and occasionally attained rather than stably relied on. In *The Leftovers* those who were snatched abruptly away by 'The Disappearance' did not undergo any perceptible dying and may not have died, though their loss has plunged the survivors into mourning. The novel tells of a recovery of day-to-day equilibrium in most of the characters, and ends with the appearance of new life, but the recovery is tentative. and the novel's ending is also marked by a death, by suicide. The inconclusiveness yet absoluteness of 'The Disappearance' has subtly threatened and undermined the practices of everyday life on which the characters have to rely. *Girlfriend in a Coma* is again set in the familiar world of the suburbs, but here aliveness is skewed and blurred in multiple ways – a woman who remains alive but in a coma for 17 years (and gives birth during that time), a ghost bringing messages from unnamed powers and working minor miracles, continual play with fakery and simulation. All this sets the terms for an apocalyptic end of the world that is thoroughly described but then completely retracted.

Audrey Schulman's *Theory of Bastards* (2018) offers two images of death denied that point in a similar direction. The later part of the novel takes place after a catastrophe that has eliminated most human and animal life. Two scientists, male and female, wander with a group of bonobo apes; they have had to leave a primate research station. Death denied is imaged directly in the bonobo female carrying the corpse of her baby with her for days after its death, and indirectly in that they are wandering across America with the aim (impossible, as they know but do not say) of reaching the man's wife in Britain, certainly dead, as they know but do not say.

One final example reasserts the contrast of mass death and individual deaths, but in extreme, inordinate form, as if the trope has been stretched to the limit. Iain M. Banks's *Consider Phlebas* (1987) ends with a prolonged firefight deep underground on a planet about which a powerful alien presence has warned 'THERE IS DEATH HERE' (294; capitals in original). In the course of this combat all of the remaining members of the company of adventurers at the centre of the plot are killed, so is the novel's main character Horza, and so are their two antagonists, members of a warrior species that is usually immortal. There is a spectacular, very drawn out, almost orgasmic train wreck that results in several deaths. Banks next provides appendices on the huge war, which has set the context for the narrative of individual actions and deaths that is now over, with total casualties comprising 851.4 billion persons and machines, and 53 planets and major moons. Individual deaths and killings are staged, to exhaustion; mass death is acknowledged, but only extra-textually. The gap between individual and mass death and destruction is thus reduced to absurdity.

There is a series of shifts, then: individual death is reasserted as normal and killing as motivated, in the face of mass death; then chosen by individuals as self-immolation or, at least, self-destruction, and chosen in relation to the transformation that catastrophe has wrought and in some cases the conditions of transcendence it has opened up; then succeeded by a blurring of the conditions of existence that robs death of its significance or its reality. This is parallel to the series of shifts in the figure of catastrophe that was sketched above.

Power

Apocalypse involves the exertion of almost unlimited, transformative power, manifest as catastrophe. As we have seen, the way apocalyptic catastrophe is imagined has changed: from being something that could be distinguished as an intervention or invasion into preceding normality, it has become a prevailing climate of disorder and violence in which the protagonists are immersed, often to the point that they cannot define what is going on or distinguish a single cause or entity as active in it. Apocalypse in its traditional form also involves a cast of powerful figures – the Messiah, the Anti-Christ, false prophets. These give direction and purpose to the events, and structure a contest of good and evil, faithful and infidel, culminating in a Last Judgement in which individual death is given its final meaning.

The figure of power would seem to be one of the constituents of traditional apocalypse that most invites variation and critique in more recent apocalyptic fictions. The texts discussed in *Apocalypse in Crisis* feature a wide variety of would-be leaders, teachers and men of power.

The conclusion from this evidence is clear: most of these figures fail, or resign, or prove fraudulent, or simply limited. (All of them, incidentally, are male.) Charteris in *Barefoot in the Head*, who is explicitly compared to Christ, retires and leaves his followers to their own devices. Eric Packer in *Cosmopolis*, who is closest to the Anti-Christ in his power and his values, whimsically discards his vast wealth, renounces his property, sheds even his clothes and dies anonymously. In *The Lathe of Heaven* the scientist Haber, a figure of human egoism and one compared to a 'bear-shaman-god' (157) repeatedly rearranging global social life in unstable alliance with his opposite, George Orr, makes a series of botched jobs of the transformations and eventually goes mad. If Haber is a version of Anti-Christ, updated as mad scientist, Orr is the closest to a figure of Christ who is encountered in the novels examined in *Apocalypse in Crisis*, but he mostly acts in association with and subordination to Haber, and is certainly not a Messiah. Johor in *The Making of the Representative for Planet 8* is the emissary (rather like a colonial commissioner) from Canopus who teaches the inhabitants of the planet to accept the end of life on the planet and prepare for their passage away from their individuality to a new life. He is an ambiguous figure at best because he is the focus of the reader's unease at the neocolonial benevolence of the Canopeans in putting the inhabitants on Planet 8 in the first place. We have to take into account the way he educates the inhabitants towards transcendence but also the fact that he, and Canopus, cannot prevent the extinction of life on Planet 8. The central characters who are given the mission of saving the world at the end of *Girlfriend in a Coma* are self-acknowledged failures, drifting without purpose, and the subject of manipulation by unknown powers. The mission of saving the world – by preaching to it – may offer their lives meaning but doesn't have credible prospects. The Judge in Cormac McCarthy's *Blood Meridian* is a nihilistic figure, violent, killing and unable to be killed, willing to make Nietzschean speeches but not actually to take command of the gang of killers at the centre of the story. The novel ends when he murders the Kid, the novel's central character and the only one in a long narrative of atrocity who has refrained from killing another person when he had the chance to. Otherwise, failed or fraudulent prophets are common in our texts: Gilcrest in *The Leftovers* (has genuine healing powers but betrays his followers with his sexual misdemeanours); Donally in *Heroes and Villains* (works by means of cynical frauds and is eventually expelled from the tribe), Gropius in *The End of the World News* (as his habitual preaching of the end of the world has actually come about, he is deprived of a role, and scorned by his family). Focus in Ballard's apocalyptic novels is always on the single central protagonist and his drift towards death;

persons of malign power and wilfulness such as Quilter and Lomax in *The Drought* and Strangman in *The Drowned World* figure mainly as excluding the possibility of benign power. The depiction of power in *Dead Astronauts* is too complex to be easily summarised, and its bearing is different because it is exercised in a world whose conditions are so far from those of our world. If it is associated with violence, abuse and monstrous capabilities it is also associated with pain and sacrifice. The novel does, however, sketch a contrast in the way male and female power works, and this contrast is discussed in chapter 9. Moss in particular is a figure of caritas, and her power is very different from even that of the most positive of the male figures in the novel, the blue fox. This leaves President Phil Chase in *Green Earth*, eventually in alliance with the scientist Diane Chang. *Green Earth* is the text among those discussed that thinks most positively about the potential of liberal democratic society and about collective effort. The very different case of the Overlords and the Overmind in *Childhood's End* will be discussed shortly.

The summary implication is that a wide variety of apocalyptic fictions stretching from the 1940s (which involve only average people of average powers) to the present all judge that we can do without leaders or figures of exceptional power, or that we have to. This seems a reasonable inference to draw from the history of the twentieth century (to go no further back), and one confirmed by the degeneration of political leadership in the Anglo-Saxon democracies.

This sequence of depictions of individual power (in the context of the immense power of the catastrophe itself) departs from that strand of science fiction that is fascinated by the individual of supernormal powers, most often male – Odd John in Olaf Stapledon's novel of that name (1935), Valentine Michael Smith in Robert Heinlein's *Stranger in a Strange Land* (1961) and many others. The power of males, even the comparatively modest power (in the aftermath of catastrophe) of fathers of families such as John Custance in *The Death of Grass* or Isherwood Smith in *Earth Abides*, is very limited in the novels discussed here. (The powers of figures in *Dead Astronauts* such as Botch, Moss and the blue fox are very great, but they are not human.) Jewel in *Heroes and Villains* (attractive as a sex object, unhappy and confused in himself) and Gerald in *The Memoirs of a Survivor* ('no one could say of him that he was unresourceful or lazy' (Lessing 1974, 116) – moderate praise) are both seen with sympathetic but unillusioned eyes.

Other readings of history and of theory are, however, possible. A glance at Peter Y. Paik's *From Utopia to Apocalypse* (2010) serves to underline by contrast how the wide variety of novels discussed in *Apocalypse in Crisis* reflect a continuing interest in the light that apocalypse throws on the vicissitudes of the individual rather than on the politics of global disaster and the prospects of apocalyptic revolution.

From Utopia to Apocalypse is based on readings of recent graphic novels, films and mangas.[38] As Paik shows, these texts grapple with the grim, indeed, in his view, tragic dilemmas that accompany the use of extreme violence to bring about revolutionary transformation. These texts, unlike the novels I discuss, do directly and graphically depict mass death. The logic of the framework into which Paik puts them is one that is partly shared with a long revolutionary tradition, though he diverges from the optimistic premises of this tradition, which, in his view, evade the tragic fate that violent revolution has to face. Paik's premises are that reform or gradual improvement is now irrelevant or empty; that the situation is such that only a complete, revolutionary overthrow of the present, globalised ruling system is to be looked for; that this overthrow will involve violence – indeed, in the texts Paik discusses, extreme, apocalyptic violence. He emphasises, however, how we must face the fact that while this extreme violence is necessary, it will also cause many, many deaths, vast destruction, and, almost certainly, the corruption of those who wielded the violence in the pursuit of transformative change – even if they achieve it (for instance, 82; 118–119). Political realism brings the tragic face of revolutionary mass violence into view, though, it would seem, the current situation allows no other way forward.

This argument makes for intense and gripping readings of Paik's chosen texts, but it is a heavy burden for the revolutionary tradition to bear. It is worth taking several steps back and asking whether reform and gradual improvement is so readily to be dismissed (indeed, seen as part of the problem), and whether the current situation is so all-encompassing and oppressive as to require revolution with its tragic endpoint.[39] Paik's sense of the current situation, it seems to me, depends on the kind of argument for the end of history advanced by Francis Fukuyama – that there is now no alternative to the liberal democratic order – though his

---

[38] Rosen (2008) discusses films and comics including *The Hulk*, *The Matrix*, and *12 Monkeys*, seeing them as critiques of the postmodern urge to apocalypse, and their heroes as fallible or mad; Ahrends (2009) notes the ambiguity of the possible saviours and the uncertainty of the endings in his chosen texts.

[39] *Dead Astronauts*, the most extreme of the texts discussed in *Apocalypse in Crisis*, is close to those discussed by Paik in many ways. The angry and grim assumption of the novel is that modern humanity, having wrecked Earth, is played out. The scene is occupied by a series of personages, many of which have powers beyond the human, though none is a superhero, and their world seems too broken to be fixed.

evaluation of this state of affairs is of course quite different. Whether Fukuyama is correct is debateable; in his essay on 'The Ends of History' (1992), Perry Anderson concedes the strength of many of Fukuyama's arguments, notes the weakness of many of the attacks on them and, nonetheless, advances strong arguments for scepticism. The history of the repeated tendency of those who embraced the necessity for revolution to accept and proliferate violence, including extreme violence, even when in the outcome this violence advanced nothing or was pointless, should incite us to look for alternatives. Paik on the whole does not pause over this, but relies on cogent readings of the theorists of political realism. There are times when one is reading *From Utopia to Apocalypse* when the strength and complexity of the range of theorists Paik is calling on seems to act as a fence against the long evidence of historical mistake and catastrophic waste in the matter of the embrace of revolutionary – or alleged to be revolutionary – violence.[40]

The texts discussed in *From Utopia to Apocalypse* all feature superheroes (*Nausicaä of the Valley of Wind* features superheroines) who have the power to wreak vast destruction and change the condition of society, indeed, of the globe. Paik notes that this power is different from and much broader than that of earlier superheroes who obeyed the convention whereby superpowers were exercised locally and in a restricted field (for instance, crime-fighting or detecting Nazi spies); he relates this to the end of the Cold War and the release of the US from restraint as the unchallenged global superpower (10–11).[41] The upshot of this reliance on the superhero in the texts he discusses is that society tends to be seen as a more or less passive mass. As has just been detailed, the texts discussed in *Apocalypse in Crisis* dismiss the claims and pretensions of figures of power. There

---

[40] In *Upheaval* (2019, 141–215) Jared Diamond discusses two instances in which extreme violence might be said, at huge cost, to have stabilised an unstable situation and opened the way for a degree of prosperity and democracy, though not a utopia. These are the massacres in Indonesia in 1965, which led to the Suharto dictatorship, and the violence and repression of the Pinochet dictatorship in Chile, both of them succeeded by regimes that built democracy and a degree of prosperity on acceptance of the situation created by the previous extreme violence. Paik would, I assume, see this acceptance as acceptance also of the global capitalist order from which only revolution can free us.

[41] Paik's texts include *Watchmen* and *V for Vendetta* (Alan Moore: English); *Nausicaä of the Valley of Wind* (Hayao Miyazaki: Japanese) and *Save the Green Planet* (Jang Joon-Hwan: Korean). (The last of these is an exception in that superheroes are much less emphasised, in a story that welters in violence and torture, if we go by Paik's report, which in the circumstances I am happy to do.)

are huge egoists who wield considerable but not transformative or even constructive power, failed or fraudulent prophets, possible Anti-Christs who resign or make a mess of their power or wealth or knowledge. Personages with superpowers who, like those Paik discusses, wield that power to transformative effect are the Overlords and the Overmind in *Childhood's End*. Arthur C. Clarke's attitudes to these figures will receive the discussion that their ambiguity requires in chapter 2.

In most of the other selected texts, the field is left to individuals without exceptional powers, violence, as we saw, is individual, and the main work of the series as a whole is that of imagining different recourses for individuals in the face of different (sometimes no) possibilities of transcendence. None of these possibilities are utopian in the sense in which utopia involves the establishment of a transformed society of justice and welfare. Individuals with power are subject to these conditions. A way out of this, as it might seem, political deadend is not provided, not on a global scale anyway, in the novels examined here, with the exception of *Green Earth*, and it is significant that Paik turns to films, comics and mangas, where superheroes have always flourished.

Part 1

The Nineteenth Century to the Postwar Disaster Novels

Chapter 1

Modern Apocalypses and Modernism
Enter Science Fiction

Paradoxes of Literary History

Apocalypse in Crisis concentrates on the varieties and inventions of apocalyptic fiction from 1945 to the present. The great ancestor to modern apocalyptic fiction is *The War of the Worlds* by H. G. Wells. *The War of the Worlds* can be put in a diverse group of nineteenth-century fictions that devise new and dark possibilities for imagining apocalyptic threat, and that suggest human complicity with the monstrously destructive. This chapter discusses *The War of the Worlds* in detail, in relation to the earlier group of fictions, and moves on to note the complications of modernism and anti-modernism in the apocalyptic twentieth century. The First World War, apocalyptic catastrophe in historical form, helped to shape apocalyptic modernism, but science fiction tended to bypass modernism, and this tendency was confirmed by the British and American experience of the Second World War, for all that the war could be also seen as an apocalyptic catastrophe that dwarfed the individual caught up in it, and abolished the stable bases of personality and morality.

Wells's novel influences later apocalyptic fictions, as will be noted, but its darker dimensions are not at first reflected in these fictions. Chapter 2 discusses apocalyptic fiction published in the aftermath of the Second World War: *Earth Abides*, by George R. Stewart; *The Day of the Triffids*, by John Wyndham; *On the Beach*, by Nevil Shute; and *Childhood's End*, by Arthur C. Clarke. This group of novels combines depiction of global catastrophe with a basic confidence in human decency, and narrates the whole in calm realist style, reporting events and responses and occasionally drawing a moral or discoursing on the implications of what is going on. It is this genre that later apocalyptic fiction, with its complexities and ironies, and its approaches sometimes to nihilism, is reacting against.

A series of paradoxes emerges from these preliminary manoeuvres. The postwar disaster novels, to call them that in shorthand, don't quite measure up to *The War of the Worlds* in scope and power; it will be left for later apocalyptic fictions to explore and often expand the darker dimensions that Wells imagined by imagining the resemblances between humans and the invading Martians in *The War of the Worlds*. By the 1960s, the implications of the nuclear age, the stirrings of anxiety about the environment, the unsettling end of empire in Britain, and the questioning of gender and patriarchy all deepen and darken apocalyptic fiction, and the results are discussed in chapters 3, 4 and 5, part 2 of *Apocalypse in Crisis*.

There are shifts and developments in apocalyptic fiction from 1945 to the present; their outlines are traced in the section on Patterns and Shifts in the Introduction, and they make a history of increasing scepticism and experiment. Here we note some broad features of style in apocalyptic fiction from Wells to the 1970s. The postwar disaster novels follow and in some cases deepen the realism and reasonableness of science fiction between Wells and 1945, and this is paradoxical in view of the apocalyptic extremes of twentieth-century history up to 1945. However we define the manner and style of traditional science fiction (what has been called 'Golden Age' science fiction), it pays no attention to the experiments and extremities that characterise modernist writing, with, shaping them, radical uncertainties and questionings about personality and social life. The literature of modernism can itself be seen as apocalyptic and as a response to the apocalyptic events of twentieth-century history that, for many, discredited the realism and reasonableness of much earlier literature. This does not mean that the 'Golden Age' science-fiction novelists were detached from the culture and the realities of their time; in another part of the wood, where they lived, confidence in reason, scientific progress and organisation flourished, and the apocalyptic disasters that helped to inspire modernist literary experiment and radical disillusionment instead suggested the need for more reason and scientific progress, without dimming confidence that both could be attained. The postwar disaster novelists tested and in some ways reaffirmed these values when they imagined catastrophe and its aftermath.

The story of what happened after the postwar disaster novelists is different again. Writers of apocalyptic fictions in the 1960s and 1970s revolt against the reasonableness and confidence in reason of the previous generation, and draw upon the experiments and uncertainties of modernism to make their fictions. This formula is too simple, as formulas usually are when applied to complex works of art: the modernism of writers such as Ballard, Aldiss, Carter and Kavan is selective, and is still shaped and subdued by the particular necessities of making a narrative out of catastrophe and its aftermath. After the playful and provocative modernism of Ballard and Aldiss, targeting the realism and sobriety of earlier science fiction, the modernism of writers such as Carter and Kavan largely reflects the way the literary novel was absorbing and adapting the innovations and experiments of modernism. Apocalyptic fiction in the style of the disaster novelists continues to be written, and not simply because science fiction derives an independence from its position in the midst of scientific culture and to one side of literary culture: also, because technoscientific projects and dangers proliferate and ask for sober and detailed engagement. Realism in the novel gathers a second wind; one aspect of this is its alliance with comedy and satire, explored in chapters 6 and 7.

So as regards fictions of apocalypse the sweep of cultural and literary history from the nineteenth century to the present can be drawn as a series of zigs and zags. Wells's achievement adds to those of others in the late nineteenth century but is not taken up in its darker implications until long after; modernism embraces the destabilising and disillusioning shock waves of the apocalyptic in twentieth-century history, but science fiction, ensconced in another part of the cultural wood, ignores them at first, but then takes them up with a vengeance and a kind of glee.

Literary history is invigorated and vexed by the way single texts, and sometimes broad trends in writing, refuse to arrive when they are expected. Great or even simply interesting texts, of the sort that you want to read and re-read, tend to appear when their author, with his or her complex formation, decides to launch them on the world – which usually takes a while to begin to understand them. D. H. Lawrence (1961, 391) has an apposite comment near the end of his discussion of *Moby Dick* in *Studies in Classic American Literature*:

> The *Pequod* went down. And the *Pequod* was the ship of the American soul. She sank, taking with her negro and Indian and Polynesian, Asiatic and Quaker and good, businesslike Yankees and Ishmael. [...]
>
> But *Moby Dick* was first published in 1851. If the Great White Whale sank the ship of the Great White Soul in 1851, what's been happening ever since?
>
> Post-mortem effects, presumably.

One of the most explosive, shattering, of all apocalyptic fictions is 'The Earthquake in Chile', by Heinrich von Kleist (published 1810–1811).

Its pace is unrelenting. The justice of 'The Day of Judgement' that the earthquake seems to announce; human justice, rationality and decency; recourse to nature for peace and beauty; love and altruism – all are overthrown in a savage series of destructions, reversals, errors and cruelties.[1] Nothing that I have read that was written since this story equals its bleak power. It is possible to fit 'The Earthquake in Chile' into its time, the time of revolution, war and romantic revolt, but it doesn't sit very steadily in its place. The story came when it would come, and literary history struggles to put it into its own narrative.

Apocalypse in the Nineteenth Century: Intensity and Experiment

The period of the French Revolution and Romanticism is a convenient starting point for remarks on apocalyptic fiction in the nineteenth century, because the Revolution introduces the secularised apocalypse into history, and Romanticism takes apocalyptic transformation into the inner world of the self. The phenomenon is a complex one. There are sensational renditions of the traditional story, in the paintings of John Martin, for instance. There are unorthodox revisions of earlier apocalypses, in Blake's Prophetic Books (revising the Bible and *Paradise Lost*), Byron's 'Heaven and Earth' (revising the account of the Flood in Genesis) and Shelley's *Prometheus Unbound* (revising Aeschylus's *Prometheus Bound*). In these cases, it is particularly the authority of Jehovah (and Jupiter) that is undermined. Accounts of the French Revolution written later in the nineteenth century incorporate a different reconciliation of the secular and the religious. For Dickens in *A Tale of Two Cities* (1859), for instance, the revolution has secular sources in the oppression and callousness of the aristocracy, but its course is imagined in terms of fire and flood ('the deluge of the Year One of Liberty'), and the novel is structured in terms of a contrast between good and evil (Lucie, Dr Mannette, Miss Pross, Lorry, as against the Defarges and Monseigneur) and, more powerfully, in terms of a contrast between unreality and death on the one hand, and life and in particular resurrection on the other.[2] Dickens in many ways follows

---

[1] Apocalyptic fictions sometimes encourage by ending with a birth – new life; here the love-child Philip survives his parents and is adopted by Fernando – whose own child has just been savagely killed.

[2] The remark about the deluge is at 301; chapters 22 and 23 are 'The Sea Still Rises' and 'The Fire Rises'; for unreality see, for instance, the aristocrats at

Carlyle (*The French Revolution*, 1837) and there too imagery of fire and flood is pervasive, though it alludes as much to natural phenomena (volcanic eruptions, for instance) as to Biblical catastrophe.

The view that is a feature of the Christian narrative – that apocalypse is directed and determined, ushers in some form of redemption and New Jerusalem, and is overseen and witnessed by a prophet – is not given up without a struggle. Indeed, there is plenty of evidence of the pervasiveness of various forms of millenarianism in the first half of the nineteenth century, in evangelicalism as a force in politics as well as religion in Britain, and in a vigorous series of millenarian prophets and sects in Britain and the US, of whom the most famous were Joanna Southcott and Joseph Smith.[3] J. F. C. Harrison (1979, 227–228) catches the appeal of popular millenarianism:

> There is a feeling of being caught up in a vast drama involving the whole human race. Angels and demons and monsters appear before our eyes on a scale which dwarfs all earthly experience. Moreover, all complexities are reduced to a simple dualism of good and evil. The redeemed and the damned are plain to see. And as if this were not enough to capture the heart and imagination of the earnest seeker, he is assured that the persecuted minority like himself will now be on top.

It is this clarity and this attraction that many secularised apocalypses set out to reinvigorate (and, contrariwise, that Blake complicated with his radical revisions of religious apocalypse in his prophetic books). Hegel and Marx replace God with History,[4] retain the sense that events have a determined direction and, in Marx, retain the confidence that destruction (now to occur in the form of revolution) will issue in a utopia in which equivalent of the persecuted majority, the proletariat, will now be on top.

More subtly, and in a more drastic departure from the traditional narrative, a form of redemption is retained and indeed reinvigorated

---

Monseigneur's – 'unconnected with anything that was real'... 'the leprosy of unreality' (136, 137); imagery of death and resurrection is pervasive. (*A Tale of Two Cities*, London: Penguin, 1985.)

[3] For the first, see Hilton 2006, 114 and plate 12, 401–402, 405, and for the second, see Harrison 1979, and Lippy 1982. George Eliot can also stand for the ideal of retaining the structures of feeling and narrative of Christianity after the departure of faith; see the discussion of *Romola* as apocalyptic in Carpenter and Landow, 1984.

[4] In Marxism 'God is "immanentized" into historical process': Tuveson 1984, 333.

in 'The Apocalypse Within', 'the apocalypse of consciousness' (Abrams 1984, 353–356, 360). There is a reaction away from history – for instance, out of disillusionment with the French Revolution – into the inner life and the changes nature can work within it. The result is reconciliation with, in various degrees and versions, nature, ordinary life and the life of the senses. Abrams (1984, 356) quotes Wordsworth, reimagining 'Paradise, and groves/ Elysian, Fortunate Fields':

> For the discerning intellect of Man
> When wedded to this goodly universe
> In love and holy passion, shall find these
> A simple produce of our common day.[5]

To this we may add Blake, combining the epic and the local (also a challenge for more recent apocalyptic writing). For instance, from *Milton*:

> ... where Hoglah,
> On Highgate's heights magnificent, weaves over trembling Thames
> To Shooter's Hill and thence to Blackheath, the dark Woof. Loud,
> Loud roll the Weights & Spindles over the whole Earth ...

Blake locates apocalypse in familiar suburbs, as Wells does by siting the action of *The War of the Worlds* in the 'Home Counties' around London. He sees it as a matter of renovating 'each Day':

> There is a moment in each Day that Satan cannot find,
> Nor can his Watch Fiends find it, but the Industrious find
> This moment & it multiply; & when it once is found,
> It renovates every Moment of the Day if rightly placed.[6]

This capturing of transformative moments in ordinary life, especially in encounters with nature, feeds into broader currents in later English poetry that it is less useful to see as expressing Abrams's 'inward apocalypse'. Moments of revelation or epiphany in personal life, unaccompanied by catastrophe in the world at large, are only apocalyptic

---

[5] The passage is from the Preface to *The Excursion*. Abrams also suggests that Revolution was internalised in a similar way, in his discussion of Schiller in *Natural Supernaturalism* (Farrell 1980, 49, quoting *Natural Supernaturalism*, 350).

[6] Blake 1979, 119, 120.

in a very general sense, but plenty of later narratives set catastrophe and its aftermath in local and domestic life, and attempt to assess and revise its value (see chapters 6 and 7).

Monsters and Humans

Saul Friedländer (1985, 61–83) traces a broad and expanding current of 'cultural pessimism' in the latter part of the nineteenth century, and offers a compelling list of apocalyptic fictions that come to terms with it. This current expresses a fading of faith in Progress and of faith in God – both faiths, for instance, threatened by Darwin's displacement of Creation by Evolution, opening the way to fears of a degeneration in which the biological would co-operate with the social, about which the demographic and industrial developments of the century had made many pessimistic. Friedländer casts his net widely among thinkers and prophets, and it is unnecessary here to weigh this pessimism against the buoyancy with which the period is also often associated, and that sometimes stimulated opposition by its overconfidence.[7] What is relevant for our purposes is that in this context we now meet another renewal of the apocalyptic narrative. This is very different from the inward apocalypse that Abrams identified from earlier in the century.

Friedländer is uncertain how to define this set of narratives – quests, narratives of degeneration, narratives of hubris – and the upshot could be to put into question whether they are best described as apocalyptic. But as with the inward apocalypse, that is the point: radical revision is being undertaken and a new kind of narrative devised, retaining and in this case fiercely focusing on a couple of aspects of the traditional narrative and dramatis personae. Friedländer's examples make a formidable list, because they include *Frankenstein, Moby Dick, Doctor Jekyll and Mr Hyde, Dracula, The Picture of Dorian Gray* and *Heart of Darkness*. All these texts belong in the realms of nineteenth-century fiction where alternatives to social realism are sought in fantasy, the gothic and science fiction. The action takes place apart from the ordinary life of social relationships that preoccupied much nineteenth-century fiction. Friedländer sees these texts as 'fantasies of the evil demiurge, the fantasy of the human

---

[7] Some scholars (for instance, Burrow, 1966) doubt that Darwin's publications led to a crisis of doubt; evolution in various forms was already a familiar concept. Geoffrey Best (1980, 131-139) discusses the flourishing at the same time, the second half of the nineteenth century, of the Peace Movement and what he calls 'the War Movement'.

monster' (75).[8] This element does link them with traditional apocalypse (Anti-Christ; the beast from the sea),[9] as does the power of the monster in each case – its threat and uncanny or unstoppable qualities. Friedlander emphasises both the fear of the bestial in nature and the fear of releasing it by hubristic overconfidence in reason, science or enlightenment, as happens with Frankenstein, Dr Jekyll and Kurtz, for instance. The modern is involved as well as the monstrous: Melville sets Ahab's obsession with the white whale in the context of whaling as an industry; the opponents of Dracula make use of up-to-date technology such as recording machines; Marlow observes a warship shelling the jungle and finds himself struggling with rivets.

In addition, in almost all cases what is staged is a complicity, a disturbing affinity, between the monster and some other, supposedly normal and civilised person – a relation sometimes extending to doubleness, the monster as the dark side of the civilised and normal yet also as created by it. So it is with the Creature and Frankenstein; Ahab and the white whale and Ahab and the crew of the *Pequod* ('at times his hate seemed almost theirs');[10] Hyde and Jekyll; Dracula and those who hunt and on occasion brutally kill vampires; his picture and Dorian Gray; Kurtz and Marlow. Humans have imagined the white whale into power and malignancy (*Moby Dick*, chapter 41); Marlow imagines himself into affinity with Kurtz long before he sees him. Wherever we find the apocalyptic monster, the 'evil demiurge', there we also find the 'normal' human in troubling affinity to it. ('He who fights with monsters should take care that he does not turn into a monster himself', as Nietzsche warned.)[11]

This is a powerful and complex narrative form, the political and civilisational implications of which can be traced, for instance in *Moby Dick* and *Heart of Darkness*. As Friedländer says, 'these visions of a total end

---

[8] It is ironic that it is *after* the flourishing of the fictions of human monsters that Friedländer identifies that we find the most formidable human monsters in history, in the persons of Hitler and Stalin, each shaped by experience of 1914–18 and shaping the more terrible aspects of 1939–45; but these present themselves as gods, supreme beings, and are at first followed as such.

[9] In *Cosmos, Chaos and the World to Come*, Norman Cohn emphasises the prevalence of the beast from the sea in Middle Eastern and Jewish apocalyptic literature, and the association of the sea with a dangerous limitlessness. For a more general discussion of evil and limitlessness, see Flahaut 2003, which includes an illuminating discussion of *Moby Dick*.

[10] Melville 1961, 188.

[11] Quoted Boyle 2008, 102.

plunge their roots into a deeper ground than that of the social tensions or the scientific theories of the period' (80). On the other hand, these texts achieve their powerful central relationship, which is that between the monster and the complicit civilised, by means of a relatively narrow focus. There is no global scope or global destruction, though there are powerful images of destruction and negation – the icy polar waste in the last scenes of *Frankenstein*, the whiteness of the whale and the lone survivor in the ocean at the end of *Moby Dick*,[12] the wood of dying slaves and the blank white mist in *Heart of Darkness*.

The War of the Worlds: Humans and Martians, the 'Strange' and the Ordinary[13]

H. G. Wells's *The War of the Worlds* (1898) appeared in the same decade as *Dracula* and *Heart of Darkness*. This time the monsters of apparently irresistible power invade from Mars, but Wells asks us to see them as expressive of the possible future of humans when captured by remorseless technological advance, and as reflective of the way humans have exterminated the less powerful both as imperialists and in their relations with other creatures. So the novel can be seen as working a telling variation on the theme of the complicity between humans and monsters that was defined in the discussion of Friedländer's set of fictions. Humans are the victims, but the aggressors behave like humans. The Martians suggest both a capacity for savagery in humans, and also humans' capacity, when it is released by modern organisation and technology, for impersonal destruction and extermination. The disaster that is depicted in Wells is now global; civilisation is threatened everywhere, and it is largely destroyed in the Home Counties and London. The Martians are frightening, monstrous and all-conquering, but they are subject to the laws of nature. The narrator sees this from the beginning, when his description of their uncanny monstrousness has room for the observation that they are struggling in Earth's gravity, and he invokes it at the end, when he explains their deaths as due to their lack of immunity to the microbes in an alien environment. Close-up,

---

[12] With China Miéville's *Kraken* in mind, note the apparition of the giant squid: 'No perceptible front did it have; no conceivable token of either sensation or instinct; but undulated there on the billows an unearthly, formless, chance-like apparition of life' (Melville 1961, 272). Melville and Miéville connect the giant squid with the legendary, apocalyptic kraken.

[13] References are to the London: Pan edition, 1975.

the Martians are sensationally repulsive (tentacles, tendency to slobber), but as they tower above humans and stalk the land they are hidden in their formidable, effective technology: a disconcerting combination that prevents us settling into a single view of them.

Earth is invaded; the threat is global, and it comes from elsewhere. Wells trumps the contemporary fashion for stories of an invasion of Britain from Europe.[14] England is the scene of the novel's action, but the whole world is being invaded. He also avoids the elements of chauvinism and optimism in the invasion stories that were popular at the time, whereby the Germans or the French are treacherous, and are defeated in the end. There will be many more stories of alien invasion in the twentieth century, and they will be joined by other apocalyptic fictions in which the threat is a matter of the incursion into the human world of a natural phenomenon: a comet, a purple cloud, a black cloud, an incurable disease, a wind from nowhere.[15] Nature can be seen as perverted by human action, by pollution for instance, or seen as proceeding indifferently and without moral agency. In the former case the threat comes from within the human world, but here it is worth emphasising that many stories of apocalyptic threat after *The War of the Worlds* begin from outside the human world and arguably figure a general sense of the power of the impersonal and abstract, of System.

Monstrous invaders return in numbers in novels and films of the 1950s, often as more straightforward antagonists to humans, reflective of the way twentieth-century history can be read as conflict of Good and Bad in traditional apocalyptic terms (the World Wars, the Cold War), though there is a subset of stories that are shaped by fears of the alien who cannot be distinguished from the rest of us, as in *Invasion of the Body Snatchers*. In more recent fictions relations of the monster and the human again become ambiguous, as in China Miéville's *Kraken*, or complicit, as in the intimate sexual connection between Slothrop and the V2 in Thomas Pynchon's *Gravity's Rainbow*. (The V2 is of course a human artefact, as is the container of the giant squid that turns out to be as important as the giant squid in *Kraken*.) In Jeff VanderMeer's *Dead Astronauts* one who is a human monster, morally speaking, is responsible through his abused son for bioengineered monsters, and in this context natural monsters, such as Botch, and bioengineered monsters, such as

---

[14] Clarke 1970 gives the history.
[15] Respectively, *The End of the World News* (Anthony Burgess, 1982), *The Purple Cloud* (M. P. Shiel, 1901), *The Black Cloud* (Fred Hoyle, 1957), *Earth Abides* (George R. Stewart, 1949), *The Wind from Nowhere* (J. G. Ballard, 1962).

the dark bird, can be viewed with some sympathy: the original of real monstrousness is elsewhere, in humans.

Wells is introducing global catastrophe in a new way, then, and we can observe him grappling with the problem of expressing this dimension while personalising and localising the story around a couple of witnesses, the narrator and his brother, and around familiar places in London and the Home Counties. The narrative involves a controlled oscillation between the local and the panoramic. Wells is engaging with problems of narrative that will face most later writers of apocalypse: how to handle the experience of a single individual in the context of vast, global disaster that is killing many or most people, and what kind of ending to offer (who survives, how is the catastrophe brought to an end, or averted, or become total and absolute). In the face of global disaster, the individual is insignificant, yet in the face of social breakdown and the threat of annihilation the individual is released from rules and inhibitions. The insignificance of the individual in the face of disaster gives rise to problems of plausibility if the author wants to centre their fiction on one or a few central, knowable, sympathetic protagonists and/or witnesses.

The problem is even more pressing with films: the more resounding and convincing the images of universal destruction, the less convincing the film's focus on a small heroic group of protagonists. Hence, the film finds itself (often, very willingly) vindicating the individual hero or clever geek, after its images of destruction have put the powers and survival of the individual into doubt. Tate (2007, 122–127) discusses the critical debate on the individual heroism of characters such as Katniss Everdene in *The Hunger Games* (Suzanne Collins, 2008–10). The problem tends to be exacerbated in fictions that differentiate sharply between society (responsible for the catastrophe) and the individual (capable of heroism): when the individual is part of society, he or she is assumed to lack the decency and courage that he or she displays as individual fighting the damage done by the catastrophe.

The release of the individual from inhibitions and rules (exemplified in *The War of the Worlds* in the views of the artilleryman) can open the way for depiction of apocalypse as making for transcendence of the old, destroyed or discredited or simply irrelevant ways of being human. This happens in J. G. Ballard's apocalypses, for instance, and Doris Lessing concludes that transcendence can only happen if the protagonists depart altogether from this earthly existence – planetary existence in the case of *The Making of the Representative for Planet 8*. The problem with endings can be seen in the context of a more general situation affecting the modern novel, as Frank Kermode has argued: the realism of dailiness, what Kermode calls 'chronos',[16] conflicts with the narrative impulse towards closure.

It might seem that this problem is less pressing with science fiction, which has usually ignored the innovations and restrictions of modernism as they apply to the making of narratives. Wells solves the problem of the ending in the case of *The War of the Worlds* by the wonderful, science-fictional stroke of having the Martians succumb to a virus carried by a tiny microbe, though it is the way this outcome is signalled by the eerie wailing 'ululations' of the dying Martians that makes this so haunting, and that is due to Wells's imagination as a novelist, period.

The Martians invade, they cause vast destruction and death, social breakdown and mass panic. They reduce humans to a state like that of animals. The narrator finds himself reconsidering what it is to be human. He is sure that human assumptions of power and superiority must be gone forever, though he can also see that humans resemble Martians in ways that are equally chastening. Then, all the invaders die, killed by microbes against which they have no immunity. They leave behind a desolation and a silence; a rupture such that the narrator as he tells us his story can speak of the times before, 'in those days' (20), even though the whole event takes only a couple of weeks, from the first signs of the launch of the projectiles from Mars to the moment of the narrator wandering the deserted streets of the great metropolis and hearing the weird 'ulla, ulla' of the dying invaders. We are given at once the intensity of a few action-packed, extraordinary days, and the awesome scope of an epoch. All this has the narrative shape of an apocalypse, and there is plenty of apocalyptic imagery and allusion. But this apocalyptic effect is moderated by the many sober descriptions of the Martians and their actions, descriptions that avoid the epic and rely on the everyday, Kermode's realism of dailiness. The fire and flood that accompanies the Martians may suggest the apocalyptic, but the black dust and the red weed are also botanical phenomena. And after the death and destruction and breakdown, after the gap in time and feeling that it opens up, there is no New Jerusalem; so this element of apocalypse, often lacking in modern apocalyptic fictions, is lacking here as well.

There is no sign that the Wells of *The War of the Worlds* sought a New Jerusalem, then, though he several times embraces and explores the utopian in later works; instead, the novel is full of an imagination of the ordinary that we could almost call pastoral ('the scent of hay was

---

[16] Kermode 2000, 54; see also Kermode's remarks on 'our lack of confidence in ends', in relation to 'The Modern Apocalypse' (101, and chapter IV).

in the air', 48), though it is also modern and mundane – a matter of excursion trains, the *Daily Mail*, men smoking in shirt-sleeves and the human geography of what is customarily called the 'Home Counties', which is meticulously traced in the narrative. Further, the imagery of traditional apocalypse – 'a fiery chaos' (56), a 'valley of ashes' (60), fire and flood, the Angel of Death (180), even Sodom and Gomorrah in the curate's ravings (76) – is tested against other, and often more compelling images – the strange, the silent and desolate, the eerie. The Martians were eliminated not by 'the Angel of Death' as the narrator thought for a moment, but by humble microbes: a thought-provoking more than an awe-inspiring fact (179–180). *The War of the Worlds* ponders and assesses the traditional apocalypse. The novel refines and tests many of the easy tropes (for instance, the notion of human devolution to savagery, going down 'at last to elemental things', 141: humans in the mass reduced to insensate panic) that later versions of apocalypse are often reluctant to do without, or it refuses them (awe-inspiring ruins, spectacular devastations). This is a large part of the achievement of this novel, though it is inconvenient that it appears so early in an examination of apocalyptic fictions, because it makes many of those that come later seem facile.

The ending mixes religious suggestions – the microbes that destroy the Martians are 'the humblest things that God, in His wisdom, has put upon this earth' (179) – with dispassionate observation and explanation – the Martians must have lacked the immunity that natural selection has brought about in humans. The narrator spends time with the curate (unbalanced, degraded superstition) and the artilleryman (unstable and crude evolutionism) and rejects the attitudes of both, though no doubt it is significant that the curate is killed and the artilleryman merely left behind. The narrator is like Wells himself: capable of dispassionate insights and long and wide views, but a man of ordinary tastes and attitudes, free of convention at one moment but grounded the next.

The authority of the narration is an important matter for all apocalyptic fictions. In later fictions, opening the text to stylistic experiment and display, to richness of symbol and metaphor, means abandoning the witness's style of plain reportage. The present discussion will consider how the authority of the witness is achieved and varied in *The War of the Worlds*, and then the related matter of the narrator's ordinariness of perception, before looking at the novel's presentation of humans under extreme pressure – humans in relation to Martians, humans in relation to animals.

There are several other point-of-view characters whose experiences or views the narrator relays to us – his brother, who takes part in the panic flight of the population of London and witnesses the subsequent sea battle; the artilleryman who tells what happens to his battery ('trying to make me see the things he had seen', says the narrator, defining his own enterprise, 59), and who later expounds what he thinks humans should do to survive and regain power, as well as avoiding 'taint to the race' (book two, chapter 7). It is the narrator who gives unity to the whole, however. He wishes both to tell us exactly what happened to him, and what the whole amounted to. He wishes for a panoramic perspective but he is driven into partial glimpses, the purely visceral sensations of the victim or perpetrator of violence, as when he is caught helplessly in the fiery flood at Shepperton or when he kills the curate in the kitchen of the ruined house.[17] The variations of the narrator's perspective are not merely a formal feature, but reflect his experience, his predicaments.[18] In the long run, they figure the attempt to remain human – that is, in this context, clear and cool-headed and capable of reasoning, but also capable of seeing the limits of reason. One of his favourite words is 'strange', a word that notes but also accepts the inexplicable:

> The most extraordinary thing to my mind, of all the strange and wonderful things that happened upon that Friday, was the dovetailing of the commonplace habits of our social order with the first beginnings of the series of events that was to topple that social order headlong. (39)

He writes of 'the strange wonder, the unfamiliar routine of the Martians in the pit' (141) when he is trapped in the ruined house and has the chance to observe them, but when he finds himself playing cards with the artilleryman he exclaims at the 'strange mind of man!' (172). Strangeness is almost the atmosphere in which the story moves, and it is what brings together humans and Martians (whose 'minds' are emphasised) in an affinity that the text continually explores.

The narrator seeks the wide view, as from his upstairs window (55, 60); he will depict the scene of flight from London as it would have appeared, 'If one could have hung that June morning in a balloon' (112). He tries also to put us in the place of the witness: 'You may imagine'

---

[17] Book 1, chapter 12, and book 2, chapter 4.
[18] And behind these are Wells's restless fear of confinement or entrapment, and his attraction to flight and to a position of overview. There are many images of confinement and of flight in his novels; see, for instance, Draper 1987, 56, 92.

(32); 'It is hard to imagine that host' (105: the crowd fleeing London); 'Anyone coming along the road from Chobham or Woking would have been amazed at the sight' (26). The sight in question is given us in terms of ordinary details, though it also figures as a prevision of the desolation and emptiness that the Martians later spread everywhere:

> The barrow of ginger-beer stood, a queer derelict, black against the burning sky, and in the sand-pits was a row of deserted vehicles with their horses feeding out of nose-bags or pawing the ground. (26)

This happens early in the story; later, when the Martians have annihilated all opposition, the narrator is trapped with the feeble-minded curate in a house that has been partly wrecked by the Martians, who are busy a few feet away. Now the two men are reduced to 'peeping' through a 'slit' in the wreckage (139) and the narrator talks of 'the horrible fascination that this peeping had' (143); the narrator and the curate struggle in terrified silence for a turn at their peephole.

In one way, the narrator is an Everyman, and his descent from panoramic observation to grovelling at a peephole stands for that of humanity as a whole in the course of the invasion. The social breakdown that his brother witnesses as the population flees London – 'that swift liquefaction of the social body' (99) – has its counterpart in the narrator's delirium and breakdown near the end, after the Martians have died. He talks with familiarity of the ordinary doings of people, 'the commonplace habits of our social order' (39) before the Martians disrupt everything:

> All over the district people were dining and supping; working-men were gardening after the labours of the day, children were being put to bed, young people were wandering through the lanes love-making, students sat over their books. (39)

Even after it is all over, and in spite of his suggestion that things can never again be as they were, he is eager to get hold of the first copy of the *Daily Mail*, though he can easily tell there is almost no news in it (185).[19]

---

[19] And see his eagerness to get the papers early in the story (44). It's a modern touch: hoping to confirm (if also, to broaden) one's direct experience by way of the media. The main characters in John Wyndham's *The Kraken Wakes* (1953) work in radio, obeying the authorities' instructions to soften the truth of the crisis, though at the same time they are the source of our knowledge of what is actually going on.

In the disturbed political and social atmosphere of the interwar years, the most powerful apocalyptic fictions will express fear of ordinary people (Nathanael West's *The Day of the Locust*, 1939), or aristocratic disdain for them (Ernst Jünger's *On the Marble Cliffs*, 1939). The contrasting quality in Wells's evocation of ordinary life in *The War of the Worlds* is reinforced by the intense ordinariness of the narrator's descriptions of what he knows to be strange and unprecedented. The Martian limb, if that is what it is, is first seen as 'something resembling a little grey snake, about the thickness of a walking-stick' (24); the Martian walking machine, 'a monstrous tripod, higher than many houses', is like a milking stool ('Can you imagine a milking-stool tilted and bowled violently along the ground?' 50); a Martian out of his hood for a short time is 'oddly suggestive from that distance of a speck of blight' (92); the city and landscape on which the Martians are pouring their poison gas is *'blotted'* in black splashes (112). Of course, the alien, the completely strange and other, can only be described in terms of analogy, and the gap between the homely comparison, the ordinary word (speck, splash), and what is actually present, intensifies the sensational, vast and monstrous. Yet this habit of homely comparison underlines that perception *is* ordinary, in that we can't perceive without a frame based on what we already and usually perceive. And Wells is determined not to abandon the ordinary and peaceful. Here are the narrator's brother and the women he has joined, a few moments after the fight with the would-be rapists and a few moments before the encounter with the relentless, panicked crowd:

> They made a sort of encampment by the way side and the pony became happy in the hedge. (103)

We can set this happy pony against the many images of humans as helpless like small animals or vermin. This pony is not serving to make a point about Martians, humans and animals, but just being a pony.

Meanwhile, *is* the narrator ordinary, exactly? Not simply; he is more complex. He tells us he is capable of a curious calm and impersonality:

> I do not know how far my experience is common. At times I suffer from the strangest sense of detachment from myself and the world about me; I seem to watch it all from the outside, from somewhere inconceivably remote, out of time, out of space, out of the stress and tragedy of it all. (36)

Perhaps this is Wells's way of acknowledging that he is writing the book, arranging his imaginary beings and destructions at his desk.

The narrator's view of the Martians is dispassionate, even though he feels revulsion from them (their outer covering, bulging and 'glistening like wet leather', 24). He sees the contrast between their laboured clumsiness in their own bodies (explicable as the result of the weight of Earth's gravity) and their swift, sure and easy movements once ensconced in their tall walking machines. They have almost no bodies, yet their machines articulate with things like muscles; they deploy very advanced technology but they don't have the wheel. They are vampires, casually preying on humans whom they carry in a container like a workman's basket (125), yet this is a matter of economy and utility – making do without a cumbersome digestive system, and injecting (human) blood straight into their veins – and doing this with 'a little pipette' (133). We are often told of the Martians' intelligence, their 'minds'; the narrator has a little of this coolness of mind, and knows that he has. But this is less an indication of the narrator's character than of the resemblance of humans to Martians. The Martians are coolly intelligent, 'minds'; evolution has in effect discarded their bodies and they have replaced them with wonderfully efficient machines, yet they are vampiric, and remorselessly destructive.

As all readers notice, the Martians are to humans as humans are to lower creatures – or as Europeans are to 'lower' races, as Wells suggests at the beginning of the novel – but from then on the images are of ants, wasps, rabbits, dodos, sheep: mostly, commonplace and domestic elimination and extermination. The Martians' bodies give rise to 'horror', but they are explicable in scientific terms, as are their frightening eating habits; they are powerful, indifferent, alien and efficient, and all this gives rise to a kind of envy or admiration as well as the remorse and, more, the 'sense of dethronement' (154), that is implied by the comparison of their actions to those of humans against other animals and Europeans against Tasmanian Aborigines. Adam Roberts (2006, 48) says that in their grotesqueness the Martians could also suggest the invading 'Eastern' hordes of the imagination of the time.[20] I'm not sure of this, but, if so, it adds another layer to the significance of the Martians. Yet they don't figure only as a significance, a set of sobering perspectives on the human. They remain odd, 'strange', unable to be assimilated. They help to do what fictions of apocalypse often do: they take us to another place. The images of the source of the catastrophe in later fictions are seldom either as detailed or as haunting.

---

[20] Roberts has good comments on 'Wells's impeccable sense of the interlinked beauties of the familiar and the strange' (46).

The Martians are in a sense secure in their complexity: they are alien and uncommunicative; much of their technology will remain an unsolved mystery. They can be seen as strange, even as eerie, as, for instance, in the sound they make: 'an exultant deafening howl' (51), 'a furious yelling' (70), 'siren-like howls' (91). This seems animal-like, and also like the noise of a machine (a siren), and thence primitive; but it is not their way of communicating; in fact, according to the narrator, they communicate telepathically (137).

The novel suggests how the Martians resemble humans and how we cannot think of what they are without thinking of what humans are. The means of apocalypse, that which brings about catastrophe and changes (almost) everything, has about it this complexity.[21] And we are given humans in degraded states (the curate, the artilleryman, the narrator himself) and society in states of panic and dissolution. The panic of the mass of fleeing Londoners, every social type and class (and vehicle) jammed together, inseparable yet violently competing, is succeeded by the panic of the swarm of comparably miscellaneous ships that have come to the coast to profit by taking the refugees off, and are surprised by the Martians. As is usually the case in this novel, however, the effect is complicated, and the conclusions are both emphatic and provisional. Humans certainly are squirming and scuttling 'Under Foot' (book 2, chapter 1). The crowd of refugees is the victim of a kind of primitive monomania ('Push on!' was the cry. 'Push on! they are coming!' 106), though out of this emerges both the death of the miser (almost medieval, like an incident in a Triumph of Death) and the more dignified end of the Lord Chief Justice (108–109). Neither of these deaths is a profound piece of writing, but they do suggest how the novel refuses to forget the individual in the mass. More, the sense of people in the mass shifts and varies according to the situation. The narrator is clear enough on what panic reveals, for instance, in the crowd fleeing London and in the swarm of ships, but at other times he evokes the peace of common life, and this on the same basis of variety, a multitude of familiar types and activities. Apocalypse tends towards one dominating and destroying global event, a pressure towards uniformity, so that any countervailing imagination of multiplicity can be significant.

---

[21] This is well brought out in Mark Rose's discussion of the novel in *Alien Encounters* (1981, 69–77). He sees the novel as built on contrasts of life and death, with the Martians – coming from a dying planet – suggesting the latter, but with important complications (70 and 74 – the later passage is on how the dying Martian seems to give life to the deserted city).

The narrator's brother meets two women, one of whom shows 'pluck' (102); the narrator, less lucky, meets the curate and the artilleryman. People strike out in furious panic in the flight from London; the narrator is succoured by unnamed strangers during his breakdown near the end of the story. The final chapters move from the immediate and domestic to a grand evocation of London, 'that mighty desert of houses', 'this city of the dead' (175, 176), modulating, after the realisation that the microbes have eliminated the Martian threat, to a powerful evocation of crowded life: 'the multitudinous hopes and efforts, the innumerable hosts of lives that had gone to build this human reef' (181). It was a 'host' that fled London ('It is hard to imagine that host', 105), but here this host lives and works together, the social mixture of the crowd, often a sign of disorder, is here something creative, the implied comparison of humans to tiny creatures (coral polyps) an epic rather than a demeaning one. Yet the deserted city also foreshadows the inevitable end of London as of every civilisation (and see the comment on images of ruined London below at p. 99, n.17).

The narrator was moved by the cry of the dying Martian, as if it was a communication after all:

> The one had died, even as it had been crying to its companions; perhaps it was the last to die, and its voice had gone on perpetually until the force of its machinery was exhausted. They glittered now, harmless tripod towers of shining metal, in the brightness of the rising sun ... (181)

The narrator does not decide whether the Martian was crying out, or its machinery was making this noise, or signal. It doesn't matter: its formidable machinery has become one of the sights of reborn London. The narrator's thought that this might have been the last of its kind to die recalls the sensation he has himself had of being the last man (157, and again in his delirium, 184), and, even more poignantly, anticipates his feeling that he and his wife have returned from the dead (192, the last sentence of the novel). The Martians are safely dead, reduced to 'gnawed gristle' (177), the narrator and his wife have returned from the dead, London is as if new and its crowded ordinary social mixture can again be seen as creative.[22]

---

[22] The treatment of ordinary people in Wells's *The World Set Free* (1914) is in strong contrast. They are seldom mentioned without being characterised as 'little'. This novel avoids the complexities of *The War of the Worlds* by having characters purely as mouthpieces, by an exclusively panoramic point of view

Global Catastrophe, Science-Fiction Anti-Modernism and Science-Fiction Modernism in the Twentieth Century

Global destruction was to become real in Europe's plunge into giant disorder and destruction in 1914: 'The Deluge', which introduces 'The Age of Catastrophe'.[23] Notice Ian Kershaw's language, in a sober history of the period of the World Wars, as he sums up:

> This war brought an assault on humanity unprecedented in history. It was a descent into the abyss never previously encountered, the devastation of all the ideals of civilization that had arisen from the Enlightenment. It was a war of apocalyptic proportions, Europe's Armageddon.[24]

In European culture, the First World War marks a break, overlaid by the rise of modernism, which preceded it and was strengthened by it, and reinforced by its sequel or continuation in the Second World War. In this series of shocks, disasters and horrors, images of the apocalyptic proliferate, and often become so intense as images as to escape from the category of the apocalyptic altogether. What results is images of violence, destruction, disorder that can just as well be seen in terms of, for instance, Hell. After all, there are only flickers of narrative in many of the most haunting poems and paintings that came out of the First World War, and those that we can discern are often savagely ironical. So it is with the German Expressionist poems that reflect or are immersed in the conflict,[25] Otto Dix's images of the war, Ludwig Meidner's from before the war and T. S. Eliot's images and vignettes of the last days in *The Waste Land* from after the war. This is not the whole picture; the revolutionary breaking of all forms – including narrative – that modernism had begun before the war and that was intensified to

---

that avoids the immersion in events that makes for drama and conflict, and by declaring Science to be sacrosanct, immune to the corruption that is said to have afflicted other social activities such as Law and Politics in the bad old days before catastrophic nuclear war jolted humanity into setting up World Government and a rational society.

[23] Adam Tooze, *The Deluge: The Great War and the Reordering of Global Order*; Heinrich August Winkler, *The Age of Catastrophe: A History of the West 1914–45*; Niall Ferguson, *The War of the World*: apocalyptic book titles are common for works of twentieth-century history.

[24] Kershaw 2016, 347.

[25] See, for instance, the selections (Trakl, van Hoddis, Heym, Schrack) in Forster 1957.

craziness in Dada during and after the war intended a New Jerusalem, a renovation at least in the realm of art, building something new and vigorous on the ruins of what was seen as exhausted. To Meidner's paintings of explosion and destruction we can compare, for instance, Franz Marc, 'Tyrol' (1913–14), or Natalya Goncharova, 'Electric Lamps' (1912), both prismatic explosions of brilliant colour.[26] Surrealist fiction celebrates transformation, which often happens from one part of a sentence to the next, and the transformation always reaches for the revelatory.[27] Bruno Corra's *Sam Dunn is Dead* (first published 1915) is a zany futurist apocalypse, celebrating the collapse of order and sense as enjoyable release. Its narrative is just enough like the sober narratives to be discussed in the next chapter to underline how very different is a text produced in the buoyant reckless early days of modernism. By way of contrast, however, Alfred Kubin's *The Other Side* (first published 1909) gives us the catastrophic collapse of the city of Perle as a nightmarish series of riots, massacres, orgies, plagues, incursions of wild beasts, floods and eruptions.[28]

Does all this mean that the experience of catastrophe, the end of stable order, destroys narrative, and so apocalyptic narrative, as part of that order? Certainly the assertion can be made of the creative destructiveness of modernism and of the experience of the First World War, and underlined if one turns, for instance, to the poetry of Paul Celan as reflection on the Holocaust, the further catastrophe that has seemed to some to destroy art itself. If this is so, then the science-fiction disaster narratives that come after the Second World War will have to be categorised as parochial survivals. This is not quite so; each of them struggles with the challenges that apocalypse poses to narrative. Each also reflects a different view of the Second World War, a view that saw the coming of the war as more predictable and less shocking than that of the First World War, and its outcome as a victory for normality and decency. Their response and their vindication of, or simply reliance on, decency and normality builds on the kinds of apocalypse that had proliferated in science fiction after H. G. Wells – alien invasion, ecological catastrophe – and bypasses the innovations and destructions of modernism.

The challenge to the old logic of narrative that modernism poses in the aftermath of the First World War remains in reserve, however: a

---

[26] Reproduced in Vergo 1977, plates 33 and 46.
[27] See, for instance, *The Automatic Muse* (Hale 1994) that prints surrealist novels by Robert Desnos, Georges Limbour, Michel Leiris and Benjamin Péret.
[28] Kubin, a painter and illustrator, was a member *of Der Blaue Reiter*, a group of expressionist painters. Corra is best classified as a futurist.

potential that finds expression in contemporary apocalyptic fictions in multiple ways, as will be seen when the discussion turns to novels by J. G. Ballard, Brian Aldiss, Angela Carter, Doris Lessing and others. It is arguably the cultural ferment of the 1960s that jolts (some) science fiction into modernism, when the Holocaust and the threat of nuclear annihilation had not done so. The shift is manifest most often in terms of style (play with language, literary allusion, richness of metaphor and symbol) rather than in the nature of the imagined catastrophe, where there is no more than variation on the previous stand-bys (epidemic, nuclear destruction, ecological crisis). The end is total in Nevil Shute's *On the Beach* (1957) as it is in J. G. Ballard's *The Drowned World* (1962), but the style and ethos are utterly different in the latter novel. Fredric Jameson (2002, 123–124, and 128) discusses modernism as a succession of moves to rewrite and exceed previous realisms and notes that 'the older technique or content must somehow subsist within the work as what is cancelled or overwritten', and this is true of Ballard's relation to earlier science fiction, for instance.

Complications and backtrackings of the imagination of apocalypse require a degree of urbanity from us. Evidently neither science-fiction writers nor many 'mainstream' novelists of the 1930s to the present stick to the modernist script that says there is no going back after a radical break. It is as late as the 1960s that Brian Aldiss, for instance, discovers modernism (James Joyce in particular) with a rush in *Barefoot in the Head* (and he also discovers the *nouveau roman* with *Report on Probability A*, 1968). His wholesale enthusiasm might seem a bit gauche to the sophisticated, but it is energetic and enjoyable, and more generally the flamboyance of (so-called) 'New Wave' science fiction of the 1960s and 1970s might suggest that coming late to modernism has its pay-offs. In addition, it has to be admitted that in his explicit stylishness and richness of evocative, sometimes mannered diction J. G. Ballard often goes back beyond modernism to the *fin-de-siècle*.[29] We can see this embrace of style and the subjective as a liberation when we compare it to the very different approach and scope of the postwar disaster novels, but we can also see that it is dangerously close to driving apocalyptic fiction into a cul de sac. Most of part 3 of *Apocalypse in Crisis* explores the various ways in which later fiction escapes this danger.

---

[29] Ballard is scornful of the Modern Movement (contrasted to Salvador Dali); see Ballard 1996, 92–93.

The Scientific Enlightenment and Pastoralism

As Patrick Parrinder has discussed, the ethos of science fiction from Wells to the 1950s (and beyond in many cases) owes much to 'the Scientific Enlightenment': confidence in rational progress, fuelled by science, and usually led by an elite of scientists.[30] 'Modern scientific optimism' reached its peak in the 1920s, an opposite kind of response to the First World War from that of Dada and the modernists, and one that exerted a powerful influence on subsequent science fiction. Modernism of style, for instance as a way of registering the consciousness of someone in an imagined world different to or alien from our own, makes an appearance in Zamyatin's *We*, but is not taken up by science fiction, even in the case of Orwell's *1984*, which was otherwise heavily influenced by *We*. Science fiction follows Wells and the publicists of the Scientific Enlightenment such as Haldane, Bernal and Skinner, in its plain, lucid style, the style of the reliable and rational witness.

The aspect of science fiction that Parrinder discusses can be put into a broader context, that of what James C. Scott calls 'high modernism', the modernism of rational planning and control, shared by many architects, engineers, administrators and visionaries and, in Scott's account, embracing everyone from Lenin and Le Corbusier to Robert McNamara and Robert Moses, with at its centre 'a supreme self-confidence about continued linear progress'.[31] In this respect, as regards ethos not style or form, science fiction of the period from Wells to the 1950s is the literature of Scott's high modernism, whereas the response to modernity in its history of unpredictable change, destruction and disorder, and indeed catastrophe, is the high modernism of the literary critics' categorising of Joyce, Woolf and Eliot. Scott's perspective is a useful one, though inconvenient for the terminological clarity of the present discussion, and his high modernism can be seen in such texts as H. G. Wells's *The World Set Free* and Arthur C. Clarke's *Childhood's End*. The other postwar disaster novels to be discussed in the next chapter do not, however, exemplify Scott's high modernism or Parrinder's 'scientific enlightenment' as clearly as does *Childhood's End*. They also feature a different imaginary, which will be discussed shortly as pastoralism.

---

[30] Parrinder 1995, especially chapter 9 on the Scientific Enlightenment and 119–126 on Zamyatin and his influence, and lack of it. On the wider British scene, however, science and scientists also contributed to the pervasive gloom and sense of crisis of the interwar years; see Overy 2009, 4, 47–48.

[31] Scott 1998, 89, and for the more general discussion of high modernism, 88–95.

Coexisting with this confidence in science is a strand of domestic pastoral that we can find in Wells and in the authors of postwar disaster fictions in the 1940s and 1950s – fictions that have been called 'cosy catastrophes'.[32] Wells sets *The War of the Worlds* in the partly rural, partly suburban world of the English Home Counties, and Parrinder (93) remarks that this element recurs in his later works. Wells does not, however, try to suggest that retreat to the countryside is a long-term option in *The War of the Worlds*; the huge population of London, and the vitality of the city, rule this out. Catastrophe leaves the cities ruined and desolate in the later British apocalypses, and the survivors retreat to the countryside; this even happens in *On the Beach*, where the countryside is Australian. One of the Australian characters is surprised that her American lover should find the Australian bush beautiful (Shute 1957, 128); it is England that is assumed to be beautiful. They are enjoying one of several rural interludes together.

The country may be greener and more peaceful as a result of the catastrophe, as in Aldiss's *Greybeard* (1964), set in the now flooded Thames Valley, or the structure of the novel may express two clashing aspects of Nature, that which led to the catastrophe and that which figures as refuge from it, as in Wyndham's *The Day of the Triffids*, which contrasts the triffids, which are plants, and the green countryside they have taken over, but in which they seem alien. Similarly in *Childhood's End* the transformation of the world wrought by the Overlords puts nature under human protection, while the destruction of the world wrought by the Overmind obliterates it.

Yet these complexities seem more like anomalies in these texts. The spirit of pastoral is pervasive.[33] The city is ruined and uninhabitable;

---

[32] Imagination of nature as refuge is widespread in the period: for instance, the interlude that Winston and Julia share in the sunlit wood in the otherwise totally grim and deprived world of Orwell's *1984* (1948): 'It's the golden country – almost […] a landscape I've seen sometimes in a dream' (quoted in D. J. Taylor, *TLS*, 3 March 2017, 5). For 'cosy catastrophe', see Aldiss and Wingrove 1986, 253–255, with reference to John Wyndham and John Christopher. In chapter VII of *The Great War and Modern Memory* (1975), Paul Fussell demonstrates the pervasiveness of the 'arcadian' in the English response to the conditions of trench warfare. He reads the poems and memoirs of Edmund Blunden as showing how strong this sensibility could be. In English apocalyptic fiction, it is still strong in, for instance, P. D. James's *The Children of Men*, 1992, though in this novel the countryside is a place of danger as well as arcadian peace (see, for instance, 215, and 256). For the cultural and political roots of idealisation of the countryside, see Hawkins 1986.

[33] I. F. Clarke (1970, 168–169) discusses a set of stories published between the

those taking refuge in the country may have to fight for their piece of it, against the triffids for instance, but there is a kind of relief in the movement, a return to what is natural and is felt to be English. Those participating in this movement are usually middle class in the British disaster novels; in Wyndham's *The Kraken Wakes* (1953) the main characters own a country cottage in Cornwall to which they retreat. In these novels nature is humanised, cultivated – very different from the unkempt and dangerous nature unleashed by apocalyptic catastrophe in Ballard or Carter.

Yet if nature is no longer domesticated in later apocalyptic fictions, it remains part of their imaginary, a possible source of value, needing constantly to be re-evaluated. Nature is destroyed, threatened and threatening, but it doesn't cease to stand over against Humanity (which may well be responsible for the catastrophe) or Society (which is usually destroyed or faced with destruction) as a possible source of value.

Of course, confidence in science is always liable to rebuffs in apocalyptic fictions, where science may have facilitated the catastrophe and may be impotent in its aftermath (hence the return to rural life). In addition, Parrinder (in his chapter 9, 127–151) narrates the decline of the ethos of scientism, a decline always potential in the hubristic grandeur of its vision. It tends over time to be crudified into a simple materialism, whose premises ignore or dismiss much of what humans in fact want and enjoy, especially if the humans in question are more various and stranger than the decent, practical, active males that figure in so much science fiction. The ethos also tends to rely on a version of evolution, in which humanity is somehow destined to transcend the material and even the human – a version that is dubious intellectually, as will be touched on later in the discussion of *Childhood's End*. More recent science-fiction apocalypses depart from the line of 'Golden Age' science fiction and its successors, here represented by Clarke, Stewart, Shute and Wyndham. Science and reason are sometimes rejected or, at least, seen as surpassed, in the fictions discussed in part 2, or what science tells us about nature is reassessed.

In later fiction nature as concept as well as entity is under stress. Ethical appeal to the natural is undermined by post-modern scepticism, yet the onset of climate change makes the desire to preserve nature more urgent, and nature shows more complex faces as the climate changes: in the cascading consequences of climate change nature becomes both

---

World Wars that greet with joy the replacement of modern civilisation by 'Arcadian blessedness'; he sees these stories as driven by hatred of urban and industrial society.

victim and threat: hundreds of species cease to exist, while fire and flood become more frequent and more extreme. Nature is both something over against humans and something humans have to see themselves as part of, and hope to manage.[34] In recent novels such as Audrey Schulman's *Theory of Bastards* and Kim Stanley Robinson's *Green Earth*, we find a double change: in the era of climate change, nature is reimagined as both threatened and powerful, and human nature is reimagined as part of nature, as the nature of the human animal, in the light of a different, less utopian, interpretation of evolution. Humans work on and try to understand nature, in recognition of the fact that they are themselves unusual and fallible animals. In both novels we have also a re-imagination of science: science as hard work, where the confident ethos of the scientific enlightenment can no longer be relied on, and as social work, the work of a knowledgeable but fallible and struggling social group.

[34] See, for instance, the essays assembled in *Entangled Worlds: Religion, Science and New Materialism* (Keller and Robinson 2017), especially those by Beatrice Marovich and Terra S. Rowe and, in a very different field, works by Frans de Waal, *Primates and Philosophers*, and *Are we Smart enough to Say How Smart Animals Are?*

Chapter 2

The Postwar Disaster Novels
Apocalypse Contained

In Britain, the Second World War comes as no surprise; apocalypse renewed loses some of its power to shock and terrify:

> Not the twilight of the gods but a precise dawn
> Of sallow and grey bricks and newsboys crying war
>
> (Louis MacNeice, 'Aubade')

War seems all-encompassing:

> This is all anyone talks about, thought Ambrose; jobs, and the kind of war it is going to be. War in the air, war of attrition, tank war, war of nerves, war of propaganda, war of defence in depth, war of movement, people's war, total war, indivisible war, war infinite, war incomprehensible, war of essence without accidents or attributes, metaphysical war, war in time-space, war eternal ...

This is from Evelyn Waugh's *Put Out More Flags* (1942, 87) – of all texts: but *Put Out More Flags* shows how war releases people from rules and inhibitions, as often happens in apocalyptic fictions, too.[1]

The Second World War gives everyone in Europe experience of the local manifestations of global emergency, if no worse: rationing, refugees ('displaced persons'), panic flight, resort to the bomb shelter. When J. G. Ballard embarks on his set of apocalyptic novels, in 1962, with *The Wind from Nowhere*, he equips the crisis with these appurtenances of Britain in the Second World War: the elite hiding in bunkers, the struggles of the emergency services, the masses fleeing to the shelter of

---

[1] Then again, from the time of George W. Bush: 'rumors of war, images of war, "preemptive" war, "preventive" war, "surgical" war, "prophylactic" war, "permanent" war' (Judt 2015, 242).

the Underground as they had in 'the war', only, this time, to be drowned in a yet more extreme disaster.[2] When a small band fight their way north from London to refuge in a secluded valley in Westmorland, in John Christopher's *The Death of Grass* (1956) the men in the party call on their experience as soldiers in the war, and the narrative traces a series of ruthless small-unit engagements.

In the US, the experience was different again, the technological sublimity of the war more a matter of the vast mobilisation of industry and armament than the scale of extermination and destruction, the revealed power of nuclear energy as impressive as its threat of annihilation. The 1950s saw fictions, especially films, of invasion, but as the Cold War deepened and led to suspicion and mistrust, much imaginative energy went into stories of infiltration and treachery, the product also of anxiety about conformity. Mistrust of one's fellow citizens was more corrosive than fear of a foreign enemy.

It will be suggested that the fictions of apocalypse discussed in chapters 3 and 4 come out of Britain's post-imperial moment – not America's problem. In Britain the fiction of Cold War mistrust comes somewhat later in the form of the espionage novel.[3]

A. J. P. Taylor (1967, 328–330) contrasts the British responses to the two World Wars: 'World War I seemed unique, a cosmic catastrophe. [...] World War II startled men less. They were dejected at having to go through it again, but they were not surprised. [...] After World War II men's aspirations were lower and their achievements higher than after World War I.'[4] The issues were clearer, the stakes were higher and the victory counted for more. It could be seen as vindicating decency and normality rather than as rendering them meaningless.

Cultural awareness struggled to keep up with the implications of the war's huge atrocities: the leading Nazis were tried for crimes of aggression as much as or more than for genocide. People had to some degree normalised and accepted mass bombing of civilians so that it was

---

[2] See, for instance, Ballard 1967, 54–57; 107 (the ruins of Genoa remind a character of the ruins of Berlin at the end of the war); 117 ('The scene reminded Marshall of the last hours in Hitler's führer bunker').

[3] There's an interval between the novels of unease and betrayal of the 1930s (Eric Ambler and Graham Greene) and the espionage novels of the 1960s and later (John le Carré, Len Deighton); perhaps the gap is filled, or papered over, with Ian Fleming's James Bond novels of imperial nostalgia.

[4] See also Judt 2005, for the prevailing modesty of expectation (David Lodge quoted, 163) and the 'fading' but still warm embers of nineteenth-century 'cultural habits and social relations increasingly at odds with the new age of airplanes and atomic weapons' (227).

possible to accept the decision to bomb Hiroshima as a decision simply to use a bigger bomb. It was later that the notion was introduced that the bomb was dropped to avert the likelihood that an invasion of Japan would cost up to a million American lives. This figure has no foundation in the military prognoses of the time, and cannot have figured in the original decision (Walker 1996). It is perhaps as important to emphasise these lags in awareness as it is to emphasise prophetic leaps of awareness such as were made by writers of science fiction and by some of the atomic scientists and by those who formulated the idea of crimes against humanity. Fictions of nuclear dread would come, but after a delay.

Nonetheless, apocalyptic fiction is renewed in the aftermath of the Second World War in both Britain and the US, and it is to four examples of this fiction that discussion now turns: George R. Stewart, *Earth Abides*; John Wyndham, *The Day of the Triffids*; Nevil Shute, *On the Beach*; and Arthur C. Clarke, *Childhood's End*. (Wyndham and Clarke wrote genre science fiction, while Stewart and Shute can't be classified as genre science-fiction writers; yet the four novels have a lot in common.) The above general considerations about the effects of the Second World War might help to prepare us for the element of sobriety, the interest in the local and ordinary, that is to be found, for instance, even amidst the uncanny mutation of children and the destruction of Earth in Arthur C. Clarke's *Childhood's End*. In these novels apocalyptic catastrophe (nuclear war, unexplained epidemic) comes out of the blue and far from any control or knowledge that the protagonists could ever exert. If it is the work of human beings, as is the case with the nuclear war that has spread deadly fallout over the globe in *On the Beach*, or the concatenation of events that has rendered most humans blind in the face of the (human-bred) triffids in *The Day of the Triffids*, then this signifies how the human – the group of ordinary people the novel follows – has become separated from that other human that is the 'they' responsible for the war and the triffids. The separation is not so emphasised that we can talk of alienation, and in the course of the novel the protagonists advance some distance towards understanding the catastrophe, as well as engaging in practical action to survive it or at least go on living as long as they can, but it is as if the global has passed out of human control and only the local can be narrated or acted on. Nonetheless the catastrophe or transformation is clear to the characters, and its representation (the triffids in Wyndham's novel, for instance, or the Overlords in Clarke's) is often what most strikes the reader.

The Quiet Recession of Modernity
Earth Abides

George R. Stewart's *Earth Abides* (1949)[5] is distinguished from most subsequent post-apocalyptic fictions by its air of calm acceptance and its dispassionate analysis of the likely consequences of the disappearance of humans – and what we are given is a disappearance more than it is a mass death. There is nothing sensational, very little that is dramatic and the narrative works its way from the initial registration of the 'Great Disaster' to a series of deaths that are on a more individual scale and that deliberately reconnect the history of the survivors of the apocalypse to the history of all humans who have to face death and grief. In *Earth Abides* dispassion is softened by sympathy with the central character, Isherwood Williams, known as Ish. The novel's analysis is panoramic and confident, Ish is fallible and full of doubts. Nature will go its own way now that the period of man's dominance can be seen as a mere 'interval'; the behaviour of the surviving humans is more wayward, swayed by emotion. Ecology is a reliable guide to what happens in nature, anthropology a less certain guide to what the humans do and suffer. Stewart thus has some divergent and possibly conflicting schemas to reconcile in *Earth Abides*. We can see this process of reconciliation at work in the two strands of the text, one centred closely on Ish, the other a series of impersonal, italicised commentaries; in the shifting registers of the prose, from the Song of Songs to the impersonally scientific; and from the text's dealings with various elementary things – light, water, Ish's hammer – dealings that shift between the contingent and the symbolic. Stewart is negotiating problems of authority and perspective, the local and the panoramic. The first is fallible and immersed in the day to day in a small district of California, and second, knowledgeable, but external to the characters and their struggles and fates. Knowledge of what is happening and of the shape of the future is, however, available to the reader, and authoritative: a much more stable situation than what prevails in later apocalyptic fictions.

Most humans in America are wiped out by a mysterious epidemic. We know this because Ish tours the country shortly after epidemic has done its worst and finds only very few survivors, and many of them too traumatised by the disaster to be likely to live long. We are given no reason to believe that matters have fared differently in the rest of the world, but the focus is definitely on the US: Ish in old age will be 'the

---

[5] References are to the Greenwich, CT: Fawcett edition, 1972.

Last American'.[6] *Earth Abides* is, then, certainly a post-catastrophe novel, but it is sceptical of the traditional apocalypse as a point of reference for what has happened. Here is Ish examining his 'qualifications' for living on; one is that he is not superstitious:

> Otherwise he would even now [...] be fighting the fear that the whole disaster had been the work of an angry God, who had now wiped out his people by pestilence as once before by flood, leaving Ish (though as yet unsupplied with wife and children) like another Noah to repopulate the wilderness. But such thoughts opened the way to madness. (41; and see 132)[7]

In fact he does become a patriarch, accumulating a mystique as, eventually, the last relic of the old times, but the notion of God's anger and purpose remains rejected.

The novel offers secular meditations on civilisation, law and religion, among many other topics, though the Bible shapes its prose, and is explicitly invoked. Ish feels that the figure of Christ as depicted in the Gospels is too involved in the social to serve as a guide (93); the angry punishing God of the Old Testament is rejected by Ish's wife, Em (258): yet the history of the 'tribe', the small group of survivors that Ish founds, is a social one, and the coming together of Ish and Em is told us in terms taken from the Song of Songs. Stewart wants to give the story an elemental – in this case, Biblical – resonance, yet is anxious to control this resonance.

Willis McNelly suggested that 'Ish' and 'Em' echo the Hebrew words for Man and Woman (personal communication). Thence we can see Ish and Em as Adam and Eve, founding a new race of humans. They certainly are depicted as the patriarch and matriarch of the growing tribe, though Stewart qualifies this, for instance by the way the aged

---

[6] Kim Stanley Robinson's Tom Bernard echoes Ish in his post-apocalyptic *The Wild Shore* (1984). Tom, another ageing survivor of a catastrophe that has reduced the survivors to a simple life, is also anxious to pass on rudiments of the old civilisation, such as the ability to read. Like Ish, Tom calls himself 'the last American' (246). Tom has more success as a teacher, but both history and what it means to be an American are much more problematic in *The Wild Shore*.

[7] Contrast Anderson, the leader of the survivors in Thomas M. Disch's much harsher *The Genocides* (1965). Anderson sees himself as Noah, and is not far from madness. His power is limited; humans are helpless before the power of unseen aliens who are turning Earth into a monocultural forest and eliminating humans as vermin.

Ish is a stranger among the new people, honoured but puzzled. That the last or apparently last man and woman are seen as Adam and Eve is common in earlier novels of the end, and parodied or subverted in more recent versions, for instance in Angela Carter's *Heroes and Villains* and Arno Schmidt's *Nobodaddy's Children*. In Ballard the protagonist usually abandons a relationship with a woman that was already tepid. Kerans in *The Drowned World* is compared to Adam, but there is no Eve.

The initial annihilation of most humans is got over quickly in *Earth Abides*, and happens while Ish is off stage, camping in the wilderness. Ish enters the new, post-apocalyptic world without attachments. We hear nothing of friends or family and his thoughts about the world that has gone, or is going, are impersonal and contemplative. He is not really bereft, however: he is beginning the world again, though as time passes there is a slow fade, a parting from the world. The text settles into a meditation on the recession of the remnants of what turns out to be a terminally damaged civilisation and a permanently disrupted human control of nature, and on the slow evolution of what replaces it, at least in the community that Ish helps to set up and to lead. There is time for thoughts about many fundamental topics in sociology and ecology, threaded through a loose plot that is shaped to pursue this or that topic when the time seems ripe in the broad stream of a chronicle of changes, losses, births and deaths. Gary K. Wolfe (1983, 8–16) sets out a schema for novels of the end, comprising five stages: experience or discovery of the cataclysm; journey through the wasteland; settlement and establishment of a community; re-emergence of the wilderness; decisive battle of the elect. They can all be found in *Earth Abides*, as he notes, if sometimes in unusual form (for instance, the episode involving Charlie is both a symptom of the re-emergence of the wilderness and can be seen as standing for the decisive battle). But my impression is that the unfolding of the novel is directed mainly by Stewart's interest in a particular cultural stage or problem on which there is the opportunity for meditation.

The style and form of the novel expresses what Ish sometimes thinks, which is that the disaster has simplified and purified, brought the elemental to the fore, relieved those who have survived of the burdens of civilisation, and meant that those who are born and who replace the survivors as time goes by will never even know of these burdens – or know of either the achievements or the power of that destroyed and forgotten civilisation. He notices, for instance, that his group is free of many diseases: 'That fact, when he thought of it, sometimes even made the Great Disaster seem beneficent – a magnificent wiping off of the slate which allowed man as a species to escape from most of the aches and pains he had been accumulating for so many centuries, and start anew' (251). (Later, however, there comes the disastrous epidemic of typhoid fever.)

Unlike *Childhood's End*, *The War of the Worlds*, and *The Day of the Triffids*, *Earth Abides* has little interest in power and its manifestations. These other novels are of course invasion stories, and invasion is a manifestation of power. In *Earth Abides* there is no struggle for domination of the tribe such as is common in narratives of the aftermath of social collapse. Stewart has a refreshing confidence in ordinary Americans' habits of co-operation and in their lack of ambition. There are parallels with Brian Aldiss's later novel *Greybeard* (1964), in which the disappearance of humanity, now sterile and ageing towards extinction, is contemplated calmly in the setting of the richness of the Thames valley ('Man had gone, and the great interlocking world of living species had already knitted over the space he once occupied', 157), and the survivalist struggle for power is muted and a touch ridiculous given that everyone is now old (one of the petty tyrants is called Big Jim Mole).

Everything in the style of *Earth Abides* is calm, patient, a trifle elegiac, and so are many things in its content. As has often been noted, Ish, who is never far from the centre of the book, alludes in his name to Ishi, the last survivor of his Native American tribe (or so it was supposed at the time, when Theodora Kroeber wrote Ishi's story). Ish will in turn become 'the Last American', that is, the last of 'the Old People', the people of the time when this was the United States. Civilisations come and go, and the (US) Americans filled an interval of time as did the Native Americans; by the time Ish is 'the Last American', an American is a person of myth rather than history (217). 'The Last American' ironically echoes 'the Last Indian', the stereotype that for the nineteenth century symbolised the inevitable extinction of Native Americans (Fritszche 2005, 185). Ish's community call themselves a 'Tribe', though the novel is careful to underline that they are slow to develop the skills and traditions of actual tribespeople. Their home is near a place where Native Americans once went about their business.

> He walked on across a broad surface of smooth rock that sloped with the hillside. It was pitted with small round holes marking the places where squaws had once pounded with stone pestles.
> 'The world of these Indians passed away,' he thought. 'And now our world that followed theirs has passed too.' (31)

In *Earth Abides*, America (the US) is wiped out, and its civilisation fades and then winks out like the lights of the city that had continued to function for a while after the catastrophe. Other pasts emerge, in the traces of Native American civilisation, and perhaps they come to encompass the surviving Americans, whose culture is tribal and peaceful and whose technological breakthrough is the discovery of the bow and arrow.

In the name Ish there is perhaps also an allusion to the Christopher Isherwood of 'I am a camera', the dispassionate observer, because we are told that Ish likes to watch; he is a witness more than he is a doer.[8] He does in fact act, sometimes decisively, but he is certainly not an action hero; he is not actually dispassionate, being often melancholy or depressed, but he is objective. His attitudes suit those of a book that wants to examine and weigh up and that avoids the sensational.

In the opening section Ish has been isolated in the woods, ill with the snakebite that almost kills him but gives him immunity to the epidemic. When he emerges, most people are dead. The quiet and the absence of people lead him to feel 'a certain amount of surprise' (10); the sight of a corpse makes him think he should contact the Coroner, though he already senses that this is futile (15). He has qualms about swinging his hammer to break into a locked store, and even about driving through a traffic light (17, 23). He reflects on humankind's dramatic imaginations of catastrophe, 'But actually mankind seemed merely to have been removed rather neatly, with a minimum of disturbance' (20). When he thinks what the future might hold for domesticated animals in a world without humans, 'All he held fairly certain was that in twenty-five or fifty years some kind of moderately stable situation would result' (54) – nothing sensational or tragic; in fact, at this early point, not even an elegiac note, though that will be sounded as time passes.

Later he investigates further, and realises that many survivors must have been traumatised:

> These people were physically alive, but more and more he realized that they walked about in a kind of emotional death. He had studied enough anthropology to realize that the same phenomenon had been observed on a smaller scale before. Destroy the culture-pattern in which people lived, and often the shock was too great for individuals. (77; and see 146)

(Again there is an implicit parallel between Americans and premodern peoples.) Ish's knowledge will become irrelevant later – he doesn't even

---

[8] The relevant texts are *Ishi in Two Worlds*, Theodora Kroeber (published in 1961, but the story of Ishi was known before this); and Christopher Isherwood, *Goodbye to Berlin*, 1939.

succeed in teaching the young of the tribe how to read – but this kind of reflection never ceases to supply the novel with a calm standpoint. Still, the effect is very low-key. Ish is confident that civilisation went out with decency and that the authorities organised mass burials (19).

The way is cleared for a 'laboratory experiment' concerning what will happen to civilisation in the aftermath of disaster (155). Ish infers the suffering and even glimpses it, but he is protected from experiencing it. We hear of his loneliness and that of many survivors ('the Great Loneliness') but that is almost all. In this novel, the fading of civilisation into oblivion and irrelevance will be calmly watched in its stages and ramifications, but sensation, trauma and violence will be rationed, present only in moderate doses (a single drunk; a menacing intruder, Charlie, who is disposed of by vote; rumours of groups elsewhere who have formed white-robed sects or worse (198, 222)). And certainly the reader can hardly open the door into fictions of apocalypse without stumbling over sensation, trauma and violence, so he or she has plenty of reason to allow Stewart his moderation and to see where it takes his novel.

This moderation and decency are embodied in Ish, the observer and witness. To vary and reinforce this element in the text, Stewart includes a series of passages that are marked off in italics and shaped both by the language of science, and by the language of the Bible (a certain sonority, a simplicity that emphasises the timeless and pays no attention to the local and immediate). For instance:

> *In those days when there had been death in the air and civilization tottered toward its end – in those days, the men who controlled the water looked on one another and said, 'Even though we fall sick and die, still, the people must have water.' [...] Then they set the valves and opened the channels, so that the water flowed freely all the way from the great dams in the mountains and through the long siphons and into the tunnels and finally to the reservoirs from which it would flow, all at the pull of the earth, through all the faucets.* (81)[9]

In these passages we are shown what is already happening and will continue to happen – most often, unresting, gradual natural process. Ish

---

[9] We can contrast these engineers, more heroic than they could have known, with the encyclopaedic, unsentimental knowledge of the passage about the water supply in the Ithaca chapter of *Ulysses* (Joyce 1960, 782–783), where the context is a catalogue of the encompassing variety of water in its natural forms.

recognises this kind of thing too, and he often feels in biblical cadences, especially about his wife, Em ('Mother of Nations') and his favoured son, Joey ('Child of the Blessing', 'the Chosen One'): so there is not a sharp break between the passages in italics and the passages that give us events and thoughts from Ish's point of view. The former do, however, particularly give us the processes that unfold once humanity's control of nature has lapsed: what will happen in the deserts and the cities, what will happen to all that has been domesticated – sheep, cattle, domestic pets, garden plants, wheat, rats, lice.[10] Stewart wittily sees in lice an example of racial harmony:

> *They existed as three tribes, taking as their domains, respectively, the head, the clothing, and the private parts. Thus, in spite of racial differences, they amicably maintained a tripartite balance of power, setting for their host an example which he might well have followed.* (61)

This is just after Ish has encountered a family of peaceful 'Negro' survivors, in his tour of the continent (59–60). Em herself is presumably African American (see 99, 102 (her 'dark face') and 115). It's interesting that no one in the tribe (typical white people of the time) mentions Em's race. Perhaps the novel's lack of emphasis on the point is itself Stewart's way of making a point about the irrelevance of race in the aftermath of catastrophe.

The italicised passages give the broad shape of time after the catastrophe; time is not human-centred, as in traditional apocalypses, and its logic unfolds because humans are now, in effect, absent. (Even those water engineers fade into an undefined past.) The context is ecology, the interdependence and interrelations of species and environments, all of them changing, and the logic is Darwinian: some creatures ('soft exotics', 69) will die out or be killed; others will prosper or revert to what they were before they came into interrelationship with humans, a period that now seems a mere interval (for example, wheat: '*After a while there was no more wheat, except that far off in the dry lands of Asia and Africa, here and there, the little spiked grass still was growing, as it had grown before an incident called Agriculture ...*' (248)).

This strand of meditation, in the italic passages, is tougher than most of what Ish thinks. For example, from a passage on the survival of the house-fly:

---

[10] Deserts and cities, 51 and 67; sheep, 56; cattle, 53; pets, 69; plants, 45; wheat, 248; rats, 111.

> *Thus, even though man should be reduced to the vanishing point or disappear altogether, the house-fly was secure as long as the larger animals still lived and continued to leave droppings behind them. The eggs of the fly, thus deposited, soon hatched out, and the larvae found themselves embowered in rich and succulent food on which to feast, as snakes upon rats, woodpeckers upon grubs, and men on the flesh of dead animals. (252)*

Indeed, the food of the surviving humans never seems to be 'rich and succulent'; it is mostly scavenged from cans in the supermarkets.[11]

Ish's attention is on the more directly social. He meditates on civilisation, its costs as well as its achievements, and on law and religion. Even in their bereft and rather mediocre state, humans feel and imagine, and their fates have different qualities from those of the sheep and rats.

He is more aware of the afterlife of civilisation, which means that the survivors in the tribe can go on scavenging, eating canned food, using and discarding razors, drinking the still running water from the still functioning water system and so on: a tribute to the impersonal efficiency of arrangements before the disaster, and a symptom of a dangerous cultural stagnation and idleness in the survivors. The text deals in specifics (why cattle will probably survive the absence of man but sheep will not, for instance (53 and 56)), but also elementals: light and water, for instance.

The weave of symbols through the text may be read as Stewart's attempt to set the human in a different context from that of the ecological; the text shifts between the contingent and the more grandly symbolical. It traces the fading of the electric light, from the early scenes in which Ish looks out over San Francisco with the street lights and even the traffic lights and some of the neon signs still functioning, to the scene in which he sits in his living room and watches the light bulbs burn low and expire (27, 89–91); meanwhile he begins to suggest how light can symbolise faith in the future, as when Em, the figure of health and profound positiveness, strikes a match (107). This symbolical resonance of light is never securely established, however; the tribe's delight in bonfires is seen as an aspect of the new people's childishness and readiness to be distracted. Similarly, the narrative shows us how the survivors rely unthinkingly on the water that flows from their faucets,

---

[11] In contrast, the post-apocalyptic survivors in Douglas Coupland's *Girlfriend in a Coma* (1998; see chapter 7 below), also scavenging in supermarkets, indulge in gross pig-outs. Coupland writes about a consumer society grown wasteful and purposeless. Coupland's survivors are heavily into drugs and alcohol; Stewart hardly mentions either.

until it fails, and they only then investigate how the pipes have rusted and given way, and make desultory attempts to dig a well. The stress in the passages about water is more on how the flow of water now follows its own course, undermining roads and streets, changing the landscape.

The most important of the novel's symbolic but contingent objects is Ish's hammer, which he brings with him from the wilderness after his snakebite. The hammer becomes his talisman, his lucky object; then he realises that the others associate it with his leadership; it becomes an object with a religious aura. Yet it is still a hammer; when Ish first meets Em:

> [...] he could think of nothing better than an apology for the ridiculous hammer which still dangled from his hand.

– Or maybe it is not just a hammer:

> 'Pardon me for bringing this thing in,' he said, and he set it down on the floor upon its head with the handle sticking stiffly into the air. (99)

Stewart is thus in two minds. He is dealing with new humans, a new beginning for humanity, or American humanity anyway, in which much is lost but something elemental is regained, and Ish and Em can figure as patriarch and matriarch. He is also dealing with a sample of ordinary Americans who don't really have very much cultural knowledge or tradition to lose, who stumble placidly into a future in which the past will be forgotten altogether, while nature proceeds inexorably on its way, following lines that can be reliably predicted, so that the predictable outcomes expounded by Stewart's passages in italics sometimes spill into the mostly carefree and unthinking lives of the tribe in a way that surprises them. Mostly the two aspects are held in balance, and the humans in the story are given dignity without implausible depth, although the combination in Em of a symbol of wise inarticulate life-force, 'Mother of Nations', and a woman who says she wants to go to sleep whenever Ish starts to discuss things, can be an awkward one. The book at these moments is trying to combine an idealism about thinking and understanding (in the depiction of Ish as well as the italicised passages) with an idealisation of a woman (really, a Woman) who understands without thinking.

The survivors settle into placid stagnation – or so Ish fears – and the text likewise for a while is episodic. Then Ish persuades the tribe to send out a pair of younger men to explore the rest of the continent. When they return, they bring with them Charlie, a casual acquaintance, and Charlie's arrival sparks a tighter sequence of events. Charlie is from the first seen as 'dirty' (219), untrustworthy and a threat; he has sexual designs on Evie, whom the group have secluded from sexuality because she is simple. Ezra, usually the most equable of the adults, bursts out in loathing: Charlie is rotten inside with 'Cupid's diseases' (239). The four senior adults vote on what to do about Charlie, and decide to kill him. They do. As Ish reflects, with this drastic action they have made Law, and with Law has come death. They have a State. But it turns out that the threat Charlie carried was not venereal disease but typhoid fever.[12] An epidemic follows and among those dead is one of Ish and Em's sons, Joey.

A story that begins with mass death that happens off stage and need not be contemplated directly, comes to end with an execution, and a series of deaths that are natural, in the course of the slow unfolding of time; the most painful, however, that of Joey, happens as a result of a local disaster. Here, as often in apocalyptic fiction, a single death in a small disaster can be faced, whereas the mass deaths in the almost total disaster could not be faced.

With Joey's death, and Ish's coming to terms with his grief, the novel stages death and grief in the form that can be felt and comprehended. The circumstances are particular, not as it were elemental. The exploration that Ish had planned brings them Charlie, who is killed only after he has brought them disease: unintended and unpredictable consequences. Joey is Ish's beloved son in whom his hopes of future intelligence and civilisation rested. Now Joey is grieved for and buried, and after Ish recovers a little he rethinks what he might give to the future of the tribe – not the kind of abstract intelligence and intellectual interests that he and Joey alone shared, but something more practical. He works this out while idly smashing bits of the stone steps of the Library with his hammer (269–271). Later he makes a bow and arrow; it becomes a kids' toy and is soon imitated (275: 'creative force had returned to the world'). In the closing pages of the novel we see that the bow and arrow have been much improved and have become the weapon of choice. In recovering from his unreal hopes for Joey, he has given something useful to the tribe, without their knowing it. He has submitted to the fact that the tribe will develop without the technology or culture of the (modern) past, and will become more like Native Americans in their skills and feelings. The aged, fading Ish recognises in Jack the kind of

---

[12] Gary K. Wolfe (1983, 18) says the epidemic is venereal, but it seems clear that it is typhoid fever (see *Earth Abides*, 253).

successor he must expect, and accepts how different Jack is from himself and from any of 'the old people'. The hammer is still important, the sign of his sometimes uncomfortable status as patriarch, or oracle, but he hands it on to Jack as he dies.

Earth Abides can be seen as reflecting on the history of the United States. American history, completing the conquest and settlement of the continent at the coast of California where *Earth Abides* is set, can be seen as triumphant – destiny fulfilled. American history can also be seen as littered with losses – the elimination of the Native Americans, the abandonment of areas of New England as the population moved west, the dust bowl, the rust belt.[13] Perhaps this melancholy alternative history is behind *Earth Abides* as the story of the end and the forgetting of the United States and the fading of Isherwood Smith, the Last American, its conscientious and thoughtful representative, towards his death.

Nature and the English
The Day of the Triffids[14]

We can work our way into a sense of the fate and the task of the humans we meet in *The Day of the Triffids* – a set of average, mostly middle-class English people – by examining the nature of the catastrophe and its threat. Seemingly, the catastrophe results from an accident, one that affects the globe as a whole. Earth passes through what is taken to be a spectacular shower of comets – cometary dust; everyone who can, gazes at the sight, and they are all struck blind overnight. Only a few are left still sighted, those who for one reason or another (accident or luck, again) were unable to look at the night sky. The narrator was in hospital for an eye operation; the woman he meets later – definitely the novel's love interest – was asleep and hung over. The sighted are far too few to care for the helpless blinded, though some of them do try. Almost all of the blinded die miserable deaths, accelerated by an unknown epidemic

---

[13] See Fritszche (2005, especially the Conclusion, and 162–164) for an account of the melancholy of the modern history of the West, including the United States.

[14] References are to John Wyndham, *The Day of the Triffids*, London: Penguin Essentials, 2014. (First published in 1951.) The title of *The Day of the Locust*, Nathanael West (1939), alludes to Revelation and to the plagues of Egypt, by way of Gilbert Seldes's *The Years of the Locust* (1933); does *The Day of the Triffids* do the same, if less directly? There are many science-fiction novels and films whose titles follow this form (for instance, *The Day the Earth Stood Still* – also 1951 – though there too is an allusion to the Bible).

disease that soon breaks out. Next, the life of the survivors is complicated and threatened by the triffids, Wyndham's big science-fiction invention here and the main reason the novel is memorable.

Triffids are plants, exploited for their valuable oils, with many unusual features: they are mobile, equipped with deadly whip-like stings that were docked when they were under human control, and carnivorous (we are not told what they are fed on when they were cultivated by humans). We gradually learn that, in addition, they probably communicate with one another (by rattling stick-like appendages) and definitely learn to co-ordinate their attacks on humans, perhaps by a kind of hive mind.

The triffids are the stars of the novel, as the Martians were of *The War of the Worlds*. They are not horrible or gross, they seem insensible or indifferent and are quite easy to kill, but they have a quiet, sinister power, massing in dark patient ranks round the fenced farm where the characters have taken refuge, or waiting hidden until starving, blind survivors venture outside their houses in hitherto peaceful English villages and are then stung to death, and eaten when they have begun to decay. It's hard to say what the triffids might stand for, in contrast to Wells's Martians who are an alien presence in the novel but suggest many things about humans, about 'progress', technology and violence. Perhaps this lack of symbolic power and suggestion is the point: in that case they simply figure the brute meaninglessness of things. Even given this air of menace, however, they seem a bit obviously to have been constructed by Wyndham for their role of alien invader: mobile, deadly, carnivorous, faceless, intelligent: a formidable list of innovations for a plant, though a plant that, as we are told early in the novel, was genetically bred in the Soviet Union and (again) escaped by accident, or at least by way of unintended consequences of an attempt to steal the seeds.[15]

In the background then is a story of capitalist greed up against communist secrecy, and in the foreground the malfunction of the military satellites that causes mass blindness and thus makes humans vulnerable to the triffids, a malfunction, if it was a malfunction, whose causes or motive can only be guessed at. Both the annihilation of most of Earth's population and the release of the triffids can be ascribed

---

[15] In an earlier version, Wyndham had colonies on Venus as the source of the catastrophe (Binns 2019, 197); with *The Day of the Triffids*, Wyndham is establishing his particular variety of near-future science fiction in which sensational changes from the present day are kept to a minimum (see Binns, 192, 201).

to the Cold War and more broadly to human hubris, notably in the cultivation of a very unusual plant that nobody properly understood (35–38). This would seem to give the catastrophe a good deal of political and moral weight, but ordinary people had no control over and almost no knowledge of the doom that was threatened by the satellites, and people in general had quickly got over their early misgivings about the wisdom of cultivating triffids (32). Ordinary humans are so far from control and knowledge that questions of general human responsibility for the disasters are moot. The authorities (government, police, army) are never sighted. Bill and Josella, the narrator and his lover, do engage in some philosophical conversations, but to limited effect. Humans seem made for specific, practical tasks, such as face them after the disaster. There is talk about what will have to be given up, and of the dangers of a slide into the primitive and the savage (127, 133, 173), and a good deal of the plot is taken up with these matters, but we get no sense of the vast collective achievement, the human version of the triffids' hive mind, that produced cities such as London, which the narrator traverses after the disaster. There is a contrast with *The War of the Worlds* here; Wells's novel imagines the power and strangeness of the Martians, but also the multiplicity and energy of human society, of London for instance.

Josella responds to Bill's interpretation of how humans brought about the disaster:

> 'I suppose in a way that should be more horrible than the idea of nature striking blindly at us. And yet I don't think it is. It makes me feel less hopeless about things because it makes them at least comprehensible. If it was like that, then it is at least a thing that can be prevented from happening again – just one more of the mistakes our very great-grandchildren are going to have to avoid. And, oh dear, there were so many, many mistakes! But we can warn them.' (212)

The Day of the Triffids is confident in the virtues of normal Englishness. Bill and Josella are educated and middle class, but Coker, who is a working-class chancer, has the same virtues – reason, realism, commonsense. Bill is not all that unlike one of John Buchan's heroes: steady, thoughtful, positive; Josella is similar – beautiful, sensitive and given to saying 'Oh darling' as did heroines in films from this period – and perhaps actual young women did also – but basically a good sort.[16]

---

[16] Amy Binns sees 'the Wyndham heroine' as feisty and independent (Binns 2019, 252 and passim in chapter 12, 'Wyndham's Women'). My assessment

(Contrast the much edgier group at the centre of John Christopher's *The Death of Grass* (1956), whose middle-class leaders are driven to ruthless measures; yet for all that evocations of pastoral peace have their place also in this novel (see, for instance, 14, 25, and 80 in the Penguin edition of 2009).

Those who have thought things through get out of the city and move to the countryside, and this is logical, but it is also a move back into an authentic England, an England whose spreading greenness, as growing things begin to take over again in the absence of humans, gives the atmosphere a pastoral tinge (for instance, 207). Even the passage in *The Day of the Triffids* about the gradual decay of London emphasises the slow encroachment of grass and weeds, and leaves – the buildings 'beginning to wear a green wig' (197). The ruination of the World City is not in the epic key, not portentous, not even when Wyndham gives us a version of the trope that Macaulay made famous (128).[17] The narrator's spirits rise when he leaves the city:

> I began to feel the lightening of the spirit that Coker was already showing. The sight of the open country gave one hope of a sort. It was true that the young green crops would never be harvested when they had ripened, nor the fruit from the trees gathered; that the countryside might never again look as trim and neat as it did this day, but for all that it would go on, after its own fashion. It was not like the towns, sterile, stopped for ever. It was a place one could work and tend, and still find a future. (138)

In this situation the weird and exotic triffids are intruders and invaders, and it seems a defence of authentic nature to eliminate them, as if they were kudzu or lantana.

---

is that this largely means that she is a more interesting and intelligent partner for the male character than a conventional romantic heroine – indeed, sometimes the more capable of the two, as in *The Kraken Wakes*.

[17] 'Alongside, the Thames flowed imperturbably on. So it would flow until the day the Embankments crumbled and the water spread out and Westminster became once more an island in a marsh' (128). Lord Macaulay introduces a New Zealander from the future to witness this; Wyndham is a Little Englander. See also Ballard's rendition in *The Wind from Nowhere* (1967, 123) – significantly, a more conventional apocalyptic novel than those he would write subsequently: 'The time-familiar façade of Westminster had vanished, and high seas washed across the ragged lines of foundation stones, spilling over the supine remains of Big Ben, stripping the clock faces as they lay among the rubble in Palace Yard.'

It is perhaps rather more than that. Humans have been eliminated, killed off, by nature that has gone wrong – actually this is the result of human action, as we have seen, but it hits the mass of ordinary humans, who had no responsibility for it, as if nature itself were the agent. Now they must strike back to protect themselves, and defend their patch of green England; having been killed, they can freely kill. Even Susan, a girl of 12 whom Bill rescued on his journey to find Josella again, takes a hand: 'It became her department to work daily vengeance on them' (190). They make use of mortars and flamethrowers. There are immense numbers of the triffids, so killing a few dozen makes only a temporary difference. It's like the killing of crowds of barbarian attackers or faceless enemies in action movies. So the novel's return to the pastoral also involves in the killing of triffids a kind of revenge for the impersonal, in many ways accidental evil that humans have suffered. There is an oddity in this combination of a kind of Wild West/Last Stand violence with sensible Englishness, and perhaps this expresses uncertainty about England's place in the world in 1951.

Not long after the catastrophe, the main characters assemble with others to hear speeches on what might be done, and we have this comment after one of the speeches:

> It must have made quite a number of the members of his audience begin to feel that perhaps they were at the beginning of something after all, rather than at the end of everything. (97)

Both the language ('quite a number', 'perhaps') and the sentiment suggest a degree of calm and even optimism. The incidents of violence and the fears of a descent into savagery do little to change this impression. Yes, savagery is a worry, but Bill is more affected by loneliness, the realisation of how much humans need one another (177), and Josella says that 'as a rule I don't go much beyond getting a little sad – the sort of gentle melancholy that the eighteenth century thought so estimable' (209). Bill and Josella define their feelings of regret in a thoughtful, civilised way. They wonder if they would be 'justified' in telling their children an apocalyptic 'myth':

> A story of a world that was wonderfully clever, but so wicked that it had to be destroyed – or destroyed itself by accident? Something like the Flood again. (210)

Bill's thoughts about savagery are similarly held at a distance, a matter of contemplation:

Since I was sixteen my interest in weapons has decreased, but in an environment reverting to savagery it seemed that one must be prepared to behave more or less as a savage, or possibly cease to behave at all before long. In St James's Street there used to be several shops which would sell you any form of lethalness from a rook-rifle to an elephant-gun with the greatest urbanity. (127)[18]

Is violence a matter of savagery or of urbanity, then? Bill collects the weapons; guns are indeed fired later in the story, but mostly they miss or serve to warn, until we come to the triffids, who are slaughtered with enthusiasm and by means of a range of weapons including flamethrowers. The novel ends with the resolution to annihilate the triffids, utterly:

We think now that we can see the way, but there is still a lot of work and research to be done before the day when we, or our children, or their children, will cross the narrow straits on the great crusade to drive the triffids back and back with ceaseless destruction until we have wiped the last one of them from the face of the land that they have usurped. (233)

The expectation of wiping out the triffids is accompanied by confidence that for the humans there will be children, and their children. The occupation of the land by the triffids (the 'narrow straits' here are between the Isle of Wight and the mainland of England) seems a bit like the occupation of the continent of Europe by the Nazis, a problem to be solved after 'work and research'.[19] The human attempt to exploit nature (the breeding and cultivation of triffids) has backfired; the results are mixed: a retreat to the green countryside and the employment of flamethrowers.

---

[18] Contrast the similar scene in the much tougher story of resort to violence in *The Death of Grass*: the main character goes to a gun shop to obtain weapons (chapter 5), but this time the proprietor insists on accompanying him and his friends. This man is Pirrie, an excellent shot, but ruthless: at each encounter he advises and implements violence, and each time his calculation is correct. The party as a whole acquiesce in violence, and Pirrie, who completely lacks scruples, can serve as their cover, though he is careful not to try to displace their leader.

[19] Wyndham served in the British army from Normandy to Germany; his letters often catch the grim, disillusioning side of the war (quoted in Binns 2019, 157–158, 162–163, 173). In his novel, where he sets out to appeal to a wide audience and avoid sensationalism, this element is played down.

Doom, Decency and Denial
On the Beach[20]

> [I]t is not only no fault but a primary requisite in an Epitaph that it shall contain thoughts and feelings which are in their substance common-place, and even trite.
>
> (Wordsworth, 'Essays upon Epitaphs')

On the Beach is unlike other novels discussed in this chapter, and unlike most other apocalyptic novels discussed in this book, though not *Childhood's End*, whose ambivalent elimination of humanity is discussed next. In *On the Beach*, everybody perishes – no exceptions. Everyone among the dramatis personae of the novel dies, even their pets die, everyone on Earth dies. There has been a disastrous nuclear war, involving thousands of bombs (4700 (81)) and a range of countries including Albania and Egypt as well as the great powers. The resulting fallout has killed everyone in the Northern Hemisphere and is making its way inexorably south, towards Melbourne where the novel is set. Investigations of the Northern Hemisphere by submarine confirm that no one has survived; there is nothing to be done, and in the end suicide pills are provided by the government, and taken, or administered to the young.

On the other hand, *On the Beach* is very like the other novels discussed in this chapter in that its setting is pastoral and its cast list is domestic. In fact it is the most domestic of all; set aside the approaching doom (and this is what many of the characters do) and the scenes of gardening, fishing, spreading manure on the fields, buying the baby a playpen and the garden a lawn mower and so on, would be about as dull and undramatic as a novel can afford to be. Precisely because the approaching death is inexorable, we can conclude that nothing is left for the characters but their ordinary, decent lives. No one feels anything out of the ordinary, or even does anything very far out of the ordinary, for most of the novel. The effect is a strong one, and it is best to set aside the judgement that ordinariness is here defined exclusively in middle-class terms, and also the suspicion that even ordinariness is not usually as ordinary as it is here.

Nevil Shute has invested a very great deal of the novel's interest, its potential to work its effects, in the contrast between the coming doom and the domestic lives of the characters. If this is successful, then the scenes of ordinary life will attain poignancy in the shadow of the

---

[20] References are to Nevil Shute, *On the Beach*, London: Heinemann, 1957.

disaster, a poignancy that doesn't have to be dramatised or sensationalised because the contrast with the disaster is so great; and this novel that is so thoroughgoing in its insistence that nuclear war might end all human and animal life, will become also a hymn of quiet praise for ordinary low-key decency.

It is true that the disaster is not dramatised. It is a kind of emptiness. When the submarine on its voyage of investigation surfaces off this or that city that has succumbed to the fallout, there is mostly nothing to be seen – no people, but no destruction, everything as usual in the sunlight; no piles of corpses – just emptiness. There is a barking dog in one place; the lights are still functioning in another; there are signs of localised destruction in another: all this underlines the eerie empty peacefulness encountered everywhere else. When a seaman is sent ashore to investigate mysterious and possibly hopeful radio emissions from near Seattle, he discovers that the possible signals were caused by the random movements of a fallen window frame. He has some spare time to read the *Saturday Evening Post* before returning to the submarine.

'They spent a domestic afternoon in their own garden' (142): this is Peter and Mary Holmes. Life has become difficult, because Australia is cut off from the resources of the Northern Hemisphere – there's no petrol available and people rely on horses for transport, and have to make arrangements with the dairy farmer for milk and so on. It's very like – reassuringly like – the regime of rationing in the Second World War. Even in this respect, daily life actually becomes easier as the end approaches – people bring out their hoarded petrol and run their cars again, shopkeepers aren't fussed about payment for purchases. There's some drinking – pink gins at the Pastoral Club on one occasion – but no orgies, no violence. The city's streets get dirty ('it was evidently some days since the street cleaners had operated', 259).

The novel is mostly set in the countryside around Melbourne. Peter and Mary cultivate their garden. Dwight, the American submarine captain, stays with Moira and her parents and helps around the farm, spreading dung on the fields (123), crutching sheep and spreading silage (134). Later Dwight and Moira go on a fishing trip up to Mount Buller (on the edge of the Victorian Alps), but only after Moira has used her contacts to get the date of the fishing season brought forward (there is a discussion at the club about the advisability of this, in the circumstances, 228–229). Is this an almost parodic version of the stiff upper lip, an exaggeration of the stoicism of the 'we are all in it together' days of the recent world war? Shute depicts Australian society as very British, very Anglo, in its attitudes and mores and the picture he gives is selective, but not wrong. Australian society was more homogenous and inhibited, more modelled on an idea of Britishness, in those days. Australia is depicted as a place where the British and the Americans can calmly co-operate: Anglo-Saxonia. Nonetheless, Shute is clearly going out of his way to emphasise the pink gins at the club, the spreading of silage and the purchase of a playpen or a pogo stick. Perhaps what is really valuable is the ordinariness of doing your job conscientiously, marital collaboration or collusion (Peter knows that Mary is refusing to see what is happening), keeping things going: 'Still, we go through the motions' (269) (compare Scott of the Antarctic's heroic stoicism: 'We shall stick it out to the end'). 'All our friends seem to be having baby after baby', says Mary (140), and Dwight tells us that half his crew have found girlfriends in Melbourne and want to stay with them. This is what counts – indeed it is the only thing that we see.

Perhaps, on the other hand, the characters are retreating into an ordinariness that is starting to become absurd. To investigate this we need to look at the novel's depiction of the prevalent *denial* of disaster. Does this signify a breakdown, normality now become insanity? Or are we to feel that it is better than any alternative, given that *any* persistence in ordinary behaviour can be seen as insane in the impossible circumstances? It is Mary Holmes who insists on planning for the future; it is she who gets her husband to work and plan in the garden (sowing bulbs that won't flower until after everyone is dead), and sends him off to buy useful domestic things. Peter goes along with her behaviour, which is depicted as typically female – worrying about the baby, treating the world outside the home as intrusive and to be as far as possible discounted. Yet the world of the novel *is* domestic, even though in pre-feminist fashion the men do the important jobs and take responsibility for the wider world.

When Peter at length takes it upon himself to repeat that they are all going to die, and to show Mary how they will dispose of themselves and little Jennifer, she is horrified and repelled. Her façade of preoccupation about house, garden and baby is cracked, but we can understand the atrociousness of her having to think about killing her baby. We don't glimpse the deaths of children in most apocalyptic novels, and perhaps for many authors in the 1950s it would be indecent to dramatise this. Shute, however, has followed the logic of his almost exclusive focus on domestic life, and it has led to this scene. (Arthur C. Clarke chooses a different but also disturbing fate for the world's children in *Childhood's End*.)

Denial also comes to rule in the second of the two relationships the novel concentrates on, that between Moira and Dwight. Dwight had a wife and two children back in the States, and now he is marooned in Melbourne with the submarine he commands. Peter and Mary delegate to their friend Moira the task of keeping him distracted. She does this at first by acting the wild girl who drinks and flirts, but then falls in love with Dwight. Soon she is taking a shorthand and typing course on his advice, and doing his mending. Dwight is steady and unimaginative and a stickler for the rules, to the end, but Mary discovers that he is behaving as though Sharon and Dwight Junior and Helen are still alive so he can expect to re-join them. He won't sleep with Moira. She accepts all this; she gets him a pogo stick as a present for his surely dead son. So this denial is never cracked, but is reinforced, and the behaviour of Dwight, an experienced and calm naval officer, cannot be discounted as that of a woman confined to her domestic concerns and come to believe that nothing else is real.[21] This outcome in *On the Beach* is striking in a novel that is apparently so uninterested in sophistications of conduct and psychology. Shute's plain style, without figures of speech or nuances, is an advantage here. We can't take refuge in the notion that he is presenting this normal decency ironically when it leads to Mary's and Dwight's denials. It is just as likely that he accepts that this is how it had to be.

So, we have blankness: no human life after the end of the novel, and in several of the characters flat refusal to acknowledge that the end is coming. Later novels envisage a post-apocalyptic future, discard the plain domestic realism of *On the Beach* and imagine a landscape shaped as much by the inner lives, the desires and fantasies of the characters as by the material event of catastrophe. Catastrophe destroys, the imagination in response creates; but the blank dead end that *On the Beach* delivers still makes a challenging point.

This account can be qualified. We are told of the tensions and plans behind the war and the accidents and mistakes that precipitated it. There are outbreaks of distress and angry (verbal) protest among our characters, and recourses to uninhibited behaviour in the face of the coming end, some hard drinking, motor races with very high casualty rates. Mostly, however, everybody behaves with remarkable calm and decorum. Just as the lethal fallout advances steadily and inexorably until at the end of the novel it has arrived in Melbourne and all the characters have been

---

[21] It's true that authors from this earlier generation were more likely to suggest that truth and openness are not the only values. In Herman Wouk's *The Caine Mutiny* (1951) the officer who had led the effort to convict the ship's captain of mad incompetence is eloquently ticked off after the court martial has confirmed his actions: discipline should have been preserved. In Arthur C. Clarke's *2001* (1968) we are to accept that people in general could not have coped with the facts of the alien monolith's presence, so they had to be deceived.

killed or have suicided, so this decent ordinariness, this quiet unexciting domesticity, persists until the end, even when this seems to require denial that the end is coming (Mary) and will be total (Dwight). From time to time the characters say that, after all, death comes to everyone anyway and at least its coming in the form of deadly fallout is known and clear (for instance, 89, 155–157). What they don't or can't say is that while death comes to everyone, everyone is born, those newly born succeed the inevitably dead and life goes on. The novel has to say this for them, by the scenes around the killing of baby Jennifer and, less explicitly, by the characters' worry about what will happen to their pets and livestock if they die first.

This concern for the future in humans is, arguably, ineradicable. This is the contention of Samuel H. Scheffler in *Death and the Afterlife* (2013). Scheffler argues convincingly that we could not continue with our life projects if we came to know that humanity as a whole was going to be extinguished in the immediate future. The characters in *On the Beach* continue with their life projects while refusing to know that humanity is being extinguished. Here it is useful to foreshadow how the presence or absence of children or pregnancy works its way through some, mostly later, apocalyptic fictions. The desire that there be signs of new life when it seems that there is no or almost no future for humanity can find expression even in some of the grimmest of apocalyptic fictions – on the very last pages of *The Road* (Cormac McCarthy, 2006), and of *Oryx and Crake* (Margaret Atwood, 2003), for instance; the former novel is intensely concerned with a father's care for his young son, and the latter is bitterly concerned with perversities of biogenetic reproduction, yet both end with this glimpse of new life, though *The Road* also ends with the death of the father. The prospect of a child is suggested in the last pages of *Greybeard* (Brian Aldiss, 1964), which concerns a world in which all humans have (so it seemed) become sterile. The heroine Marianne is – unenthusiastically – pregnant at the end of *Heroes and Villains*. There are new babies whose arrival hints ironically at redemptive continuance in *The Leftovers* (Tom Perrotta, 2011) and in *The End of the World News* (Anthony Burgess, 1982). In P. D. James's *The Children of Men* it appears that all humans have become sterile, as in *Greybeard*, but the climax of the novel is a birth – indeed a miraculous birth that is staged – in a wood-shed – as another birth of the infant Saviour.

Childhood's End is a text that faces this aspect of the apocalyptic situation very intriguingly, by dividing humanity into adults who all perish (along with Earth and everything else on it), and children who are all transformed and lost to humanity. Discussion now turns to this novel.

Apocalypse – Utopia – Apocalypse
Childhood's End[22]

Childhood's End (1953) is not a cosy catastrophe, although, as will be discussed, there are elements of the elegiac, and the voice of the narrative often offers to be reassuringly knowledgeable. It takes more risks, aims higher – towards the transcendental – and runs into more problems than *Earth Abides* or *The Day of the Triffids* or *On the Beach*. The conflicts and uncertainties that were outlined earlier press more closely and at times confusedly here: the problem of reason and its limits, exacerbated in a novel that invokes the ineffable but offers many confident explanations and knowing asides; and the questions of voice and authority – who tells the story and where it is told from, from what standpoint. *Childhood's End*, after all, tells of several alien invasions, several apocalypses, the end of human society and of Earth, not to mention the institution, if only as a passing phase, of a utopia. It also offers a haunting image of the loss to humanity of its children – arguably more disturbing than the total extinction of (adult) humanity that follows shortly afterwards.

Childhood's End is an alien-invasion story. Unlike the invasion in *The War of the Worlds*, or those in many later stories and films,[23] it is a benign invasion, and the invaders are wise and non-violent: the Overlords. Arthur C. Clarke is positive and confident about science and reason, and confident also in his own powers and opinions. *Childhood's End* presents particular challenges to this confidence. It might appear that the challenge is less testing because the invasion is benign, and the apocalypse is presented as a sublime transcendence, but this is not so, and the double movement of apocalypse that the novel presents is the clue here. There is a second invasion, and another apocalypse. The alien that brings this about, the Overmind, can hardly be considered benign, or wise, either because its invasion leads to annihilation or because it is so transcendently other that words like wise cannot apply to it. It is pure power, a kind of essence of what alien invaders almost always have, and the novel makes us think about the lure and fascination of power, and the awe it arouses. The Martians in *The War of the Worlds*, like many other invaders, are mainly seen as wrecking and killing, like stereotypical barbarians in this respect, for all their advanced technology; the first invaders in *Childhood's End* had subtler purposes, and the second had subtler purposes still, and in both cases the invaders' power served

---

[22] References are to Arthur C. Clarke, *Childhood's End*, New York: Ballantine, 1973.
[23] There is a brisk discussion of the disaster films of the 1950s in Sontag 1976.

these purposes and had no limits other than those they imposed on themselves.

First, intelligent creatures from Outer Space arrive on Earth, take over, and under their regime the world is transformed and a utopia results. These highly intelligent and superlatively wise aliens are the Overlords. There is no violence and, as the course of events is depicted, the trauma of the fact that humans have lost their autonomy is limited, and those who are aggrieved at it are shown to be immature; but there is certainly a complete break in history, indeed an end to history, which is succeeded by what could be taken as an ideal state, so in these respects we have an apocalyptic sequence. In addition, there are plenty of revelations: the narrative is structured as a series of revelations and in that broad respect is like John's in *Revelation*.

Then, after the utopia has been surveyed in considerable detail, all this in turn comes to an end. The children of humans develop psychic powers; they can control material things, and also, as they change yet further, they free themselves from dependence on material things and from contact with them. The change is described as a mutation, but it doesn't conform to the usual nature of a mutation: it is predicted and awaited, by the Overlords; it happens to all children, without exception; and it is not exactly adaptive, since it has the effect of enabling the children to control and then obliterate their environment.

The children become other than human and more than human. Behind the Overlords is the Overmind; it is revealed that the Overlords are mere servants of the Overmind, the utopia was no more than a preparatory phase, and the Overlords have been readying the scene for the evolution of the children into union with the Overmind. That is, if we assume that it is an evolution, as the novel does, though from a mere human point of view it could also be seen as a devolution. The children are as it were uploaded into the Overmind, and as with fictions and fantasies of downloading the self into the digital realm, there is, in the assumption that this is an advance, an ambiguous or dismissive attitude to the body and its pleasures and awareness. As George E. Slusser (1987, 50) puts it, 'To become disembodied mind, man must completely abandon his old physical form. To create it, the green Earth is totally consumed.'

The Overlords themselves, for all their abilities, are incapable of this evolution: 'Yet [the race of the Overlords] had no future, and it was aware of it' (177). The Overlords' virtually unlimited intelligence and indeed wisdom lacks some indefinable ingredient that humans, unstable as they are, are capable of evolving, en masse as regards the children. They don't appear to have gender, or they are all males, and it is their fate, as much as their privilege, to lack autonomous purpose – they serve the Overmind.

The children of Earth lose (or shed) their individuality and separateness and are swept up into the Overmind; Earth is emptied, becoming a lifeless husk, but before that happens the remaining humans (everyone more than the age of about ten) perish, mostly by suicide. This second time, the destruction that accompanies apocalypse is clear enough; indeed it is ultimate and total (Clarke has reserved a single human, Jan, to witness the final moments of Earth before he perishes).[24] The equivalent to a New Jerusalem, the state of grace and transcendence that follows the destruction, will strike various readers in various ways, though it seems that Clarke embraces it, in the form of union with the Overmind, with a religious fervour. (It is hard to find clear assessments of this matter in critical commentaries on *Childhood's End*. Is it thought that the text's stance is so clearly positive that the matter is not worth discussing, or that the text's stance is so clearly detached and impartial that the matter is not worth discussing?)

Hierarchies and Revelations

The novel's procedure is a clear one. Discussion of this will lead to some of its problems and interesting uncertainties. There is a series of secrets and revelations: who the Overlords are, what they look like (they rule without revealing themselves for many years: then it turns out that they resemble stereotypical devils), what they have planned for humanity (utopia), what they have *really* planned for humanity in the service of the Overmind (transcendence and extinction); who seems to be in total, masterful command of Earth (the Overlords), who is *really* in command (the children, as they evolve to assumption into the Overmind); what time and history now are (featureless and peaceful since the arrival of the Overlords), what time is approaching (an end, once the assumption of the children has been consummated). Each of these revelations opens a new, vast, almost borderless perspective. When we don't have important revelations, we have little surprises, as when Clarke describes Jan's journey for a while before revealing it is towards the bottom of the sea (115), or when the Overlords make the light of the sun blank out over Cape Town:

[24] Slusser (1987, 45) reads this as a kind of vindication of the extinct human race, since Jan passes on the story of the end to the Overlords. I can't see this.

> The demonstration lasted thirty minutes. It was sufficient; the next day the government of South Africa announced that full civil rights would be restored to the white minority. (20)

This structure of concealment and revelation also prevails both socially and cosmically: we have subordinates, and behind them, but above them hierarchically, will be found a more powerful and capable elite. In contrast, the social structure of the other novels discussed in this chapter is open: government is irrelevant, the characters must cope by themselves, and sometimes a leader emerges, sometimes not. In *Childhood's End* we encounter underlings, then we encounter those above them. We have humans, seen often as short-sighted and immature, with over them the Overlords, not merely of immense intelligence but of unfailing wisdom (which often leads them to deceive their human pupils), and over them the Overmind. The latter, for all that it is 'mind', is superior by some quality that goes beyond intelligence or knowledge but manifests itself as pure power. Certainly – by the stage of the climax of the novel, the assumption of the children and end of Earth – this power cannot be expected to justify and explain itself by means such as using words and offering reasons. As will be illustrated shortly, Clarke is a very candid and forthcoming narrator, full of opinions and information, but the structure of the novel, and of the cosmos, as the novel reveals it, consists of a series of surprises, deceptions and revelations, of underlings and elites ranked in hierarchies. This is not what the actual cosmos is like nor what liberal democratic society is actually like (for all its flaws), but it supplies a clear structure analogous to that of traditional apocalypse in Revelation, with its Son of Man, angels, elect and infidels, and successive openings of the Seals.

The notion that the next stage in evolution is in effect reserved for humans and that it will take the form of the emergence of beings beyond the human conforms to what Mary Midgley calls 'infallible, escalator-type evolution' and, as she says, this has nothing to do with Darwin's theory of evolution (1985, 33, and also 58–59, 61–62). With its assumption that the next stage in human evolution will produce beings somehow superior, it also encourages 'a contempt for existing people' (46). We can see Clarke as both embracing the escalator theory of evolution, with its (un-Darwinian) focus on humans (Midgley, 69–70), and its assumption that the universe is hierarchical and ruled by elite beings, and also as exhibiting some of the disquieting aspects of this, most obviously in the fact that humans more than ten years old are eliminated, together with Earth and all that it contains. People in Britain and America were not so intensely aware of the Holocaust in 1953 as they are now, but they certainly were aware of it, as was Clarke. Edward James (2005, 438) quotes from Clarke's *Prelude to Space* (1954):

> Out of the fears and miseries of the Second Dark Age, drawing free – oh, might it be forever – from the shadows of Belsen and Hiroshima, the world was moving towards its most splendid sunrise.[25]

This puts the historical catastrophe of the century in an apocalyptic context, because the catastrophe is followed by a New Jerusalem, a splendid sunrise. The transformation is sublimely colourful in *Childhood's End* (215).

Further, if the life of the Overmind consists in contemplating the universe, as is suggested, it is odd that it proceeds by eliminating that which it might contemplate. In this respect the Overmind is to be imagined as so much higher than either humans or the Overlords as to be ineffable, like God, but as Midgley points out God created the universe, rather than living in solitude – He expressed Himself in that way.

In the period of the utopia supervised by the Overlords, George and Jean and their children take up residence in New Athens, a planned artistic community. We learn how it was planned:

> Behind this spectacular façade of temperamental talent, the real architects of the colony had laid their plans. (145)

The 'handful of the world's most famous artists' who are convinced by the plan – they are the 'spectacular façade of temperamental talent' – are of minor importance in comparison to 'the real architects', whose knowledge of 'applied social engineering' and 'social dynamics' underpins the plan and the 'battery of psychological tests' that decides whether one is admitted to the colony (140, 144, 141). Clarke wrote *Childhood's End* when optimism about social engineering, planning, modernisation theory, cybernetics as 'the human use of human beings', and much more was still strong, and there is no use submitting this optimism to contemporary disillusionment. Nonetheless it is striking how thoroughly controlled by social science this *artistic* project is. Given that the first planner sees the project as an 'insurance policy' against the dying out of art under the Overlord peace (145), it is not surprising that the best the text can do is to talk of 'worthwhile results', in sculpture, music and so on (147). Discussion will return to the possible significance

---

[25] Belsen was not an extermination camp; Clarke is evoking the horrors of the Second World War more generally.

of the novel's unease about art, so closely and confidently controlled by science in New Athens.

At one point we meet Rupert, who is giving a party and is depicted as frivolous and fun-loving; he has a job, however, the medical care of wild animals over a wide area of southern Africa:

> 'Rather a full time job.'
> 'Oh, of course it isn't practical to bother about the small fry. Just lions, elephants, rhinos and so on.' (87)

The 'charismatic megafauna', as they will be called in our time, get the medical attention; the 'small fry' miss out. We meet some megafauna later, when a model of a sperm whale in combat with a giant squid is to be shipped to the Overlords' home planet (this is where Jan will stow away before the end of Earth):

> 'No, the whole thing will be faked up with plastics and then accurately painted. By the time we've finished, no one will be able to tell the difference.' (128)

Jan has managed to find where in the universe the Overlords' home planet is located; Karellen comments:

> 'Though it is part of our directive not to reveal our base, there is no way in which the information can be used against us.' (104)

A secret without point then, like many a bureaucratic secret, but another detail in the novel's pervasive pattern of secrecy – or deception – and revelation, of ignorant underlings and aloof elites. (When the Overlords arrive, one of their giant ships hovers over each of the world's major cities, to intimidating effect. Later we discover there was actually only one ship, Karellen's: the rest were 'phantoms' (70).)

The novel gives a good deal of weight to intelligence and thence to reason, but has little time for democracy. The organisation of matters after the arrival of the Overlords is undertaken by Karellen and Stormgren the Secretary-General of the United Nations. The Overlords hate cruelty, and one of their few explicit directives after they take over forbids cruelty to animals. All animals, and everything else living, will perish when the children destroy Earth and join with the Overmind. There are passages on Jeff's dog Fey and its sadness and devotion when Jeff leaves to join the Overmind (187); on the whale as site of Jan's stowing away; on the familiarly named 'Lucie', Lucifer, the giant squid that hangs around the undersea base; and on Rupert's job as 'supervet'. It is as if the mind of the book keeps remembering that there are other living creatures on Earth than humans, and that they too will perish.

On other matters the Overlords, to return to them, are indifferent, or tolerant:

> The Overlords seemed largely indifferent to forms of government, provided they were not oppressive or corrupt. Earth still possessed democracies, monarchies, benevolent dictatorships, communism, and capitalism. This was a source of great surprise to many simple souls who were quite convinced that theirs was the only possible way of life. (27)

Benevolent dictatorships are OK, then, also communism; and perhaps Clarke means 'theirs was the only admirable way of life', or something more like that, since you would have to be a simple soul to believe yours was the only possible way of life. The Overlords themselves are benevolent dictators, though the analogy the novel hints at is with hard-working and burdened colonial administrators, hoping to bring the natives, members of 'a more backward society' to a more advanced level (29; see also 45, 62). In this respect *Childhood's End* is very different from *The War of the Worlds*.

The small confusion in the passage quoted just now points to a larger problem, that of the voice of the text, which is knowing, confident and prepared to inform the reader what is the case, what humans are like, what grand problems are readily soluble. We have to acknowledge the usefulness, perhaps necessity, of this quality in a novel that stages such sweeping changes; there's not much room for hesitation and qualification when one is recounting universal transformations. We have to overlook remarks that might have seemed fresh or uncontentious in the 1950s: that after the Overlords had established 'One World', 'there was no one on Earth who did not speak English' (72);[26] that Rashaverak, one of the Overlords, reads a page every two seconds, like a graduate of one of those speed-reading courses advertised in the 1950s (82); or this:

---

[26] The same thing happens in the post-catastrophe utopia depicted in H. G. Wells's *The World Set Free* (1914). In this novel we are told that the language was greatly simplified in grammar, and also that its vocabulary was greatly expanded. On the same page the calendar is reorganised and the date of Easter is fixed (1988, 147–148). Parrinder (1995, 94) suggests that Wells sees world government developing out of British imperialism, so perhaps it is assumed that it will bring the English language with it.

114 APOCALYPSE IN CRISIS

> Women had fainted – not always without foresight – since time immemorial, and men had invariably responded in the desired way. (105)

The novel's range, from evocations of 'Time's impassable barrier' (131) and of the slow work of geology, laying the foundations of lands to be in the eternal night of the deep sea (118) to the sadness of the family dog when its child master is transformed (187), invites us to take these things in our stride.

The text exists in an uneasy tension of ineffable and explicit – for the sweeping confidence of the latter, see the remarks on education (111) and on idleness (112). An alternation of concealment (what can't be told, or at least is not told) and revelation (the amazing, awe-inspiring clarification) is the result of this tension. It's the project and approach of much 'Golden Age' science fiction: the balancing, or the combination, of sublime wonder and explicit and often practical and no-nonsense explanation and rationalisation. Here in *Childhood's End* it is under pressure because of the breadth of the novel's ambitions towards sublimity and transcendence, *and* towards explanation (the unfaltering confident voice of the text). Apocalyptic fiction usually involves a tension between the global and the local; in *Childhood's End* the narrator's air of assurance tends to exacerbate rather than relieve this tension. Later apocalyptic fictions often approach the problem from a different direction, relying more on images of transformation than on comments and explanations – the catastrophe is shaping local things and experiences in ways that are imagined and evoked rather than explained.

Similarly there is a division between the valuation of intelligence, science and reason, the 'fierce and passionless light of truth' (75) that, for instance, with some help from the Overlords' advanced technology, refutes the claims of all existing religions to possess the exclusive truth,[27] and on the other hand the introduction of the Overmind as superior being, union with which is arguably fit recompense for the end of humanity and the earth (including all those animals that the Overlords

---

[27] Compare Iain M. Banks's late novel *The Hydrogen Sonata* (2012): the narrative traces a quest, sometimes frenetic, sometimes violent, to find a document rumoured to demonstrate the falsity of the religion prevailing in the world of the novel. The document is found; it does demonstrate the falsity; then the overlords of this universe, the Culture, decide it had better not be published. Then most of the inhabitants of the novel's world proceed to a transformation into another state of being, 'the Sublimation', which may *also* be a fake. Technology is stunningly efficient in the world of the novel, but the narrative asks whether it is possible to trust any authority.

spared from human cruelty). The division has about it a kind of bravery, of risk-taking, because the confidence in science and intelligence is so sweeping and yet its apocalyptic surpassing is so spectacular and unqualified. This split, one between science and religion, is reflected in the double apocalypse itself. The first is scientific (the achievement of intelligence, deployed by the Overlords), and the second is religious (as Eric S. Rabkin has noted).[28] In the case of the second neither the mutation of the children nor the power of the Overmind can be explained or even (as regards the Overmind) given content. The problem is that the voice of the text, reasoning, explaining, telling us that 'a sound knowledge of social engineering' will do the trick (changing Earth and its people 'almost beyond recognition', 69) is the voice we hear until the very end. This voice pities human beings in their parochial and ignorant moments, but is clearly not one of them; it is present, to observe their end and that of Earth itself, and it survives Jan's departure, to tell us what Karellen was thinking and feeling as the story closed:

> For a long time Karellen stared back across that swiftly widening gulf, while many memories raced through his vast and labyrinthine mind. In silent farewell, he saluted the men he had known, whether they had hindered or helped him in his purpose. (218)

The novel's voice of reason and explanation is not aligned with humans, about whom it is condescending, but with the Overlords, oppressed by their hard task as colonialists and servants of the Overmind. So the suffering is that of Karellen as much as or more than that of humans, and it is certainly interesting that the novel ends with the burden of living on, as Karellen has to, with his memories, rather than with the deaths of the living of Earth. The outcome is neither triumphant (for all the gesturing at the idea that humans are privileged to become part of the Overmind, if at the expense of their humanness), nor tragic, but elegiac. This acceptant sadness is evoked in *Earth Abides* over the course of Ish's ageing and the emergence of a new society in which he is a stranger; its entrance into *Childhood's End* is less secure – it is another of those revelatory gestures that are frequent in the novel.

The second apocalypse, that brought about by the children and the Overmind, destroys the utopia of science and reason that the first, that

---

[28] Rabkin 1979, 27–29. Rabkin feels that we should look past Clarke's scientific errors (for instance, on the nature of mutation) for the sake of his religious vision; but then he says that the latter shows that the Overmind 'loves us', and this I cannot see in the novel, whatever Clarke may have intended.

organised by the Overlords, had introduced, and Clarke can't really say what it is replaced with. If the Overlords are bereft, so is he: hence, perhaps, the intensity of his sympathy for them. It is a clue to what is going on in the economy of the novel that the utopia of art, New Athens, is completely controlled by (social) science, and there is no sign that it creates any art (unless you think that 'worthwhile products' make the grade). Art is a kind of reflection of the ineffable human quality that the Overlords lack and that leads to the transformation of the children and the end of humanity, but it is also something that, in New Athens, needs to be controlled and supervised by science. Science in turn falls silent before the transformations that mark the end, and so does intelligence, which is frequently invoked in the novel. An end to humanity is what the Overlords were supposed to have spared humanity from when they first arrived and their arrival enforced peace, but it is consummated in the final chapters, with the compensation, assuming that there is one, happening somewhere else, to or maybe *in* something else. This something else, the Overmind, has no knowable or accessible content. It's really an Overpower. The aporia that the novel reaches does point to the difficulty of presenting a benign religious apocalypse in the twentieth century.

We are left with the haunting, uncomfortable power of the passages on the withdrawal of the children from humanity. What Clarke dramatises there, the loss of children, continues to gnaw at the imagination of contemporary makers of apocalypse, as a threat that is realised or is overcome, in *Oryx and Crake, Greybeard, The Children of Men, The Road, The Leftovers,* and *The Memoirs of a Survivor*: imaginations of humanity coming to an end through sterility, of parents withdrawing from children or of children becoming alien to their elders.[29] The postwar baby boom released a flood of children into the world, to puzzle and disturb their elders as children, as teenagers and later as student rebels. Doris Lessing's *The Memoirs of a Survivor* (discussed in chapter 5)

[29] Robert Galbreath (1983, 66–67), discussing this aspect of the novel ('In *Childhood's End* humanity simultaneously ends its childhood and loses its children') notes a series of uneasy imaginations of mutant children from the time of Clarke's novel: Theodore Sturgeon, *More Than Human* (1953); John Wyndham, *The Chrysalids* (1955) and *The Midwich Cuckoos* (1957) – and later Ira Levin, *Rosemary's Baby* (1967). The entry on 'Children in SF' in Clute and Nichols 1993, 212–213, groups *Childhood's End* with a set of novels about 'children in league with aliens'. With chapter 3 in view, J. G. Ballard's novella *Running Wild* (1988) can be added to the list: children as murderers, the murders stemming from the sheer imprisoning niceness and tolerance of their parents and (closed) community.

views social breakdown through an older woman's observation of and puzzlement about a young woman and her peers; paranormal children are born at the end of Lessing's *The Four-Gated City* (1972).

The postwar disaster novels reflect the feeling that the Second World War ended in the victory of decency, rather than expressing horror at its atrocities and its human cost. This is the case even with *On the Beach*, where it is the more striking because nuclear disaster is bringing human life to a complete end. The result is that these novels do not feel the need to depart from the prose of journalistic clarity and directness, though they vary it at times, as with the italicised strand of discourse in *Earth Abides*. Instead, the end of civilisation reaffirms ordinary virtues, makes way for a revival of English pastoral as if it were a norm that modernity and the city had overlaid (*The Day of the Triffids*, *On the Beach*, Aldiss's *Greybeard*) or, in *Earth Abides*, an American variant, the end of civilisation sees cultural life begin again in an unavoidable, and accepted, return to a tribal way of life, indolent rather than savage.

The matter is not quite as simple as this. The pastoral England to which the survivors retreat in *The Day of the Triffids* is the scene of war between civilised (those who have the flamethrowers) and savage (the flesh-eating Triffids with their whips). The intruder Charlie is executed in *Earth Abides* because he brings with him the disease and the mentality of corrupt urban society. In John Christopher's *The Death of Grass*, the peaceful green of England is evoked (2009, 14, 25, 180), but has now gone forever because all grasses have been killed and mass global starvation threatens. Those at the centre of the novel do fight their way to a rural refuge, but they calculate and kill on the way, and are thoughtful enough to define what has happened to them – not quite primitivism or savagery, but a kind of feudalism. The direct reporter's style is here stripped back to quick curt reasoning; nothing has the resonance of, for instance, Wyndham's triffids. In *Childhood's End* human life is exterminated and Earth itself destroyed, though only after an orderly utopia reflecting the One World idealism and faith in Science of earlier science fiction had been established for a while, and the whole sequence of invasions, changes and mutations is a matter of ordered stages, planned and successive. We saw above how the narrator's determination to rationalise and clarify in *Childhood's End* sometimes falls into bathos. Decent, domestic life is carried on to the very end in *On the Beach*, but at the cost of a painful blankness and denial.

The language of all these novels reflects a confidence that no radical change in feeling and virtues is needed, or it can at times be seen as a refusal to conceive it. *The Death of Grass* is the exception that proves the rule: the civilised virtues do have to be discarded, but the novel's prose is stripped bare, and after the opening delineation of the global catastrophe, the novel's focus is relentlessly on the struggles of its central group. An emphatic change will come, in the form of fictions in which apocalypse is an ongoing process rather than an abrupt catastrophe, a process that releases other, less socially acceptable or even comprehensible, impulses and subjectivities, and is couched in prose that blurs external and interior worlds and feelings, and works by imagining rather than explaining.

Part 2

Post-Imperial Subjects

The next three chapters of *Apocalypse in Crisis* discuss British apocalyptic novels from the 1960s and 1970s. Important developments in the science-fiction genre are put into relation with wider counter-cultural currents. The overall effect, in all these varied cases, whether usefully classified as part of science fiction or not, is a turning away from the practical reasoning and reporter's narrative style of the fictions discussed in part 1, and a turning towards explorations, and occasionally indulgences, of subjectivity, and towards death. The logic of apocalypse, the narrative of destruction, death and transcendence, is clearly open to this turn, and we have seen how *On the Beach* registers it by a blankness and denial, and *Childhood's End* by the uneasy relations between the first apocalyptic invasion, that of the Overlords, and the second, that of the Overmind. The culture of the 1960s and 1970s also throws light on this turn, though this effect is less easy to sum up in a formula, because it involves both the exuberance and the self-destructiveness of the 1960s, and the disturbance and disillusionment of the 1970s in Britain, though this way of putting the matter is tendentious, since these novels were themselves part of this culture, for instance of the way pleasure and performance was accompanied by violence and narcissism.

Chapter 3 examines apocalyptic fictions by J. G. Ballard: *The Drought* (1965), *The Drowned World* (1962) and *The Crystal World* (1966).[1] Chapter

---

[1] *The Drought* was published in the US as *The Burning World*, underlining how these three novels make a set of variations. The trio was preceded by *The Wind from Nowhere* (1962), also an apocalyptic novel, but different in that it focuses on the struggles of the authorities to cope with the disaster – precisely what is abandoned in the three later novels, in which the authorities are close to invisible. So, it is set aside in the present discussion.

4 discusses two novels published in 1969, *Barefoot in the Head* by Brian Aldiss and *Heroes and Villains* by Angela Carter, exuberant expressions of the 1960s opening to pleasure and experiment. The third chapter in the series moves from the 1960s to the troubled 1970s and 1980s to look at *Ice* by Anna Kavan (1967) and two novels by Doris Lessing, *The Memoirs of a Survivor* (1974) and *The Making of the Representative for Planet 8* (1982). All the novels discussed in part 2 reimagine apocalypse as heading towards an ending that – provocatively or ambiguously – involves both death and transcendence. Apocalyptic catastrophe sometimes precedes the action of the novel, as in *Barefoot in the Head* and in *Heroes and Villains*, and sometimes accompanies it, as in all the other novels discussed in this part, but each novel tends to culminate in this ambiguous and transcendent ending in a way that is in contrast with the novels discussed in part 1. The actions of the protagonists have a different, more wilful and driven, more psychologically complex quality, and the centre of gravity of the narrative is shifted towards its ending.

Ice was published in 1967 and its preoccupations can be fitted into those of the darker 1960s, preoccupations with destruction and unbridled or fated subjectivity, as is also the case with Ballard, but Kavan is a writer who goes her own way throughout her career, and there are limits to depicting her as shaped by the decade, or any decade. The apocalyptic fictions by Doris Lessing discussed in the third of the chapters in this part are likewise shaped by her own preoccupations as she moved on from her earlier work, most obviously into science fiction with the *Canopus in Argo* series of five novels, of which *Planet 8* is one, but *Memoirs* and *Planet 8* share an interest in death and transcendence with the other novels discussed in part 2. Their indifference to or rejection of the practical coping with catastrophe that had figured in the postwar disaster novels also aligns them with Ballard, Kavan, Aldiss and Carter. Like the other novels discussed in this part, they investigate the dimensions of subjectivity, but by blurring its boundaries, questioning or dissolving individual distinctness. There is no reckless following of impulse or engaging in performance, as often happened in the aftermath of the destruction of civilisation in the 1960s novels; in Lessing the protagonists have little scope for action, and find themselves having to learn their limits.

The postwar disaster novels discussed in part 1 tend to be firmly located, in England, California and Melbourne, and this helps to make plausible the way they concentrate on a small group that is using its reason and common sense to cope with catastrophe; the apocalyptic fictions to be discussed in part 3 are unlocated, or nomadic. Kerans in *The Drowned World* doesn't know that the submerged city he is living over and diving into is actually London;[2] the characters in *Barefoot in the Head* wander through Europe; in *Ice* unnamed characters wander unnamed continents. The setting might be England in *Heroes and Villains* and London in *The Memoirs of a Survivor*, but it is never named and specific details are avoided, even though *Memoirs* surely reflects the disturbed condition of Britain in the early 1970s. These novels are set in worlds in which the characters have to find their own bearings and courses without place names or familiarities: their worlds are ungrounded. The protagonists no longer practise their profession (the doctors in *The Drought* and *The Crystal World*, the scientist in *The Drowned World*), or have no occupation (the Survivor in *Memoirs of a Survivor*) or no means of support (the narrator and girl in *Ice*) or drift ecstatically (Charteris in *Barefoot in the Head*): they are beyond the necessity of making do. They find themselves in tense, often mutually hostile groups and relationships – the sado-masochistic central trio in *Ice*; the unusual family made up of the Survivor, Emily and Hugo in *The Memoirs of a Survivor*; the passionate but antagonistic relationship of Marianne and Jewel in *Heroes and Villains*, with the prophet Donally as an uneasy third party. Charteris in Aldiss's *Barefoot in the Head* is at one moment involved with a woman called Angelina and at another with a woman called Angeline, and this points to the way the persons of this novel drift: in *Barefoot in the Head* the exuberance and play is all – but only – in the language. The main character in each of Ballard's novels is departing from a relationship or has already left it behind, and his connections with others are always loose and uneasy. In these ways the novels to be discussed in the next three chapters build on and deepen the unease and uncertainty of the times, in relationships, in the individual's sense of where he or she is and where or whether he or she belongs.

Ballard's formative experience was in China; Aldiss was intensely affected by his wartime and postwar experiences in Burma and Sumatra, which he recounted several times in autobiographical fictions; Carter's emotional and sexual life was transformed by her years in Japan and Lessing's political views and her characteristic detachment from whatever society she was in were importantly formed by her growing up in what was then Rhodesia. These were all, in different ways, post-imperial experiences. All were experiences that prepared these authors for a degree of alienation from the now weakened imperial centre when

---

[2] Contrast the references to London in *The Day of the Triffids* (2014, 128) and *The Death of Grass* (2009, 107), and indeed the passage on London in Ballard's earlier, more conventionally postwar novel, *The Wind from Nowhere* (1967, 123).

they returned to it, and indeed for a feeling that there no longer was a centre, reflected and expanded in the post-apocalyptic settings of their novels.[3] Ballard's youthful experience in Shanghai helped to shape his characteristic imaginative vocabulary as an author (dereliction, drained pools, low-flying aircraft, aridity). The empire of the Sun of his autobiographical novel is that of the Japanese, victorious at first over the British and Americans, as well as that of the Sun that dominates *The Drowned World*. In *The Kindness of Women* (1991, 78) he writes of the strangeness for him of England when he came to live there after the Second World War ('I had left Shanghai too soon, with a clutch of insoluble problems that post-war England was too exhausted and too distracted to help me set aside'). In *Forgotten Life*, the second time Aldiss put his experiences in the campaign in Burma and in the postwar British occupation of Sumatra into fiction, his protagonist underlines the futility of the campaign and, still more, of the occupation: the British spent their blood in Burma, then left Burma and India, they left Indonesia, and then the Indonesians expelled the Dutch and massacred the Chinese.[4] The main character's affair with Mandy in Sumatra brings sexual initiation and bliss – then he leaves her and never sees her again. As Edmund Gordon puts it in his biography of Angela Carter (2016, 137), Tokyo was 'the city in which her life was transformed', because of her affairs with two much younger men, experiences of sexual freedom and power – rather less conventional than happened to Aldiss but even more important for Carter's later free-ranging imaginations of power and pleasure in sexuality. Doris Lessing left behind a husband and children when she moved from Rhodesia to London, already an activist and fiercely determined on her own course as a woman. One sequel was her altruistic adoption of the young Jenny Diski (Simmonds), which is reflected in the main character's relationship with Emily in *The Memoirs of a Survivor*. Susan Watkins shows how the white activists in *The Golden Notebook* (1972) are adrift, between Africans and settlers, suffering the

---

[3] Phyllis Lassner (2011, 123) makes the point: 'Because England was an unknown and alien place until they were adults, these writers saw English political and social culture from an in-between distance.' Lassner is discussing women writers from the British Empire.

[4] Aldiss 1989, 79–80, 89–90, 147, 175: 'Such was the price to pay for being a cog of Empire – an empire which was even then disintegrating, just as I felt myself to be.' The earlier novels treating the protagonist's experiences in Asia were *The Hand-Reared Boy* (1970), *A Soldier Erect* (1971) and *A Rude Awakening* (1978). Paul Fussell (1989, 110–114) discusses these novels. They fit his fiercely anti-idealistic argument about the British and American experience of the Second World War.

loss of 'a straightforward relation to English culture and identity'.[5] The original plans of Canopus for the people of Planet 8 (in *The Making of the Representative for Planet 8*) are, however, colonialist in being based on an assumption of the Canopans' right to manipulate others for their own good. *Planet 8* narrates the failure of a colonial project, though the transformation that the people of the planet undergo at the end may be read as compensation for this. Certainly Johor, the representative of Canopus on Planet 8, is a much more ambiguous figure than Karellen, whose feelings as a kind of colonial administrator among the backward humans receive sympathetic treatment in *Childhood's End*. As for Anna Kavan, her whole life seems to have been spent in fierce unhappy disillusionment, whether in London or elsewhere.

The New Wave: Against Commonsense Practicality

In the 1960s Ballard and Aldiss were very much part of the British science-fiction scene, publishing prolifically in *New Worlds* magazine.[6] *New Worlds* was itself taking British science fiction in a new direction, christened 'New Wave' science fiction.[7] Ballard in particular contributed to this movement, in his literariness, stylishness, readiness to provoke and (later) interest in sex, violence, perversity and satire of, especially, US politics and culture. These were manners and matters absent or downplayed in most previous science fiction, and certainly not provocatively underlined when they did appear. New Wave science fiction in general departs from the kind of science fiction that had prevailed up

---

[5] Watkins 2010, 61. Watkins (65) sees Lessing as critiquing Britain's 'post-imperial melancholia' (the term is Paul Gilroy's).

[6] The editor of *New Worlds* and inspiration of the New Wave was Michael Moorcock. Moorcock's *The Dancers at the End of Time* is an over-the-top extravaganza of apocalypse; the dancers, privileged, decadent grandees of the far future, are free to indulge in carnivals of spectacular destruction, in which nothing is finally destroyed or dies. The point that catastrophe is very easy to imagine, and imagine again, is definitely made, though the effect, for me, is like that of too much rich cake. *The Dancers at the End of Time* (1993) comprises three previously published works: *An Alien Heat* (1972), *The Hollow Lands* (1974) and *The End of All Songs* (1976).

[7] There is a good discussion by a participant in the movement, Norman Spinrad, 1990. He suggests that the New Wave – a British enterprise, though with American involvement – initiated a split between British and American science fiction, the first winning literary readership and acceptance at the expense of popularity, the second retaining its broader appeal. Whether the split persists after, say, the 1980s, is another question.

until then, but science fiction is what it is. Plenty of its exponents, such as Brian Aldiss, or those swept up in its publications, such as Philip K. Dick, already had prolific publication histories in the older style or under the older regime – which means that the older regime was not as set in its ways as the publicists of the New Wave sometimes asserted. As with many revolutions, a second look after the excitement and sometimes the hype of the break suggests that the break was not as dramatic as first thought. Ballard's trio does make a striking contrast with the British disaster fictions that we considered in the previous chapter – in fact, it makes a more striking contrast with this group of science-fiction novels than with the science fiction of the 1940s and 1950s more broadly considered, where the painful and the zany and the grim found varied expression, for instance in the work of Alfred Bester and Philip K. Dick.

So Ballard and Aldiss are writing within science fiction and – if restlessly – within genre science fiction. But they are also writing anti-science fiction in that they refuse much of the ethos of science fiction as it had been written. Their protagonists refuse, or neglect, common sense practicality of the sort that tends to be normal in science fiction both in that it is met with very frequently and in that the protagonists are felt or simply assumed to share it with most other people. Protagonists of science fiction often behave very ingeniously, but this is just the exertion of common-sense practicality at a higher level. Not so in Ballard or Aldiss, and the difference is itself almost enough to make Ballard's science fiction, in particular, into anti-science fiction, especially when the protagonists of his apocalyptic novels carry their indifference to the practicalities of survival to the point of submission to the oblivion that apocalypse is bringing about. In his *Obsolete Objects in the Literary Imagination*, Francesco Orlando posits as important to modern literature (literature since the late eighteenth century) 'the return of the repressed antifunctional' (2006, 6–7). Things are taken away from rational function and given new meanings and resonances. We can see this happening in Ballard and Aldiss, in the context of the particular allegiance to reason and practicality of earlier science fiction, and, as Orlando would predict, in Ballard and in Aldiss the embrace of the anti-functional is accompanied by an unleashing of performance and impulse in the characters, and of style in the text – style as itself a kind of performance and an assertion of connotation, as against the unadorned denotation to which earlier science fiction was committed.

Style

In the novels discussed in chapter 2 the emphasis was on reportage and the provision of information. The text offers the observations of a witness or the perspective of an impersonal, knowledgeable narrator, and the occasional expansion or inflation of this – the italicised passages in *Earth Abides*, the elegiac notes in *Childhood's End* – does not disrupt the overall steady beat of reliable reportage. Ballard, Kavan, Aldiss and Carter all offer a richer mixture of information and impression. The reporter's style of earlier disaster fictions, which imitates the absence of style, or at least the manner of absence of style, that prevails in non-fiction, is abandoned. The text is open to the wider resources of the literary. Literariness can function to frame a reader's expectations, inviting the expectation of pleasure in language for instance, just as generic conventions can frame a reader's expectations of, for instance, sober explanation and practical calculation. More important is the effect of impression, simile and analogy – often ironic or simply unexpected, and this is true also of the literary allusions. It's not primarily the facts and objects, the information and rational explanation or hypothesis, that we are given. 'As if' is one of Ballard's favourite formulas. We are given a penumbra of comparisons and resemblances and reflections, and these very often locate the situation and the setting in a new reality, in which time itself is different and the protagonist has to sense and intuit because reason is inadequate. Things seen and done come to merge with things felt, dreamt and remembered. Ballard, Aldiss and Carter are allusive, and this calls attention to the literariness of their texts. Density of allusion shadows the present text with others, in an effect of double exposure.[8] Aldiss clearly offers his text for the enjoyment of play with language; in his interchapters he translates the events of the chapters (bizarre already) into diverse sets of poems. In Carter and Kavan, inner and outer worlds are blurred, almost anything can be read as metaphor or symbol; indeed, to say that much in a text is presented as metaphor or symbol is to say that the world of the text

---

[8] It will be argued below that the allusions in Ballard and Carter do not cohere into an underlying structure of meaning, except perhaps in *The Crystal World* in relation to Conrad's *Heart of Darkness*. The effect is different in apocalyptic fiction of the romantic period, responding to the apocalyptic turmoil of the period that puts both political revolution and the Enlightenment into question. Blake in his prophetic books is directly rewriting the Bible and *Paradise Lost*, and Byron in 'Heaven and Earth' is writing against the biblical account of the Flood: in these cases, the reader has to bear closely in mind the text that is being rewritten.

is a reflection of the inner world of the characters, though it need not only be that.

In these novels, that ungroundedness discussed above in terms of their authors' post-imperial experiences figures as an invitation to experiment and to proliferate imagery. One product of this is a crowded, haunted landscape, desolate but peopled with the louche and eccentric. These qualities of style mean that these novels offer a different economy, a different interaction of aspects, most obvious in Ballard, where the pleasures of art can interact for the reader with the stark, reduced qualities of the world that is presented. The fact that catastrophe has transformed the world is more present to us than the implication that it has involved mass death, or the end of civilisation, and the novel's language works with image and dream to make this transformation real for the reader; the style of reportage would not have done the job.

By contrast, in Doris Lessing it is precisely the refusal of many of the elementary pleasures of style that pulls the reader up short. As the disaster is inexorable, the telling of it is to be unadorned, even inelegant. If the postwar disaster novelists aim for the contrary of literariness, plain reportage, then Lessing aims for the contradictory of literariness, anti-literariness. It is perhaps as a consequence of this anti-literariness that the supernatural enters awkwardly into *Planet 8* when the characters transcend death, and awkwardly into *Memoirs* when they enter another, transcendent space. In Ballard in the midst of desolation and devolution in *The Drought* we have allusion to Yves Tanguy (*'Jours de Lenteur'*);[9] in Carter as *Heroes and Villains* approaches its bittersweet ending we have a tableau that recreates Henri Rousseau's 'The Sleeping Gypsy'; but in Lessing 'the great birds' that attack Alsi in *Planet 8* (128–129) are just 'the great birds', and Alsi is not her name, just the name of her social function.

---

[9] Gasiorek 2005, 42.

Chapter 3

Style and Immolation
J. G. Ballard

Nature Remade

The most striking and haunting thing about Ballard's apocalyptic novels is their creation of a transformed, desolate or hostile landscape – one that is so all-encompassing as to embrace and express the subject, the life of the psyche. In the postwar disaster novels, the narrative concentrates on what happens after the catastrophe, and tells of a recovery of initiative and responsibility as the survivors struggle to make do, and even re-establish stability. In many of these novels, the aftermath to catastrophe takes place in nature, in a return to the simple and pastoral – in *Earth Abides, The Day of the Triffids, The Kraken Wakes, Greybeard*. If nature in the form of a disease, or a set of creatures from outer space behaving as nature (evolution) dictates, has almost annihilated us, then nature in the form of the English countryside or a California returned to the wild is the setting for our recovery, and, more than that, our recovery is positive because it is happening in nature.

Ballard strikingly departs from the earlier valuation both of nature and of a decency and normality that is itself imagined as if it were natural for humans. He can be seen as revising and intensifying the trope of the invasion of nature in the aftermath of, or as part of apocalyptic catastrophe.[1] The nature that invades in *The Drowned World* and *The Crystal World* is primitive, proliferating and threatening; in the latter novel Ballard is adapting the image of the luxuriant, menacing jungle

---

[1] Orlando traces the history of this imagery of desolation (2006, 162–168; see also 141, and 417, n.211). This history stretches from the Bible ('the vulture and the hedgehog/shall lodge in her capitals/the owl shall hoot at the window/the raven croak on the threshold', Zephaniah 2, 14) to Pope's *Windsor Forest* (1967, lines 67–72), to visions of the weeds in the ruins of blitzed London. It is so pervasive that it is its *absence* after a catastrophe that is striking, for instance in *The Leftovers*.

that enters the Western imaginary with imperialism – Conrad's *Heart of Darkness* is the important precedent. The irony is that this invading nature is also productive. What could be a more productive force in nature than the Sun, so powerful in *The Drowned World*? And the process of crystallisation is powerfully creative in *The Crystal World*. Further, Ballard's protagonist refuses the task of survival in the aftermath of a catastrophe that comes from nature. He accepts the intimation – in *The Drowned World* it is actually a message, transmitted by dreams – that nature is a dark power that must be submitted to. He does this the more readily because it echoes his own impulses, impulses that look like apathies if viewed in the light of traditional science-fiction practicality. The catastrophe in *The Drought* is caused by pollution but those in *The Drowned World* and *The Crystal World* are outside human responsibility or control, and there is no prospect of re-founding human society. (Colonel Riggs in *The Drowned World* appears to be trying to do this, but his sympathy for the psychopathic scavenger Strangman betrays him, and he is last seen threatening and machine-gunning from a helicopter.)

In all three novels the protagonist rejects as futile or unengaging any attempts to re-found human society. He embraces lack of responsibility. The voice of his deep self, which is also the voice of the universe in its new and inexorable configuration, says the same thing in each novel: renounce relationship, love, practicality, everydayness; choose, or submit to, death or absorption – which in the view of many critics is also new life, a transcendence to a new order of being. The work of apocalypse is to remake the world so as to produce a landscape so powerfully present as to carry an inescapable meaning to the protagonist. Apocalypse is more release than destruction. In this transformed landscape human things (towns and cars in *The Drought*, the edifices of a great city in *The Drowned World*) are part of a new reality. The process of transformation is active and under way in *The Drowned World* and *The Crystal World*, so that we can't exactly talk in terms of a post-apocalypse. The protagonist is part of the process: it reflects his dreams and wishes. The transformation of nature and the way the protagonist carries a rejection of practicality as far as the embrace of oblivion are interdependent. In fact the protagonist doesn't exactly 'embrace' oblivion. Oblivion is already present in the way that the landscape is haunted and time is deranged. The protagonist simply moves into it and with it. 'Even those who survive collective catastrophe have already experienced their death' (Sebald 2005, 73): this is not quite true of Ballard's protagonists, because they and their creator are so interested in the images and possibilities released by the catastrophe and present in the landscape, but it does help us to understand their somnambulistic passivity.

Ballard's rejection of the reasonableness of earlier science fiction in his apocalyptic novels has its origins in more than literary provocation. His short stories from about this time suggest not merely dull uniform materialism, but a kind of nullity, as if the goods and houses were just facades – a shadowless institutionalised uniformity riding on emptiness. They are full of loners, disregarded as eccentric or crazy, who have seen some oppression or emptiness or flaw in consensus reality that everyone else has missed (Hathaway in 'The Subliminal Man', Franz in 'The Concentration City', the narrator in 'The Venus Hunters') or have felt and responded to the lure of the primeval (the central characters in 'Now Wakes the Sea', 'The Delta at Sunset', 'The Gioconda of the Twilight Noon').[2] There is nowhere for these outsiders to go in these stories, unless into death or madness. In his apocalyptic novels of the 1960s global catastrophe provides a way out. Society itself, with its imprisoning illusion of reality, of which Ballard gave relentless disenchanted pictures in his short stories, has now been abolished. People are now able to wander in the post-apocalyptic landscape, sensuously vivid, subjectively rich, stimulating dreams and desires, often grim and threatening but certainly not a hollow façade. For a time, this wandering, even to oblivion, is enough, because of the power and fertility of what the catastrophe has released. In *The Day of Creation* (1987), however, the new river emerges, transforms the landscape for a while, then dries up again: the moment has passed. In later novels Ballard will tighten his depiction of the emptiness of modern consumer society (the suburbs and appliances of Britain's 'you never had it so good' prosperity) into the air-conditioned nightmare: empty wealth and ease that leads to outbreaks of violence or transgressive sexual practices (*Running Wild*, *Super-Cannes*, *Millennium People*, and, from earlier, *Crash*).[3]

The Drought[4]

As *The Drought* opens, the sea has become covered with a molecule-thin coating, due to pollution; the result is that there is no precipitation, a

---

[2] 'The Delta at Sunset' and 'The Gioconda of the Twilight Noon' were published in *The Terminal Beach* in 1964; 'The Concentration City', 'The Subliminal Man' and 'Now Wakes the Sea' in *The Disaster Area* in 1967; 'The Venus Hunters' in *The Overloaded Man* in 1967.
[3] *Running Wild* was published in 1988, *Super-Cannes* in 2001, *Millennium People* in 2003, *Crash* in 1973.
[4] References are to *The Drought*, London: Granada, 1978. The novel was first published in 1965.

disastrous, global drought and the end of life as we know it – the end of modern civilisation. We are informed of all this in a brisk and lucid passage after the novel is well under way (33–34): the ocean is now coated with 'a thin but resilient mono-molecular film formed from a complex of saturated long-chain polymers', generated from industrial wastes. Having put this nemesis of our reckless industrial civilisation in place, Ballard has no interest in its *global* consequences, and little in what might be done to alleviate it.[5] In *The Drought* the catastrophe is a negation: no rain; in *The Drowned World* and *The Crystal World* it is, in contrast, emphatically productive. This is why *The Drought* is here discussed before the other two novels, though it was published between them.

The setting is an unspecified but circumscribed landscape, now barren and becoming drier; this is the site of the wanderings of the central character Ransom and the activities, often self-indulgent and colourful, of a series of others whom he encounters but barely connects with. It dominates the novel. Ballard introduces into apocalyptic fiction this compelling, mesmerically described and evoked landscape of apocalypse. If anything haunts and possesses the reader of *The Drought*, *The Drowned World* and *The Crystal World*, it is this landscape. It's the landscape of obsession, from which the narrator can hardly withdraw his eyes; it seems to have come into its own in the aftermath of disaster.

Rain does fall at the end of *The Drought*, after ten years (as predicted, 175), though perhaps too late for Ransom to benefit from it – or, given his state of soul, even to want to benefit – but *The Drought* has no interest in telling us how this relief has come about and whether the drought might really be over. (The end of *The Wind from Nowhere* is similar – the disastrous wind simply dies down.) The novel is interested in the condition and behaviour of its selected group of survivors – it might as well be a castaway novel.[6] Earlier disaster novels frequently concentrate on a very small group of survivors, with the activities of the authorities, the signs of grander social conflicts and the desolation of great cities just noises off; it is as if Ballard seizes on this confinement and goes close to abolishing the larger scene.

[5] Contrast Kurt Vonnegut's *Cat's Cradle* (1963), in which 'Ice-9' coats the ocean with a similarly disastrous effect; this time the energies of the novel go into satirical critique, for instance of the invented religion, Bokonism.

[6] Ransom contemplates Philip, the waif he has befriended: 'Standing in the stern with his legs astride, his back bending, the outstretched wings of the dying bird dipping into the water from the bows, he reminded Ransom of a land-locked mariner and his stricken albatross, deserted by the sea' (24). The allusion, as often, is multiple: castaway stories, 'The Rime of the Ancient Mariner'.

Apocalypse as Aesthetic Opportunity

For the survivors whom we meet, the ruin of civilisation and desolation of the landscape comes as expressive opportunity, not as crisis, loss or challenge to rebuild. There's something in the soul that will be satisfied – germinated and released – by the coming of apocalypse, and *The Drought* will examine what this is, against the backdrop of a landscape that is both dominant and reduced to a few sparse elements. As we are told early on

> [...] the failure of Ransom's marriage was less a personal one than that of its urban context, in fact a failure of landscape, and that with his discovery of the river Ransom had at last found an environment in which he felt completely at home, a zone of identity in space and time. (13)

It's true that there is an episode in which many of the survivors have been organised in the common post-catastrophe dictatorship – 'semi-feudal' – to harvest water and fish from the retreating, salt-saturated sea. Ransom participates for a while, then leaves. The spectacle of Ransom frantically herding fish when the tide comes in (114–116) is close to a parody of the practical, suggesting how demeaning and futile it is. For the characters on whom we focus in the rest of the novel, disaster has in fact brought *release* from this sort of practical and more or less rational activity, while the past world in which it might have made sense has faded into unreality. This unreality is imaged in the abandoned cars that litter the landscape:

> [...] a light coating of dust covered the bodywork and seats, as if the car were already a distant memory of itself, the lapsed time condensing on it like dew. (30)
> [...] stalled in motionless glaciers of metal that reached over the plains as far as the horizon. (90)
> [...] idealized images of themselves, the essences of their own geometry. (154)

The characters are set in a context of literary allusion and carnival theatricality, and what occupies most of them is behaviour as signification and expression. They are free to improvise vivid costumes or customs. Quilter, the most malign of the characters, first appearing as if an idiot, becomes dominant towards the end (Ransom is glad to submit to him). His unpredictable murderousness and the hints of cannibalism are less prominent than his wholly impulsive actions and his weird improvised costume (stilts, a headdress made of the corpse of a black swan (163), a dead peacock around his neck). Similar, if less histrionic, is Catherine Austen's obsession with the escaped lions from the zoo. Then we have Richard Lomax, effete and camp millionaire and self-conscious joker and wit, with his silk suits and fireworks: 'like some kind of hallucinatory clown, the master of ceremonies at a lunatic carnival' (77), like 'a grotesque pantomime dame' (174), 'a demented Prospero' (181), 'a plump, grinning Mephistopheles' (47). His sister, Miranda – 'puckish cheeks, hard eyes and the mouth of a corrupt Cupid' (47) – is later compared to 'the yellow-locked, leprous-skinned lamia who pursued the Ancient Mariner' (52), and to 'an imbecile Ophelia' (78). The cluster of allusions here invokes both 'The Rime of the Ancient Mariner' and *The Tempest,* with Lomax, Miranda, 'Quilter, the grotesque Caliban of all his nightmares, and [Philip] the calm-eyed Ariel of the river' (67). Later we have Johnstone as 'a demented Lear' (130). Quilter's name perhaps alludes to the malign Quilty in *Lolita*. This dense and emphatic literary allusiveness of *The Drought* is refined by the time we reach *The Crystal World*, where the relations to Conrad are subtler than those to Shakespeare and Coleridge here (see below, 146–148).

Ransom is drifting out of the present and into a continuum that is haunted by the future but also by the re-emergence of the stripped down, essential residues of the past. This is what the catastrophe has effected, to so saturated a degree that it might as well be the point of the whole supposedly destructive and supposedly global event: the catastrophe itself is a reductive simplifier. So while Ransom is by no means an assertive or active figure, it is as if the whole thing has happened for his benefit, or to help him to come to see what his benefit is. His benefit is this release from the present time of actions (he is a doctor) into a temporality that is made up of images, figments, memories and hauntings. This in turn can constitute a compelling image of subjectivity. Ballard caps this aesthetic interpretation – for what the main characters are doing is aestheticising the apocalypse – by including a character who is obviously reminiscent of the archetypal aestheticiser of catastrophe, Nero. This is Lomax, epicene to the point of caricature, who burns the city for his own entertainment; that is, he doesn't merely resemble Nero, he re-enacts Nero: an instance of the novel's theatricality.[7]

The Drought celebrates and indulges the inner life, which finds its place less in the character's consciousness or feelings than in the landscape

---

[7] Ballard's dictators, such as Manson in *Hello America* (1981), tend to be mad emperors.

and in costume and impersonation. The inexorable material situation, consequence of the facts of chemical reactions and the conditions of modern industrial production (waste, pollution) is turned by an impulse to symbolise and self-express that is equally (in the context Ballard elaborates) inexorable. *Vermillion Sands* (1971) is a collection of linked stories, set in a similar desert, which are explicitly about the making of idiosyncratic works of art. There's no apocalypse in *Vermillion Sands*; in *The Drought* a set of individuals wrest apocalypse to aesthetic ends. They are compared to so many figures from literature that it is tempting to say that they enter textuality, as if they were impersonating literary characters at the same time as acting on their unchecked impulses – though Ransom is an exception here.

Dissolution

Ballard often writes his novels as pageants, as sequences of tableaus, in which the mise en scène is more important than any actions that might take place in it. Time is suspended, and images and performances pass in review, strewn artistically about a transformed landscape. The chapter titles refer to places, as it were way-stations, in the wanderings of the main character ('The Draining Lake', 'The Drowned Aquarium', 'The Terminal Zone', 'The Burning City', 'The Bitter Sea') or to encounters that are like manifestations ('The Dying Swan', 'The Lamia', 'The Cheetah'). They wait to be encountered, like the bowers and castles that Spenser's wandering knights come across in *The Faerie Queen*.

Ballard's landscapes are present as images in dreams are but also present because insisted on – wrecked cars, burnt-out buildings, drained pools or lakes, exotic desert villas. We can feel he initiates apocalypses in order to get things sufficiently wrecked or transformed to open the scene of his favourite landscapes. If the scene of the fall of Shanghai revealed to the young Ballard how things really are, then that scene is to be repeated with variations. Apocalypse doesn't make a new world so much as reveal one that has a primal authority. And this, like so much else in *The Drought*, adds to Ballard's anti-science fiction, because the landscape is a field of symbols and the protagonist comes to accept or to greet it as expressive of his inner self. Mention of dreams and hauntings in this context could be misleading. As regards Ransom, the individual seems to be *emptied into* the landscape. The landscape is rich and suggestive, a field of symbols, but the individual seems vacant, a field of habits and symptoms, though the habits and symptoms are interestingly irrational and often picturesque. We hear of 'the vacuums and drained years' of Ransom's memory (44), and of 'an increasing sense of vacuum, as if he was pointlessly following a vestigial instinct that no longer had any real meaning for him' (92). At the end, just before we learn that the rain has returned, it is as if Ransom has died, or become no more than a reflection:

> To his surprise he noticed that he no longer cast any shadow on to the sand, as if he had at last completed his journey across the margins of the inner landscape he had carried in his mind for so many years. (188)

This suggests a fulfilled destiny as well as a state after death, and connects it with the landscape, which is the most powerfully memorable thing in the novel. *The Drowned World* takes the process a step further; once again the main character travels towards a death that might also be a fulfilment, but this time the process is intimately and powerfully connected to the global heating that is transforming nature and making human life unviable.

The Drowned World[8]

In *The Drowned World*, the apocalyptic catastrophe is already well under way. The ferocious increase in heat and sea level brought about by Earth's new exposure to the Sun has inundated the city where most of the novel happens, and this must have taken place a long time ago. Kerans, the main character, doesn't recognise that the city is in fact London; he was born after the great cities had to be abandoned and is 'indifferent to the spectacle of these sinking civilizations' (19). We are told of the nature of the catastrophe early in the text, and in impersonal terms, without comment: unusual solar activity blew away the ionosphere that protects Earth from solar intensity, Earth's atmosphere has begun to heat up to an intolerable, unlivable degree, and will continue to do so (20). Unliveable for humans, that is; a natural event (not caused by, for instance, pollution or any other human activity) has released a process of rapid evolution, which is also devolution. This is not the gentle settled nature that was evoked in earlier novels of disaster as alternative to whatever it was in human action or in nature (triffids, invading aliens, epidemic disease) that produced the disaster. It is what is producing both

---

[8] References are to J. G. Ballard, *The Drowned World*, New York: Berkley Medallion, 1962.

the disaster to humanity and the new life that is replacing it. Unlike the drought in *The Drought*, but like the crystallisation in *The Crystal World*, it is a positive force, unresting and insistent. We have jungle, lagoons, silt, ferns, alligators, iguanas, a huge pitiless blazing Sun. The novel draws on the Western imagination of the tropics as the place of luxuriant, liquid, overpowering growth and the home of primitive creatures and plants – iguanas and giant ferns in this case. The world is drowning in fertility.[9] Humans have retreated to the once-freezing fringes of the now torrid planet. The fetid and proliferating, muddy and liquid, primitive and reptilian has taken over the rest:

> An immense profusion of animal life filled the creeks and canals: water-snakes coiled themselves among the crushed palisades of the water-logged bamboo groves, colonies of bats erupted out of the green tunnels like clouds of exploding soot, iguanas sat motionlessly on the shaded cornices like stone sphinxes. (49)

It is the energy of the transformation that powers the description, rather than the eeriness or poignancy of desolation, which is what is most often emphasised in earlier vignettes of ruined cities. (There are passing references to the relics of ancient civilisations – sphinxes, the Cloaca Maxima.) The humans on whom we focus, Kerans, Bodkin and Beatrice, tend to inertia and indifference, so that the narrative is in a way waiting for them to be affected by the energy of the new world that so energises the writing. Meanwhile, the city is smothered:

> Everywhere the silt encroached, shoring itself in huge banks against a railway viaduct or crescent of offices, oozing through a submerged arcade like the fetid contents of some latter-day Cloaca Maxima. Many of the smaller lakes were now filled by the silt, yellow discs of fungus-covered sludge from which a profuse tangle of competing plant forms emerged, walled gardens in an insane Eden. (48)

Kerans and Bodkin drift away from the orbit of their practical and brisk commander Riggs, and Kerans and Beatrice find themselves for a

---

[9] Byron notices that when the flood has drowned everything else, it will give the creatures of the sea 'boundlessness of realm':
　　When ocean is earth's grave, and, unopposed
　　By rock or shallow, the leviathan,
　　Lord of the shoreless sea and watery world,
　　Shall wonder at his boundlessness of realm.
　　Byron 1970, scene II, 80–83.

while in the power, instead, of a new arrival, the piratical Strangman with his motley crew. Strangman is aggressive, cruel and indulgent, perhaps less the opposite to Riggs than the completion, the one reason and the other impulse and libido.[10] Like Lomax and Quilter in *The Drought*, Strangman is theatrical, an impresario of carnival, into which he ropes Beatrice and Kerans for a while. Carnival is part of civilisation even as it subverts its rules; Strangman, like Lomax and Quilter, is marked by the civilisation he has rejected. Kerans, for all that he lacks flamboyance and tends to drift, will end up somewhere else, far from civilisation, though while he is with Strangman he finds himself impersonating figures of myth ('acting out the role of Neptune into which he had been cast', 124).

The narrative in Ballard's apocalyptic fictions follows the central character's or characters' uncertain drifting and their periodic recognitions of a fate to which they are gradually submitting and that requires the refusal or rejection of conventional, practical action. The commentary that follows will trace this in *The Drowned World*, noting how the story of Kerans accrues symbolic weight in the process, though noting also Ballard's refusal to commit himself to a single symbolic schema or myth, and his persistence in blending different kinds of story (science fiction, myth, adventure story). The quotations above illustrate Ballard's habit of vivid simile and metaphor ('like clouds of exploding soot'; 'like stone sphinxes'; 'walled gardens in an insane Eden'). As in *The Drought*, the effect is that people and things are set in a shifting penumbra of resemblances and possibilities, suggestive, but not definitive as the description in earlier science fiction can often be.

We have repetition and routine – temporary, desultory or insubstantial. Kerans, Beatrice and Bodkin wait in the heat, meeting periodically but without much purpose. Kerans and Beatrice are having a passionless love affair; Bodkin has theories to impart. The narrative fragments into a series of scenes, marking an overall trajectory, the emergence of something, and also fusing with the devolutionary process that is going on everywhere in the scene, in the landscape, but without onwards drive as regards the humans. We can say that these repetitions exist for the sake of their settings, in that the mise en scène, the lagoons, iguanas, half-submerged and deserted buildings and so on, is what they mainly deliver. This serves to express the main force in the world of the novel, which is not human but the power of the Sun and the energy of nature.

---

[10] Gasiorek 2005, 37–39. If Riggs represents reason, as Gasiorek suggests, then the picture is complicated by Bodkin, who also reasons, if we accept his Jungian premises.

Solar Power

The energy and power of the transformation of Earth gives rise to certain theories among the novel's characters, and the novel itself largely endorses them. It is Dr Bodkin who explains what is going on, and thereby defines the destination to which they are inexorably drifting (39–41). The dreams that Bodkin, Kerans and Beatrice are experiencing, as are many of the soldiers in Riggs's party, are the throbbing, beating presence in them both of the Sun, the huge powerful god of the world they are now living in, and of the past. The past haunts and gradually becomes real for Ransom in *The Drought*; here in *The Drowned World* it is given a scientific – Jungian – substance in the circumstances of the new Sun-dominated world. So Bodkin argues. The past, sedimented in the 'lower' layers of every psyche, is now emerging, taking them over. The later, 'higher' layers of the psyche are now superseded, and practical rationality, as represented by Colonel Riggs, 'still obeying reason and logic' (68), on hand to evacuate them to what remains of civilisation in Greenland, is now obsolete. The movement of the book, when it eventually resumes, after the impetus lent it by the Strangman episode (Strangman and his crew don't seem to suffer any of the powerful, devolutionary dreams), is towards the heat and jungle of the south, Kerans's destination in the last chapters. Beatrice serves as a kind of bedecked idol for Strangman for a while, then leaves with Riggs; Bodkin is murdered by Strangman.

So only Kerans of the three heads south – but all three have essentially been isolates all along. Their 'growing isolation and self-confinement' (13), indifference and self-sufficiency are underlined (Beatrice, 'courage and self-sufficiency', 65; Hardman, who precedes Kerans in setting out for the south, 'tough self-sufficiency'). There is a new world, and a new state of being, but – as in *The Drought* – only for the isolated individual. Beatrice, Kerans and Strangman are brought together in very uneasy intimacy for a while, but as impersonators, masked figures in effect. The postwar disaster novels work with a group of survivors, learning to co-operate in the new, radically changed world; Ballard discards this pattern and focuses on isolates.

Bodkin's theory is scientific in form. It posits the reactivation of archaic buried layers in the brain as well as the psyche, which in turn are put in tune with the rhythms of the now all-powerful Sun by way of dreams. Humans, therefore, are also devolving, but in this they are in touch with a stupendous increase in fertility and power. This explanation, stemming from Bodkin's theory, becomes more and more a religious position, with the Sun as god, but still the language is that of science. (To add another layer, the characters' experience is also played out in terms of myth; they are linked to a variety of Biblical and classical tropes and figures; more on this below.) Ballard has invented something that combines science and religion under the cover of C. G. Jung, has given it the text's endorsement as the best explanation of what is happening to the humans we see in the novel and suggested that it shapes the central character's decision to head further south, suicidal though it may be, and that his decision is logical. Others, notably Hardman who also heads south, may be in the grip of a compulsion they can do nothing about, but Kerans has made a decision, though only after a kind of ordeal at the hands of Strangman.

In this novel, science is absorbed into religion, or anyway into the kind of alternative view of existence that we can associate with religion; science's authority is not denied but surpassed. Meanwhile, for much of the novel, the aesthetic is released, and we have symbol-making and performance, as in *The Drought*. In *The Drowned World*, the symbol-making and performance is assigned to Strangman. Strangman is a more powerful figure than is either Quilter or Lomax in *The Drought*, as well as being somewhat more pragmatic, in his interest in scavenging. Still, the emphasis is on Kerans's decision to head south, and how this gains authority from the novel's endorsement of Bodkin's theory.

Not only is the catastrophe ongoing, a process that the novel observes in motion from moment to moment and for which it has a framework in evolution (and devolution); it opens the way to a revelation – a framework of religious meaning – and a New Jerusalem, or more precisely a new Garden of Eden. As we saw, characters in *The Drought* – but not Ransom – are compared to a variety of figures from literature; they undergo a kind of ironic canonisation, but in *literary* terms; they don't enter myth. The last sentence of *The Drowned World* has Kerans as 'a second Adam searching for the forgotten paradises of the reborn Sun' (158). The implication is that the Sun has been the true god all along, and is now 'reborn' in the sense of coming back into its own. In keeping with its enthusiasm for this revelation and new beginning (accompanied by the death of the old Adam, as is traditional), the novel pays minimum attention to the mass death of humans and indeed of all non-tropical life forms, including even those that once inhabited the Arctic regions, since it is now hot even there. We are simply left to infer all this death and extinction while the novel dwells on the overwhelming teeming of new life. The mass of humanity is present only as what it left behind – ruins – desolate, sinking into the lagoons and the silt, temporarily inhabited by some of the novel's characters, and plundered by others. There are none of the glimpses of what happened to the mass of people that we get in *The Drought* – if only briefly, and by way of a pause in the novel's main action – in the chapters set on the coast.

Carnival as Ordeal

As in very many of Ballard's works, we do get the seductive pleasure of sojourning amid the ruins, able to pile up and use whatever you care to use; so it is for Kerans, Beatrice and, to a lesser degree, Bodkin. But this is caricatured, or rebuked, by the looting and vandalising of Strangman and his crew, whose behaviour is in contrast to the desultory and apathetic self-indulgence of Kerans and Beatrice, because it is accompanied by riot and carnival, caprice and cruelty. Overall, the scene is a phantasmagoria of the sixties as a release of libido, pleasure and violence in the midst of a supersession of the old ways.

Strangman's crew of obedient but dissolute and feckless blacks draws on a repertoire of the exotic and primitive that writers were going to have to learn to discard as soon as possible after 1962. (And that Ballard did discard.) The set-up does, however, usher in a series of images of blackness and whiteness; Strangman is like a white vampire (93; but in his decline later in the novel, 'like a decaying vampire glutted with evil and horror', 146); seen as a 'white devil' by Beatrice (121) and by Kerans (143); accompanied by albino sea creatures. It looks as if Strangman is offered as a god of death, but he also prompts lots of images of decadence, caprice and madness.[11]

Strangman has seized on the new state of affairs to act on his impulses and desires, but he serves to induct Kerans into a role in myth, though it is hard to label the latter as a single figure, Christ or Adam or Neptune. Kerans and Beatrice are caught up in Strangman's performances and then in his violent play. Kerans is made to impersonate a victim-deity, pelted and mocked, dragged around on a kind of palanquin, with an alligator's head shoved onto his own head. It seems that he has become a second Christ, mocked and spat upon. The episode figures as an ordeal, after which he is ready to pursue what he has recognised as his destiny.

---

[11] Umberto Rossi (1994, especially 88–91) compares the imagery of *The Drowned World* and *Hello America*. Pop culture reference replaces allusion to history and art; the mad dictator Manson in the later novel differs from the violent grotesques such as Strangman, and Quilter and Lomax, in the earlier novels; he figures in a 'telematic' America in which the simulacral takes over. On allusion, often to modernist writers (Eliot, Conrad, Joyce, Camus), but also to Keats, Donne, Defoe, Dante, see McCarthy 1997, and below on the relations of *Heart of Darkness* and Ballard's *The Crystal World*.

In his discussion of the novel in *Alien Encounters*, Mark Rose (1981) gives a more coherent account of the symbolic structure of the Strangman episode than I can accept. He sees Strangman as a 'pivotal figure in the narrative' (133–134), and in his interpretation Kerans when captured by Strangman and made into a carnival figure is Neptune (Rose, 135; 'acting out the role of Neptune into which he had been cast', *The Drowned World*, 124). The sea is the site of the limitless, 'another version of the incomprehensible, shapeless infinite, the void of the prehuman' (Rose, 131).[12] Even if Kerans as Neptune is overlaid by Kerans as other figures, this emphasis on the sea is useful in a novel full of images of the liquid. It fits Ballard's revaluation of catastrophe as introducing new life that the sea, threatening in its 'shapeless infinite' in traditional apocalypse, should bring a new state of being closer in *The Drowned World*.

The Strangman episode hinges on two encounters with the drowned city. In the first, Kerans dives into a flooded planetarium, which is seen as a womb-like unconscious ('amniotic'); there he confronts his own image in a mirror (97), and, perhaps, attempts suicide – or perhaps he was almost killed by Strangman. Kerans has to decide for himself, if he can, as Strangman points out, and thereby he has to face the prospect of his death if he heads south (101–102). Later Strangman and his crew succeed in draining a portion of the drowned city. He introduces this as his biggest spectacle, laid on for Beatrice and Kerans, though he is also doing it in order the more easily to loot the place. As will be seen shortly, this reclamation has a strong effect on Kerans, and complicates the novel's imagery of the power of the unconscious.

It is after this that Strangman's manic play turns vicious, we have the period in which Kerans is captive as a mocked deity, and in fact Strangman is on the point of killing him when Riggs and his men return.[13] They rescue Kerans, but Riggs surprisingly says there is no

---

[12] On the sea and sea creatures in traditional apocalypse, see Cohn 1993; on the sea in China Miéville's *Kraken*, see chapter 8 below; and this, from Richard Lloyd Parry's *Ghosts of the Tsunami*: 'The tsunami was a thing of a different order, darker, stranger, massively more powerful and violent, without kindness or cruelty, beauty or ugliness, wholly alien. [...] It stank of brine, mud and seaweed. Most disturbing of all were the sounds it generated as it collided with, and digested, the stuff of the human world: the crunch and squeal of wood and concrete, metal and tile' (Parry 2017, 134).

[13] 'Looks as if you have been having a bit of a party here', says one of Riggs's soldiers (140), perhaps echoing the naval officer's words to the boys on the point of killing Ralph at the end of Golding's *Lord of the Flies* (1958, 223): 'Fun and games'.

evidence against Strangman and that his achievement in reclaiming part of the city will probably be praised back in civilisation (142–144). The effect of this is to make us think again about Riggs's rationality and that of the remnant of civilisation that he represents, while deepening the ambiguity of Strangman, at once an associate of Riggs and a god of death and disorder. Strangman replaces Riggs as obstacle and alternative to what Kerans plans to do; only one whose values are also inverted and indeed deranged can do this in a world in which ordinary values and behaviours are irrelevant. It is Strangman who is challenging Kerans's desire to head towards death; that is, the challenge comes from this violent and by no means sane and sensible source; meanwhile any labelling of Riggs as sane and sensible is also undermined.

Yet if Strangman is challenging Kerans he is also fitting Kerans and Beatrice into patterns of myth, though these seem to have the incoherence of his nasty play.

Further, the series of events after Kerans manages to escape from captivity seems like Ballard's rendition – or caricature – of adventure story action, in which a woman has to be rescued and a ferocious African guard fought off (the latter happens again in *The Crystal World*, though less sensationally). Kerans arms himself, sneaks onto Strangman's ship, kills the enormous hunch-backed one-eyed mulatto, Big Caesar, who attacks him, and rescues Beatrice. This episode from adventure fiction fizzles out with the arrival of Riggs and his men in the nick of time, and then the favour Riggs shows to the mad and violent Strangman. And as we have seen the symbolic tends to be improvised, or, more precisely, subject to a musical variation, so that, for instance, Kerans's appearances as Neptune or Christ or Adam, or Beatrice's appearances as Esther or Venus or Minerva or 'a tribal totem' or Nefertiti (106–107, 119, 136) need to be heard as similar motifs in different keys.

Southwards

If Riggs praises Strangman's feat in draining the city, the action appals Bodkin and Kerans. Bodkin is murdered after he fails in an attempt to blow up Strangman's barrage and let the lagoon back in. Kerans finds the remainder of Bodkin's store of explosives and succeeds. Then he sets off on his journey south, pursued for a while by Riggs, machine-gunning from the helicopter. Given that the draining of the city so alarms Bodkin and Kerans, we have to ask how it fits into the symbolic milieu of the novel. It seems to figure as a contrast to the suggestions of the 'amniotic' rich underworld that Kerans experienced in the drowned planetarium.

Does Strangman's action expose an alternative and less glamorous view of the depths of the psyche as a mess of muddy incoherent vestiges, not the profound source of a powerful Triassic re-emergence? Kerans is shocked by 'this total inversion of his normal world' (109), and also disgusted:

> Everything was covered with a fine coating of silt, smothering whatever grace and character had once distinguished the streets, so that the entire city seemed to Kerans to have been resurrected from its own sewers. Were the Day of Judgement to come, the armies of the dead would probably rise clothed in the same filthy mantle. (114)

The novel does not – and need not – commit itself to the choice of a single significance from this cluster of clashing actions and images; instead, it journeys onwards with Kerans.

Kerans was, however, preceded by Lieutenant Hardman, the grounded helicopter pilot who was the first to be possessed by solar dreams. The lieutenant's self-immolation, even more extreme, painful and driven than that of Kerans, perhaps blunts the edge of any scepticism the reader might feel about what Kerans is doing. Kerans meets Hardman after some time in the wilderness, though he is now blinded by the Sun, emaciated and delirious – or absorbed in the emergent new reality – so that he doesn't recognise Kerans.

> The man was no more than a resurrected corpse, without food or equipment, propped against the altar like someone jerked from his grave and abandoned to await the Day of Judgement. (155)

In a moment, on the last page of the novel, we will be given the resonant image of Kerans heading further south, lost, but 'a second Adam, searching for the forgotten paradises of the reborn Sun' (158). It doesn't seem that the Day of Judgement that Hardman awaits, or the Day of Judgement in which the dead would arise 'clothed in the same filthy mantle' is likely to be followed by any entrance into Paradise. Kerans's fate is inexorable but ambiguous. And we notice that as he heads south Kerans is 'attacked by alligators and giant bats' (158): Ballard can't resist throwing in the giant bats.

Landscape into Art
The Crystal World[14]

The Crystal World is the last and the most successful of Ballard's trio of novels about the end of civilisation and the transformation of nature. It offers the most compelling and continuously dazzling transformation of Earth, and the first in which Earth and human civilisation are not merely wrecked, but nature is made over by an unearthly beauty. If we take the aesthetic to be that which can be seen as existing in and for itself, and as valuable (wonderful, fascinating in the sense of compelling) in and for itself, then in *The Crystal World* the aesthetic is proliferating, revealing more of itself, self-enhancing, and this is happening in nature itself. Human responses, actions and attitudes are secondary. This novel, more than its predecessors, contrasts the messy clumsiness and violence of human actions, the ambiguous uncertainty of human motivations and impulses, with the precision and tireless creativity of natural process. Nature doesn't only invade, it appropriates art, and outdoes it, and this happens in the jungle, the classic site, in the Western imagination, of unchecked, disorderly growth – the opposite of intricate artifice.

It was suggested that in *The Drought* and *The Drowned World* the apocalypse is consummated by the submission to it of the protagonist; this amounts to a provocative rejection of the reason and practicality that usually shapes action in science fiction, and it can be seen either as a choice of death, or as a transcendence of the previous limits of conventional humanity and the entrance into a new state of being. The same might be said of *The Crystal World*, but it goes much further. The protagonist Sanders is captivated and captured by the crystallisation; he abandons his previous commitments, weak as they already were. His case is paralleled by that of the others who wander and clash in the metamorphosing forest. The movement of the novel, however, is beyond the human altogether. The crystallisation is an imagination of something more powerful, totally other, though its basis is in chemistry. It is as if this is a novel of invasion, like so many apocalyptic novels, but one in

---

[14] References are to J. G. Ballard, *The Crystal World*, London: Jonathan Cape, 1966. An earlier version of the novel, 'The Illuminated Man', can be found in Ballard's 1964 story collection, *The Terminal Beach*. Given that this story is roughly 30 pages in length, Ballard includes in it a remarkable amount of what would become *The Crystal World*. The main differences are that the setting is Florida, not Africa; there is more emphasis on scientific investigation of the outbreak; and we don't yet meet Louise and Suzanne. The evocation of the crystallisation is almost the same in the earlier text. Page references to passages from 'The Illuminated Man' are preceded by 'IM' here.

which the invader cannot be seen as even remotely creaturely, cannot be seen as having qualities that we can recognise, in a more or less chastened or horrified spirit, as like our own – purpose, inventiveness, desire to feed, desire to conquer and possess.[15] In general Ballard carries off his provocative refusal of practicality with a style of unruffled impersonality; this impersonality finds its most extreme expression in the imagery of *The Crystal World* – a kind of armoured sensuousness that attracts and fends us off at once.

There are parallels between the luminous, intricate beauty of the crystallisation that takes over the jungle in *The Crystal World* and the experience of drugs such as mescalin. Aldous Huxley in *Heaven and Hell* (1956) details how the visionary experience to which he felt mescalin gave him access was one of light, of brilliant colour, best compared to jewels, geometric in form, elaborately decorated and figured, like carvings, and intricately patterned.[16] All these features can be found in the dazzling phenomenon of crystallisation as Ballard details it (see 150–154 below); the difference is that the art of these passages in Ballard is as much verbal in its richness as it is visual, whereas Huxley accompanies his descriptions of visions with assertions of the inadequacy of language and appeals to 'Being', 'ultimate Reality' and so on. Ballard's crystallisation is never ineffable.

Carnival, harlequinade, dressing up, prominent in *The Drought* and *The Drowned World* as expressive and hedonistic, sometimes as violent and challenging, makes only a fragile appearance in this novel in the form of the 'saraband' of the lepers in the forest (206–208). In *The Crystal World* nature makes art, art that is continually compared to human artefacts (the baroque, the embellished, above all the bejewelled); humans stumble repeatedly, victims of the obsessions that lead them on. Process triumphs in the form of crystallisation, and action (what humans attempt, violent, drifting, desultory, clumsy) flounders. The beauty of the crystallisation is intense because it seems like art but is in nature, nature in the act of transformation and creation. Because it produces beauty it is compelling; because it is a process it seems mechanical, the victory of the mechanical, the systemic, over the human – one of the

---

[15] Later imaginations of the invasion of the other can be found in the work of Greg Egan, for instance, 'Luminous' (1995) and *Schild's Ladder* (2001), and in Jeff VanderMeer's Southern Reach Trilogy (*Annihilation, Authority* and *Acceptance*, 2014).

[16] See Huxley's quotations from A. E. (George Russell) and Weir Mitchell, at 69 and 72. Ballard wrote a foreword to the 1994 edition of *The Doors of Perception* and *Heaven and Hell* (London: Flamingo). Of course the New Jerusalem in *Revelation* itself features gold and jasper, glass and emerald.

nightmares of modernity. It is not enough to wonder at it, however, as at a beautiful scene or painting; here it seems one must do something – penetrate further into the forest, surrender, escape. This imperative results in odd narrative rhythms and repetitions.

The Crystal World's presentation of the apocalyptic catastrophe will be effective if that which is presented as beautiful, the transformation of the forest and everything in it into intricate reflections and crystals, is indeed felt to be beautiful – birds, butterflies, rivers, buildings, humans. It's hard to think of another novel that invests so much in this particular enterprise, and so thoroughly reorganises the relations of the human and that which is not human in pursuit of the aestheticisation of nature.

This enterprise does succeed, but the paradox is that nature is found to be beautiful insofar as its productions approach those of (human) art. The novel is indifferent to the Romantic enterprise of finding in nature a beauty and vitality that is intrinsic to nature *and* is shared with humans, given that they are part of nature. Images of reflection are everywhere in *The Crystal World*, and the process of crystallisation that Ballard tirelessly depicts – mostly by means of similes and metaphors – turns nature into a reflection as well as an outdoing of human art. Yet, as was suggested, the humans who appear in the novel are incompetent. It is as if nature has triumphantly appropriated the products of human art, leaving humans bereft, while at the same time bringing life on Earth – indeed, in the universe – to an end. It's a high price to pay for unearthly but jewelled beauty, but from sentence to sentence the novel is prepared to pay it. It might be commented that, no matter how beautiful the crystallisation is, there is a lot of beauty and preciousness elsewhere in the world, and this is now about to be obliterated. The novel's recourse is to pull as much as possible of this into the crystallisation – birds, trees, jewels, effects of light, works of art, indeed birds, trees and jewels *as* works of art, this being the effect of the process of crystallisation. We can entertain the illusion that the crystallisation includes as well as obliterates the beauty of the world.

The phenomenon that is transforming the world and will transform the universe involves a change in Time; in crystallisation, we are told, 'the element of time replaces the role of light' (81; IM 81). The novel's explanations of this are given with Ballard's usual confident fluency. The aesthetic trumps the scientific in *The Crystal World*, however, and shortly we will examine the temporal qualities of the process and the products of transformation as they are imaged rather than as they are explained. It is, however, useful to begin by examining the world in which the novel is set – the jungle and the bewildered or obsessive personages who wander through it.

Heart of Light

The point of reference is Conrad's *Heart of Darkness* – not the historical setting of Conrad's novel, the Congo in the time of Leopold of Belgium, but the mythos, the imagined realm, which Conrad's novel creates.[17] We arrive at the coast of Africa in chapter 1, 'The Dark River', proceed upriver and enter a forest where ordinary rules and realities are abandoned. It's a 'landscape without time' (19); the river is 'like an immense snake' (25), a 'sleeping snake' (47), the dawn illuminates 'the serpentine course of the river as if revealing a secret pathway' (57; this and the preceding quotation fall resonantly at the ends of their chapters). As for the forest, 'there is something minatory and oppressive about its silence' (31). We even have 'sombre', one of Conrad's favourite words (13, 22: 'Suzanne's sombre beauty', 58 and 65, of the forest). The crowd of lepers waiting helplessly on the fringes of the forest outside the hospital, to which they are not admitted, can remind us of the wood of the dying African slaves in *Heart of Darkness*, as can the African encountered by the track 'dying quietly' at Sanders's feet a bit later (143).[18] Ballard borrows and varies Conrad's imagery of light and dark, white and black: the white bandages on the black African (126; and see 198) echo the white cotton around the neck of the African in the wood of the dying slaves. All these echoes and variations thicken the atmosphere of powerful gloom and obsession, and prepare us for a world in which time and identity will be transformed. The tangle of insights into colonialism along with fears and horrors about Africa, Africans and Kurtz that Marlow has to cope with, that is, the human and political concerns of *Heart of Darkness*, are surpassed in a process of dehumanisation, and, as already suggested, the life of this jungle is not that of rampant primitive fertility but of intricate artifice.

The time and place of the novel are unspecific, colonial rather than post-colonial, and redolent of the colonial imaginary (Conrad, Graham Greene, Edgar Wallace) more than of colonial history. *The Crystal World* was published in 1966, and is ostensibly set in Cameroon, which achieved independence in 1960, but all the important characters

---

[17] See McCarthy 1997, 302: 'Ballard denied that *The Drowned World* was influenced by Joseph Conrad's *Heart of Darkness*, claiming that he had not read Conrad's African tale before writing [*The Drowned World*] and might not have read it even by the time he wrote *The Crystal World* (1966).' McCarthy refers to Gregory Stephenson's discussion of *Heart of Darkness* and *The Crystal World* in his *Out of the Night and into the Dream: A Thematic Study of the Fiction of J. G. Ballard*, 1991.

[18] Conrad 1973, 24–25.

are European, and Africans appear only as subordinates – servants, onlookers, Thorensen's violent sidekicks.[19] There is a helicopter (which crashes when it flies too low and its rotors are crystallised), there is a reference to the conflict in Katanga (49), but little to locate us in the 1960s rather than in some unspecific earlier period. Many of the main characters are given surnames with quite definite associations, but these seem random in that they don't fall into any pattern, though as will be seen the novel is rigorously patterned in other ways:[20] Sanders (Edgar Wallace's Sanders of the River, appropriate in that the river is very important in the novel, but ironical in every other way);[21] Radek (the bolshevik: no relation to the Radek of the novel); Balthus (the controversial painter of young girls: no relation to the Balthus of the novel); Ventress (perhaps Ventris the decipherer of Linear B: if so, a random association); Aragon (surrealist poet, no relation to the Aragon in the novel, who figures as an enigmatic Charon). We can find a mythic pattern in the action of *The Drowned World* (see above, 138–140), but Ballard refuses this in *The Crystal World*, and perhaps the associations that go nowhere are a sign of this refusal, though it is true that characters' names are often deliberately empty in Ballard's novels. You would, for instance, get nowhere with the name Ransom in *The Drought*, while the same name in C. S. Lewis's trilogy of science-fiction novels is freighted with implication.[22]

Even the location is mythical rather than specifically African; there are scarlet macaws, which do not belong in Africa, and golden orioles, which can be found there but are more characteristically Eurasian birds (203).[23] After *The Wind From Nowhere*, each of Ballard's apocalyptic novels

---

[19] Brigg (1994) locates the novel in 'French West Africa' (49), 'a French equatorial colony' (50); this is basically right, though we are told, 'Politically, this isolated corner of the Cameroon Republic was still recovering from an abortive coup ten years earlier' (*The Crystal World*, 12).

[20] The female characters are more often denoted by their first names – Suzanne, Serena, Louise – and the male by their surnames; indeed, Sanders is sometimes more formally called 'Dr Sanders'; but the practice was common in literature of this period.

[21] Wallace's novel was published in 1911; the film directed by Zoltan Korda is from 1935.

[22] C. S. Lewis, *Out of the Silent Planet* (1938), *Perelandra* (1943), and *That Hideous Strength* (1945). Lewis's Ransom begins as Everyman and ends as Christ. (Ransome is, however, the name of the main character in Conrad's *The Shadow Line*.)

[23] Or perhaps Ballard liked the exoticism of scarlet macaws and couldn't be bothered checking. See the salutary and witty discussion of writers' mistakes in Barnes 1984, chapter 6.

refuses the imperatives – and the pleasures – of practical making do that many apocalyptic and post-apocalyptic novels respond to; *The Crystal World* also refuses history and politics, though these were pressing in *Heart of Darkness*, its direct model.[24]

'I doubt if any of you really know what you're after' (139)

Sanders, like the central male characters in most of Ballard's fiction from early to late, from, for instance, *The Drought* to *Super-Cannes*, is a drifting, uncertain, isolated person, not just a witness, but not much of an agent either. Gasiorek (2005) sees him as a quester. I see the point, but his questing often seems a wandering. His past has left him carrying the memory of failures and compromises, never detailed, but usually involving a failed, or faded out, marriage or affair. Like Ransom in *The Drought*, Sanders is a doctor who has slight interest in practising his profession. He seems to have come to Port Matarre to seek out his ex-lover Suzanne, though he doesn't really think about why, and his liaison with Louise, Suzanne's counterpart, light as against dark, enables him to set himself indecisively between the two women for most of the novel, as well as enabling Ballard to add to his structuring pattern of contrasts. Once Sanders makes it upriver to Mont Royal and the crystal forest, he finds Ventress and Balthus, two men with whom he had become involved at Port Matarre, already mysteriously present, and then finds himself entangled with Ventress and with Thorensen. This pair are violent rivals for the wan, bedridden Serena.[25] There follows a pattern of repetitions: each antagonist uses Sanders as ally, confidant and decoy; each sends him off into the forest with guides who neglect to guide him. The effect is that the forest dominates the scene and with its strangeness and beauty asks for a new kind of behaviour from the humans who now wander it; they know this, but they are continually distracted into violence, and fall into repetition. Further, amidst all this icy, hard-edged but enthralling beauty their actions seem clumsy. Thorensen smashes his

---

[24] Baxter 2009 provides a contrary reading. The novel is seen as a 'critique of emergent US Neo-Imperialism' (39), the crystallisation signifies the spectacular in Debord's sense (49) and 'critical distance' and 'critical agency' are asked of Sanders (50–51). Baxter's reading of *The Drowned World* is similar; Strangman is seen as a Situationist (30–32), and Beatrice and Kerans are allotted critical duties, which they fail to perform (30, 33).

[25] Serena is 'Emerelda' in 'The Illuminated Man'; Ballard dropped the Emerelda/emerald pun when he wrote *The Crystal World*. He does have Sanders refer to Thorensen as 'a rough diamond', however (89).

cruiser through the crystallisation that is coating the surface of the river by shooting off his cannon; the boat does advance but it is wrecked in the process. Sanders saves Radek, who seems to be in danger of being killed by the encrustations growing on him, by tying a branch across his shoulders and launching him into what remains of the river's current; Radek doesn't want to be saved, and staggers back into the forest still bearing the branch across his shoulders. Sanders himself runs through the forest 'propellering' his encrusted arm before he finds Balthus's chapel, and contact with the jewelled crucifix melts the growth away. These actions and episodes are sometimes haunting and strange as we would expect in this forest, but it is as if we are given only fragments of the order that usually emerges in fantasy; for instance, the discovery that jewels can dissolve the crystallisations results in no further order, no further coherence in the actions of the characters, which remain sporadic and repetitive.

Characters deceive one another (Ventress deceives Sanders and uses him as a decoy), withhold information (79: Sanders with Radek; 162: Sanders with Max Clair), postpone decision or suggest that a decision was unconsciously formed some time earlier so they can now proceed without needing to decide. Feeling becomes mood, rumination sets action or motive in the past or the unconscious. When Sanders realises that Suzanne has leprosy,

> He realized that he had been waiting for Suzanne to catch the disease, that for him this had probably been her one valid role. (158)

We are left to guess what 'valid' means here. As Louise says, 'Edward, for a man so uncertain of his real nature you can be very calculating' (168). There's a wonderfully characteristic moment near the end of the novel:

> 'Someone's got to make a decision' [Sanders says to Louise – and then:]
> 'Actually, I haven't made up my mind yet.' (215)

He does journey back to the forest on the last page of the novel, but whether this is because he has made a decision, or because Aragon and his boat have reappeared and made it easier for him to do so, is hard to say.

All this registration of clumsiness and repetition, of complexity of motive and feeling, makes a contrast with the process that transforms the forest, which is beautiful, inexorable, precise. The end of the world does not come from humans, as it does in many apocalyptic fictions, and it mainly underlines their uncertainties and obsessions, their sheer lack of elegance and intricate beauty. Meanwhile the beauty that is produced is imagined in terms of human art and craft, though never anything modern, or anything primitive or primeval (as is the case with the call of the Sun in *The Drowned World*); the descriptions and images evoke the medieval and baroque.

'Jewelled Words' (210)

The Crystal World is a work of art about nature as a work of art. Both things, the text and what is imagined in it, are clearly structured; the descriptors the text applies to the crystallisations – 'trellis', 'lattice' – might equally apply to the patterns by which the text organises its material. The shape of the novel is clear and its artfulness hard to miss. In a formula, we could say that dualistic contrasts structure the text, which moves towards an ambiguous synthesis or surpassing of the contrasts.

The approach of death is underlined on the first page of the novel, where 'the straggle of warehouses and small hotels that constituted Port Matarre' is 'like the pavilions of an abandoned necropolis' (11; see IM 99); Arnold Böcklin's painting 'Island of the Dead' is referred to a few pages later (14); and when the enigmatic and deceptive Ventress is told that the incubation period for leprosy can be 30 years he responds, 'Like Death. Good' (17). Sanders sums up in a letter to a friend:

> It's obvious to everyone now that in the forest life and death have a different meaning from that in our ordinary lack-lustre world. Here we have always associated movement with life and the passage of time, but from my experience within the forest near Mont Royal I know that all motion leads inevitably to death, and that time is its servant. (102)

These remarks begin to associate the jewelled fixity of the forest with death, and the connection of treasure that is located in an exotic place (under the sea, on a tropical island) with death and corpses is a traditional one, though it is perhaps only in Ariel's song in *The Tempest* that the treasure is made by nature rather than hidden in it.[26] Other remarks and images suggest a different consummation. 'You make

---

[26] Francesco Orlando details the trope (2006, 306–312); his examples include Sinbad the Sailor, *Paradise Lost*, *Das Rheingold*, 'The Gold-Bug' (Poe), *Treasure Island*, and *Nostromo*.

it sound like a New Jerusalem', says Max to Suzanne, his wife and Sanders's lover (173); Sanders sees the dancing lepers in the forest as celebrating 'their new-found paradise' and shortly after that he revives a leper child with the jewelled cross that Balthus has given him for his own protection.[27] These suggestions are ambiguous; Suzanne is afflicted with leprosy, the cross is a kind of antidote to the crystallisation and those such as Suzanne, Radek and Ventress who seek a kind of salvation in the forest all seem deranged. Yet the forest is depicted both as a place of inexorable blind process and as the scene of the wonderful. Towards the end of the novel, Sanders regrets that he has left it:

> [H]e had felt like the empty projection of a self that still wandered through the forest with the jewelled cross in his arms, re-animating the lost children he passed like a deity on his day of creation. (216)

It's no surprise that the very end of the novel finds him again journeying upriver to the forest. (*The Day of Creation* (1987) is Ballard's later novel about the emergence and burgeoning and then drying up of a river in Africa.)

The pattern of light and dark, black and white, that structures the novel is laid out for us explicitly (44) and discussed by the characters (87, 170): day and night, Louise (day) as against Suzanne (night); Ventress (white suit) as against Balthus (the priest's dark soutane); a game of chess; white bandage on black skin, dark sunglasses on white face (Louise). Just as the crystallisation produces reflections, indeed is a process of endless replication, so there are patterns of counterparts and doublings among the characters, as when Louise seems a younger version of Suzanne, and of images of reflection, as when Sanders imagines he is seeing a dark reflection of himself, only for this to emerge as one of Thorensen's African servants, who attacks him with a knife (115). The images are sometimes complex, as in the way the novel associates the forest both with death and with renewal; for instance, the river is dark, 'serpentine', in Conradian style, but also a source of safety because water is slower to crystallise (this is why Sanders immersed the crystallising Radek in it). Nonetheless it seems fair to say that just as the process of crystallisation produces hard, jewel-like

---

[27] And see 'The Illuminated Man': 'I had a curious premonition, of intense hope and longing, as if I were some fugitive Adam chancing upon a forgotten gateway to the forbidden paradise' (91). The forgotten gateway might echo H. G. Wells's story 'The Door in the Wall' (1911). *The Drowned World* ends with an image of Kerans as a second Adam.

fixity, so the imagery of the novel lends the text a fixed structure, maybe a lattice or trellis.

To investigate this further it is necessary to define the kind of art that nature makes in *The Crystal World*. Here are some recurring words and images – examples could be found on almost every page; every encounter between Ballard and what he is creating and evoking for us prompts more images and descriptions. Words: 'myriads', 'pavillion', 'baroque', 'embellished', 'encrusted', 'congealed', 'annealed', 'diaphanous', 'glacé', 'heraldic', 'transparent', 'translucent', 'conflagration'. This already gives the flavour: a touch of Yeats's jewelled bird, out of nature, a touch of Wallace Stevens perhaps, a resemblance to the paintings of Gustave Moreau with their extensively worked surfaces like coloured reliefs. It is possible that not one of these words appeared in any of the texts discussed in chapter 2: a sign of the spectacular entrance of Ballard as stylist into the world of science fiction. These impressions might suggest something too deliberately opulent and ornate, and indeed that is part of the effect – again, something as far from the Nature of grass and sparrows and daisies as possible, a repudiation of the traditional English pastoral.

Ballard delights in a resonant paradox: 'now rainbows glowed in the dead man's eyes' (121; said of Radek, who is not actually dead at this point). He pushes a comparison as far as it will go, or further: Louise's body lying next to Sanders is said to be 'like a piece of the sun, a golden odalisque trapped for Pharaoh in his tomb' (177; why 'trapped for Pharaoh in his tomb'? and who is Pharaoh? – surely not Sanders; here the elaboration of a schema – Louise as woman of the light, Suzanne as woman of the night – and a theme – the approach of death – has led Ballard into lushness).

Ballard's descriptions often render the sheer strangeness of the crystallisations: 'a congested mass of rhomboidal spears like the barbs of a reef' (85; IM 82); 'huge fragments of opalescent candy' (106; IM 93). More often, however, the evocation is of the exotic, intricate and expensively worked piece of art or craft:

> This huge jewelled gauntlet, like the coronation armour of a Spanish conquistador, was drying in the sun, its crystals beginning to emit a hard vivid light. (61)

The phrasing catches the paradox of fixity (something hard and jewelled) and process (the gauntlet beginning to dry, but still emitting a light that is 'hard'). The associations are usually with the intricate art or craft of the past, 'medieval Japanese jeweller's art' (40), 'heraldic beasts carved from jade and quartz' (101), 'exquisite curlicues and helixes' (106 – on furniture; IM 93 – on a house), 'intricate crests and cartouches' (185; IM 99), 'exotic minarets and baroque domes' (92; IM 87), a cannon 'transformed into a medieval firing-piece, its breach embellished with exquisite horns and crests' (196). The prose has a formal elegance:

> the water ahead was touched by a roseate sheen, as if reflecting a distant sunset or the flames of a silent conflagration. (83; IM 81)

The sunset is 'distant', the conflagration 'silent', adding to the effect of subtlety in 'touched'; and there is another instance of reflection. Here is another, itself redoubled:

> After the endless glimmer of the vitrified forest the trees along the road, the ruined hotel and even the two men with him appeared to be shadowy images of themselves, replicas of illuminated originals in some distant land at the source of the petrified river. (150)

The sentence is shaped towards its dying fall, with the rhyme of 'petrified' and 'vitrified'.

A final example:

> Embedded at various points were the almost motionless forms of birds with outstretched wings, golden orioles and scarlet macaws, shedding brilliant pools of light. The bands of colour moved through the forest, the reflections of the melting plumage enveloping them in endless concentric patterns. The overlapping arcs hung in the air like the votive windows of a city of cathedrals. Everywhere around them Sanders could see countless smaller birds, butterflies and insects, joining their cruciform haloes to the coronation of the forest. (203; IM 103)[28]

It's a kind of cadenza, with its sound patterns ('melting ... enveloping ... endless concentric ...') and its succession of mutations, from pools of light to bands of colour to overlapping arcs, and then to a city of cathedrals and the coronation of the forest. We are not going to quibble over the exact point of 'votive' and 'cruciform'; they contribute to a general air of the sacred. Chapter 1 touched on the late arrival of modernism in 1960s science fiction; with Ballard the point is strengthened if Walter Pater is counted as an early modernist.

---

[28] The golden oriole also appears in a slightly different image at IM 94. Gasiorek (2005, 53) notes the echo of Yeats.

The forest is at the centre of the novel; the process of encasing it in a series of image patterns (for instance, reflection and replication) is at the centre of the writing. The prose is cool, almost fastidious, calculated, commanding:

> At sunset, when the disk is veiled by the crimson dust, it seems to be crossed by a distinctive lattice-work, a vast portcullis that will one day spread outwards to the planets and the stars, halting them in their courses. (212; IM 106)

A delicate effect of colour (again), a medieval artefact (again) and, at the same time, the End of the Universe.

At the end of the novel, Sanders returns to the forest, and no doubt he will submit himself to crystallisation – both a death and a transmutation into something jewelled and beautiful. This outcome, however, has less salience than Kerans's journey towards his death and the realm of the omnipotent Sun in *The Drowned World*. It is not humanity – even as dehumanised into crystal – that occupies the centre of the novel's attention, but the eerie beauty and endless creativity of the processes the text observes with such fascination. Crystallisation is both the catastrophe and the new state of being in this apocalyptic novel, and this takes one tendency in Ballard's imagination of apocalypse about as far as it can go. A condition for this development is the split between characters, always uncertain and drifting, and here more wayward even than before, and the impersonal narration, the 'omniscient narrator' and 'the absolute terms of omniscient description', as Peter Brigg says (1994, 51, 47). The language is both precise and lyrical, providing the unexpected word and the suggestive simile; the language comes as if from another planet, an observant but indifferent Martian, or Flaubertian; the characters are floundering about in the forest. The narrator is making a world as one might make a work of art; the characters are suffering it. The question of where the narration is coming from has received a variety of answers in the novels discussed so far – from a rational but immersed witness, from the point of view of a domestic group isolated from the global catastrophe and coping in a more domestic setting, or in the case of Arthur C. Clarke, partly from the burdened view of the alien Overlords and partly from a position of editorial wisdom. Ballard's answer emerges more and more clearly over the course of this sequence of apocalyptic novels: omniscient, impersonal to the point of inhuman, detached to the point of separate.

In Ballard's apocalypses we have a terrible simplification and reduction: everything is reduced to dry sterility, to teeming tropical life under the unrelenting Sun, to relentless, unstoppable and beautiful processes of crystallisation. Ballard seizes with a new ruthlessness and certainty on a feature of any apocalypse – any apocalypse reduces natural and social life to itself, and no independent plot or behaviour has much chance. Practical activity, which is what Ballard's protagonist refuses in favour of the drift towards death, is something of a distraction or stopgap in science-fiction apocalypses, in that anything one does is trivial against inexorable global catastrophe, and the main character in most science-fiction apocalypses figures more as a witness. Ballard enforces the logic of this as he sees it: resistance is futile, one must embrace what the apocalypse means, a reduction towards death.

Chapter 4

Apocalypse in 1969
Brian Aldiss and Angela Carter

Barefoot in the Head and *Heroes and Villains* present apocalypse as release into pleasure, even indulgence, and thereby make a contrast with Ballard's apocalyptic novels of the 1960s, where the release is palpable but is, ultimately and inexorably, towards oblivion. They share a fullness of expression, a grasping of possibilities, that can be seen as reflecting the basic condition and achievement of the counter-cultural 1960s – the expansion of feeling and imagination, the desire to be honest that accompanies the enjoyment of the uninhibited.[1] This counter-cultural enthusiasm was no doubt often clumsy, incoherent and self-important, and its expressions require from us some suspension of hindsight if they are to be appreciated. With *Barefoot in the Head* and *Heroes and Villains*, vitality, exuberance and readiness to improvise and go over the top, is the reader's reward. There is a clear difference between these texts, and it can be related to the two phases in the history of sexuality that overlapped and clashed in the 1960s, the sexual revolution, to call it that, and the gender revolution. The pleasures of *Barefoot in the Head* are mostly those of language, of play with language. It is not interested in relations between the sexes, or indeed in relations at all; it is interested in what can be said, on how language can be turned every which way. There is more talk about sex than sex, and the female characters in the novel are not of much interest and not given much to do. The philosophy the novel plays with for a while is 'Man the Driver': mobility, change, onwardness and a don't-look-back energy. There's no real point in labelling the philosophy masculine, or masculinist, but 'Man' the Driver seems right. *Heroes and Villains*,

---

[1] Arthur Marwick in his history of the sixties (1998) shows how widespread this urge and movement for frankness and honesty was – reaching beyond sexual explicitness in art, the liberalisation of censorship and the provocative bluntness of radicals and demonstrators.

published the same year as *Barefoot in the Head*, is similarly rich and exuberant in its imagery, and similarly concerned with pleasure, but it exploits the openness and disorder of the post-apocalyptic world to explore the relations of men and women: sensuous, brutal, fluctuant. It reflects on the feminist revolution in that it imagines how openness about power and sexuality between women and men brings with it new and involving vistas and problems.

Barefoot in the Head: A European Fantasia[2]

With *Barefoot in the Head* and with *Report on Probability A* (1968), Aldiss is seizing the chance to experiment. His earlier post-apocalyptic novel, *Greybeard* (1964), belongs with the novels discussed in chapter 2 in its quiet unfolding and its pastoralism; later he will return to the procedures of genre science fiction in his great Helliconia trilogy, elaborating cultures, religions, political histories and natural histories on his invented planet, while narrating the failure of empire and the fragility and violence of civilisation. In *Barefoot in the Head* technology (cars, film-making) roams free but civilised order has ended, and the fact that the war with the Arabs has abolished European hegemony is unlamented.[3] *Barefoot in the Head* alludes several times to the traditional apocalypse (the Messiah, the New Jerusalem), though it also alludes to a great deal else. In *Barefoot in the Head* Aldiss initiates the expression and elaboration of apocalypse as breakdown of ontological as well as of social coherence, something that recurs in very different guises in Doris Lessing's *The Memoirs of a Survivor*, China Miéville's *Kraken*, Jeff VanderMeer's *Dead Astronauts* and Jeff Noon's *Falling Out of Cars*.[4] *Barefoot in the Head* combines clever and at times frantic language play (puns, poems, allusions, coinages) with an embrace of sex, drugs and rock and roll. This combination can stand for the presence and varying influence of much wider cultural shifts, running their course from exaltation to disillusionment in the 1960s and 1970s, but leaving behind more substantial changes, and also more testing problems to be engaged with. The *images* of eccentricity that Ballard and

---

[2] References are to Brian W. Aldiss, *Barefoot in the Head: A European Fantasia*, London: Faber, 1969.

[3] *Helliconia Spring* (1982), *Helliconia Summer* (1983) and *Helliconia Winter* (1985).

[4] In *Falling out of Cars* (2002) an epidemic disease has affected memory and language, breaking continuities and connections, making sustained action difficult. The novel's three protagonists wander through a series of places that are like tableaus or pavilions, and are sometimes granted momentary glimpses of coherence in these places.

Aldiss provide with enthusiasm – Charteris's motley crew in *Barefoot*, the carnivalesque grotesques in their weird costumes in Ballard – are best seen in the long run as placeholders. Diversity is imaged rather than investigated. Investigation of choice and freedom, the body, pleasure and pain, takes place at another level in later apocalyptic novels, still in the shadow of death and potential annihilation.

The Prophet as Hedonist

Barefoot in the Head is the story of a prophet, Colin Charteris, who proclaims his message and gathers his disciples in the wake of apocalypse, the Acid Head War, in which 'PCA' (Psycho-Chemical Aerosol) bombs were dropped on Europe by the Arabs. These bombs blew the minds of most of the population, who now stumble about confusedly in the aftermath. 'Wesciv' has disintegrated. Authority survives only in enclaves, themselves unstable and tatty. Cities are drab, darkened, decaying – we see this especially in the scenes set in England (for instance, 94, 106), but France, not directly affected by the war, in which it stayed neutral, is if anything drearier (17). People are moody, unstable, inclined to violence, but ready for a good time, if someone will offer it to them. Charteris does so, unleashing and embodying a different sort of release from the conventional and orderly than what is found in Ballard's apocalyptic novels of the 1960s.

Charteris is actually Serbian, and has named himself after Leslie Charteris, the author of the books starring The Saint, Simon Templar: he is called 'the Simon Temple of himself' (135); later when he becomes a prophet and moves towards becoming the desired 'new messiah' (46) he is called a saint.[5] We first meet him in Metz, heading across France to Dover, thence, meandering by impulse and chance encounter, to London, Loughborough, back to the continent and via a violent sojourn in Brussels, to Strasbourg. He is gradually shedding – or losing – irrelevant or alternative selves (this is depicted literally; 50), accumulating companions and followers, and refining a philosophy of possibilities into a prophetic spiel that consolidates his power and enables him to follow his impulses. Like many a prophet, he goes with the flow; unlike many, he commits himself to no firm predictions, since the essence of his position is that

---

[5] Leslie Charteris (1907–93) had himself changed his name, and was born in Singapore to an English mother and a Chinese father. The Saint ran from 1962 to 1969. *Barefoot in the Park* is dated 1963 (play by Neil Simon) and 1967 (film).

everything should be as open as possible. It is suggested that Charteris realises that he has to avoid being pinned down or trapped as Christ was, for instance in his death. At Strasbourg, where his meander across Europe comes to a halt in encounters with the epicene police chief Laundreis, he parts from his disciples and heads into retirement as an enigmatic sage, and eventual placid death (this part of the novel is based on anecdotes about Gurdjieff). So far, so good, as regards the plot, or anyway the progression of scenes that makes up the bones of a text that has a lot of flesh on it and many colourful swathes of garments on top of that.

Picaresque Chaos

This hectic plot summary might begin to give an impression of the post-apocalyptic chaos that is collected round Charteris and his trajectory and the encounters that punctuate it, but it misses what is extraordinary about the novel, a 'fantasia' indeed. What is extraordinary about the novel is its language. *Barefoot in the Head* is written in a mad, joyous, anything-goes stream of consciousness, marked by puns, as many puns as can be improvised, and by thickets of imagery that mostly replace rather than serving description and enactment; more on the puns and other linguistic inventions and decorations in a moment.

The book began as a series of stories in *New Worlds* and it remains a collection of interludes, with jumps in between to new settings. Aldiss made changes before publishing the work as a novel.[6] There are interchapters, added for the novel, consisting of songs and poems that replay the feelings and images of the rest of the text, and usually echo the shape of the incidents in the preceding chapter. The poems in turn are varied – games with syllables, concrete poems, poems in stanzas with (some) rhymes, renditions of popular songs, a 'Fragment of a Much Longer Poem'.

Each interlude revolves around an encounter between Charteris and someone met by the way, or attracted to his growing fame and notoriety – for instance, the chambermaid in the hotel in Metz; here Charteris has a vision of himself at the heart of a web of interconnectedness, and it is symptomatic of this interconnectedness that the maid is called Angelina, overlapping with Charteris's girlfriend Angeline. Rather than being

---

[6] Aldiss and Wingrove (1986, 256) comment on two early novels by James Gunn: 'Both suffered from a difficulty more widespread at that period than today: the problem of structuring a coherent novel from disparately published short stories and novellas on a common theme.'

agents, people are nodes in a web, or symbols (35), and are often as it were disseminations of Charteris himself in that bits of what might have been associated with him as new messiah are instead connected to them.

Each interlude is more chaotic than the last, and the text is carefully modulated in that respect. This modulation, plus the exuberant writing, is what carries the shape and structure of *Barefoot in the Head*, more than the wisps of plot. Metz is drab (a gloomy almost-deserted hotel, a canal filled with rubbish outside the window); Loughborough is more crowded, but at this point individual acolytes can still be singled out as having their own fairly straightforward purposes; Brussels is much more sinister and violent, culminating in mayhem in the main square after the intended showing of Nick Boreas's film of a car crash turns into a psychedelic light and colour show and then a riot; Strasbourg begins a diminuendo in the text, teeters between farce and pornography, and resembles the scenes in the Zone in Pynchon's *Gravity's Rainbow* (1973). (The interpolated poems and goofy songs can also remind us of Pynchon, though Aldiss's poems are on the whole better.)

There are flashbacks, for instance to Charteris's memories of when he couldn't make it to his father's funeral and was stuck on the other side of a river – a scene repeated and varied at the Rhine late in the novel when he is challenged to walk across the water and seems to appear on the other bank as if he had (62–63, 239–240). There are flashes to a reminiscence of a scene with Gurdjieff in Moscow. There are transferences or bleedings across, for instance in the episode with the Koninkrijks, where Marta (like Charteris) is haunted by her father, and Jan sets off, after Marta has left with Charteris, to seek a woman in a hotel in Maastricht who seems an echo of the maid in the hotel in Metz whom Charteris encountered.

'Man the Driver', a quasi-futurist philosophy of speed and danger, is emphasised at first; it modulates into scenes of car wrecks, and finds a parallel expression, another sideways leakage, in Boreas's film, and then leaks out of the novel. Likewise, the notion that one has a series of 'I's', egos that peel off and go their separate ways, is literalised frighteningly in the early scene in which Charteris arrives in Dover: the Charteris that we have been with sees his (other) self driving away and realises the latter is 'a discarded alternative' (50). Then it fades out of the novel, perhaps because Charteris has accepted that his I, the I that stays with him or that we stay with in the text, is itself a fuzzy, indeterminate thing. The latter notion congeals into a series of images of and references to photographs, carrying the idea that each instant of our lives can be taken as a photo and discarded. All this – the text's accumulation of leakages and shifts and short circuits of meaning and situation across times and persons – can be seen as reflecting the state of addiction that most people are stuck in since the Acid Head War. More interestingly, it can also be seen as reflective of the new temporality and logic of the post-apocalypse, in which the old rules and reasons, sequences and separations, no longer apply. Charteris is trying to exploit, encourage and understand this new condition as he intuits his way into his role as prophet, so he evolves a philosophy, or at least a set of attitudes and assertions, of multivalency, of not either/or but both – and more than both, many. This philosophy is most successfully and enjoyably expressed in Aldiss's puns and other games with language.

Carnival of Language

The art of the puns here is the art of doubleness, or tripleness, the art of having several meanings shoot off at tangents from a single word – meanings sometimes counteracting one another, sometimes connecting with other suggestions, half-meanings that had shot off from other puns. This verbal play expresses the notion of networks and nodes as replacing linear before-and-after, and expresses the condition of meaning being liberated and disseminated and never settling. Charteris also articulates this condition more directly in his prophetic raves, and he lives it out in his refusals to take decisions, to be pinned down, to be faithful or loyal. Ballard in his apocalyptic novels asserts that catastrophe has brought about a new temporality (see, for instance, *The Drought*, 120, and *The Drowned World*, 58) but his narratives retain an onwards drive as they carry their protagonist towards death or transformation, and, as was suggested above, catastrophe in Ballard simplifies and reduces, as well as releasing new energies. Aldiss goes further, in this respect.

The art of the novel's word-play cannot but remind the reader of James Joyce, but this influence can be overstated: John Lennon (*A Spaniard in the Works*, 1965) is equally relevant. We have an inrushing of modernist style but also a particularly English playfulness of the sort that flourished in the 1960s. There are puns and portmanteaus – where two or more different meanings, or meaning-traces, fly apart, and where two or more different meanings or meaning-traces are jammed together. There are coinages, some of them making a set of allusions to other science-fiction writers, Heinlein (223), Spinrad (225), Van Vogt (249) and so on; but the puns and portmanteaus are already coinages.[7] There are allusions

---

[7] Some examples: Masadistrick (248), gadarine (as a verb, 171), lemanster (183; Le Mans roadster), marakeshed (181), exinbintion (159 – somehow

and echoes, fragments of quotation in drastically new contexts ('Time like a never-rolling stream', 223; 'We shall all follow that impulse to the last fracture and serial of recorded time', 107).[8] There is play with names – the names of suburban streets – Herbivore Drive, Woodbine Walk, Placenta Place – and the names of bungalows – Neptune Tiles, The Bushes, Shaggy Shutters (43–44); the running through of a *combinatoire* of syllables ('Such sounds seemed sexplicable, nexplicable, inexplicable, plicable, lickable, ickable, able, sickable' (177)). We have systems of allusion, for instance to the story of Christ (the crucifixion, John the Baptist, the agony in the garden). Laundrei who is just about to offer himself as Charteris's John the Baptist says, 'I I have watched an parayed all nightlong now morning climes again and I must make a last taste of you' (236; See Mark, 14, 38). Cass refers to 'our great triumphal entry' into Brussels, and it is Ensor's painting of Christ's entry into Brussels that comes to mind (186). But allusions are liable to shoot off in almost any improvised direction, as when the same Laundrei is termed 'the fat commander', in allusion to the fat controller in the Reverend Awdry's children's books, who in turn has been interpreted as a figure for God. Sometimes the text lurches into 1960s zaniness and whimsy, as with the silly laws passed by the still drug-addled Belgian parliament (157). Elsewhere there are abrupt shifts into understatement ('There had been a war, a dislocation', 51). All this linguistic play and tireless (but sometimes tiring) doubleness or fuzziness of language is where the text responds to the post-apocalyptic condition, the openness of possibility and the chance of a New Jerusalem that rests in the wayward hands of Charteris as messiah. These inventions and improvisations don't exactly *express*, as if their task were instrumental; they take over, they flood the surface of the text, so that actions and characters are figments of the language of the text rather than the other way about. It is as if the text dips into its narrative meander across Europe when it becomes bored with its puns and coinages, its games and inventions.

But it is useful to sample the mad rush of the writing from close up:

> Burton was bellowing something at the top of his voice, but the engines drowned out what he said as they began to roll along the grey deserted front, away from littoral meanings, between echoing shutters and the sea. The new autorace, born and bred

---

Aldiss has smuggled in the World War II slang 'bint', as well as exhibition and inhibition), 'human detestiny' (153), 'this was the spontaneous generation' (151).

[8] From Isaac Watts and *Macbeth*, respectively.

on motorways; on these great one-dimensional roads rolling they mobius-stripped themselves naked to all sensation, beaded, bearded, belted, busted, bepileptic, tearing across the synthetic twen-cen landskip, seaming all the way across Urp, Aish, Chine, leaving them under their reefer-smoke, to the Archangels, godding it across the skidways in creasingsack selleration bitch you'm in us all in catagusts of living. (137)

The passage picks up speed at 'beaded, bearded', and so forth, copies the style but rejects the satirical disdain of Aldous Huxley in 'twen-cen landskip', and hits full speed with the mentions of Europe, Asia and China, with the speed actually splitting words apart in 'increasing acceleration' and 'bitumin', ending at 'catagusts of living', one of a series of variations of words like 'cataclysm' and 'catastrophe'. This is not a breakdown of the signifying chain, such as occurs in the aftermath of apocalypse in Jeff Noon's *Falling Out of Cars*, but it is certainly a stretching and twisting of the chain.

A Second Coming

Barefoot in the Head stages the adventures of Charteris as a kind of Second Coming, with allusions to Christ and assertions that Christianity is past and gone.

> 'Whatever you all think you think you all think in the old stale repeating masadistrick Judeo-Christian rhythm because it's in your bloodshed. Your heritage taken or rejected dominant.'
> ... he saw the old dimensions all shagged out and Christ on the clockwork cross with in his sly brown eyes that frantic glimpse of progress on the astralplane and from our deathbeds that vanvogtian upward surge into heaven's arms. The cult of the third day the White House open to any mother-loving son. (249)

The novel imagines a New Jerusalem, a new condition of humanity, at least of European humanity, a condition in which going back is impossible and there is no alternative to a radical reorientation. It is flooded with images of carnival, of masks, performances, riot and promiscuity. It reflects New Wave science fiction in its embrace of stylistic self-consciousness and experiment and it reflects the late 1960s, a time of somewhat febrile hope and excitement, centred on drugs and rock and roll; the 'Clapton is God' moment for (at least)

British rock fans, or for those more inclined to the queer, it anticipates the Ziggy Stardust moment (1972; rock star as saviour at the end of the world),[9] and maybe also the Woodstock moment (1969): the rock festival as temporary utopian interval. It embraces the notion of the liberated condition as a festive one in which art is freed and sex is everywhere (as in Charteris's riff at 234). So, as regards art, we have the poems in the interchapters; Charteris himself has taken the name of the author of what is in effect fantasy fiction, fiction that stands for his own fantasy of England; in Loughborough his companions include the members of a rock group with shifting names (the Escalation, the Genosides,[10] the Dead Sea Sound); later his anarchic procession across Europe spawns Nick Boreas's film as a kind of side-product, though this certainly doesn't express the joyous side of art (Boreas's previous film appears to have been a snuff movie). But then the 1960s version of festive liberation is itself part of a narrative that always slides downwards – to sordid death, punk machismo, the return of the Right, the war on drugs and so on; if that devolution is clearer in hindsight there are plenty of suggestions of cruelty and waste already in *Barefoot in the Head*.

Discussion now turns to a more focused, less madcap imagination and questioning of apocalyptic liberation into pleasure in Angela Carter's *Heroes and Villains* (1969).

Sex, Death and The Maiden
Heroes and Villains[11]

A juicy, overblown, exploding gothic lollipop
        (Angela Carter's comment on *Heroes and Villains*)

The cataclysm, the great overturn, which figures in *Heroes and Villains*, is not primarily the destruction of the preceding civilisation; it is the change in relations of men and women. It is not that this is dramatised or proposed; it is assumed to have happened, Marianne embodies it

---

[9] David Bowie, *The Rise and Fall of Ziggy Stardust and the Spiders from Mars*, 1972, tells of a messianic rock star who believes he is alien and preaches peace, love and hope as the end of the world approaches; the arrival of the 'infinites' does not bring salvation and leads to Ziggy's death. 'Everything had to be infinitely symbolic' (Bowie as interviewed by *Rolling Stone* in 1993).
[10] *The Genocides* is Thomas M. Disch's apocalyptic novel of 1965.
[11] References are to Angela Carter, *Heroes and Villains*, London: Heinemann, 1969.

without needing to have thought it out and its consequences and pains are explored.

Heroes and Villains is richly descriptive and lyrical. There is room in the luxuriantly natural setting (itself seen as released by the apocalypse's destruction of most of modern civilisation) for a complex but improvised symbolic patterning, involving Adam and Eve, the serpent, snakes, lions and tigers. This also introduces the aesthetic; Marianne sometimes views Jewel as a work of art, and he has a work of art on his back, a tattoo of Adam and Eve and the serpent. This aspect of the novel will need further attention, but in my estimation it complements the depiction of the relationship of Marianne and Jewel – the depiction of their experience of each other – rather than setting the meaning of the novel in a tight structure. The allusions prompt us to think of the distinctness of the relationship and fate of Marianne and Jewel, which is not that of Eve and Adam.

The novel's focal character is Marianne. Marianne grows up among the Villagers who shelter in enclaves of order and organisation, but finds herself living, and experiencing sex and conflict, with Jewel, in a tribe of the other main human group on the post-apocalyptic scene, the Barbarians. The tribe is led by Donally, a modern cynic acting as a tribal shaman, though his power is intermittent. The division between Villagers and Barbarians is conventional – we have repressive and sterile organisation, based on reason, as against unrepressed wandering tribalism, based on ritual, gaudy but superstitious. This dualism is complicated by Marianne and Jewel, who do not represent either group in any stable way. The disaster that destroyed most of the old world has released a rich luxuriance in nature that is easier to associate with the libidinous and wayward Barbarians than with the Villagers who have separated themselves from it in their fortified enclaves. The opening move of the novel has Marianne leave her home in one of the villages and join (and be captured by) the Barbarians, though the rest of the novel centres on her restless, challenging, thwarted feelings as an outsider among them. Marianne's relation to the Barbarians is less stable than Charteris's relation to his followers; her story is a version of a female captivity narrative such as Patrick White's *A Fringe of Leaves* (1976).

The Barbarians are tribal, but Marianne and Jewel, like Donally, are ironic and self-conscious, analytical even. 'I see you are an intellectual' Jewel remarks to Marianne, 'obscurely' (27): this seems like a joke about the passionate, changeable Marianne, but it has a point. Later we have

> 'Had a bad day?' inquired Jewel with some irony.
> 'I haven't decided, yet.' (72)

Not long afterwards Jewel comes across her in the woods, and rapes her, so his question is answered, but afterwards they converse calmly; she hates him, he is afraid of her: even given the rape, their power relations and feelings fluctuate. Later still she refers to 'the Yahoo who raped me yesterday afternoon about what used to be teatime' (87) – not that she places much stock in teatime, or really feels Jewel is a Yahoo. Perhaps only irony could express so many shifts of feeling and such a density of shocking or sensational incident. Jewel and Marianne carry a modernity with them – and one that is more interesting than that of the Professors in the Villages. They act and feel impulsively but watch themselves doing so. The tribalism of the Barbarians was in fact partly invented, by Donally, originally a Professor from the other world of the Villagers, now performing as shaman. He has a plan for Marianne and Jewel, a plan that develops into an ambiguous destiny even while Donally himself loses his power in the tribe.

The Maiden

The novel's opening sentence is, 'Marianne had sharp, cold eyes and she was spiteful but her father loved her' (1). Marianne is feisty, wayward, intelligent, restless and irreverent. She is easily made angry, and enjoys her anger. She is sceptical and abrupt; she stands up for herself, and has an eye for adult absurdity, but she is also readily entranced, taken out of herself – by solitude in the woods (grown very lush as well as wild in this England, if this is England), or by the sex with Jewel that she discovers that she enjoys, and becomes obsessed by. In all this she much exceeds the demands and dimensions of the witness to apocalypse and its aftermath that shape the depiction of many of the protagonists of the novels so far discussed. Ballard's interest in the psyches of his protagonists is inseparable from his imagination of the landscape of his apocalyptic novels; Carter's interest in Marianne's emotional and sexual life challenges the primacy of apocalypse itself, even though apocalypse has released that life. It expresses a different response to the energies of the 1960s than is to be found in Ballard or Aldiss – more engaged, more riskily emotional.

If the two post-apocalyptic groups of humans have been split between the intellectual and the sensuous, the over-rational and the superstitious, then the contrast is worked out in the relations of Marianne and Jewel, with the twist that in important ways neither of them is typical of their respective group. Marianne has wandered away from hers and more or less wilfully joined his; he chafes confusedly at the roles his group puts upon him. And in their relationship they are not only contending with their differences as members of the Villagers and the Barbarians respectively, but also with the contest of man and woman, and with the mysteries of sex.

Jewel is himself an enigmatic, restless character, often cruel and sarcastic, but fearful and gloomy as well. He has been chosen by Donally, to mate with Marianne, and also, as he increasingly feels, for death. A great deal happens between Marianne and Jewel – he rapes her, she is forced to marry him (and he to marry her), he hits her several times, she hits him, she saves his life at least three times, he oppresses her, she desires him, and perhaps also needs him, he fears her: a crowded gamut of possibilities as regards gender relations. For Marianne, Jewel is a source of pleasure, a beautiful thing, someone to resist and to enjoy; to himself he is both a burden and a darkness. Because each has been thrust into intimacy with the other it is understandable that each often regards the other as a specimen of the Other, as the person from the other world that they have to cope with and that they fear, suspect and hold in some contempt, and some awe. Yet each has also chosen this intimacy, though they don't admit to this. The more the complications of liberated libido in Marianne and Jewel pile up in attraction and rejection, enjoyment and sarcasm, the denser the patterns of incident, the more Angela Carter improvises patterns of imagery and symbol in the attempt to structure the meanings of their relations.

Sex

At the beginning Marianne is living in a tower like a fairy-tale princess – then she is shut in her high room because she has misbehaved, and it is from here that she sees a Barbarian (Jewel) kill her brother. (Her seclusion also alludes to that of Shakespeare's Mariana in *Measure for Measure*, and Tennyson's rendition of the same character in his 'Mariana'.) This is a kind of primal scene in her life, the origins of her fascination with the Barbarians and eventual departure with Jewel. Jewel, for his part, is terrified by the sight of 'the severe child who watched him' (8). After a later Barbarian raid, she helps one of the raiders (the same man) who has been wounded; he takes her with him by force (but perhaps she knew he would; 24–26). Her joining the Barbarians, then, is partly willed, partly fated and much of the rest of her time with them – the main part of the novel – is like that. She resists, is caught or forced, succumbs bitterly, finds her own way again, sees through what is going on, is fascinated and disgusted, enjoys sex with Jewel but not a personal relation with him. It's full of Carter's sense that each gender is fascinating and necessary but alien and hostile to the other (see also, for instance, 'The Bloody Chamber', 1979: the bride's feelings about and the story's steamy depiction of the Marquis, Bluebeard).

As for the Barbarians, they seem to express an outpouring of libido, careless, forgetful, violent, infantile (living in their own mess and excrement). This chimes with the land, the woods and marshes around them, almost trackless, bursting with life, dangerous. The high room (set in contrast to the tower where we first see Marianne) in which Marianne and Jewel live after their marriage is open to the elements, a place of darkness, the moon and sex, in which birds from time to time perch and sing (125).

> Marianne could almost feel the wind beneath her feet. It was like climbing up to the moon. At last they reached a little door, so low that Marianne had to stoop, and they entered Jewel's room. It seemed that he preferred the open air, for much of the roof had fallen in, revealing a large expanse of rich, blue night sky scattered with a handful of stars. (106)

The world of the Barbarians is not idealised. The Barbarians are sinking into the nature that they live in (its fluids and their fluids, 'their abominable refuse', 50), and they are dominated by Donally, educated, fluent, a charlatan. They are superstitious, impressed by Donally's invented rites and his sham fits, and inclined to value and to fear Marianne as a stranger from the other world. They belong in the forests and wetlands that are taking over, but not in the cultivated fields that the Villagers protect, and perhaps not in the ruined cities or by the seashore that they trek to at the end of the novel.[12]

In all this the text expresses a sense of release that the old restrictions are gone – an enjoyment of the fecundity of nature (31, 74), even if it is messy and smelly where the Barbarians are squatting in an abandoned mansion; enjoyment of the costumes of the barbarians: furs, tattoos, jewellery, face paint, shiny things. The flamboyant adornment is a kind of play, as well as something that Donally encourages, as he sees himself recreating a primitivism that might need to be invented (but

---

[12] Parrinder (2002, 227) sees these last scenes as Ballardian. The way one incident is based on Henri Rousseau's painting of the lion and the gypsy is like passages recalling works of art in Ballard, with an added touch of reflection: '[The lion] looked exactly like the pictures of itself', *Heroes and Villains*, 198.

then again it might not; not all that many of the Barbarians' habits and decorations seem to be due to him). Donally resembles one of those carnival figures we met in Ballard, decadent violent jokers, such as Lomax and Strangman. He is also like other figures in Angela Carter – dominant, untrustworthy, capricious older males, such as the father in *The Magic Toyshop* (1967).

Death

At the end of the novel Donally is rejected and thrown out of the tribe, though it is uncertain how much this amounts to, because his power over the tribe never seemed secure. The important change comes with the death of Jewel, and leaves Marianne in charge, though she does not want the position. We can possibly see this outcome as the working out of a symbolic pattern, but, if so, it is a shifting pattern.

Donally has made Jewel into a work of art, by means of the tattoo of Adam, Eve, the snake and the apple that covers his back. Donally painfully engraved the tattoo on Jewel when he was 15, and he himself cannot see it. The tattoo is Donally's mark on Jewel, but also perhaps a sign of his frustrated love. Marianne too sometimes sees Jewel as an object, even a specimen she might keep in a huge jar. She wishes to have him as a beautiful object (194). She is equally fascinated, however, by Jewel's long black hair, which several times she rhythmically combs for him, and his hair seems to say something about his richness of nature that is mostly hidden, or only potential – something very different from her feelings about his face, with its 'opaque' eyes and stark bone structure, the latter felt as much as seen. The moments when Marianne combs Jewel's hair, then, suggest something quite different about her feeling about Jewel, and about the clash of the sexes, given that long hair is more stereotypically female (110, 146; and Marianne has cut her hair short, 33), and the men of the tribe are bedecked with jewels and charms. (But they are also violent hunters smeared with the blood and mud of their occupation (65).) Jewel and Marianne sometimes provoke thoughts in the reader about typical masculinity and femininity, and sometimes confuse them. Similarly, the complexity of Marianne's changing feelings about Jewel is such as to sweep the image of the tattoo into its turmoil, and make it difficult to label.

There is a set of images of snakes in the text – the asp that bites Marianne when she and Jewel are escaping from the Village (it is her surviving this bite that suggests to the Barbarians that she is uncanny and powerful); the snake that Donally keeps in a cage as part of his shamanic equipment, which turns out to have been dead and stuffed all along. In relation to the novel as a whole, the tattoo seems to suggest that Marianne will work her way through a revision of the story of Adam and Eve while Jewel will succumb to it. The tattoo is a burden from the past of culture, imposed by Donally: 'Observe the last work of art in the history of the world' (Donally, 135). For Jewel Marianne is the Eve who allies with the snake and brings about his death; for herself she is bitten by the snake but survives, and his death might bring power and a kind of freedom for her as 'the tiger woman'. In this case we connect the tiger and the lion, remembering the moonlit scene when the lion pauses over the sleeping Jewel and then decides not to eat him, and oppose both to the snake, remembering that the snake is associated with Donally as well as with Marianne. But Carter's patterns of imagery and allusion are haunting and not readily to be schematised, so the above interpretation won't take us all that far.

While *Heroes and Villains* emphasises necessity, because the characters are born into tribes that seem predetermined as regards customs and material provision, or even as regards genetics (suggested here by the malformed, half-animal Outcasts who are glimpsed at one point), almost every action in the novel has also a quality of the willed, resisted or gratuitous. This is the field that Carter opens for the characters and the story through the novel's density of incident and lushness of setting. Yet again, if there are these flashes of intuition and waywardness from all the main characters – Marianne, Jewel, Donally, even the idiot boy – who are each given a degree of ironical, self-aware speech, there is also a patterning of images (snakes, knives, towers, lions) that set the characters in archetypal positions.

The characters find themselves experiencing an intensity of desire and need, and also an intensity of separation and hatred. There emerges from this quality a series of stops and starts, convergences with a fate that does not yet come, that is willed and resisted – thinking of killing, saving from death or suicide; treating another as already dead or abstracted, as inanimate, an object, pared to the bare bone;[13] treating the other as hardly individual – a masked appearance, a performance of ritual, a specimen of the other, whether it be the other tribe or the other sex, but mostly both. There is a strong contrast with the fated, determined aspects of the narratives in *Ice* and *The Making of the Representative for Planet 8* to be discussed below. Carter treats a new situation in which

---

[13] See, for instance, 125, just after the wonderful image of the nightjar singing above Marianne and Jewel in their tower room.

new feelings and decisions are possible, and it seems plausible to see this as her response to the energies of the 1960s.

Towards the end, as Jewel approaches his foreseen death, we have the setting of the shore and the ruined resort, and the incident of the lion that comes upon the sleeping Jewel but does not eat him. This makes a series of images of change and loss and gain: the once vulgar resort transformed by the sea, the lion indifferently turning away from the man (though the man wants to die), the names of seaweeds and corals that are now lost and unknown ('all the wonders of the seashore, to which Marianne could scarcely put a name, though everything had once been scrupulously named', 193). This is the lyrical context for the departure of Donally from the tribe, and the death of Jewel. *Heroes and Villains* for all its playfulness and Marianne's stroppiness is involved with transience, loss, growth: Marianne's discovery of sex, Jewel's despair, Marianne's pregnancy, her initiation of the idiot boy into sex, the joyful burning down of the old, many-roomed house, the moment of contact with the lion, as if dreamt.

The death of Jewel is very different from the steadily approaching deaths of Kerans and Sanders in Ballard; it doesn't come from the nature of the apocalypse. It is also different from the deaths in various apocalyptic fictions in which we can see a 'normal', painful individual death substituting for the mass death that the novel can't directly contemplate, as with the death of Joey in *Earth Abides* (discussed above, 95). Nor is the death the completion of a symbolic pattern, as might be argued of the death of Kerans in *The Drowned World*. As in *Ice*, the central relationship captures or surpasses in its energies all the forces released by the disaster (whose event is well in the past in this novel), but Marianne and Jewel are not simply prisoners of their relationship as are the central trio in *Ice*. They are exploring and exploiting their feelings and their intensities of perception and response, though they are also captured by them – marked, as Jewel is by the tattoo; raped, as Marianne is by Jewel; forced to marry, as both are; fated, as Jewel feels he is. Being captured is the cost paid for their release into intensities of perception and response. In this way the apocalypse – the new situation in society and in nature that has followed the nuclear disaster – is not just a pretext for what can then be a freewheeling, picturesque and uninhibited story. It overshadows and conditions what is felt and what happens. The disaster that conditions life in the novel and the new state of affairs it has released are intertwined, but the new state of affairs *is* new – its possibilities prompt the novel's and the characters' continual restless changes of feeling and perception.

Chapter 5

Darker Imaginations, Harder Lessons
Anna Kavan and Doris Lessing

Discussion of developments in apocalyptic fiction in the 1960s and their aftermath now turns to less provocative, less dandified, departures from the traditional science-fiction apocalypse: by Anna Kavan (*Ice*, 1967), and Doris Lessing (*The Memoirs of a Survivor*, 1974, and *The Making of the Representative for Planet 8*, 1982). These are novels in which the shadow of death, waiting at the end of the narrative, is darker than in the novels by Ballard, Aldiss and Carter considered in chapters 3 and 4. This darkness stems from the fact that the protagonists have little room for choice, and no room for play. They are driven (*Ice*), puzzled and confined to witnessing (*Memoirs*), confined to pupillage (*Planet 8*). Apocalypse is all-encompassing, and those facing it are dwarfed and left with little power. Kavan and Lessing move away from emphasis on the individual to consider sets of characters whose relationships are painful (*Ice*), uncertain and shifting (*Memoirs*) or slight (*Planet 8*), but though they return to the collective they do not return to the collective that finds some solidarity in working to cope with disaster, as in the postwar disaster novels. Ballard in effect shunts aside questions of relationship to elaborate a landscape so saturated with the individual's psyche that the individual is emptied out; the secondary characters who perform more violently and wilfully in the space the central character has vacated are isolates, or anti-social in their habits. In *Barefoot in the Head*, Charteris is central, though unattached, wayward and fragmented as a personage. The intimacy of Marianne and Jewel in *Heroes and Villains* often underlines their antagonism or apartness. The apocalyptic novels by Kavan and Lessing to be discussed in this chapter take a different route into investigation of the breakup of the subject. *Ice* is centred on three individuals locked into a relationship that is at once antagonistic and all-defining, even to the point that their selves overlap. *The Memoirs of a Survivor* is also centred on an odd trio, but this time their relationship, conveyed to us by the narration of the Survivor, is shifting, uncertain, puzzling. *Planet 8* treats the fate of a people whose individuals are only roughly, problematically, differentiated.

Ballard and Aldiss departed provocatively from earlier science-fictional apocalypses by abandoning the style of sober reportage for one of wild invention, allusion and image. *Heroes and Villains* is similarly rich in imagery and symbol. Just as the individuals at the centre of these novels are dispersed, shifting and changeable, so the patterns of symbolism and allusion add colour and depth but don't cohere into a schema or progression. Kavan and Lessing are more austere. There are uncanny moments, hard to fathom time-shifts, in Kavan, but on the whole the concentration is on the imprisoning, pathological central relationship and everything else in the novel works to thicken the atmosphere around this relationship. In Lessing the body and its pleasures tend to be rejected, selfhood sought elsewhere, and found if at all only on the last pages of *Memoirs* and *Planet 8*. The pleasures of language are not to be found, and arguably not sought after. In each novel there is a reaching for the authority of pedagogy – the drawing of conclusions, the teaching of lessons. In neither case is this authority really found. In *Memoirs* the survivor offers opinions but hesitates, withdraws; not surprising, as her own position is confined (she never goes outside her apartment) and the situation of the city is shifting and confused. In *Planet 8* the course of events inexorably strips joy, comfort and hope from the inhabitants, while the envoy from Canopus, Johor, teaches by silence and by question. He has no practical remedies to offer, and no consolation. The depths of the psyche appear in a darker light in *Ice*, *Memoirs* and *Planet 8* – painful, unsettling memories surface, rather than transformative energies being released.

The shifts from the 1960s novels of Ballard, Aldiss and Carter to the novels of Kavan and Lessing are marked, then. It's tempting to connect them to the change in feeling and perceived prospects from the 1960s to the 1970s and beyond, a time of political reaction and disillusionment, and a time also when the indulgences of the sexual revolution (in frequent actuality, more fun for men than for women) came under the scrutiny of the gender revolutions led by women and gays.[1] The temptation should probably be resisted. *Ice* was published in 1967, and anyway Kavan is hard to place in any period; even her drug addiction lasted from long before the 1960s to long afterwards. *Ice* would

---

[1] Arthur Marwick discusses the complexities and varieties of the sixties as 'cultural revolution', qualifying many blanket generalisations about it, including mine just now on how it was more fun for men than for women (Marwick 1998; for instance, 680–682).

not have seemed out of place had it been published in the 1930s, when Kavan was already writing. Its haunted atmosphere can be illustrated from an early poem by W. H. Auden:

> The horns of the dark squadron
> Converging to attack;
> The sound behind our back
> Of glaciers calving.[2]

Yet *Ice* makes an impact here because it offers so grim an alternative to Ballard's imagination of the way apocalypse releases a desire for death, and, even more, to the exuberance of apocalypse in Aldiss and Carter, for all that it is accompanied by violence in Aldiss and death in Carter. Lessing's trajectory from feminism to Sufism, and from the novel of social struggle and pain to science fiction, especially in the form it took in her *Canopus in Argo* novels, is a very individual one. It is better to see the two contrasting groups of novels as suggestive of the possibilities of the whole period, liberating and disillusioning, and to infer a pressure to experiment, in language and depiction of the subject, issuing in one instance in the exuberance of Carter and Aldiss and the jewelled words of, for instance, *The Crystal World*, and in another instance in the austerity of *Memoirs* and *Planet 8*.

Ice[3]
Sex and Deadlock

Ice resembles Ballard's apocalypses in that a world in the grip of destruction and devolution intersects with and enlarges a particular, peculiar state of the protagonist's soul. There are three protagonists in *Ice*, but they are so tightly bound together in their relationship as to function, or malfunction, as one person – and this is the nub of the novel.

Ice very definitely has an end of the world setting: an Ice Age is coming, and this will inevitably eliminate all life on Earth, and at the same time as this is happening humanity is being torn apart by relentless obscure wars and rumours of war. Anna Kavan evokes both of these forces very grimly and vividly – the atmosphere of extreme cold, snow, blizzards, and of hostile, icy, monotonous landscapes, glimpses of walls of ice visibly advancing across the sea; and purposeless fighting, grim

---
[2] Auden 1966, 39 ('The Bonfires').
[3] References are to Anna Kavan, *Ice*, New York: Norton, 1967.

destruction, suspicious locals, anonymous troops of callous soldiers, mob violence and helpless refugees (for instance, 103).[4] These images and glimpses recur and recapitulate; we are told that the situation is getting worse, but this is not particularly evident from the passages of scene-setting and evocation, and there are also episodes from the distant past, seeming to erupt into the present – brutal barbarian horsemen, the sacrifice of a girl to the dragon that lives in the depths (53–57). The soldiers, stooges and military leaders or bosses are always impersonal; the countries at war and the causes of war are never named. ('It could have been any town, in any country. I recognised nothing' (104)). The implication is that giving names and details, specifying causes and ideologies, would be pointless. None of the characters has a proper name.

So far, then, we have an apocalyptic novel, catching the sense of doom and imminence, of rumours and emergencies or crises blending into a state of affairs that has made crisis and emergency into routine, and affecting not only societies (a succession of small towns and border regions) but also the climate, the state of Earth. But the coincidence of political breakdown and the advance of the ice begins to change the bearing of the novel, because there's little suggestion that the two are connected, for instance that the climate is being changed by human action, action that might have about it the same selfishness or fecklessness as is probably behind the political disorder (some remarks on p. 22 are an exception). The narrator does feel that the Ice Age and the imminence of extinction is a kind of punishment, but, basically, we have the two disaster-complexes converging so as to produce an atmosphere of maximum gloom and death. Maximum gloom and death in one field is an encroaching Ice Age, maximum gloom and death in another field is political and social breakdown, and the two are combined to produce a world that is completely closed off, closed out.

The narrative centres on two men's pursuit, and virtual enslavement, of a single, fragile and elusive woman. It is as if the constituents of global catastrophe that were just surveyed are drawn into the vortex of this story. The evocations of disorder and disaster frame an obsessive quest, obsessively detailed. The obsessive quester is the narrator. It would not be adequate simply to say we are dealing with a fantasy, because the images of disaster have so much reality. We could borrow

---

[4] At one point the main character asks a contact for news of 'the latest developments': 'It appeared that the situation at home was obscure and alarming, no precise information was coming through, the full extent of the disaster was not yet known' (79). That is, there is no news, just uncertainty.

Tzvetan Todorov's formula[5] and say that we have here the kind of fantasy that hesitates between real and imagined (or causes the reader to do this), though the text doesn't hesitate so much as drive from the external real to the internal and obsessive imagined and experienced. The effect is that the novel is emphatically human-centred, because it centres on this relationship, and emphatically death-centred, because the relationship, like the climate and the disorder and violence, drives towards destruction. In *Heroes and Villains*, Marianne's relationship with Jewel may be said to begin with her rape and end with his death, but it also involves exchange, pleasure and mutual testing and curiosity, not to mention Marianne's pregnancy. The depiction of sexual entrapment and pathology in *Ice* is much darker.

The narrator is involved with a young woman (often called a girl), thin, sometimes painfully so, fragile, silver-haired. He tells us that she has been mistreated in childhood (by her mother) and as a result of this cannot defend or assert herself.

> Her prominent bones seemed brittle, the protruding wrist-bones had a particular fascination for me. Her hair was astonishing, silver-white, an albino's, sparkling like moonlight, like moonlit venetian glass. I treated her like a glass girl; at times she hardly seemed real. (8)[6]

He presents himself as sometimes unable to explain his obsession with the girl and the quest to find and catch her that it leads him on, and as sometimes wanting to rescue her, a plausible motive given her helplessness and the dangers of the world of the novel. The narrator has a rival, a figure of much more power and confidence than him, indeed a figure of charisma. This rival is usually uniformed and surrounded by underlings, and is usually called the warden or the consul as he crops up in different settings. The warden gains power from the prevailing disorder, and seems to have no motives other than the gaining of power. The narrator by contrast drifts and struggles, moving through the scenes of cold and of breakdown with difficulty, a loner, tricking or persuading others to help him from time to time but then leaving them. From time

---

[5] See Jackson 1981, 27–31.
[6] There is a suggestion that the girl is a kind of ice maiden; but the ice itself is beautiful but cruel, and she is its victim: 'As her fate, she accepted the world of ice, shining, shimmering, dead; she resigned herself to the triumph of glaciers and the death of her world' (21). Then again, the warden, one of her pursuers, has 'an ice-blue gaze' (36).

to time he promises himself that he will return to a better place, that of the 'Indris' and the singing lemurs, somewhere in the tropics and his past life. Indris is a faint echo of the pastoral that provided a recourse in the postwar disaster novels. The narrator never sets out for Indris; instead, he repeatedly encounters the warden in a position and place of power (a labyrinthine castle, a military headquarters), confronts him over the girl and is then helpless, almost abashed. He thinks of giving up, but then he sets out travelling again in search of the girl in the disorder of war and breakdown, in danger of being arrested by whatever set of police and soldiers is on hand in this new – but essentially the same – setting of conflict and emergency.

There is a scene in one of the early encounters of this kind in which the warden rapes the girl (36–37; the narrator does not even mention this to the warden when he talks with him shortly afterwards), but after a while we realise that there is a sadistic streak also in the narrator (he rapes her, 75–76). He begins to blend with the warden:

> 'In an indescribable way our looks tangled together. I seemed to be looking at my own reflexion. ...I continually found I was not myself, but him.' (98)[7]

The realisation doesn't discourage him, and presumably cannot discourage him, since they are in effect the same person, in a variation of Edgar Allan Poe's 'William Wilson'. They are co-operating in a practice of torture of which the girl is the victim, and the narrator's quest has become a pursuit, angry and at times cruel, a kind of stalking. The narrator presents himself as somehow goaded and driven on by the very fragility and vulnerability of the girl that at other times he offers as the motive for rescuing and helping her. The objective drive towards destruction and an end to Earth – objective in that it seems to be at work in the external worlds of climate and politics – serves as setting for the sadistic obsession that drives the behaviour of the two men towards the girl – if there are two men.

The power and gloom of *Ice* is sometimes explained in terms of the will towards death that it seems to express: a review in *The Times Literary Supplement* calls the novel 'a love-song to the end of the world' (20 June 1997). There is clearly something in this, but a comparison with Ballard's

---

[7] In an analogous way, Ballard pursues his theme of the dissemination of the self by way of images of reflection and doubling in *The Drought* (for instance, 31, 39, 95, 148) and *The Crystal World*, and Aldiss plays with the notion of alternative selves in *Barefoot in the Head*.

apocalyptic novels, especially *The Drowned World*, suggests how much more troubled *Ice* is. In *The Drowned World* the coming doom of humanity, the rise in Earth's temperature to unliveable levels, is greeted as a release from practicality, from the effort to survive, and the drive towards death is given an explanation: the Sun is summoning humans to self-obliteration in the heat of the expanding tropics. A buried, primeval aspect of the psyche is being called forth. The nature of the drive towards death and oblivion in *Ice* is more complex and uneasy. There is no summons; the encroaching ice is dead and indifferent; the wars and violence are presented as without purpose. These forces are always on the point of arriving (a gloom of imminence, a series of shapeless rumours) or they have always just left, having wrecked the town and left mess and broken survivors behind. Both the ice and the wars have a fascination about them, and Kavan expresses this in passages of resonant gloom, but they do not really arouse a yearning for destruction. They have only the power of what has now become routine, the way things are. Everything is recurrent (visions of ice entrapment, ruined towns, night flights in a big vehicle, confrontations with the warden, appeals to flee) or has happened in the past (sacrifice, enslavement, massacre, ruination). In Ballard, for instance in *The Drought*, the past, the dreamt and the future have come to occupy the present, the protagonist Ransom realises this, and it comes as a revelation. In *Ice* disaster has already happened or is always happening:

> I should have to start searching for her all over again. The repetition was like a curse. (99)

> [And the girl exclaims,] 'With *you*? Oh, no! Surely we haven't got to go through all *that* again!' (150)

This element of repetition is stronger than the suggestions that things are getting worse and the end is nigh, though these suggestions are made repeatedly and with more and more emphasis ('The whole world was turning towards death', 141). Ends can be nigh for a very long time, evidently, and meanwhile the element of repetition in the passages about the ice and the wars finds a counterpart in the repeated scenes between the three characters at the centre of the novel: confrontation, reproach; appeal from the narrator that cannot be properly articulated, apparently because the warden is too steely and intimidating and because the girl is too childlike and vulnerable – the warden is too utterly sure of himself and the girl is so totally lacking in ego. So this repetition redoubles that which we find in the passages about the cold and the passages about the wars, and adds a quality of neurosis. There is a drive towards death and the end, but there is also a blockage, as in a sadomasochistic relationship. The two aspects share a quality of nullity.[8] The fact that the narrator and the girl both perceive the merged identity of the narrator and the warden, and the narrator and the girl both see that they are condemned to repetition, adds to this element of blockage: awareness does not lead to any change of behaviour.

None of the three personages is fully present as distinct and independent, so no exchange can really happen between them. The warden and the narrator continue to pursue the girl who continues to submit and be tortured by them; the narrator is sadistic towards the girl and masochistic towards the warden; the girl cannot make a life apart from the two men and – since they are compelled to pursue her – exerts a kind of masochistic power over them. When the narrator decides (again) to leave the girl, she reproaches him, though she has reproached him for pursuing and torturing her (119). When he announces to the warden that he has given up his pursuit, the latter turns on him in fury, 'So you've abandoned her' (133). The relationship is irresolvable, and this returns us to the apocalyptic setting.

The narration is from the narrator's point of view, but it shifts to the girl's (48–49, 68, 148)[9] without warning, just as it shifts from the actual to hallucination (7, 13, and elsewhere, for instance, 136) or from the present to the past, without warning (52–57). During the interlude in a primitive past the narrator comes across the girl lying with a cruelly broken arm:

> I felt I had been defrauded: I alone should have done the breaking with tender love; I was the only person entitled to inflict wounds. I leaned forward and touched her cold skin. (54)

> [And later]: A girl's arm protruded from a heap of detritus; I took hold of the wrist, pulled gently; it came away in my hand. (59)

---

[8] Similarly, the lack of information about the political crises deepens to a blank, 'the implacable spread of those unnerving areas of total silence' (100) – and again: 'To speak of the catastrophe was an offence under the new regulations. The rule was to choose not to know' (117). *Ice* resembles Howard Jacobson's more recent *J* (2014): an ongoing catastrophe that is not to be defined, and is the worse for that; a blocked relationship infected by these broader, not-to-be-defined conditions of catastrophe.

[9] 'The man drove the car brutally throughout the short day. It seemed to her that she had never known anything but this terrifying drive in the feeble half-light; the silence, the cold, the snow, the arrogant figure beside her' (68).

The relations of Naptha and Settembrini in Thomas Mann's *The Magic Mountain* (1924) are locked in repetition, though they do produce some illuminating arguments, and can only be resolved by death. The relations of Gudrun and Gerald and Loerke in D. H. Lawrence's *Women in Love* (1920) are locked in conflict, but they are again resolved by death, and as with Naptha and Settembrini the antagonists stand for something and make arguments. In *Ice*, the blocked relationship of the trio has no content other than its own dynamic – the antagonists don't stand for anything and are hardly separate beings; death accompanies, threatens, looms; but death does not arrive. Neurosis – the sadomasochism at the novel's heart – is stronger than death, stronger than apocalypse.

The primacy of the objective and material – the way in which we are asked to believe that the catastrophe is really happening in the world of things – is thrown into question. Perhaps the subjective, the relations, feelings and fantasies of the protagonists, is primary, and the catastrophe, in its dual form, only expresses that subjective reality. Apocalypse haunts the imagination, prompting story after story; once the subjective dimension of apocalypse is depicted as the desire for death, we face this deadlock in repetition. The inexhaustibility of apocalypse, the fact that there is always another to be imagined and this even after – or more after – apocalyptic events like the World Wars, the Holocaust and Hiroshima – can be reduced to nullity. If we look at *Ice* in the context of its appearance in the history of apocalyptic fictions, that is, in the context of the moment when fictions faced the *desire* for apocalypse, then it suggests a dead end, an aporia. In earlier apocalypses, there are usually some who survive and carry on; in Ballard's apocalypses, the protagonists choose death; in *Ice* the protagonists survive in a kind of death-in-life of repetition:

> I was aware of an uncertainty of the real, in my surroundings and in myself. What I saw had no solidity, it was all made of mist and nylon, with nothing behind. (31)

The Memoirs of a Survivor[10]

The Memoirs of a Survivor (1974) and *The Making of the Representative for Planet 8* (1982) stand in emphatic contrast to Doris Lessing's earlier fiction, and also to genre science fiction. They come during a period of

---

[10] References are to Doris Lessing, *The Memoirs of a Survivor*, London: The Octagon Press, 1974.

experiment, when Lessing adopted very different styles and points of view: *Memoirs* is very different from *The Summer Before the Dark* (1973); Lessing's venture into science fiction was a new departure for her; the novels in the *Canopus in Argo* series differ from one another; and the series in turn differs from *The Diaries of Jane Somers* that followed soon after.[11] The created worlds in both *Memoirs* and *Planet 8* are drab and unlovely, and the most vividly present creatures are the yellowish hybrid dog Hugo in *Memoirs* and the withered, ageing Alsi in *Planet 8*. The sensational, dramatic and attractive is almost aggressively eschewed, though the extinction that comes to all life on Planet 8 might seem material for the dramatic and sensational. The narrator in the first case, the Survivor herself, certainly does not confine herself to reportage, but is full of opinions; and *Planet 8* carries a message. *Memoirs* refuses the pleasures of language, as if they would be a distraction or evasion; yet it elaborates a complex allegorical structure. Similarly, although it was published in 1974 and concerns social breakdown in a big city, it avoids direct reference to the crisis coming to a head in Britain at that time – the three-day week, strikes, the fall of the Conservative government. (Perhaps this context would have been obvious to a contemporary reader.)[12] *Planet 8* is inventing a new world for us, and this usually offers simple pleasures to the reader, but in this instance the effect is austere to the point of bare.

Reviewers were often decisive in their criticisms of these novels, and more recent critics, much more positive, equally decisive in classification and evaluation – for instance, Susan Watkins's *Doris Lessing* (2010). The discussion that follows is more tentative, because it seems to me that the force of both novels lies in their bleakness and their alternations of asperity and austerity. It does seem that if you put *Memoirs* and *Planet 8* into the context of fictions of apocalypse then different and more disturbing effects come into light than if, for instance, you put *Planet 8* into the context of post-colonial feminism, as Watkins does, though with reference to the whole *Canopus in Argo* series.

In discussing *Memoirs*, it is useful to begin with Hugo, who offers a way into the novel because he affects the emotional range of the novel in a significant way. Hugo belongs to Emily. He is ugly, yellow, with a cat's body and a dog's face, the habits of a cat (inactive, purrs, likes to be stroked) but the fierce loyalty and uncomplaining devotion of a

---

[11] See Susan Watkins 2010, chapter 4 (83–118).
[12] See, for instance, Beckett 2009. Beckett discusses novels and plays of decline at 179–181, mentioning, among many others, Lessing's *The Summer Before the Dark* and Ballard's *High-Rise* and *Concrete Island*.

dog. His devotion, his unhappiness when it seems Emily is deserting him, his willingness to be loved anyway when Emily remorsefully remembers him, is all kept in view, so that Hugo definitely makes a trio with the narrator and Emily, and in addition adds an unqualified love and emotional directness that no one else in the story can provide. So we are glad he is present – glad even though he may represent the fact that Lessing has given up on humans and can find something to admire only in animals (see 70–71). Why he is yellow and ugly, and a kind of hybrid, is a puzzle, though it is true that animals don't know when they are ugly, or care, just as they don't judge their owners, and this quality is, again, a relief in a book that is full of registrations of self-consciousness (Emily) and the offering by one human of confident judgements about other humans (the narrator).[13] The inclusion of Hugo might be one way in which Lessing compensates for other, harsher elements in the novel. The novel's allegorical approach might mean that love and loyalty is embodied in one personage rather than allotted naturalistically in imperfect quantities to several, though if so the fact that it is an animal, and an uncanny one, that stands for love and loyalty, is significant. These other elements now need to be detailed.

The basic structure of the novel is binary. There is the mundane world of social breakdown and fragmentation, and there is another world, experienced only by the narrator until near the end of the novel. In these comments reference will be to 'the mundane world', because 'real' raises too many questions, and to 'the other world', because 'alternative' doesn't quite fit. In the other world the narrator finds herself passing through the wall of her apartment into rooms and a garden, with, sometimes, other people, as well as a 'Presence' who is not seen until the end of the novel. No time passes in the mundane world when the narrator is in this other world, and scenes from the past of Emily and her family are sometimes enacted in the present of the other world. But it is not quite right to suggest (as Betsy Draine (1983) does, for instance) that the contrast is between fantasy and realism. In the mundane world in *Memoirs* events seem to be tied to place just as are events in the other world, so that events inside the narrator's flat, events in the street, and events on the higher floors of her building all happen according to different rhythms, different rules even, just as do events in the different rooms in the other world into which the narrator passes sometimes. At one point we are told that as groups of young people go about their

---

[13] Roland Barthes's observations (1980, 51–52) on the Abbé Seguin's yellow cat in Chateaubriand's *Vie de Rancé* are suggestive: the choice of yellow to describe this cat introduces an anomaly, a gap in meaning.

new communal life on the street, the windows of the buildings looking down on the street are lighted and alive with watchers (34). This seems to be repeated exactly, never changing, never further developed – for instance, we never see the narrator chatting with the other watchers. It's an image, not a moment from a continuing narrative. Then again, the narrator's apartment is on the ground floor of a tall building and the upper floors of this building undergo a number of abrupt changes. They are inhabited by those middle-class watchers, then they have become the scene of a bustling market (98–100), then they have been taken over by Emily's lover Gerald with a gang of feral and dangerous children.

The binary – mundane world, other world – breaks into shards. As regards life on the streets, this fragmentation is no doubt a sign of the twists and strains that humans, especially the young, are undergoing while orderly social life of the old kind breaks down. There is a re-foundation of order and production based to some degree on mutual co-operation and caring – fragmented (society is divided into small groups with armed guards) but full of invention (growing food, using draught animals, obtaining water, heat and light in improvised ways). The narrator notices also new and more promiscuous sexual customs, as well as an exaggeration of some old customs (young women competing for the prize young man), but the trend, so far, is positive. Meanwhile, in the opposite direction, there are gangs of feral kids, hardly human, hardly gangs if the term suggests some order and co-operation among the members, primitive of speech, violent, cannibalistic, and 'inconsequent' (143, 175) – vicious one moment and friendly the next moment. So there are two contrary developments in the mundane world.

The implication might be that movement should be inwards, into the other world and away from the broken mundane world, and this indeed happens at the end of the novel, but the other world is itself a shifting and sometimes painful place.

Scenes here happen in, roughly, three different fields. Sometimes the narrator encounters order and peace, a garden, a blue sky, a kind of Eden, with intimations of a 'Presence', a reminder of the image of nature as refuge that was given larger dimensions, though less mystical qualities, in the postwar disaster novels.[14] Sometimes she encounters wrecked and

---

[14] There is a rich tradition of Edenic gardens, discovered, lost, refound – for instance, the garden in H. G. Wells's 'The Door in the Wall', or the rose garden in T. S. Eliot's *Burnt Norton*, which, as in Kipling's 'They', one of its sources, features mysterious presences. There are several fleeting glimpses of Edenic places in *Dead Astronauts*. See also the entry 'Secret Garden' in Clute and Grant 1999, 847–848.

vandalised rooms, as if people from outside had broken in there too, and done what they are doing to deserted buildings all over the city. Sometimes she encounters scenes from Emily's past life, which are experienced by her as if from Emily's point of view. These scenes stage a nightmare of the nuclear family. The adults are huge, clumsy, clumping, dysfunctional. The father is ineffectual and bewildered, the mother ('the large carthorse woman', 128) endlessly nags about how exhausted she is by the effort of looking after Emily (60–62). Neither of them is capable of any tenderness. The rooms in which they appear are chokingly white, painfully overheated. The vein of disgust or contempt, especially for the clumsy complaining mother, is surely the narrator's or Lessing's. This is particularly obvious in the scene where we come across Emily as a bit older, wearing a red dress that is too adult for her (158). (The novel was at first subtitled 'An Attempt at Autobiography'; the subtitle was later dropped. The parents in these scenes can be seen as reflections of Lessing's feelings about her parents – the mother harsh and unloving, the father enfeebled by ill-health and failure – and the child in these scenes as a reflection of Doris as a child, ill-treated and rebellious.)[15]

The series of scenes of Emily's family comes across as a version of the bad old days for women, infantilised and reduced to nagging by motherhood, sexualised too young (the scene in the red dress). The narrator at times seems to feel that women in the throes of the crisis have slipped back to their old, pre-feminist ways – captured by love, by the need to serve and be giving, incapable of leading or being independent. Then at other times, as in the passionate meditation on women's weeping, on Emily's 'archaic and dreadful grief' (145), this behaviour seems archetypal.

Meanwhile, the Emily of the mundane world suffers and is torn, for instance, between her life on the streets with Gerald, and her life in the narrator's flat with her pet Hugo, but she matures, becomes capable, a leader (for instance, 140), and aware of emotional complications and different needs. This development in Emily seems to have less and less to do with the increasingly overwrought scenes in the other world, which don't work as helping us to understand how the troubled girl we first met might have been shaped by unlovingness in her childhood; we are learning about the survivor rather than about Emily.

These scenes suggest what can happen to someone who lets unlovingness prey on their mind so that it assumes a monstrous

---

[15] Carole Klein (2000) details Lessing's childhood and her conflicted and angry feelings about it in her biography of Lessing. On the subtitle and its deletion, see 207; on the red dress, see 55.

quality. This resembles the way the main character in *The Summer Before the Dark* experiences the world as nasty and disjointed when she is undergoing her breakdown. It might then be possible to see *The Memoirs of a Survivor* also as depicting a breakdown. There is an element of constraint in the narrator's relations with the mundane world – though she is opinionated, she is passive and powerless. Perhaps, then, the split and sharply opposed realms of the other world express the reaction inwards of a thwarted and unhappy psyche. Yet we are dealing with another *world*, not a series of hallucinations or, as in *The Summer Before the Dark*, bitter and out of control responses to ordinary occurrences such as a visit to the theatre (Lessing 1973, 170–179). The narrator is unstable, and this registers how destabilising, indeed traumatic, the experience of social breakdown might be, something that many apocalyptic fictions overlook; but *Memoirs* does not fold everything into the narrator's psyche as might be the case with a novel of personal breakdown.

Lessing is catching an experience that is fragmented, non-continuous, repetitive and sluggish, then abruptly shifting. Perhaps this is an expression of the ways in which coherence and orderly temporality break down when society is breaking down. Lessing has redoubled this effect by introducing the other world in which three separate kinds of event (thence, three distinct temporalities?) unpredictably alternate, and at least one seems to signify something sacred, the Presence. In addition, the narrator invokes ordinariness in the mundane world by talking of the puzzled mass of ordinary people of whom she says she is one, but then hides these people from view, replacing them with the young, who are developing new ways of living in response to the crisis. So in this last respect Lessing has inserted into this series of expressions of fragmentation and incoherence a picture of practical responses to social breakdown. She has then inserted into *this* picture the feral and violent gangs of children who express an alternative view of how the young might respond to social breakdown: except that it is not alternative; it is additional. It cannot be said that *The Memoirs of a Survivor* is giving a simplistic picture of breakdown into primitive violence, as many apocalyptic fictions do.

The Narrator and 'It'

Near the very end of the novel, and at a climactic moment of vision, the narrator says of this vision, 'and all I can say is ... nothing at all' (182). This is the moment of transcendence, when 'One' appears and

DARKER IMAGINATIONS, HARDER LESSONS

all – the survivor, Emily, Hugo and Gerald – are changed and released from the disorder of the world. 'All I have to say is ... nothing at all' is a surprising remark from one who has talked a great deal, and has told us that the official class are full of nothing but 'Talk', and has told us that she and others among ordinary people of the city spend much of their time moving around the city, talking, exchanging gossip and information (45). Yet it is also true that the narration, the memoirs of the survivor, is shaped by very distinct decisions, or impulses, about what we are to be told and what we will not be told. Moreover, the text is full of disquisitions and opinions that are put into the words of the narrator, but as a character in the story she is usually passive. The heart of the story is her relation with Emily, who comes to her as a child and grows to a woman in the course of the story while her growth is extensively commented on by the narrator – but the narrator scarcely talks to Emily until page 67, and their first real conversation is on pages 112–113 (of 182).

The context of the relation between Emily and the narrator that is at the heart of the story is a situation of complete social breakdown. We are not told anything of the origins of the breakdown. When it looks as if we will be told about 'It', we are given a series of manoeuvres around the word 'it' (130–133):

'Perhaps, after all, one has to end by characterising "it"...' –

She compares 'it' to water vapour, giving us eight lines on water vapour, then ten more lines on all the things 'it' is, or might be, including 'everything' and 'nothing' and (almost) concluding: '"it" was, finally, what you experienced...' By which time the maddened reader is ready to reject the original thought because it has been so blurred and fogged in appositions and generalities.[16]

Perhaps this circling round 'it' reflects the idiom of powerlessness (as when people say, 'What does it mean?' and 'When will it end?' and so forth), and suggests that 'it' is any and all of the troubles and sufferings that people are experiencing as part of the general condition that prevails. Apocalyptic fiction frequently expresses the common feeling that history is something that happens to its subjects: the alien invasion is one way of expressing that; the narrator's blurred vision of social breakdown in *Memoirs* is another. A particular account of

---

[16] Yet it is from this passage that Jeanne Murray Walker (1988, 97) derives the interpretation that the root of the trouble in the world of the novel is the breakdown of social exchange.

how things began to go wrong might be seen as banal or redundant, because any writer of apocalyptic fiction can toss off a variety of causes and factors. As the number and variety of apocalyptic fictions piles up, writers feel a need to find an angle on what can be a habituation to apocalypse: they play with apocalypse (Aldiss), or parody its conventions (Le Guin, who also offers repeated apocalypses), or depict apocolypticism as a trendy subculture (Miéville), or write with the polemic assertion that we already know how badly the world is wrecked, because we are wrecking it (VanderMeer). Lessing, arguably, responds by assuming that the details of the nature of the apocalypse she is treating are redundant.

Nonetheless, it is striking that her narrator won't give the reader a bit more detail here, while she is very confident in commenting on or digressing into dozens of topics (how young women are captured by love, what humans have ignored in the lives of animals, how law and government still functions, why we need air and water). She hesitates, tries alternative phrasing, fills in obvious details as if gripped by nervous uncertainty as to whether we will understand, disclaims confidence and authority and ability to do anything. She presents as one of the helpless mass of ordinary people without power or wider knowledge; but, for all this, she is free with her opinions, insights and summary dismissals. One way of catching the resulting conundrum is to say that we are faced with passive-aggressive behaviour. It is this complex passive-aggressive authority in the narrator that makes *The Memoirs of a Survivor* at once involving and infuriating.[17]

The narrator notices how Emily keeps her at a distance, and sympathetically explains this as the result of whatever happened to Emily before she was left with her at the beginning of the story; but equally, by seeing her as a kind of specimen of what life is now like for a girl becoming a woman, and making her the subject of disquisitions on this topic, the narrator keeps Emily at a distance.[18] The young are clearly a puzzle as well as a problem in *Memoirs*; the apocalyptic setting serves to dramatise this puzzle and problem, and in that respect *The Memoirs of a Survivor* resembles earlier novels such as *Lord of the Flies* (1954) and *A Clockwork Orange* (1962), but there is not really anyone in *The Memoirs of a Survivor* with whom we find ourselves empathising as we do – with a jolt – with Ralph in Golding and with Alex in Burgess. Hugo is lovable, but alien: he might as well be a creature from

---

[17] On Lessing's passive-aggressive side, see Bertelsen 1988.
[18] In *In Gratitude* (2016), Jenny Diski ponders her experience of being fostered by Doris Lessing as a troubled teenager. Each was puzzled by the other.

another planet. Emily is a subject for disquisition, and (for me) this puts her at a distance, even though the disquisition is often insightful and sympathetic.

At the very end, the characters escape into the dimension presided over by the Presence. They escape into another dimension of being. There is a great deal, both in the mundane world, and in parts of the other world, to escape from, but the text has been sketchy in suggesting what the world of the Presence is like. We perhaps need from the text the sense that 'humanity is being watched over by benevolent, Godlike creatures' (Watkins, 2010, 78); but this we don't really (to my sense of it) get.

The Making of the Representative for Planet 8[19]

The Making of the Representative for Planet 8 is narrated by Doeg, an inhabitant of what is simply called Planet 8; he is a narrator by social function, and his story has ended up in the archives of Canopus in Argo, basis of a series of science-fiction novels by Lessing. (No doubt Canopus gave the planet a number; we never learn what the inhabitants call it.) The story is about the extinction of Doeg's people, and indeed of all animal and vegetable life on his planet. The planet gradually succumbs to a very severe Ice Age, one that ends up covering the entire planet under a thick ice sheet. The text often insists that everything changes, nothing is stable, so that some other condition will eventually succeed the ice. The planet may revive, but the people will have gone.

Modern humans are aware that they will end but the universe will not, and this is crucially different from the attitude behind traditional apocalypse, in which History ends and Earth is destroyed but humanity continues in Eternity. Even in *Planet 8*, the end is that of the inhabitants not of the planet, and not of the universe – not the absolute death of which for instance, José Saramago has death (*sic*) talk in *Death at Intervals*: 'you human beings only know the small everyday death that is me, the death which, even in the very worst disasters, is incapable of preventing life from continuing, one day you will find out about Death with a capital D, and at that moment, in the unlikely event that she gives you time to do so, you will understand the real difference

---

[19] References are to Doris Lessing, *The Making of the Representative for Planet 8 (Canopus in Argos – Archives)*, London: Grafton (Collins), 1983. The novel was first published in 1982.

between the relative and the absolute, between full and empty, between still alive and no longer alive'.[20]

So – these considerations aside – *Planet 8* is unusual among apocalyptic fictions in that the desolation is not only inexorable but also total. This assertion may have to be qualified when we come to the very end of the novella, when the Making of the Representative is consummated, but it will do for now. Apocalypse is about bitter ends, after all; however, for Lessing the story of annihilation will be framed and changed by the teaching of transcendence that is knit into the novel: a version of the traditional end of history and entrance into bliss. *Planet 8* is in the last resort a religious novel, and this makes political readings hard to develop.

In addition, as will be examined below in discussion of Tom Perotta's *The Leftovers*, apocalyptic fictions seldom treat grief and trauma. *Planet 8* does this.[21] The end is predicted, it comes slowly and its coming cannot be avoided. The people of the planet feel grief, loss, disorientation, resistance, nostalgia, anger. They take some steps to resist the coming of the ice, and to survive as long as possible, but almost everything they feel is under the sign of the coming end.[22] We are not in the aftermath, wherein most novels of apocalypse are set, to dwell on survival or sometimes on the embracing of the end. There is no chance of life being protected, as the father protects his son in Cormac McCarthy's *The Road*, or renewed, as with the arrival of the baby on the last pages of *The Leftovers* or the hint that new life will arrive at the end of Aldiss's *Greybeard*; indeed, babies and children are never mentioned in *Planet 8*. No one is to be blamed, if we assume that ascribing blame can be a way of avoiding the work of grief.

The ice advances, the climate becomes colder and bleaker, the vibrant aliveness of birds and animals and people is extinguished, so is the colour itself of birds and landscape and people, which only figures as a memory. The vegetation becomes sparse, the animals mostly become heavy, sluggish and sullen (roughly like musk ox or bison); everything is black and white and then everything is grey. The people, once slim and

---

[20] The quotation is from death's letter to the newspaper explaining why she signs herself 'death' and not 'Death'. Saramago 2008, 103; see also 65.

[21] Susan Watkins suggests that making something positive of loss (personal, cultural, political) runs through a great deal of Lessing's fiction in the 1970s and 1980s. Watkins 2010, chapter 3, 'The Politics of Loss: Melancholy Cosmopolitanism', 53–82.

[22] Betsy Draine comments, 'The most convincing portions of the novel are Doeg's detailed descriptions of those times of grief' (1983, 175). She quotes Doeg's feeling for the small creatures that have taken refuge from the ice in a cave where the representatives find shelter (*Planet 8*, 9–10, 28–29).

lithe and alert, now buried in their thick garments, become yellowish, greasy, unhealthy, slowly starving on a diet of the meat of the sluggish animals and some scant remains of vegetation, a diet they find repulsive. In contrast to *The Memoirs of a Survivor* and to most novels of catastrophe or its aftermath, there are no recourses, improvisations, resistances. Most of the people of Planet 8 recognise there is no hope, and the form that this recognition takes is sometimes complaint and violence (brawls and murders and eventually small wars, though violence was never known in happier days), but most often passivity, inertia, sleep. The text treats these people, the mass of the population, with the kind of cold sympathy that accompanies the feeling that you didn't expect any better of such as these. In a moment discussion will turn to those on whom the story does focus, the representatives (in the plural for most of the story), together with Johor, the delegate, or guardian, or teacher, from Canopus. Canopus is a more developed and enlightened planet, or so we are to understand.

So far, in terms of the examination of apocalyptic fiction, *The Making of the Representative for Planet 8* offers lots of invitations and challenges. But there is a further aspect to the novel, stemming paradoxically from another way in which *Planet 8* pursues the apocalyptic. This is that *Planet 8* is concerned to discard the flesh, the life of enjoyment in the world, to gain insight into the spirit, and eventually attain a kind of afterlife beyond individual life in the flesh.[23] The grief, the varied and painful signs of which were just summarised, is to be got beyond. The novel has an agenda, a determined sense of the place of each stage and each experience in the unfolding of that agenda, and it has a didactic purpose. This gives rise to a problem, which can usefully be approached through Johor, the envoy from Canopus who is the means of a lot of the teaching; also relevant to this problem are the form of the novel, which is entrusted to a character (Doeg) who sets out to tell what happened as a witness does, but that is best read as a parable, or fable; and the readiness of the locals to be taught, their innocence and obedience. This last is a datum that carries with it certain implications. The specification of these qualities of submission as native to the locals takes a lot of heat out of the novel. The situation is tragic, but there is no Lear or Medea to rage against it. In *King Lear* – to choose a text that is in extreme

---

[23] Ursula Le Guin, reviewing *Shikasta* (1979), the first novel in the Canopus in Argos series, sees Lessing as Calvinist: salvation is by grace not works, ordinary humans and their decisions don't count and Lessing has no interest in the colour or texture of the worlds she is setting before the reader (Le Guin 1989a).

contrast but is, after all, also apocalyptic – everybody who figures tries to wrest the situation, the world, to their perception and feeling and will; in *Planet 8* none of the inhabitants does.[24]

Meanwhile the form and manner of the story needs more definition since it might be retorted that it is not a tragic drama, even if a comparison with a tragic drama is allowable. *Planet 8* is a kind of parable or fable. Parables usually have a moral point – use your talent, be kind to strangers and so on. *Planet 8* comes from the years during which Lessing was much involved with Sufi teaching, and it carries a zen or sufi lesson.[25] The point of this parable is an austere, uncompromising one: 'They [the people of Planet 8] are nudged into understanding the inadequacy of reason, the futility of guilt, the terror of choice, the community of dreams, the flavour of death and the duplicity of gods' (Leonard 1986, 206). There is a tension between Doeg as narrator, thoughtful and conscientious, and Lessing's will to unillusion, if that is the right word, which is driving the novel.

The story begins when Johor arrives (with some others from Canopus) and tells the people they must build a high wall round the equator of their planet. This is to hold back the snow and ice when the climate changes and the ice spreads, and it does so for a while, and then fails. The people's labour produces a gleaming black monolith, fifty feet high. Because the wall is so stark and simple, monotonous and undeviating, it seems more a symbol than a piece of practical defence. Canopus (always the name at once of a planet, a people and an authority) has ordered it, and Canopus is benevolent. Maybe the wall is a kind of teaching machine, intended to convey that whatever you do, even something as gigantic and logical as this, will be futile: not exactly built to fail, but built to demonstrate the inevitability of failure. The refinement would be that, after all, the wall did work for a while, so that the lesson becomes: you have to do what you can, even though it will be futile. But the wall, so simple and bare in its logic, also seems a refusal of the practical ingenuity that so often rules in science fiction. It's not science or technology, with their improvisations and experiments; it's a wall, massive and singular. If that doesn't work (and it won't), nothing else will (and nothing else is tried).

But assessment of the significance of the wall leads us to the problem of Canopus, represented for most of the novel by a single envoy, Johor.

---

[24] On *Lear* as apocalyptic, see Wittreich 1984.
[25] See Klein 2000, 215–222, for this phase. Lessing's mentor was Idries Shah: see the illuminating anecdote of his relations with John Bennett, an admirer, on 217–218.

Canopus colonised Planet 8 with the people whose fate is determined in the story. They were selected because of certain genetic qualities; it seems that these are that they are happy, not very aggressive, and obedient. The plan was that when they reached a certain level of development they would be removed to another planet, Rohanda, and there blended with the people already in place, to produce a good mix. Judging by this plan, the people of Canopus go in for confident, long-term shaping of the fates of other peoples, though that is not the initial impression that we get from Johor in this novel. He influences feelings and actions, but he never tells people what to do, or even answers questions. So the envoy Johor represents Canopus and exercises authority on Planet 8; his behaviour is not typical of Canopus's colonising confidence, but he can nonetheless be seen as manipulative. The novel invites a political, anti-colonial reading, but it also ignores it and proceeds in a different, zen-religious, direction.

Things went along well for a while; Canopus visited from time to time, introducing new technologies and possibilities, and the people of Planet 8 progressed, remaining happily vegetarian and (in the moral/utopian sense) pastoral, but diversifying into textile manufacture and the mining and working of iron, at the prompting of Canopus. (Since their planet is not called anything other than Planet 8 the inhabitants don't have a collective name: more, below, on names in this novel.) They don't revolt or complain or decide to go off in different directions, as do people in colonised territories in our history who are supposed to develop and modernise but don't follow the agenda, or redefine it, and as the inhabitants of Lombi do in the course of *The Sirian Experiments* (1982). They feel they have to do 'what he [Johor] wanted. What Canopus wanted...' (132) – the sentence tails off, as if the wanting is indefinite (again on 133, 'Canopus says...'). Lessing doesn't indicate any reservations about this neo-colonialism; instead, the implication seems to be that, setting aside whether Canopus's policy was a good one when it was working, it proves to be good after it has failed, because this people so happy in tutelage are equipped to submit to an inexorable fate, and to learn and mature under Johor's guidance. (Though the majority degenerate, understandably, given the stress they are under, the text is centred on the representatives, and they trust and learn.)[26]

Rohanda turns out to be unsuitable. It becomes Shikasta, corrupt and in turmoil, as told in *Shikasta*, the first in the *Canopus in Argos*

[26] Contrast Susan Watkins's account: 'some of those on the planet give up and die quickly while others gradually learn to adjust, under Canopean guidance ... abandoning physical life in the body and individual personality' (2010, 92).

series (1979). The people of Planet 8 might have decided they would nonetheless take their chances on Shikasta, rather than all die where they are, but there are vague other objections, and the choice is never offered. The Ice Age on Planet 8 was not at first predicted, nor was the degeneration of Rohanda. Canopus doesn't seem to possess the practical wisdom to go with its grand plans for its pupils, so the attention shifts to its moral or spiritual wisdom. It might be objected that to read the novel like this is to read it as genre science fiction, or simply as realist fiction, rather than as a religious fable. The latter reading would require one to dismiss thought about Canopus's failures as irrelevant to the fable, but it is hard to do so, since the failures are so obvious.

Johor visits from time to time while the ice is advancing, life is becoming harder and prospects narrowing. There is a general expectation that Canopus will rescue the inhabitants of Planet 8, for whom it might be seen as responsible; this fades; it comes to seem implausible, or unreal. There is an expectation among the representatives that Canopus will rescue them, at least; this fades, too, in the same way. Johor sits with people; he requests a certain kind of discourse from them and persists and nudges when he doesn't get it (see the dialogue, though it is not quite that, with Alsi, from 118). He doesn't answer questions or respond to complaints. If he were an ordinary person, his behaviour would be annoying, if not insulting, and if he were a bit less lucky in those subject to his behaviour, he would be beaten up, or worse, given the grim situation on Planet 8 and Canopus's part in marooning these people on it. But we are probably to accept that he is not an ordinary person, and that his silence is a wise Sufi technique for getting people to make for themselves the discoveries or acceptances that they need to make. Annoyance at this, or resistance to it, is presumably to be ascribed to a faith in ordinary secular exchange, a faith in give and take in conversation, with its assumptions of equality. Lessing has set this faith aside in the case of Planet 8, though she seems to invoke it in her 'Afterword' (162–190) as if it were applicable to our judgements about the First World War or Scott's expedition to Antarctica, these being her topics in the Afterword.

This interpretation of Johor, as prevailing upon the inhabitants to mature and submit by exerting a wise silence, is not an inescapable one as regards most of the novel. We infer that he responds as he does so as to nudge them towards wisdom, and the representatives feel the same, but it is possible that he responds as he does because he can't respond in any other way. Since the novel clearly has a message, we set ourselves to understand what it is, and this leads us to accept that Johor is to be seen as wise and justified. But if we decided not to follow this readerly logic, based on respect for the author's evident intention, we could see most of the text as depicting Johor as a kind of automaton.[27] In the last analysis, it doesn't matter – the crucial thing is whether the people of Planet 8 learn from Johor's Sufi silent treatment, or at least whether the representatives do, because it is the latter he visits and sits with.

The shape of this part of the tale is clear: the flesh declines, and the spirit gains insight. The majority become sunk in apathy, reluctant even to help themselves, choosing somnolence. The representatives become withered, aged, ugly even to themselves – this is poignantly expressed when Alsi, whom we first saw as a vigorous young woman, strips and shows her withered flesh and shrunken, hanging breasts (119). The representatives also choose sleep, but the dreams that come in sleep prompt a series of meditations in Johor's presence, and putatively at his silent prompting. The meditations concern the self – the self as seen in a mirror, but not the image in the mirror of the present declining flesh. The meditations focus on individuality, whether individuality is something we paradoxically share with others, and then, as the end comes nearer, they concern the soul or spirit as an evanescence, a mist or net, in the body but somehow not of it. In these passages the novel's language becomes hesitant and exploratory, continually trying different, overlapping formulas for the elusive possibilities that are being sensed. It is through this change in language that the representatives' change of insight and condition is best approached.

The style here is in contrast with the simple, stripped language of the rest of the novella, where the variety of things and creatures was always narrow and is becoming narrower as the ice advances and variety leaves the planet, and nothing has a proper name except the representatives and Johor – not features of the terrain, not kinds of birds or animals, or implements, not the planet itself or its single, sacred lake. Doeg refers in general terms, for instance, to great white birds; at first, they seem to appear from nowhere, and we suppose they are part of the coming of the Ice Age, unfamiliar to Doeg and the others, as are the rough creatures like musk ox that they come to depend on as the weather eliminates almost all other food sources, and that are never given specific names either. Later, in a powerful story that Alsi tells from her childhood, we learn that the great birds have always been on the planet (129). If the inhabitants have given them a specific name (snowy owls, pale vultures, whatever) we never hear it. This kind of

---

[27] See Ursula Le Guin's response (1989b, 277) in her review of Lessing's *The Sentimental Agents* (1983): 'Can it be that Lessing is playing her own double agent?'

local colour, as it were translations from the (of course invented) local language, which is to be found away from Earth in almost all science fiction, and in fantasy, is eschewed here.

I remarked that only the people have proper names in this novella. This is not quite so. The names of persons that we come across in the text, Doeg and Alsi and Marl and so forth, are not the names of individuals but of functions. Doeg is the narrator, the person to whom is given the task of telling stories; whoever takes on this task becomes Doeg, as Alsi does at one point (117), before reverting to being named Alsi because she is the keeper of animals. There is some suggestion that the narration, from beginning to end, from the sentence at the beginning to the same sentence at the end, is given us by one Doeg; but it might have been given us by many who took on that name as they narrated – in which case their struggles to define individuality are thrown into a different light. And this is perhaps why Lessing doesn't as far as I can see define the gender of Doeg, or indeed of anyone except Alsi and her friend the boy Nonni who dies on an early expedition into the ice and snow. Certainly, gender is underplayed. Almost always we have 'we' for the representatives and 'they' for the rest of the people; two other representatives figure as 'he'. Alsi is the only person whose body is evoked for us (119), and the only person who gives us a glimpse into her own, individual childhood (the anecdote of the great birds that harass her and take her basket of food; 128–129). It is also Alsi who protests when she ceases to be Alsi because her role (nurturing growing animals) is no more: 'since this is not Alsi, Johor, who am I, *and what is my name?*' (146). Only at this point do the other representatives, who have also lost their roles, ask the same question. Johor, as commonly, says nothing.[28] The novel's practice with names keeps the inhabitants of Planet 8 at a distance, as it is easier, for instance, to execute someone who is simply 'the prisoner'.

Doeg cries to Johor that he feels more for the coming death of Alsi than for the deaths of his whole people – an attachment to the individual

---

[28] Names figure in complex ways in Lessing's life and fiction. Her parents were Emily and Alfred Taylor. Shortly after they were married, Emily decided that they would be known as Maude and Michael, and so they were from then on. After a difficult labour, Maude was delivered of a girl, to her disappointment. She wouldn't give her a name, so the doctor, anxious to complete the formalities and get away, suggested Doris. Later Lessing uses the name Emily for the foster-daughter in *Memoirs*; when she publishes two novels as Jane Somers, the dying old woman whom the main character nurses in *If the Old Could...* (1984) is given the name Maudie (Klein 2000, 10–12, 237).

that he evidently has to learn to surpass (89). Alsi makes a fissure in the novel's impersonal emphasis on the anonymous and collective, a fissure that reopens in Lessing's comments in the 'Afterword' on the very different individualities and deaths of Scott and his companions in the Antarctic. Johor is the only outsider on Planet 8, and perhaps the only one with a personal as distinct from a functional name – but we can't be sure of this on the evidence of the text. Johor is not physically described until he is starving and beginning to resemble the others; and he is mostly characterised in terms of his omissions – he won't answer questions or explain.

This simplifying blankness in the overall treatment of things and people partly follows from the fact that we are told only what Lessing thinks we need to know to pursue the strong central trajectories of the story. We do learn of textile making and the working of iron, as new developments in the past history of the planet, but if we are curious to know whether these pursuits cause people to invent new names for the performers of new functions or for tools of the new trades, our curiosity will not be indulged. The inhabitants of the planet are already less individualised than is common in human groups, since they share names in taking on functions. The representatives are separated from the others, so we might wonder whether the others have distinct functions and therefore names; but we don't find out. As fits this minimal or different individuality, we learn that when the representatives meet with the people in general and decisions are to be made, there is not usually any discussion, let alone debate. A consensus emerges from the silence of the meeting.

So when the representatives, with Johor, make a final trek towards the North Pole, the heart of the cold, from where the ice at first descended, they are ready for the shedding of an individuality that was already attenuated. And this is what happens. There is the period of learning, sponsored by the silent, insistent Johor, which eventually images the self/spirit as evanescent, light and mist-like, that is, images it as everything the ice-suffocated and burdened planet and the wizened body burdened with heavy coverings are not. After this, the representatives go on two treks. These are part of an ascesis, not an exploration. First, they go to the South Pole of the planet, where there is a beacon erected by Canopus to guide the ships from Canopus. They sit, wait and come to the final realisation that no help or rescue will arrive. Then they trek again, with great effort and difficulty, towards the north, come to a point where they can go no further, and die. That is, they shed their bodies and become as one. This is 'the Making of the Representative'. There is a hint that those who have died earlier such as

Nonni, and the otherwise dismissed remainder of the population who have not undergone this ascesis, are also present in this afterlife. Some other future state awaits them. The state of being alive, not in the body or in social exchange or in thinking about the self as an individual thing, but in being a released, light, mist-like thing, which is what they attain at the end, is also what they apprehended earlier, in that phase of hesitant, exploratory use of language that as it were vindicated the novel's abstention from proper or specific names. A state that is newly discovered, and is separate from the experienced life of the body and of social exchange, can only be described, or suggested, in this way.

The transcendence that happens at the end of *Planet 8* is more carefully prepared than that which happens to the survivor and her companions at the end of *Memoirs*; the manner and style of the novel has been shaped to lead to it, as was not the case with the fragmented world and shifting focus of *Memoirs*. Interpretation and evaluation of *Planet 8*'s trajectory depends on a series of judgements: of Johor, of Canopus, of the refusals and indifferences that are entailed by the novel's form (parable or fable) and of its specifications as to the nature of the inhabitants of Planet 8, which in turn will take us back to our judgements of Johor and Canopus. Further, it depends on the shift from this being a novel about grief in the context of apocalypse to its being a novel with a religious orientation, leading to a discovery of the true nature of being and thence to a passage beyond death – which means that in the last analysis there is nothing to grieve, at least if you accept the loss of the body, social exchange and life on the planet as you gain transcendence.

After this, we have an 'Afterword' in a quite different style. Lessing admits candidly that this Afterword might have been better placed after the previous novel in the series, *The Sirian Experiments*, but says the publisher wanted it here, after *Planet 8*, because *Planet 8* is so short (162–163). The essay picks up when Lessing comes to Scott's last expedition to the Antarctic. She is moved by the idealism, 'nobility' and quixotic courage of those who took part, both in the amazing journey in winter and darkness and extreme cold to collect the eggs of the Emperor Penguin, as told in Apsley Cherry-Garrard's *The Worst Journey in the World*, and in the wasteful, possibly incompetent, certainly impractical journey to the South Pole that ended in death. This illuminates the icy world in which *Planet 8* is set, but it has an ironic ring. Those who went with Scott shared an ethos that, as Lessing emphasises, is now part of history and hard for us to share, but it was impressive, and in addition many of them were strong, individual, intensely idealistic. (Lessing concentrates on Edward Wilson.) They are all very unlike the submissive, conscientious people of Planet 8, doing their best to respond to Johor's nudging, and learning to accept death. Lessing talks of the 'high drama' of the Scott expedition; there is not much of that – not much action other than the emblematic – in *The Making of the Representative for Planet 8*. As often in the *Canopus in Argos* series, Lessing's attitude to her readers is a puzzle.[29]

In some ways we end part 2 of *Apocalypse in Crisis* with Lessing where we began with Ballard, in contact with a relentlessly personal vision, and one in her case, given that it is didactic, that comes without acknowledgement that it is personal. Most readers are accustomed to the stamp and flavour of the personal in many writers, but in Ballard and Lessing it can shock. It is an indication of what apocalypse as the story of death and the End can release, especially in a pair of novelists who are driven to re-imagine the New Jerusalem, the passage through destruction to a place or state beyond death. It is very largely this version of apocalypse, with its reimagining of death and transcendence, that is resisted in the fictions discussed in chapters 6 and 7.

---

[29] See Lorna Sage's comments on the novel's attitude to the reader and its use of the Canopeans: '"I" becomes "we": and "we", fairly clearly here, is an imperial, imperative pronoun'; 'Lessing's Canopeans employ a doublespeak that appropriates the voices of others' (Sage 1988, 165).

Part 3

Resistance and Revision

The discussion in part 3 of *Apocalypse in Crisis* ranges from texts first published in the 1950s (Arno Schmidt's *Nobodaddy's Children*) to one published in 2019 (Jeff VanderMeer's *Dead Astronauts*), and from texts that treat apocalypse with comedy and scepticism or reassert the values of everyday life to those that press it to extremes and in the process dissolve linear temporality and the boundaries of identity. It moves away from the historical orientation of the first two parts of *Apocalypse in Crisis*, but in focusing on resistance to apocalypse and radical revision of apocalypse it highlights how the makers of fictions of apocalypse have increasingly responded to our culture's habituation to it, the sheer weight of fears, actual threats and fictions of apocalypse.

Part 3 looks at where apocalyptic fictions have resisted underlying features of apocalypse itself, its domination of the narrative, its alliance with death and its haunting by unqualified doom, and it looks at how recent apocalyptic fiction has revised prevailing narratives, often in radical ways. Resistance to apocalypse can take the form of comedy, or parody, or the interweaving of apocalyptic with other narratives, or questioning the material reality of catastrophe itself. Revision has behind it a variety of impulses and changes. A set of cultural shifts and reorientations have become apparent over time; they include the contemporary habituation to apocalyptic thinking and feeling; the inadequacy of imagining catastrophe as a delimited figure and event rather than as a condition in which those involved are immersed, and, more broadly, contemporary unease about the pretensions of the individual subject and the reliability of truth. These conditions have not abruptly appeared on the scene, but the texts discussed in part 3 suggest that they have attained special salience in recent years. The result is that the central constituents of an apocalyptic fiction – the nature of the event and whether it is an event, exactly, and the persons and their relation to the event – have been revised. Catastrophe is imagined as a condition more than as something that can be delimited and figured, such as an invasion – or its existential status is seen as uncertain; in consequence the challenge and task catastrophe sets the individual is less clear.

Recent apocalyptic fictions, then, are markedly different both from the postwar disaster novels discussed in part 1 and from the products of the cultural moments and movements that were examined in part 2. Part 1 discussed novels dealing with apocalypse as it unfolded in ordinary middle-class life, examining how the characters responded and coped. The novels to be discussed in chapter 7, 'Apocalypse and Everyday Life', return to the world of ordinary, even domestic, lives and anxieties, but with a difference: in both *The Leftovers* and *Girlfriend in a Coma* the solidity of this domestic scene is thrown into doubt by anomalous features of the apocalyptic catastrophe itself.

Part 2 traced an intensifying focus on death and transcendence in apocalyptic fictions of the 1960s and after. This development was not the only one in this period, but it had a degree of coherence; it was launched by Ballard's and Aldiss's provocative dismissal of much of the ethos of previous science fiction, and fertilised by the counter-culture of the 1960s and 1970s. Apocalypse involves catastrophe, even annihilation but, properly speaking, it also holds the promise of recovery, or liberation, or transcendence: a form of equivalence to the New Jerusalem of traditional apocalypse. The direction of history is towards doom, final and total destruction, but something can be retrieved from this, though it will have to be reimagined in a secular age. In the texts that were examined in part 2, something *is* retrieved, but not necessarily what might have been hoped for. We arrive not at recovery but at death submitted to, immolation chosen, or, in Lessing, a somewhat strained overstepping of death into a being beyond that is only glimpsed. Perhaps the project of imagining apocalypse needs reassessment or a dose of scepticism. Perhaps apocalyptic imagining simply releases nihilistic pleasures.

As we saw with *Memoirs* and *Planet 8*, however, the counter-culture that animated the provocative explorations of pleasure and subjectivity in Aldiss, Ballard and Carter could in turn prompt a reaction. In Karl Mannheim's term, the 1960s were 'dynamic-antinomial' (1952, 314). Lessing reacted into austere refusal of style and play, of the sensuous and even the material, and moved past death in the form of immolation to a glimpse of transcendence beyond death. She also experimented with the nature of the catastrophe: in *Planet 8* it is clearly imaged (the invading ice); in *Memoirs* it is a matter of scattered, confusing symptoms and behaviours – more like what we will encounter later in, for instance, *Cosmopolis*.

Nor was this the only reaction. To examine others, we can begin from earlier. Chapter 6, 'Apocalypse, Comedy, Multiplicity', discusses *Nobodaddy's Children* (1951–63), *The Lathe of Heaven* (1971) and Anthony Burgess's *The End of the World News* (1982). These texts from the 1950s to the 1980s don't make a coherent corpus the way the English postwar disaster fictions or the Ballard–Aldiss apocalypses did. Indeed, Schmidt's trilogy is discussed not only for what it has in common with the texts of Burgess and Le Guin, but because it is brilliant, quirky and little known. What these texts do have in common, and what differentiates them from the apocalyptic fictions discussed in parts 1 and 2, is a sceptical attitude to apocalypse itself; events in the aftermath of catastrophe refuse to narrow towards either death or transcendence, and apocalypse is delimited by being set against other possibilities.

Apocalypse claims a kind of global hegemony in any fiction in which it appears. The ultimate End surely demands the full attention of the text, and dictates or releases what all the characters do and feel. Apocalypse can become Doom, and this possibility, which always haunts the tradition, itself asks for scepticism and critique. Hence, narratives that confine apocalypse to one strand of a multiple text, or, contrariwise, stage it repeatedly, or question its validity; and narratives that imagine how catastrophe can be averted or mitigated. In each of these cases the global hegemony of apocalypse stimulates contrary imaginations. Apocalypse may be forced to compete with a plethora of other stories. In *Kraken* London is thronged with 'apocalyptists', and the text shifts between satire, comedy and horror in the effort to accommodate their competing or cross-purposing agendas; a single apocalyptic threat eventually fights its way to the forefront and is averted. There is no question of this apocalyptic outcome threatening the stability of reality: reality is already unstable in a variety of ways, some of them fun, others horrifying. In *The End of the World News* the apocalypse is only given a third of the text, and even there the tangled strands of the characters' activities culminate in farce at the gates of the armed complex where the starship is being readied for flight away from a doomed Earth. The text of *The End of the World News* as a whole, with its three strands, and the actual end of the world story, as one of the strands, amount to a resistance to the finality that is built into the notion of apocalypse.

On the other hand, apocalypse as a form of imagination – as fiction, discourse, epithet – is habitual as well as ultimate in our culture. Any new apocalyptic story is shadowed by the hundreds already written. There will be more to come. Many a crisis, or even problem, nowadays strives to raise its threatening head above the others that are proclaimed and imagined from day to day, by asserting that it is apocalyptic. As I write, the Covid-19 crisis is giving the government in Australia another excuse to postpone action on climate change. These conditions can give rise to anger, or scepticism, or comedy.

There is no hard and fast rule for determining when a tradition such as that of making fictions of apocalypse has entered a phase of belatedness, but it is arguable that this has happened since – we had better say approximately – the 1970s. Because it is a literary form that makes much use of conventions, tropes and sub-genres, science fiction tends to self-criticism, parody and inventive revision of standard tropes, and there are examples of this in, for instance, *The Lathe of Heaven*, *The End of the World News* and *Kraken*; but the signs of belatedness extend more widely. In a phase of belatedness, the naïve imagining of the sudden arrival of the end of life as we know it is scarcely possible. The belated maker of an apocalypse has to manage the fact that imagining apocalypse has become habitual, a cultural reflex. The topic is as much how we imagine apocalypse, and how it imagines us – how its tropes and assumptions can dictate our imaginations – as it is the continuing power, salience and threat of catastrophe.

Contemporary apocalyptic fictions sometimes examine the split between knowing and explaining apocalypse, on the one hand, and suffering it on the other. Contemporary fictions sometimes examine the prevailing culture of apocalypse: attitudes and attractions to apocalypse and the language we have devised for it (Don DeLillo's *End Zone*, 1972), or how we receive and enjoy apocalyptic stories (A. S. Byatt's *Ragnarök*, 2011), or how we can hardly tell any other kind of story (Douglas Coupland's *Generation A*, 2009). *End Zone* juxtaposes the languages of American football and Mutually Assured Destruction, their tempting pleasures as well as their absurdities and their hermetic isolation from the rest of existence – which is itself often absurd and punctuated with unpredicted deaths in *End Zone*. *Ragnarök* begins by recalling how the story of the Norse apocalypse entertained and convinced a young girl during the Second World War, and then proceeds to recount the story, bringing out its challenging view of Nature as both vulnerable and dangerous.

Generation A tells of a group of five young people of the same generation, singled out and brought together because of their apparent ability to attract bees, previously thought to be extinct. They are required to tell stories, for experimental purposes. Zack's story is about the people at the rock concert who lose the meaning of words and numbers altogether; it's called '666!' and begins with a conversation in which the characters can no longer get the point of this apocalyptic Death Metal cliché (227–231). Julien's story is about the prehistoric birth of language, and its contemporary death as it is replaced by the gabble of texting (241–248). Serge's story is about the man who finds that decomposing *Finnegan's Wake* in his head helps to drown out the insistent voices telling him to gamble (269–273). Harj's story (183–187) is about the king who witnesses the utter destruction of his kingdom from a balloon; when he eventually descends to earth he finds that the few survivors can't read – letters are now nonsensically jumbled for them. The king stumbles over to a destroyed car: 'With his index finger, he wrote the words THE KING IS DEAD on its dusty window, and when he was asked what he had just written, he told his subjects, "A map"' (187). Most of the stories are about disaster and in many the disaster takes the form of incoherence of language and communication: for this generation, disaster infects the imagination and corrupts language.

In earlier apocalyptic fictions, catastrophe is sometimes confidently explained by the voice of the text, or the nature of the catastrophe is reasoned out by the characters. Science, common sense and the governing authorities retain a degree of trustworthiness. In recent years, the instability of truth has mutated from being a complex topic of interest to post-modernists and their critics to being a cultural and political threat and disease. Truth can be particularly vulnerable when disaster makes a rupture in routine. Rumour runs wild: 'no clear fact to be discerned'. Social life cannot proceed without trust, and in modernity we have to trust not individuals so much as systems, for instance the multitude of interlocking systems and institutions that make safe air travel a routine experience. As Niklas Luhmann says, trust in systems is 'trust without effective possibility of mistrusting';[1] but when something goes disastrously wrong, as when hijacked planes are crashed into the Twin Towers, mistrust is released. Hence, allegations that the CIA was responsible, or that the Covid virus is a hoax. Recent apocalyptic fictions have taken the logic of the instability of truth to the point of narrating apocalyptic catastrophes that are fake (in *Girlfriend in a Coma*), or very probably fake, as in Iain M. Banks's *The Hydrogen Sonata* (2012), or very probably illusory, as in Miéville's *The Scar* (2002), which culminates in an apocalyptic catastrophe that seems both to have happened and not to have happened. In Jeff Noon's *Falling Out of Cars* (2002) the catastrophe has taken the form of an epidemic that breaks the signifying chain, impedes memory, makes coherence of meaning a quest rather than

---

[1] Shapin (1994) discusses how trust is essential in any society, and all the more necessary in modern society, because of its complexity. See chapter 1, 'The Great Civility: Trust, Truth, and Moral Order', especially 8–15. Shapin quotes Luhmann when he returns to the topic at 411–413, on 412.

an ordinary experience; the protagonists wander a phantasmagorical England. Their situation is very different from that of the protagonists of the postwar disaster novels, or from those who wander the wrecked landscape in *The Drought*, where the causes of the disaster are clearly explained. Yet the distance between sensational and bewildering disaster or catastrophe, in the media and in fiction, and the safety and dullness of everyday life (in the suburbs, say) opens an opportunity for apocalyptic fiction that bases itself in that everyday life, and rejoins the two, though the recent versions examined in chapter 7 present everyday life as uneasy and deceptive in its ordinariness.

Our habituation to apocalyptic thinking and feeling prompts a series of variations in the depiction of catastrophe and what it leads to. Apocalypse is imagined less as an event and more as a condition. The figure or image of apocalypse as a kind of entity (like an invading monster) that can be grasped and witnessed is, at the least, attenuated. There is a sense that the threatened apocalypses are ongoing, as if in suspended imminence (especially true of climate change) or are less to be seen as events, such as invasion, than as processes, movements with multiple causes and symptoms, such as overpopulation and climate change. Apocalyptic catastrophe is often experienced not as a single event but as a bewildering concatenation of emergencies. 'Where the prospect of disaster once had a galvanising effect', observes David Runciman (2018, 6), 'now it tends to be stultifying. We freeze in the face of our fears.' The moment of apocalypse is one of overload and bewilderment, rather than one of inescapable disaster followed by a call to work, rebuild, survive or (in Ballard, for instance) to submit. *Cosmopolis, Kraken* and *Dead Astronauts* capture this condition of immersion and overload; catastrophe becomes both more diffuse and more extreme; the boundaries of identity (not necessarily that of humans in *Kraken* and *Dead Astronauts*) are thinned in magical and terrible ways.

When events *are* dramatised, they tend to be spectacular, to involve a multitude of participants and centres of attention, and to reach for an almost orgiastic intensity of violence, destruction and confusion. (This is the prevailing condition in the mangas and films that Peter Y. Paik discusses in *From Utopia to Apocalypse*, 2010.) Events become hyper-events. Yet while multitudes are swept up in the story, individuals have to strain to be effective and, in response to that, they tend to be violently self-assertive or fecklessly wayward. The sobriety of report by a witness whose role in the events is a modest one (lucky to have survived, working to pull together a small community or face the inevitable end) no longer suits the confused and accumulating quality of events. The main character may well be self-assertive and active; there are heroes (not simply witnesses) but the hero is not so much eclipsed as exacerbated. In the earlier fictions discussed in part 2, apocalypse took the protagonists deeper into their subjectivity; in more recent fictions intensified subjectivity is depicted more sceptically, and often as closer to madness. In Eric Packer, the main character in *Cosmopolis*, individual will and self-assertion is intensified almost to insanity. Almost any of the main characters in Iain M. Banks's Culture novels from the 1980s could also be cited; Horza in *Consider Phlebas* (1987) is a good example, because his repeated and often feckless violence is directly posed against the vast impersonal violence of intergalactic warfare, as if he hopes to equal or exceed what is almost immeasurable.[2] (Both Eric Packer and Horza are hyper-masculine.) The protagonists of Jeff VanderMeer's *Dead Astronauts* dispose of menacing and uncanny powers, but these powers seem as much stigmata or burdens as capacities to shape the world. In contrast, recent apocalypse fictions that put the emphasis on everyday life, such as *The Leftovers* and *Girlfriend in a Coma*, stress the necessities and pains of collective action, and the fallible ordinariness of the main characters, who are coping, if they can, with vast overturns that have been brought about not by human agency but by hidden, possibly supernatural forces. Similarly, George Orr in *The Lathe of Heaven* is ordinary as well as exceptional, and only succeeds in averting the chaos threatened by the hyper-masculine and larger-than-life Haber when he summons 'a little help from my friends'.

---

[2] For Horza's violence, see his reckless flight *inside* the vast hangars and corridors of a crowded spaceship; for the impersonal violence of the war, see the meticulous long-range destruction of the vast Vavatch Orbital, an artificial planet (both in chapter 8); for the almost immeasurable scale of the war, see the appendix, 'the war, briefly'.

Chapter 6

Apocalypse, Comedy, Multiplicity
Arno Schmidt, Anthony Burgess and Ursula K. Le Guin

Apocalypse begins with a catastrophe that is global and all-encompassing, an event that changes everything and dictates what people will do and what the story will tell. Apocalypse unifies the world, in a way that resembles the unification of the world brought about by a dystopian regime, a regime that controls reality and has no outside that one can escape to. In apocalypse the science-fictional ideal of World Government controlled by science and reason meets its evil twin: a world made one by disaster. In apocalypse there is only one story to tell, that of the disaster and its aftermath; the story begins with an ending, though very often it ends with a tentative beginning – a recovery, a sign of new life or a new society.

Yet there are many imaginations of apocalypses; the label is readily, habitually applied to many possibilities and, as this practice takes hold, apocalypse blurs with crisis, a matter of weekly if not daily encounter in the media. Apocalypse is imminent, a matter for the future, just about to happen; it hasn't happened yet, its home is the (near) future and all the catastrophic wars and transformative revolutions in the modern past have left us shaken, but have not yet issued either in a New Jerusalem or in annihilation. This situation is something that many recent fictions of apocalypse have acknowledged.

The multiplicity and diversity characteristic of the novel, its appetite for breadth of social life, scenes, personalities, plots and subplots, ironies, genres and generic mixtures, has tended to chafe against the connection of apocalypse with the all-encompassing and inescapable. This chapter samples some fictions involving apocalypse that give a form to this sceptical urge to multiplicity. In *Nobodaddy's Children* (Arno Schmidt, 1953–63) and *The End of the World News* (Anthony Burgess, 1982) apocalypse is confined to one strand of a text that has several other tales to tell, and apocalypse is accompanied by comedy of eccentricity – the self-absorbed little guy – in the first case, and by the muddle of coincidences and crossed purposes that is farce in the second. In addition, both these texts offer characters who live through other texts, reminding us that apocalypse is something imagined, one of the multiplicity of imaginations, though it is also the bringer of doom and unity. In *The Lathe of Heaven* (Ursula K. Le Guin, 1971) apocalypse happens over and over again, just as it does in our cultural imaginary even though we imagine apocalypse as, by definition, a once-only event. Le Guin's novel lays bare the relations between apocalyptic transformation and the changes that we learn to normalise in modernity: the first serves as a metaphor of the second. The unforeseen rules, in spite of repeated efforts to control and reorder reality, wholesale and catastrophic changes approach insanity, and the situation is only resolved by a touch of magic. In each of these novels what is valued and asserted is the muddle and cussedness of the everyday and ordinary; the discussion in chapter 7 takes up this valuation in Tom Perotta's *The Leftovers* (2011) and Douglas Coupland's *Girlfriend in a Coma* (1998).

The works by Schmidt and Burgess with which this chapter begins come from different cultures and different times – the three parts of *Nobodaddy's Children* were first published in 1951–63, *The End of the World News* in 1982. This gap is a threat to the historical narrative that *Apocalypse in Crisis* is tracing, from postwar through the cultural tumult of the 1960s and beyond to more recent developments. The book's narrative is disrupted; but then comedy is disruptive. As regards dates of publication, Schmidt belongs with the first and second waves of the imagination of apocalypse in the aftermath of the Second World War, Wyndham and Shute to Ballard and Lessing, though *Nobodaddy's Children* illuminates his very different national situation. He belongs to a distinctly German cultural moment. His task, along with, for instance, Heinrich Böll and Günter Grass, is to come to terms with the Germany of Nazism and the Second World War. In *Apocalypse in Crisis*, however, he is discussed with Burgess and Le Guin in terms of how comedy modifies and even subverts apocalypse.

Nobodaddy's Children and *The End of the World News* are casual in their origins – three novellas in the case of Schmidt, not published as a single work until 1963; a text made up of three widely – wildly – divergent strands in the case of Burgess, probably thrown together at a late date, with one of them, the strand concerning Trotsky, probably drafted as a musical comedy, or maybe a parody of a musical comedy. A triple-stranded text such as is Burgess's is clearly different from a text made into a trilogy by taking three texts originally published separately and fitting them up as a single volume, as with *Nobodaddy's Children*. Yet they have a great deal else in common. Neither text submits to the primacy of the apocalyptic catastrophe it is narrating. The apocalyptic catastrophe treated in Schmidt's 'Dark Mirrors' is the third of three episodes from German history, though it is the only one that happens in the future, and it works no real change in the idiosyncratic style of the text or in the quirky individualism of the main character, even though it tells of life after most humans have been exterminated. In Burgess the apocalyptic catastrophe is one of three interwoven stories from the twentieth century, those of Freud, of Trotsky (sort of) and of the obliteration of Earth by collision with Lynx, an asteroid. The third, apocalyptic story has the last word – Earth is destroyed – but also the last laugh, in that its events are often farcical. Both novels rely on versions of a traditional comic figure, most familiar in Falstaff – self-indulgent, pleasure-seeking, selfish, irresponsible, improper and unquenchable. In *Nobodaddy's Children* this is the central character of all three novellas; in the Lynx strand of *The End of the World News* it is the feckless pair that we mostly follow, Willett and Brodie. In each case the form of the work refuses apocalypse's drive towards the monolithic, because a lot else is being narrated in separate stories, and the content refuses it also, because the characters ignore its call to seriousness and discipline. Willett and Brodie in *The End of the World News* and the main character (Düring/Schmidt) in *Nobodaddy's Children* are all traditionalists, at home in literature and the classics, though mostly as what gives them pleasure and a chance to orate or vent, and are not interested in science or modernity or the future.

Adventures and Opinions of an Eccentric
Nobodaddy's Children

Nobodaddy's Children consists of three novellas, 'Scenes from the Life of a Faun' (first German publication, 1953), 'Brand's Heath' (1951) and 'Dark Mirrors' (1951). It was published as a trilogy in 1963.[1] 'Faun' takes place 1939–44, 'Brand's Heath', 1946 and 'Dark Mirrors', 1960–2, which is in the future as regards when it was written. They are all set in the same area, the north German plain – heath and pine forest – south of Hamburg, a little north of Hanover, near Walsrode. The history is broad (the Second World War, its aftermath in Germany, a nuclear war in the late 1950s), but the setting, the activities and the values are local. The central character is in each case the first-person narrator;

---

[1] References are to Arno Schmidt, *Nobodaddy's Children*, translated by John E. Woods, Champaign and London: Dalkey Archive Press, 1995; the title of the relevant novella is also given with each reference.

his circumstances are different in each case: in 'Faun', Düring, a civil servant, a First World War veteran, married with kids, in his early fifties; in 'Brand's Heath', Schmidt (not named until p. 165), a writer researching for a life of de la Motte Fouqué, served in the Second World War and has just been released from a British prisoner of war (POW) camp; in 'Dark Mirrors', no name given, possibly Schmidt again, seemingly the last survivor of a nuclear cataclysm.[2] This character has very much the same personality and views throughout, so he will be discussed as if he were the one person – indeed, his insistence on remaining the same person, unchanged even by nuclear catastrophe, is the point. (Much is drawn from Arno Schmidt's own life especially in 'Brand's Heath', the first to be written: the work on Fouqué, of whom Arno Schmidt published a biography; the parcel from Schmidt's sister in the US, full of good things.)

That personality and those views are very important. It is through them that we experience the changing circumstances of the war, the postwar and in the third novella, the period five years after the great catastrophe, a nuclear war that has wiped out almost all humans. The central character's independence, learning and didacticism, idiosyncrasies, buoyancy and sensuality, and love of nature (more than of people, though he has a lover for a while in each novella) stand against the bleakness, successively, of Nazism, defeat and catastrophe. All of these disasters, he is quite sure, are the responsibility of the Germans in particular and humans, especially those in authority, in general. As he says, or rather orates, to his lover Lisa in 'Dark Mirrors':

> 'The mummers, quacks, jugglers, prestidigitators, bawds, cut-purses, and swashbucklers divided the world among them; – the sheep stretched out their muttonheads and let themselves be shorn; – while the fools gambolled and somersaulted. And the clever ones, if they could, went forth and became hermits.' (223)

The old-fashioned diction (relying on the accuracy of the translation here) is appropriate; his values are retrospective as well as local; and up until his unexpected meeting with Lisa, a second survivor, he has been happily living as a hermit himself. He has no use for particular political or historical explanations, though he values the particular over the general in many other contexts.[3] He is *l'homme moyen sensuel*,

---

[2] I refer to the character as Schmidt and to the author as Arno Schmidt.
[3] He comments on another character: '...he had got around to "the meaningful general" (as Goethe would have expressed it : and at his age he should have

eager for pleasure according to his own very definite tastes – food, sex, reading, walking in the woods or on the heath, tricking the authorities, holding forth on the writers he likes and on the things he doesn't like about Germans, or about humans: 'always a windbag of first rank' as he says of himself ('Dark Mirrors', 181). Not that his pleasures are always typical of the comic eccentric: for instance, he always describes the behaviour of the weather, the Sun or moon, the wind, how the trees and bushes respond to the weather as if they, together with the Sun, moon and wind, were living creatures. Here he does immerse himself in particulars, as if every day had different weather and the trees and bushes behaved differently every time he walked among them. He has his set of authors that he loves, few of them contemporary (Döblin is an exception), many of them Germans of the romantic period, but also with a cosmopolitan outreach (Poe, whom Arno Schmidt translated; Shakespeare). Idiosyncratic as he is, he can also stand as democratic man – not that he would ever be in a majority or defer to the majority, but in figuring what democracies need (independence, scepticism, refusal to be swayed by rhetoric).

Circumstances are different in each novella, and clearly this illuminates the drastically differing histories the Germans suffered or – as Schmidt would probably say – brought upon themselves. But so far in discussing the central character's personality the emphasis has been on what does not change; even the change of name and age from one story to another makes no difference to this personality, which is present, eagerly expressing itself, in every line of the text. In each story he walks in the woods, enjoys the weather, performs as ingenuous lover to a woman who leaves or (in 'Faun') will probably leave. In each story he denounces the Germans, avers that population reduction would be a very good idea, or welcomes the fact that nuclear catastrophe has accomplished it to the point of depopulation (for instance, 188 and 208, 'Dark Mirrors'). The circumstance that he is – as far as he can tell – the last human alive only brings out some new sides of the same personality, and even that is qualified by the fact that the exuberant, brief love affair he enjoys at the end of 'Dark Mirrors', when another human does appear, involves the same enjoyment, ardour and clumsiness as did the love affairs in the other two novellas. (In the affair with Lisa in 'Dark Mirrors' we have Arno Schmidt's rejection of the common Adam-meets-Eve motif of many post-apocalypse stories.[4] Schmidt and

known that only the meaningful particular has any meaning !)' ('Brand's Heath', 145).

[4] See the entry on 'Adam and Eve' in Clute and Nicholls 1993, 4–5.

Lisa have a good time, he enjoys her feistiness, she stays with him as long as she feels like doing so, but there is no chance that they will dedicate themselves to reproducing the human species.)

So we have Arno Schmidt's riposte to the world-shattering gloom of many fictions of apocalypse, the descent of humans into violent survivalism, or their ascent into enlightened pastoralism. The person who is the consuming interest of 'Dark Mirrors' remains as he was, just as animatedly himself as he was before, and the two earlier novellas enable us to see this very clearly. Neither descent nor ascent, just carrying on much as before, pedant become vagrant, as he says (186), though in fact in 'Dark Mirrors' he is still a pedant. Nor do the two earlier novellas really take it upon themselves to show how the world was headed for the catastrophe that arrived between the second and the third. We could infer this analysis if we tried hard, and certainly the moral laziness and gullibility of people in general could figure in this analysis, as well as the indiscriminate violence of the Second World War. 'Scenes from the Life of a Faun' ends with a set-piece dramatisation of a bombing raid on a munitions factory, with immense explosions, vehicles and people hurled high in the air; but even this figures partly as a spectacular fireworks display, and Düring and his lover set off their own private explosion in the midst of it all. The second novella in the sequence, 'Brand's Heath' gives us a defeated and occupied Germany, not so much devastated, in what we see, as levelled, reduced to poverty and improvisation; but in many ways the action is more upbeat than in the first novella, so there is no steady decline from the first to the second novella to prepare us for the absolute nuclear disaster that sets the scene for the third. If anything, the second novella shows us a world in which the protagonist has more scope than his predecessor in the first. Bureaucratic pomposity and futility have been swept away with the defeat, the main character's nocturnal trips into the woods with his lover have a more practical purpose (gathering mushrooms, stealing apples), and he now enjoys his own little family (the sisters Grete and his lover Lore, and himself), whereas he was estranged from his wife and children in what was depicted as an empty bourgeois domesticity in the first novella. For most of 'Dark Mirrors', the third novella, there are no people whatever; so, the world is terminally devastated; but for the central character this gives yet more scope for improvisation, Crusoe-like making do ('like Robinson with 2 guns', 215), walks in the woods and disquisitions on literature. (Arno Schmidt vaguely acknowledges that the bombs would have poisoned water and vegetation, but makes no real attempt to show this; the house the protagonist breaks into early in the novella in the course of his scrounging is full of human skeletons but also harbours a lively fox. Later he and Lisa work out that the war has particularly devastated two belts of land in Europe, but outside these belts it appears that humans have died out although trees and fields flourish.)

It is still necessary to fill in more of the details of what happens in each novella, in particular how each is put into relation with past history and literature, but, so far, it seems that Arno Schmidt has pushed about as far as it can go the affirmation that *l'homme moyen sensual*, as created here in his idiosyncrasy and defiance of authority, can survive almost anything. And the text's highly individual, heavily worked prose style is yet to be discussed. This style is effective in catching moment to moment mood and sensation and thought, but it is also full of flourishes and assertions of the self, Schmidt's self, unabashed by crisis and change.

Personality as Pocket Universe

The style of *Nobodaddy's Children* is full of pauses and digressions, of devices to ensure that the present moment of experience is loaded with a grab-bag of comments, asides, reflections, allusions and fancies. The opening phrase of each new paragraph is in italics, and then the rest of the paragraph is indented. (Retellings or readings from other stories or histories are conventionally paragraphed.) There are sudden thoughts:

> *Why* can't you connect other people's brains onto your own, so that they can see the same images, flashes of memory, that you do ? (But then there are the bastards who would) ('Brand's Heath', 108)

There are crowded encapsulations of a moment:

> *Tender starshine trembling in resting clouds* : four times the cry circled the house : Wish-ton-wish. Wish-ton-wish : owlet. Great man, Cooper. That's the soldier's curse : never to be alone; here I was alone : finally! Cold, true : but alone at last. Except for across the way, the two of them bustling and sleeping; that was tolerable. ('Brand's Heath', 127)[5]

---

[5] 'Cooper' is Fenimore Cooper, one of Schmidt's favourites; 'the two of them' are his companions Grete and Lore.

And a quick reflection on his changed condition as the last man, from 'Dark Mirrors' (186):

> [...] just as with Schopenhauer and Buddha, where a criminal became a saint with no transition, life has transformed me from pedant to vagrant; not that it still doesn't sometimes make a strange mix.

And see the sudden reflection at 199: '...only you needed to be very careful on the long bridge – what's this <you> ? : I ! I can in fact strike the word <you> from the language !'

His appreciation of nature, and himself in it:

> *I had lost my direction in there*, and suddenly found myself again at the woods' edge, in a little clearing, only a hundred yards from the tracks. Junipers built two delicate semicircles : to judge by their size, those must be very old plants (they get to be 800 to 1000 years old; not me). And the ground was so firm and clean that I cosily poured myself out on it with a sigh. Wonderful ! ('Dark Mirrors', 192)

Arno Schmidt makes extensive use of spaces and colons, as well as parentheses and exclamation marks and angled brackets; there is always some nuance of timing or feeling to be underlined. The effect at its best is that the writing is brisk and leisurely at the same time. As with Sterne, this always-fascinated finickyness also tends to disguise the fact that things are happening beneath the ever-active surface: there actually is a plot.

The Living Past

In 'Scenes from the Life of a Faun', Düring, a civil servant, is commissioned by his boss to assemble an archive of local history; in 'Brand's Heath' Schmidt is delving into local archives again, as research for his life of Fouqué; in 'Dark Mirrors' he is simply a collector of books and a maker of quotations, as there is no society to serve, even nominally – and in the earlier novellas he was collecting facts and documents for himself, and to spout to anyone interested, but not really for broader purposes. In his work in 'Faun' he becomes fascinated by scraps of evidence from the time during Napoleon's heyday when the district was a *departement* of France; these scraps concern a French deserter, who apparently lived in hiding for years on the heath.

But then I stopped to consider : the lonely fugitive on the moor !
And I puckered my brows and gazed at my windjacket's horsedung-
colored sleeve : had simply deserted ! In a single bound left rank
and file and leapt onto the open moor (and had apparently lived
there in hiding for years on end, <and paying thee no notice>
: even in the white desolate winter : so you can do that sort of
thing !). ('Faun', 43)

He eventually finds the tiny hut the man had built himself, though it's not on any map (he collects and pores over maps, as we would expect). The hut becomes a convenient place for himself and Käthe, his lover, to sneak off to at night; he has become the Napoleonic fugitive, the faun. The authorities start to realise he has this hideout, and he sets out with Käthe to destroy it before it can be discovered. This is the night of the huge raid on the nearby munitions factory. The resulting explosions serve to hide the small explosion that obliterates this evidence of the Napoleonic deserter's secret freedom and of his own and Käthe's secret freedom. The past comes to the aid of the present; the consensus present, the present of everybody else, is rejected, scorned, evaded; the past is collected, cherished and (here) acted on, and the point to which the past flows is always, in this and the later novellas, Düring/Schmidt himself.

The effect is more diffused, less carefully plotted, in the later novellas, but all are full of quotations, allusions, stories read or told – the past assembled to rebuke and replace the despised present. Arno Schmidt is posing the treasures, intricacies and by-ways of German literature against the empty windy rhetoric of the present. And he is posing the local, a set of fields, woods and obscure villages, traversed on foot or bicycle or at most in a local train, against the grand vagueness and randomness of war (in 'Faun', Düring's son dead near Murmansk (76), the young clerk from his office, 'little Otte, not yet 18', dead near Monte Cassino (71)).

Arno Schmidt's affirmation through his central character of the value of the local particular is in many ways a challenging all-or-nothing refusal of history. We can't read *Nobodaddy's Children* as it moves from 1939 to 1946 to the future in 1966 without engaging ourselves in the main character's personality and style, his likes and dislikes (likes Fenimore Cooper and Wieland but dislikes Balzac and Goethe), his opinions, responses, naivities, sensations, delight in his small victories (sex, trickery, food). But, on the other hand, that history which he denies and rejects – to the point of welcoming the depopulation of Germany and probably the world – may well be what shapes our acceptance of his embrace of the local, warts and all. He is like Yossarian in *Catch-22*:

his madness makes sense in the context of a greater madness that, in *Nobodaddy's Children*, he hardly need to do more than allude to: mention of a bludgeon in a randomly opened book reminds him:

> '...apparently back then in the camps of the Hun there were <light field-bludgeons 53>; and then the <doubleFB 17> for heavyweights : to what ends cannot a rhetorician be corrupted by his word supply ! ('Dark Mirrors', 189)

Even here his particular point of view can be troubling: he is, characteristically, annoyed by the misuse of language, while bludgeons are associated with more horrible and direct crimes. His rejection of contemporary history, including that of nuclear catastrophe, and insistence on his own quirky likes and dislikes, is challenging, quixotic and unstable. It depends on the tightrope act of his moment-to-moment surprisingness. The localness of the postwar disaster novels is grounded in the characters' commitment to survive and rebuild, and in the typicality of their values, decent and practical. Schmidt, in his local and historical situation, is much more sceptical and resistant.

Everything hinges on the depiction of the main character in *Nobodaddy's Children*, and it may give rise to reservations. W. G. Sebald (2005b/1983, 106) suggests that this kind of character – bluff, earthy, uncompromised because uninvolved in the horrendous crimes of the nation in the period of Nazi rule – serves as an evasion in German fiction of the 1950s: 'the myth of the good German who had no choice but to let everything wash over him and bear it'. He notices how this begins to change with Günter Grass's *From the Diary of a Snail* (1974), which recounts the fate of the Jews of Danzig, and thereby faces crimes that earlier fiction would not look at, but goes on to suggest that the result is that the story of the main character, Hermann Ott – a variant on the type of the good German – 'will not ultimately stand up to critical examination' (114). Is the depiction of Schmidt in *Nobodaddy's Children* open to a similar criticism? He is even more assertively independent of the mass of Germans and their conformism than Grass's character, and (perhaps) he is offered to us as an ideal German in his earthiness and in his love of his native region, though in the context of German history the latter can suggest a desire to return to an idealised past before Germany was unified.[6] If we follow this interpretation the

---

[6] Not that imaginative return to the past is to be rejected out of hand. See, for instance, Grass's novella about a gathering of German poets during the Thirty Years War, *The Meeting at Telgte* (1979). Also relevant to this issue is the

figure of the good German is stretched to breaking point in *Nobodaddy's Children*, and nuclear annihilation serves as an uneasy substitute for the Holocaust and other crimes of the German nation from 1933 to 1945. There is plenty of history and disaster in *Nobodaddy's Children*, but it is everywhere and nowhere, because of the way the central figure in it assertively, and idiosyncratically, narrows our perspective to his opinions, feelings and interests. This reading is possible, and if we follow it then *Nobodaddy's Children* with its quirks becomes an exercise in ingenious, and often entertaining, distraction. I don't think this is correct, but it is true that the novel demonstrates the brittle logic of the figure of the good German. If you find yourself going so far as to welcome nuclear annihilation, as Schmidt does in the novel, then your refusal of history has put you into a cul de sac. The good German in the end is a nation of one, even if he has such a multitude of opinions and sensations that he has seemed like a tribe in himself.[7]

Comedy of Apocalypse
The End of the World News

In *The End of the World News*, Anthony Burgess takes on the scope of modern history in a text whose three narrative strands are interwoven rather than successive, and gives that history much more weight than does Arno Schmidt; but in the strand that concerns apocalypse he similarly relies on idiosyncratic, irresponsible characters.

The text of *The End of the World News* is very much by Anthony Burgess.[8] He wrote the Foreword, under his given name, John B. Wilson, BA, he wrote the Epilogue, set long after the end of the earth; he wrote the blurb on the dust jacket. There is a Foreword, in which 'Wilson' is puzzled by the mess of papers Burgess left behind,[9] hazards a guess that these three stories should be bundled together, relying on a stray clue in Burgess's papers, and bestows the title, and there is an Epilogue, which declares that future generations on the starship *America* will neither remember nor believe the story we have been reading.

---

prevalence, sometimes dominance, of unpolitical 'inwardness' in German culture, surveyed in detail in Watson 2010. He sums up at 830–833.

[7] The issue of whether the survival and valorisation of the local and everyday might amount to an evasion of the global dimensions of apocalypse emerges again in the discussion of *The Leftovers* in chapter 7.

[8] *The End of the World News: An Entertainment*, London: Hutchinson, 1982.

[9] Burgess made a similar joke about 'Joseph Kell', his nom de plume for *One Hand Clapping* and *Inside Mr Enderby*. See Biswell 2006, 272, n.2.

In between is a complicated 'Entertainment' in three strands, full of speeches, songs, puns and word games, dramas, deaths and killings, and also disasters. Towards the end the last US President meditates on what he might have said to his people, honestly announcing that the end had come rather than concealing the certainty of catastrophe. He concludes instead, 'There was nothing to say. There had never been anything to say' (377). On the contrary, there is a lot to say, spilling over three stories. Stories may end in disaster, but speech comes before, during and after. There is plenty of music, too: the starship with the last survivors of Earth departs to the strains of Mozart's Jupiter symphony. The heroes of the Lynx story, the apocalyptic strand of the text, are Willett, actor, declaimer, lover of demotic insult, and Val Brodie, minor poet and writer of pulp science fiction (both of whom resemble Burgess himself in various ways); the hero of the Freud story is 'The golden-voiced Professor Sigmund Freud, Freudios Chrysostomos' (306; but this reminder comes when his speech is blocked by the prosthesis necessitated by his cancer).

One of the intertwined stories gives the history of Freud's foundation of psychoanalysis, the quarrels and treacheries of the movement, his cancer, and his exile and death, as the Second World War begins. War is announced on the radio by *'J'aime Berlin'* (Chamberlain: not the most atrocious pun in the book):

> 'They say it will be the last war.' [Ernest Jones to Freud]
> 'It will be *my* last war.' (367)

Second, we have episodes from Trotsky's time in New York as revolution is imminent and Russia and America's entry into the First World War is also imminent, ending with his being summoned triumphantly home. Third, we have the approach towards Earth of Lynx, a planet-sized body that causes chaos and destruction on its first orbital pass around Earth, and annihilates it on its second approach, some months later (here this is called the Lynx story). The Freud and Trotsky stories relate to events – the Second World War, the Russian Revolution – that were, understandably, seen as apocalyptic. The Lynx story stages the end of the world, brought about by an event borrowed from classic science fiction (for instance, H. G. Wells, 'The Star'). The book's title brings news of the end of the world, or it merely quotes what BBC announcers said at the end of the World News.

The Lynx story is based on an earlier version, unpublished in Burgess's lifetime. This is *Puma*, in turn the outcome of a project for a film script based on Edwin Balmer and Philip Wylie's *When Worlds Collide* and *After Worlds Collide* (1933, 1934). *Puma* has recently been published with very informative notes by Paul Wake.[10] In both *Puma* and the Lynx story there are signs that Burgess was very aware of the conventionality of the science-fiction story of Earth's collision with an asteroid or similar body, and very aware of apocalypticism as a cultural habit. In *The End of the World News* he manages this awareness by measuring the Lynx story against those of Freud and Trotsky: different imaginations and narratives are built into the text. In *Puma* he responds with a kind of manic play both with science-fiction conventions and with literariness. A science-fiction author usually provides even a near future setting with names of things, brand names, names of people, and in *Puma* Burgess does this almost to parody; see, for instance, the description of a living room, with 11 brand names in a paragraph (P. 41), or the list of the names and professions of 50 crew members (P. 73–75). The practice is excessive but also systematic: names allude to often obscure Americans of about the 1970s, professions are invented by Burgess on the basis of Greek. This latter gives a clue: Burgess simultaneously indulges the verbal conventions of science fiction and indulges his love of arcane and clever verbiage and allusion. Hence Willett's prolific insults come from Thomas Urquhart's translation of *Gargantua and Pantagruel* (literally Rabelaisian, then), and the titles of Val Brodie's science-fiction novels from Gerard Manley Hopkins's poems. In *Puma*, this verbal play sits like an applied screen or veneer over the surface of the science-fiction narrative of doom and the twist towards rambunctious comedy and farce that Burgess gives it. Often what is applied is an assertive literariness, a dash of modernist culture; it suggests a restlessness on the part of the author with the rest of the project, like someone spending time on his phone (maybe accessing a dictionary) because he is finding the conversation around him a bit boring. The element of busy verbal play is certainly not absent from *The End of the World News*, as we will see, but it is toned down, and the reason may be that Burgess has found other ways of expressing his unease with his apocalyptic story, by combining it with additional, different, kinds of story.

Freud's story is told in realist terms: there are scenes of argument and dispute, as the psychoanalytic movement develops and splits; quick scenes of Freud diagnosing and curing patients; passages recounting dreams and their interpretation. This story begins, in the order of the

---

[10] Burgess 2019. The points regarding Rabelais and Hopkins in this paragraph are derived from Wake's notes. In what follows, passages from *Puma* that were reused in *The End of the World News* are indicated by 'P.' and a reference to Wake's edition. Their context is often interestingly different.

text, with Freud and his family and Ernest Jones dealing with the Nazis when they leave Vienna; we have the famous moment when Freud has to sign a document attesting how well he has been treated and adds 'I can recommend the Gestapo to anyone', and it ends, in the order of the text, with Freud on his deathbed in London, visited by eminent members of the Royal Society who ask him to add his signature to those of Newton, Darwin and Einstein. In between, there are many quick scenes and episodes, but the narrative is both clear and complex. The effect is that this story acts as a kind of foundation to the text as a whole: there is a lot of irony but not much comedy, the ludic side of Burgess's writing is under some restraint, the main outlines of Freud's history are recounted, without reverence but tellingly.

Meanwhile the Trotsky story is told in the form of a musical comedy with many songs and dances. This is very much an *episode* from Trotsky's career. At several points in the song-fests a mysterious Mexican sings ('Everything ends/ In Mexico Mexico,/ An excellent place to die', 153),[11] but there is not much else to give us a wider view. We follow Trotsky's relations with Olga, who has been recruited as his secretary. A love interest, with plenty of drama: the material of musical comedy. The news of the overthrow of the Tsar brings it to a happy but abrupt end. 'Trotsky's vision of the universal socialist state' as one of the 'three greatest events of our century', to quote Burgess's blurb, hardly emerges from this comic muddle through which Trotsky himself stumbles, while the best lines go to the workers who want comfort and prosperity not revolution, and to Olga who wants gradual change and no violence. So Freud's story is fully detailed, and rounded off, not only with his death but with the signatures of the two contrasting documents; the Lynx story has the finality of an apocalypse story (end of the earth and all who are left on it); and the Trotsky story is a series of false starts, stumbles and anti-climaxes, and is at the same time the silliest, and the closest to how most of us live.

The text's form, the three interwoven but contrasting strands, sets the assumptions of apocalypse fictions in a sceptical and comic context. Apocalypse is at the same time the story to end all stories, a kind of totalitarian story, and a cliché and joke ('trashy').[12] Burgess jumbles the

---

[11] And when Olga is trying to save Trotsky from arrest by the Tsarists she says, 'Get to Mexico – you'll be safe in Mexico' (298).
[12] On Burgess's patronising but fascinated attitude to apocalypse stories, see Parrinder 2002, 229, and the appendices of Burgess's writings on science fiction reprinted in Wake's edition of *Puma*, especially nos. 2 ('The Last Day') and 6 ('The Apocalypse and After').

hierarchy of genres and their commonplaces: farce takes over at a crucial moment in the story of the end of the world; a passage in the life of a great revolutionary is told as musical comedy, with inept songs.[13] There is play with language, especially names – taking a famous name and putting it on a new character – Waldheim, Heller (280–281), Gropius, Goya, Dashiel (297), Saarinen (374). (The not-very-famous names that proliferate in *Puma* are mostly cut.) The starship is repeatedly renamed – Tallis, America, Bartlett, America. The Nazis change the name of the International Psychoanalytical Association (323). Freud is told he is 'becoming a name'; and that his name 'stinks all over Vienna' (282). Words are phoneticised, for instance 'voke able airy' (255); 'Real Eedy puss complex I calls it' (363) – this is more Joyce than Freud in style, but Joyce himself refuses to submit to word-association sessions (279). Meanings refuse to be fixed or final; names are arbitrary, contrary or forced.

In the Lynx story there are nods towards common tropes of science-fiction apocalypse – the inexorable approach of an astronomical body threatening Earth (H. G. Wells, 'The Star'; Fred Hoyle, *The Black Cloud*; Greg Egan, *Schild's Ladder*; and the Wylie and Balmer novels that Burgess began from), the flight of a tiny remnant in a starship (Walter M. Miller, *A Canticle for Leibowitz*, and 'generation starship' stories). The scene between Professors Bateman and Frame in Bateman's study (22–26) in which they discuss the grim implications of the first appearance of Lynx is surely an imitation of the scene early in *The War of the Worlds* in which the astronomer and the narrator discuss the implications of the new phenomena observed near Mars. One of the main characters, Val Brodie, is the author of trashy science-fiction novels about the end of the world.

The third story develops the inevitable – that Lynx will crash into Earth and destroy everything and everyone – by a many-stranded narrative in which a variety of actors follow impulse or calculation without much acknowledgement that they have no hope and not much future. Almost all the surviving characters converge on the compound in Kansas where the starship is being readied for a few elite escapees from the disaster. At that point, everyone takes part in a final collision, riot

---

[13] Burgess originally wrote the three stories separately. He justifies their combination as right for the present day with its multiple stimuli, and says reading the result should be like watching three televisions at the same time. I doubt that this is so: the effect is a literary one, in my opinion. See Biswell 2006, 384, 301, and Burgess 1990, 326: 'All three sat in the same folder in instalments of varying length, and when all three were finished I saw that they were aspects of the same story.'

and peripeteia. The Trotsky and Lynx stories can be classified as comedy, if comedy is the form that contains – more or less – the anarchy of human wills and interests, individuals merging into crowds and splitting into waywardness. In comedy the individual who takes himself and his purposes seriously is often a loser, as with Malvolio in *Twelfth Night*, or Bartlett in the Lynx story; but comedy enjoys the socially irresponsible eccentric such as Schmidt in *Nobodaddy's Children*, and Willett and Val in the Lynx story.

The Freud story is different, and, incidentally, the only one of the three in which people's behaviour seems even a little repressed, but in the Freud story irony is constant: the Freudians, liberating others, are themselves riven by passions, jealousies and anxieties; Freud is slowly killed by his incurable cancer, which is given a sinister voice inside his psyche. Freud and his colleagues can give brilliant, unvarnished analyses of what is going on (for instance, that Jung the son plans to kill Freud the father), but are no more effective in action than are the characters in the other two strands of the novel. Freud is reluctant to leave Vienna at the beginning of the text, and arrives in London only to die there, having come to hate Vienna as full of malice and meanness.

How is the story of apocalypse, the Lynx story, modified or broadened by being grouped with the two others in an 'Entertainment'? The most important effect comes from the simple fact that this apocalypse story has to share the text with two other stories. Here, Lynx is indeed imagined as relentless and sinister, a power that no one can resist, an intervention from outside history that brings history to an abrupt stop. Burgess can make a joke about the name it has been given (a compromise between the Americans who wanted it called Lynch after its alleged discoverer and the Soviets who wanted it called Marx) and can make metaphors on its resemblance to a fierce cat, but it is a kind of nullity really. The human achievement in predicting its course, and the rightness or wrongness of concealing that its return pass will bring doom, are both trivial in comparison to its inexorable power. So far, the novel acknowledges that apocalypse in its secular, science-fictional form means a closing down, a full stop.

Yet if the end of the world really is coming, its approach has to make its way in an America that is used to the myth, and used to uncertainty. One of the main characters is the evangelist Calvin Gropius who has spent his life preaching the end and has the texts at his fingertips. As he makes his way towards Kansas, site of the starship, the new, hi-tech Noah's Ark, his family revolts in irritated boredom. They've heard this stuff for years. Edwina, who is determined to get to the starship to save her unborn child, makes the point:

APOCALYPSE, COMEDY, MULTIPLICITY 225

> 'Christ,' she said, 'we've all seen too many movies, read too many trashy books. About the end of the world, I mean. It's just a chunk of old-fashioned folklore. But now it's really going to happen.' (295, P.163)

Val Brodie has written poems about the end (269); 'end-of-the-worlders' are part of the scene, though this time they are crying wolf no longer. New Yorkers are slow to respond to crisis:

> 'New Yorkers,' Willett puffed sadly. 'They will not be told. Everything left to the last moment. [...] Too much individuality. Too much incredulity. New Yorkers have seen everything and live in a perpetual state of apprehension. There is nothing new to make them feel new fear.' (200, P.109)

The cosmic scale of the story is tragic, or totalising; the local scale, on which the characters move, is comic: sporadic effort and purpose, distraction, imprisonment, escape, indulgence in pleasure of the flesh. Mostly we follow Willett and Val. Willett is Burgess's expression of Falstaffian greed, wit and fecklessness: cigars, whiskey and red meat, voluble streams of oratory or insult.[14] Val is the husband of Vanessa; she is a scientist, desirable, cool, capable, systematic even in sex; he is an author of pulp science-fiction, seducer of his students but impotent with Vanessa. Burgess employs a semiotic code: a character who is an irresponsible mess is coded as authentic since irresponsible messiness is human. Val joins with Willett for a last night of irresponsible indulgence, and as a result misses his flight to join Vanessa and fifty other scientists as the token humanist in the crew of the *America*. Willett is much more Val's soulmate than is Vanessa, so amid the indulgence in sex, orgies and drinking of the last days of chaos we have a reminder that sex isn't everything – a correction of Freud's insistent 'sex, sex, sex' (for instance, 209).

Val and Willett struggle to survive as New York is drowned in successively more menacing tidal storms, but there are intervals in which (as

---

[14] Willett is a reminder, in contrast to Freud, that you can sometimes get away with constant smoking of cigars; but another character in the Lynx story, Professor Frame, is dying of lung cancer 'I've always liked cigarette smoking' said Frame. 'Probably because both my parents were violent anti-smokers. They both died, incidentally, of lung cancer' (P. 69). Burgess was a heavy smoker; in 1973 he had health problems and was advised to take up cigars instead – which he did (Biswell 2006, 321). He died of lung cancer.

in Ballard's *The Drowned World* in more solemn circumstances) they can indulge in the luxuries of deserted penthouses, enjoying the absence of the regulations and barriers of property:

> They sat down to litres of fruit juice from the refrigerator, steaks, fried eggs, sausages, pork chops, cold Balmoral pie with mustard pickle, ice cream with strawberry purée, champagne (Ballart, 1984), brandy (Zacatecas, b.o.f.i), much very strong coffee. (199; 'b.o.f.i' stands for 'beware of French imitations', along the lines of 'v.s.o.p.')

When the floods recede for a time they set out for Kansas (where Val would be if he hadn't missed his flight). There are earthquakes, a huge cleft across Illinois, storms, orgies, religious panic, but also the pleasures of stealing cars and stockpiling food and guns.

At length they steal a helicopter and make it to the guarded compound of the *America*, where a chaotic denouement will unfold – a situation of mayhem not uncommon in times of extreme disaster and civilisational breakdown, but local not global. The clash of thrown together human crowds and purposes, not the dark coming of Lynx, is what determines things at this point. The mode is that of farce. Others who intend to crash through the wire surrounding the starship comprise a band of farmers, angry that only an elite is to be saved; the party of Calvin Gropius, his wife and sons, and the pregnant Edwina who has attached herself to him as the spiritual father of her baby; and a couple of Mafiosi for whom Gropius's son has been working as a hotel manager. Those on the other side of the wire comprise scientists, bewildered or brainwashed; the appointed head of the crew, Bartlett, who has rushed to make himself a tinpot dictator (and has had the actual father of Edwina's baby killed for trying to escape the compound), but has begun to lose authority because his instructions as to who should mate with whom to propagate the race after the end of Earth have met with a storm of laughter (332–333, P.186). Finally, there is a squad of soldiers whom Bartlett has distrustfully armed with blanks. Bartlett orders the soldiers out, in the teeth of the Mafiosi who are spraying the site with machine guns, they run over the hapless Calvin, and Willett and Val arrive in their helicopter just as one of the scientists sensibly shoots Bartlett. Burgess assembles all these diverse people with glee, and lets confusion resolve itself into a new and slightly better situation. 'This is the end of the world. I presume anybody can join in': the authentic note of carnival (Edwina, 355, P.199). Edwina gives birth, Vanessa and Val are reunited and Val becomes the crew's new and more moderate leader.

Willett feels he is of the earth, earthy, and can't bear the prospect of artificial food and very little grog on the starship. Willett makes the decision to die on Earth, but he is too rambunctious and vulgar to be allotted a death scene; Skilling, the last president of the USA, is given one, an eloquent end in the ruined New York that he used to run as mayor. Burgess refuses to settle into one tone or point of view. The novel presents its contrasting suicides without any sense that self-immolation or transcendence beyond earthly life might sum up the direction of the text. It adds a birth – new life as well – and the novel's Epilogue happens long after amid new generations on the starship, though these descendants don't believe in the story of the destruction of Earth, or, indeed, in Earth. Burgess has also given ironic hints in the part of the novel that is concerned with the life of Freud, his relations with his father and his 'sons' such as Jung, and in the relations of Calvin Gropius with his son Dashiel who becomes the foster father of the new baby. The new son will enter into conflict with his father, and then with his son when he becomes a father.

It is the comic, the form that takes on the muddled clashes of wills, impulses, libidos and accidents, and accepts them, that is dominant in this strand of *The End of the World News*. The arrival of the Lynx is nobody's fault and nobody's work (not God's work, though some of the characters would like to proclaim that it is) and in the last event it terminates everything, but, as in comedy, the human actors have to accept that what they are doing is as much their own doing as can be expected on this Earth, or, no doubt, anywhere else.

That apocalypse is final and all-encompassing can hardly be denied, since that is what apocalypse entails, and in fact it is vividly enacted. True, some humans escape on the *America*, but, as the Epilogue makes plain, a starship travelling for generations means the end of the civilisation of Earth if not of humans. The starship will journey into a future in which history and the long span of human civilisation are at once forgotten and irrelevant. Willett, in contrast, eloquently exalts history and the long span of human civilisation over the claims of a non-existent future and a non-existent present.

> Let us not dream of a future which does not exist and can exist only by becoming the present. Let us not dream of living in the future, since the present has no existence. Let us glory in having added more and more to the past, increased the roar of its music and the chaotic profusion of its flowers. (216; Willett is reciting a passage from one of Val's novels; P.116)

The other two strands of narrative do not simply echo or supplement the Lynx story. They assert that humans have had and will have other things to do and feel. Yet the whole text pays homage to Freud: formally, in that the transitions between one strand and another sometimes happen simply by means of an association of words (for instance, 67, 93–94, 102); and in style, most notably in Burgess's love of puns[15] and rhymes, many of the latter so comically forced as to remind us that a rhyme is a kind of pun. In addition, there are associations, some particular, some more general, and these associations combine to make a perspective. As regards particular associations – better called echoes or rhymes – we have already noted the contrast between Freud as cigar-smoker and how Willett and Val can enjoy cigars, among the pleasures made available by the anarchy of the final days. Again, we can contrast the intricacy of Freud's being very early but yet almost too late for trains, with Val's missing his plane to Kansas – but eventually getting there on time anyway. The assembled elite simply laugh to scorn Bartlett's humourless attempt to choose mates for them; Freud refuses to become Lou Andreas-Salome's lover or to choose a lover for her from his colleagues ('from among my twelve tribes, that is to say apostles, that is to say –', 'I do not ask you to choose ... I merely ask you to evaluate', 342).

In these particular cases the echo or rhyme simply allows the two stories to bounce off each other. Other conjunctions are more suggestive. Each of the stories is about exile – Freud's exile from Vienna and death in London; Trotsky's sojourn in New York and his return to Russia – but with intimations of his final exile and death in Mexico; universal death, but the exile, never to return, of the *America* and its crew. Apocalypse is what people constantly fear and imagine; exile is what people often get in modern history.[16] And there are reminders that death and war have their own finality – not very evident in the Trotsky story, where both war and revolution are imminent and offstage, but telling in the Freud story: Freud's prolonged and painful dying; Freud as killer of his father and to be killed as a father; Freud as Moses, if we recall that Moses did not live to enter Israel; Freud as Oedipus, attending a performance of the play by Sophocles and hearing this apocalyptic speech:

---

[15] For instance, a lynx is a kind of cat, CAT (Center of Advanced Technology) is where the starship will be prepared and a cat becomes the logo of the dictatorial Bartlett who calls himself Boss Cat (196).

[16] For glimpses of Burgess's feelings about exile, see Biswell 2006, 35, 77, 222, 318. He spent the last part of his life in Malta, Italy, Monaco and Switzerland.

'Dark dark. The sun has burst there
For the last time.' ...
'The eyes of the world are out.
The gods scream.
Finding poison in the wine cup.
The mountains are molten,
The sea blood.
The mounting moon
Turns her face away.
Day will never return.'

(42)[17]

Apocalypse is a cultural cliché, worn thin with repetition in fiction, religion, the media, casual remarks, but haunting us nevertheless. This chapter now turns to a novel that presents apocalypse as repetition, a spectacular transformation that is restaged, varied, adjusted, like a classic opera in the hands of an avant-garde director – or here it is a mad scientist.

Apocalyptic Dreams
The Lathe of Heaven[18]

The Lathe of Heaven (1971) is a novel of catastrophes, in the plural. Le Guin's novel plays with science-fiction tropes, and makes not a realist picture so much as a magically shifting fable. The world of the novel is repeatedly, drastically transformed, and the transformations become more extreme and dangerous until they culminate in a series of disasters. Further, we learn in the course of all this that an even worse disaster has already occurred. This was a catastrophic nuclear war, out of which the protagonist George Orr dreamed the world into the condition of grim depletion that prevails at the beginning of the novel and is then frequently restructured (7–8, 139–140). But this summary has to be modified: it is the human, social world of modernity that is repeatedly transformed, while the mountains, the sea, the rivers, remain – more

---

[17] This is Burgess's own translation of Sophocles, and it is at this point that he made a major change – having Oedipus blind himself on stage. See Burgess 1972, 77–78 (the quoted passage), 3–4 (why Oedipus is blinded on stage). See also Freud's dream confrontation with Melanie Klein and Hélène Deutsch, 345.

[18] References are to Ursula Le Guin, *The Lathe of Heaven*, New York: Avon Books, 1997.

or less – stable, and in addition serve to supply the text with a strand of imagery that evokes an alternative to the social reality that we see in its drastic and clumsy changes. Further, time itself is unhinged, as my summary implied when it said that the world of the novel was approaching a culminating catastrophe when one had already occurred. Time for humans depends on memory, which links one event to another, in comprehensible succession, but memory is broken in the world of *The Lathe of Heaven*. This breaking of memory will take us shortly to the matter of 'effective' dreaming, which is the founding premise of the fiction.

Playing with the Formulas

The Lathe of Heaven works variations, both playful and serious, on the contemporary cultural phenomenon of the repeated, almost the habitual, imagination of disaster, even apocalypse. Drastic transformations happen every couple of chapters; there are repeated disasters and apocalyptic destructions. They really happen in the world of the novel, but they happen because they are imagined.

The imagining involves a machine, the 'Augmentor', an ambitious psychologist (Haber), and his patient, an emphatically ordinary man (George Orr). There is an Infernal Machine – a gizmo – a mad scientist, and an ordinary man who has extraordinary powers. In addition, as was just suggested, there is a derangement of time, as in many a science-fiction novel about time travel or time slips. There is also an alien invasion: plenty of well-worn science-fiction formulas.

Le Guin also enjoys the game of bestowing names, which is one opportunity science fiction offers, which Burgess indulges in *Puma* and that Doris Lessing eschews in *The Making of the Representative for Planet 8*. George Orr's African-American lover Heather LeLache works for a law firm: 'Forman, Esserback, Goodhue and Rutti' (44); in a later rearrangement of reality this becomes 'an aged and otiose legal partnership, Ponder and Rutti' (153); the US President through all the changes is Albert Merdle, recalling the financial swindler Merdle of *Little Dorrit*; Haber miscalls George John at one point (25), Ringo is mentioned (131), 'Let it Be' is quoted (136) and 'A Little Help from My Friends' figures vitally at a crucial juncture. More seriously, George Orr recalls George Orwell (the Orwell is a river, and rivers are important in the novel's imagery); his complete averageness is seen by Haber as 'Either, or' (134), and one of the aliens more positively expresses this balance by calling him 'Jor Jor' ('After a moment Orr recognized his own name in this Barsoomian bisyllable', 137). Le Guin is playing with science-fiction allusions ('Barsoom' is the fantasy Mars of Edgar Rice Burroughs), but also making serious points about the uses and (with Haber) abuses of language. 'Jor Jor' may recall Churchill's 'jaw jaw is better than war war' – the aliens' arrival accidentally precipitates a short war. The text stretches out one arm to embrace familiar tropes and formulas (the mad scientist, the hero whose exceptional talent marks him as chosen, the alien invasion), while the other reaches for the mysteries of being, the deep morality of nature, in the face of repeated and steadily more dangerous rearrangements of reality.

Effective Dreaming and the Culture of Acceptance

It is the combination of Haber, the scientist, and George Orr, the ordinary man, that powers the succession of rearrangements of reality and memory. Orr has been trying not to sleep, so as to avoid dreaming, and in the attempt has taken more drugs than he is allowed, in a future society that is closely regulated and surveilled. He falls into the hands of Haber, a sleep scientist and psychologist to whom he is legally compelled to submit. Orr has been avoiding sleep by these illegal means because he has 'effective' dreams, dreams that bring about, in reality, an aspect of what they dream, and this he is sure is dangerous. The new reality that an effective dream establishes has complete authority, existential and psychological as well as material: everyone totally accepts it, and the previous state of reality is as if it had never been.

There is a ready pay-off to this fantasy premise, because a certain condition of modernity is figured and highlighted thereby. Modernity involves continual and often radical change, social, economic, cultural and political. Change is to be expected and often welcomed; hence the positive charge often borne by words such as 'development', 'progress', 'radical' and 'revolutionary'. Change – that which vast and barely visible forces and agents combine to produce for us and impose on us – is what we have to accommodate and accept and to see as the everyday and therefore the normal. When change is gradual it tends to abolish a longer-term perspective – the phenomenon of 'creeping normality' (Diamond 2005, 425–426). The result of the prevalence of change is a culture of acceptance; successful adaptation to modernity can be a matter of acceptance of the latest condition of affairs as natural, or at least tolerable. Conditions, and ideologies, conspire to enforce the idea that what is, is what has to be. In *The Lathe of Heaven* Le Guin offers an unqualified image of this: the change (wrought not by 'history' or 'progress' but by Haber and Orr) is radical and it is accepted and adapted to because the rule with effective dreams is that no one (except Orr) remembers the preceding state of affairs, which indeed is not to be remembered because it – now – has never been. People can normalise anything, it seems, because they normalise, or, more precisely, find themselves having normalised, each of these violently contrasting societies. The river dries or flows, the climate is mild or uncomfortable, the office towers rise or fall, they live in tiny apartments or dilapidated cottages, and they accept it all.

Le Guin does push this condition very far: in one of the new social realities the citizen's arrest and killing of a man discovered to have an incurable disease is accepted (131). Haber/Orr have somehow dreamt into existence, that is, into the condition of accepted normality, *this* society, in which anyone with an incurable disease can be executed by any passing citizen. Haber justifies this (137) – by this stage he justifies everything – but Orr is shocked. We are to believe that there is no persisting average decency in the mass of people such as those who witness this killing, which happens amid ordinary crowds on the street – though at the same time the average, normal decency of Orr and Lelache can be relied on.[19] Nonetheless the overall figure, that of the effective dream as a kind of speeded-up film of the transformations modernity brings and the culture of adaptation that copes with them, or values them, is a telling one.

Orr and Haber

The power of Orr's dreams is in fact intensified and coarsened by his relationship with Haber, which begins as that of doctor and patient and rapidly becomes that of master and slave. Haber's 'Augmentor', when attached to a sleeper, locates the time of dreaming in the successive stages of sleep, enhances the dream's alpha waves, plays them back and increases the power of the dreaming, and we are to understand that Orr's alpha waves were already exceptionally strong.

The proof that Orr really does dream effectively comes in their first session together. Haber told Orr to dream about a horse – a poster of a

---

[19] The gap between the exceptional averageness of Orr and the unexceptional averageness of the mass of people is wonderfully bridged for a moment when Orr feels joy on a crowded subway train and his feeling uplifts everyone around him (42). There is a less successful passage about the integrity of ordinary people on 99.

big racehorse replaces the poster of Mount Hood on the wall of Haber's office:

> 'Was it there an hour ago? I mean, wasn't that a view of Mount Hood, when I came in – before I dreamed about the horse?'
> Oh Christ it had been Mount Hood the man was right
> It had not been Mount Hood it could not have been Mount Hood it was a horse it was a *horse*
> *It* had been a mountain
> A horse a horse it was – (27)

The horse resembles Haber, this being the dream's wit. The setting at this point is the mediocre cheaply furnished office of a not very successful psychologist, and as his powers grow and the effective dreams keep coming he will have not a poster of Mount Hood but a picture window with a view of the real mountain, and a grand then a grandiose, vast office. Everyone who has an office wants a bigger, more prestigious office: Haber gives himself a very big office, by means of his relationship with Orr, and this is one, wry, measure of *his* fantasies. Another, in contrast, is what else he gets Orr to dream and effect – a series of sweeping transformations, intended to solve such problems as racism and overpopulation. All along, however, as at this first moment, he denies that Orr really is changing the world with his dreams, as instructed by Haber himself, though always the changes happen in unpredictable ways that follow dream logic. He splits himself psychically, ordering more and more fundamental changes to the world while maintaining the pretence that Orr is his patient, they are working together and reality is as he says it is: the more radical the changes, the more blustering and complacent, but also coercive, his denials. The more skewed the dreamed and real results of his instructions – dreaming being a literal and irrational process of mind – the more he persists. Eventually he decides that he himself should be the one to hook up to the Augmentor and dream, and this has chaotic effects, including his own madness.

Haber is easy to criticise, in his hollowness, his scientism, his resort to speechifying, his invocations of his superior training and objectivity. Le Guin lays a basis for this criticism of Haber in the contrast with Orr, diffident, centred – grounded indeed: an exemplification of groundedness before the term became current. Haber is big and booming – he is often compared to a bear; Orr is small and nondescript; Haber stands for doing, is confident of the end and careless of the means; Orr stands for being, and is sure that the means corrupts the end. Haber has more and more power and larger and larger offices as the world is repeatedly reorganised, Orr remains in one variety or other of modest job and rented apartment, keeping the same amiable, drug-addled landlord as at the beginning; Haber is fluent to the point of inane glibness, Orr has trouble speaking up even though he sees very clearly that what is happening is dangerous, out of control and a threat to the order of things, of Being. But this contrast, though useful as moral pedagogy, is arguably too easy and stark. Every scene shows Haber's limits and his monstrousness. Matters become more challenging if we concentrate on the fact that it is the two men *together* who bring about so many changes, and eventually catastrophe. The Anti-Christ in this series of apocalypses means to do well, and the saint brings about destruction and disorder.

Schmidt and Burgess confine apocalypse to one strand of *Nobodaddy's Children* and *The End of the World News*; this gives ordinary life and other histories play in the rest of each text, and sets each text up for the challenge that individual cussedness poses to the all-encompassing reach of apocalypse. There is a world elsewhere. Le Guin's procedure is different: there is a painful gap between the averageness of ordinary citizens who find themselves accepting whatever Orr and Haber dream for them, on the one hand, and the suffering of Orr (idealised version of the ordinary), who knows what is going on, on the other hand. There is a painful gap between the grounded sanity of Orr and the insanity of Haber, who denies what is going on; and there is a painful gap between Haber's activism and Orr's inability to act. These violent contrasts lead to problems that the novel does not always resolve, and on the level of the plot they lead to a blockage that can only be solved by the intervention of alien immigrants.

Orr has integrity and dignity; he is completely, solidly himself, 'so sane as to be an anomaly', as Haber says (133). Heather Lelache recognises this, and so do the aliens, who have been brought onto Earth by one of his dreams. Orr defends Being, the rightness of things being as they are that must not be tampered with, as he and Haber are tampering. Yet his effective dreams impart a crazy twist to Haber's – on the face of them – idealistic demands. The problem of overpopulation, for which Haber instructed him to dream a solution, is solved by a catastrophic epidemic and famine that reduces Earth's population from six billion to one billion. 'The colour problem' is solved by eliminating colour and thence race, and making every human being a dull grey (including Heather, who was previously black and is now lost to Orr among the monotoned multitude). The dreams play tricks on Haber and Orr, and on the world. After aliens have arrived, with apparent violence, on the moon (in Orr's dreamed response to Haber's instruction to bring about peace on Earth: the warring nations of Earth will now unite against the threat of the aliens), Heather (this time) asks Orr to dream them off the moon and he does this by dreaming them onto Earth, with chaotic results as earth fiercely resists them: a mistake, as they are in fact peaceful. Dreams are like that: literal-minded, indifferent to morality, tending to violence, knowing nothing of measure and proportion.

We can see that what Haber is trying to do is wrong to the point of being crazy. The law of unintended consequences is running rampant and wreaking havoc. There is an analogy with magic wishes in folk tales, as when the recipient who has been granted three wishes has to use the third to undo the unintended consequences of the first and second. Haber attempts to resist awareness of this issue with an authoritarian bluster that becomes more and more hollow and false until he goes mad. Yet Orr's effective dreams had this skewed quality before he fell into Haber's power; they become much more sweeping and drastic under Haber's instructions and with the intensification that the Augmentor adds, but they were already dangerous. Haber is heading for madness, and there seems to be no way out for Orr, whose solidity of self means that suicide is not an option. Orr's centred and grounded self connects with an undersea realm of being. Nature itself dreams – 'Rocks have their dreams', as he says to Haber (161). Yet when Orr dreams an effective dream *social* reality is disrupted and the social and cultural work that is usually necessary to accomplish change and solve problems is dangerously bypassed. The interface between the realm of dreams and daylight human reality is a zone of misfit, of things going wrong.

Haber and Orr are locked in a relationship in which Orr unchains Haber's ambition and his emptiness – the way in which, being empty, his self depends on the hugeness of his effects on the world (and the hugeness of his office) – and in turn Haber deepens the way in which Orr is blocked and passive, able to protest lucidly but not resist. The effect can be frustrating: why doesn't Orr kill Haber – dream his death, perhaps, or smash the Augmentor? These suggestions no doubt belong to the can-do pragmatism that Le Guin is criticising in Haber while she imagines its complete antithesis in Orr. Violence haunts the text just the same, in the global disorder and suffering that several of Haber–Orr's rearrangements have involved, and also in the sinister gesture by which Haber takes Orr by the throat when he is about to put him under and attach him to the Augmentor (23, 60).

Magic Words

It seems that Haber and Orr, blocked and bringing out the worst in each other, need a third term to unblock them and rescue the world that is subject to the increasingly grim changes they are bringing about together. The text first proposes Heather Lelache, sympathetic, modest and self-aware. She follows Orr to the mountain hut whither he has fled from Haber, doses him with a lot of brandy and asks him to dream the aliens off the moon. This, as was noted, just puts the law of unintended consequences into disruptive operation. The aliens arrive on earth to the accompaniment of many explosions and other collateral damage, as Earth clumsily defends itself, though it is not in fact being attacked. After a while, however, they are accepted as peaceful, enigmatic and homely immigrants, good at small business.[20]

Heather's work is done; it will be the aliens who break the blockage in which Haber and Orr are caught.

Haber uses language too easily and blandly, so as to deny what he knows is happening; Orr clearly expresses what is wrong with what is happening, but can't do anything about it; the aliens have to learn Earth's language from scratch. At first, they don't even realise that the sounds that Earth people make are their means of communication. After a time, they develop an eloquence of their own, enigmatic, stripped and bearing a strong resemblance to how aliens often speak in science fiction, derived probably from how Asians or Native Americans speak in popular fiction. A crucial exchange between Orr and an alien happens as if by accident, in the street:

> 'Please forgive warranted interruption. You are human capable of *iahklu'* as previously noted. This troubles self.'
> 'I don't – I think –'
> 'We also have been variously disturbed. Concepts cross in mist. Perception is difficult. Volcanoes emit fire. Help is offered: refusably. Snakebite serum is not prescribed for all.[21] Before following directions leading in wrong directions, auxiliary forces may be summoned, in immediate-following fashion: *Er' perrehnne!*' (137)

---

[20] Ian Watson (1992, 68) discusses whether the aliens, creatures of dream themselves, might have been attracted to Earth by Orr's dream potential. But then everything on Earth is a figment of Orr's dreams, and at the same time real, and the aliens become part of this reality – as Watson also says.

[21] The alien is alluding to a recent conversation between Haber and Orr concerning when it is right to help others (136), a conversation at which it was not present.

Orr needs a little help from his friends, who include Heather and the aliens. He listens to Lennon and McCartney's song on an old record given him by an alien; he finds strength for the moment when it is Haber who hooks up to the Augmentor and begins to dream a dream that will wreck the world in altogether new ways. At this point he utters what is in effect the magic word, *Er' perrehnne*, and turns off the Augmentor ('I did a lot today. That is, I did something. The only thing I have ever done. I pressed a button' (170)). This magic is not without cost: he loses Heather, at least for a while, and the world everyone now accepts as normal is an irrational mess as a result of Haber's aborted dream (172).

The power that Haber and Orr together had begun to exercise to such harm is dissolved by the assistance of the aliens, with their homely help and the magic word they supply Orr. It's a deus ex machina solution from the stock of science-fictional formulas, and this acknowledges that we won't always be so lucky, assuming that the reality transformations at the centre of the novel are figures of modernity in its succession of transformations. Yet the link of the aliens with Orr is more complex and suggestive than this comment about its hokeyness would imply:

> [The alien] stopped, half blocking his way: and he too halted, startled and impressed by its nine-foot, greenish, armored impassivity. It was grotesque to the point of being funny: like a sea turtle, and yet like a sea turtle it possessed a strange, large beauty, a serener beauty than that of any dweller in sunlight, and walker on the earth. (137)

The mind in dream is like a sea creature adrift in the depths:

> What will the creature made all of seadrift do on the dry sand of daylight; what will the mind do, each morning, waking? (7)

This is how the novel begins. Orr's dreams come from the depths, but he is stranded in daylight. The element of water is constantly present in the novel – the sea, rain, rivers; there are passages about how the Columbia River is bridged and tunnelled and about the strangeness of being in a train under a river (40), about the din of the mountain creek 'shouting and hollering eternal praise!' (108). Orr is even compared to 'a moral jellyfish' by Haber (143). All this presence and potential in the other world of dream is unavailable to Orr, though he is connected to it, until he is given help by the aliens, sea turtles in their carapace that protects them in Earth's atmosphere while it also conceals their bodies.

The Lathe of Heaven is a very inclusive novel; inclusive as comedy is, in its attention to muddle, inconsistency, unintended consequences, its lucky, even magical, solutions, alliances of odd-balls, ordinary cussedness – and also inclusive as poetry is. The text respects the rationality of science – the passages in which Haber outlines the science of sleep are informative ones – and it variously offers accounts of dreaming in common sense, in psychoanalytical, in Taoist and in poetic terms. In consequence it is not easy to use the text to systematise a single account of dreaming that brings together the images of dreaming as drifting undersea life and the skewed irrational content of Orr's effective dreams, but this layered openness is the ethos of the novel, and it underlines its repulsion from Haber. There is an attempt to see Haber in sympathetic terms, in his need for the world to confirm his existence to him, and in poetic terms, when in his expansiveness he is seen as a bear, indeed a 'bear-shaman-god' (157); but mostly he is a threat, in his hubris, emptiness and ability glibly to marshal every rationalist and authoritarian cliché to the service of his will. This sense of Haber as a threat, the bad side of modernity that can easily present itself as the only side, the exception to the novel's encompassing tolerance and good humour, idealism and openness (qualities that can also find a place in modernity), is redoubled when it is the Haber–Orr combination that gathers such power. Haber and Orr are in unqualified moral contrast, yet locked together in dangerous remaking of the world. Orr knows and suffers what is wrong, but for most of the novel can't do anything about it; Orr is perfect and ideal normality, but separated by a gulf from the average of the rest of humanity, though connected to the empathetic Heather. That the magical intervention of the aliens is needed to enable Orr to break these deadlocks suggests how intractable the deadlocks are.

This apocalyptic novel does not end with death, or transcendence; all those we meet at the beginning are still alive at the end, though Haber is mad and Orr and Lelache are together, but they have been joined by the aliens, invaders who came in peace and have probably got what they wanted, which was not much.

Chapter 7

Apocalypse and Everyday Life
Tom Perrotta and Douglas Coupland

> And so they all, each in his own way, reflecting or unreflecting, go on with their daily lives; everything seems to take its accustomed course, for indeed, even in these desperate situations where everything hangs in the balance, one goes on living as though nothing were wrong.
>
> (Goethe)

One of the attractions of fictions of apocalypse, for writers and readers, is no doubt the way apocalypse offers freedom from the everyday, the ordinary, the regime of common sense and shaping one's behaviour to what society does: what Agnes Heller in *Everyday Life* calls 'particularity'. Society has been destroyed, and with it the masses of ordinary people who are often seen as the enforcers of conformity and mediocrity. Hence, violence, hedonism, the unrepressed and impulsive; and hence openings to a new mode of being or a new society. Yet contemporary apocalyptic fiction often is the scene of a conflict between the sublime (extended sometimes to transcendence, and to a reversal of values) and the anti-sublime, expressed as critique or comedy, or as everyday realism. The realist novel has a commitment to the local and everyday. Apocalyptic fictions that ground themselves in the everyday can express the desire to forget or ignore apocalypse, in contrast to the yearning for it. In relation to the everyday, the apocalyptic may have to fight for recognition, for importance.

This passage from Tom Perrotta's *The Leftovers* puts the situation in the context of the contemporary habituation to disaster:

> As the weather changed, Kevin sensed a shift in the collective mood, as if the whole town had suddenly decided to lighten up and stop obsessing about dead Watchers and serial killers. He'd seen this process before; It didn't matter what happened in the

world – genocidal wars, natural disasters, unspeakable crimes, mass disappearances, whatever – eventually people got tired of brooding about it. Time moved on, seasons changed, individuals withdrew into their private lives, turned their faces toward the sun. (297)

In Anthony Burgess's *The End of the World News*, Val and Willett take the opportunity of a remission in the ongoing catastrophe:

They walked south of a very green though treeless Central Park and found people, not many, walking dogs. 'Mad, mad,' muttered Willett uneasily. 'It's almost as though it never happened.' They saw signs of reconstruction work – men working lights, floodlamps already flooding. On West 57th Street they entered Jerry Towle's Bar and Grill, a hostelry they could not recall having seen before. It smelt of a very damp grave, but there were drinkers and a cheerful barman. (254)[1]

Walking the dog or drinking in the bar (even one that smells of a very damp grave) are acts of resistance to, or refusal to recognise an aspect of apocalypse that is very different from its invitation to nonconformity and individual self-expression. This aspect is the drive of apocalypse to uniformity, the insistence that only one thing now matters, and everyone and everything else now finds meaning in relation to that. From this point of view apocalypse is as tyrannical as any Big Brother that sucks the reality out of everything but Big Brother.

This chapter concentrates on two recent American apocalyptic novels, Tom Perrotta's *The Leftovers* (2011), and Douglas Coupland's *Girlfriend in a Coma* (1998).[2] In these novels, as in most realist fiction, everyday life is domestic in setting. Ordinary things and acts – Christmas presents and a visit to the mall in *The Leftovers*, for instance – can stand against this insistence that comes with apocalypse, even though, being ordinary, and familiar, they are much the same everywhere, and so from another

---

[1] We can also see the impulse that is animating these New Yorkers as early as the Florentines in *The Decameron* (1349–51): it is behind their tales of love, trickery and sex in the face of (but also withdrawal into an idyll from) apocalypse in the form of the Black Death. One of the witnesses in Svetlana Alexievich's *Chernobyl Prayer* puts the refusal to turn away from ordinary habits more grimly: 'The wheels of evil will keep turning even during the apocalypse. That's what I've realized. People will keep gossiping, kowtowing to their bosses, rescuing their TV sets and astrakhan coats. [...] The same as always' (Alexievich 2016, 125).

[2] More properly, North American; Coupland is Canadian.

angle they could be seen as depending on a monocultural, globalised uniformity. The ambiguities and difficulties of setting the everyday against the apocalyptic in *The Leftovers* and *Girlfriend* will figure later in the chapter: the everyday is no longer stable and reliable.

Perrotta and Coupland: Middle America

> It appears that in the postmodern and posthuman era we are fated to be stricken with confusion not only over the nature of our own identities but also that of our deities as well.
>
> (Peter Y. Paik)

The Leftovers and *Girlfriend in a Coma* both reinvent the apocalyptic catastrophe in challenging ways that will need careful examination. Neither is set in the city or the country: this framework, with behind it a contrast of nature and culture, relevant to many earlier apocalyptic fictions, is irrelevant here (there some scenes set in the woods in *Girlfriend* – traces of the image of the country as natural; 47–48, 105–107).[3] *The Leftovers* is set in a small town, and *Girlfriend in a Coma* in the suburbs of Vancouver. Suburbs and small towns are quiet, safe, conformist, dull, and secluded from the dynamism, danger and sin of the city. Both novels draw upon traditional apocalypse, reminding us of ways in which it features in contemporary American culture, both Christian and New Ageist, but doing this in unexpected ways. *The Leftovers* invents a version of 'the Rapture' that figures in the fundamentalist imaginary in America, but in this case there are none of the clear rules and distinctions that, presumably, console or inspire believers in the Rapture, no division into saved and left behind, no tyrannical World Government nor crowds of those who have zombie-like succumbed to the Beast to be resisted or slaughtered.[4] In *Girlfriend in a Coma* a sort of divine plan is eventually revealed to have been behind the end of the world, but both the end and the plan are of very shaky validity, and those selected as a saving remnant are hardly up to the job. Though both novels are set in everyday life with its routine and familiarity, in both the catastrophe is

---

[3] References are to Douglas Coupland, *Girlfriend in a Coma*, London: HarperPerennial, 2004.

[4] For a brief history of contemporary fictions of the Rapture, and its place in contemporary American culture, see Beal 2018, chapter 9 and 'Postscript'; for a convincing reading of the Left Behind novels as sadistic, see Lundberg 2009.

brought about by a deity, though one that is never seen or named, and one whose purposes are unfathomable in *The Leftovers* and (arguably) unconvincing in *Girlfriend*. There is a crowded and familiar foreground but it is surrounded by a void.

The novel cannot easily discard the local and everyday, 'the ordinary, the untranscendent real, the humanist world of the down-to-earth detail', to quote Valentine Cunningham (2002, 167 and 162), stuff, a muddle, but inexhaustible, to paraphrase Iris Murdoch. Authors as different as Sterne, Austen, Chekhov and Joyce embrace it – in the process, no doubt, redefining the everyday, and making a term like 'realist' an inadequate one. Apocalyptic catastrophe abolishes the everyday as it existed before the catastrophe, so the everyday is in question, at the least. Immersion in the everyday, its immediacy and urgency, can stimulate the thinking that supplies practical ethics, the aspect of the everyday that Agnes Heller discusses in her *Everyday Life*.[5] The limitations of this ethic are as obvious as that we cannot do without it; perspective on and engagement with wider, often determinative forces and events can be lost in the myopia of the present and local. The tradition of the novel (or the traditions of the novel, if the multiplicity of the form needs to be stressed) has developed ways to highlight this, and to overcome it, in that the structures and images of the text can signify or point to wider forces and events, even when it is confined to everyday life. Alternatively, the text can be layered, or overloaded, with incidents and details, departing from the localised realism of everyday life in order to express the density of contemporary experience, its clashes of banal, terrifying and mediated. This is what is done in *Cosmopolis* and *Kraken*, to be discussed in chapter 8.

In *The Leftovers* the catastrophe is particularly null, a kind of blank. Vast numbers of people have simply disappeared – catastrophic enough – but the conditions and texture of everyday life in small town America are in most ways left exactly as they were before the catastrophe. The result of this is to put daily life, as it goes on in ordinary ways, under particular stress. The characters are trying to recover from the loss and grief brought on by the catastrophe, and many of them succeed, but the everyday life that they have to work with is destabilised, sometimes subtly, sometimes violently. In *Girlfriend in a Coma* the end of the world, when it comes, is thorough and spectacular, but it is a fake, a simulacrum. The revelation of this late in the novel pulls the rug out from under the characters and

---

[5] Heller 1984; see also Jay 1998, especially 44–46 on 'learning from experience', and Jay 2005, on the varied attempts of thinkers to define and defend the value of experience.

the reader, and risks the plausibility of the novel, but the world to which the catastrophe has happened (and then has not) was already and in a multitude of ways a world of simulacra, and one in which not only the real and the fake but also life and death were hard to distinguish, as in the coma of the novel's title. The characters keep to their routine after the world ends as they did before it – arguing, making jokes, drinking, consuming – but always, both before and after, with a glum sense of inadequacy and meaninglessness. It takes not merely a catastrophe, but the revelation that it was faked for their edification, to bounce them into a not quite plausible sense that their lives have a purpose.

The Leftovers[6]
Mourning and 'Disappearance'

Jean-Claude Carrière (1999, 110) imagines disappointed millenarians: the Sun has come up after all on the night of foretold doom, 'And life has to be resumed, a life they had thought was lost. It is perhaps at such a moment that people become truly human. One stops looking up at the sky and starts thinking about the problems of ordinary existence.'

Fictions that tell of the event or the aftermath of catastrophe tend not to confront matters to do with grief. Perhaps characters in disaster fictions would be unable to settle to their other narrative tasks or roles if the immensity of loss and grief were allowed to affect them, rather as the heroes of action movies have to be allowed exemption from the normal emotional accompaniments of violence and death (remorse, fear, nervous strain, post-traumatic stress disorder (PTSD)). There is often a transference; for instance, the destroyed and ruined buildings (monuments, cities, and so on) might stand in for the lost people, the more safely as they are usually deserted.[7] Care for those who have also survived has to replace or cover grief for those who have gone; this seems to be the case with the father in Cormac

---

[6] References are to Tom Perrotta, *The Leftovers*, London: Fourth Estate, 2012.

[7] It is common for fictions of apocalypse to omit the depiction of mass death and to skip over the immediate aftermath of destruction, its excrement in the form of waste, mess and corpses. (Waste and mess – pollution, landfill – is already a problem for contemporary civilisation.) The text can proceed to the cleaner, more poignant stage of the deserted ruin, expressive of transience and desolation, of what Francesco Orlando (2006, 218–229) calls the 'solemn-admonitory'. In *The Leftovers* there are no ruins or material remainders at all – an absence that is troubling because it doesn't express anything.

McCarthy's *The Road* (2006), who has to care for his son and seldom has time to spare to think of his dead wife, let alone anyone else. In this instance the distance between the daily struggle of the father and son and whatever happened in the past is so great that the past and everything in it can seem a kind of void. The transference is more complex in Don DeLillo's *Falling Man* (2007), set in the aftermath of 9/11, because it is the falling man, the performance artist who mimes and somehow stands for those who jumped from the towers (but how, exactly, the falling man does this is the question the novel pursues). In other fictions, the survivors are glad to be rid of the dead, in their crushing, overwhelming numbers, and, in a related genre of fiction, happy to slaughter them when they come back as mere ugly meat, soulless zombies. In apocalyptic fictions of the 1960s and 1970s, the protagonists often accept and embrace their deaths, sometimes by way of passage to a new state of being, as in Doris Lessing's *The Making of the Representative for Planet 8*, where grief and loss becomes a stage in a progress towards transcendence.

The Leftovers begins by imagining that a version of 'the Rapture', figment of the imagination of some contemporary American Christians, actually happened. Here it is called 'the Disappearance'. The Disappearance lacks sublimity. Thousands of people, of all ages and types, from the Pope to Adam Sandler, disappear in an instant, and are gone forever. The twist is that they belong to no discernible group, neither Christians (Hindus, Moslems and Jews as well as atheists disappear) nor the devout nor the good nor the bad (for one thing, there are lots of children). The Disappearance has not selected an elite of the faithful, as the Rapture is supposed to do.

Scientific explanations are unconvincing, but if the Disappearance was the work of a supernatural power His point is unfathomable. People have disappeared, but all material things are as before. There are no ruins to serve as loci of mourning or as tolerable stand-ins or substitutes for the masses of the dead/gone that the imagination might shy away from confronting directly. The plot culminates in a shocking murder that certainly is the result of irrational responses to the apocalypse (this is the context for Kevin's reference to 'dead Watchers and serial killers' in the quotation on 239 above), but all this happens amidst the problems and pains of family life, relationships, communal life. The recourse to the everyday here allows for a coming to terms with the bitterness, dismay and grief that attends mass death (or in this case, disappearance). This coming to terms is slow and difficult. In the shape of the novel as a whole disappearance (apocalyptic, inexplicable, felt as unconscionable) becomes leaving (leaving town, leaving behind) or deciding not to leave, and this works as a restoration and recovery, but there is no new state of being, no opening to the sublime.

After its 'Prologue', *The Leftovers* ignores the global extent of the catastrophe, and even its spread across the United States, and concentrates on a couple of families in Mapleton, a typical average (as Philip K. Dick would say) Middle American township. It's a novel about loss and grief, except that the loss and grief is general, so that the loss and grief of a given individual or family, in its upset and anger and disorientation, is continually interacting with, and mostly exacerbating, that of every other individual and family, so many of whom have also lost someone. Strictly speaking, the disappeared are missing, not necessarily dead, but this only adds uncertainty to grief. Death and dying may be seen as being in some trouble in the contemporary West, because we die in hospital, separated from family and community, because we expect to live for a very long time but are sometimes kept alive for too long, because there is no shared culture of the good death.[8] The conditions and culture of at least a passable experience of and response to death have been further disordered by the Disappearance. There is no rhyme or reason to the deaths, assuming that they are deaths; there are too many deaths for any given death to be given proper sympathy by the rest of the community (though people do try). God brings about apocalypse in the Bible, but this Disappearance is random, uncaused and incoherent, and hard to explain as the action of any God one would want to know, though some people do try to act on this explanation. And this disaster has wrought no material destruction and left no work of material repair and recovery to unite people and distract them from grief.

> '"The" world as fact-world is always there: at the most it is at odd points "other" than I supposed, this or that under such names as "illusion," "hallucination," and the like, must be struck out of it, so to speak.'[9]

So Husserl commented on what is sometimes called consensus reality; but 'illusion' and 'hallucination' won't do for the phenomena that Perrotta introduces into the everyday life of *The Leftovers*. The Disappearance

---

[8] On the history of this see Ariès 1981. In discussing the modern culture of death, Ariès emphasises the importance of the family: heaven, if believed in, is where people will be reunited with their loved ones, and the Beatific Vision hardly figures. This is relevant to *The Leftovers*, which centres on families and their struggles.

[9] Edmund Husserl, quoted Douglas 1970, 15.

is part of the 'fact-world'. The conventional realism of *The Leftovers* – the circumstance that this text is not avant-garde, doesn't play with temporality or the boundaries of the individual – is a condition for the shock of anomaly in the fact-world. Everyday reality opened up for a moment, contradicted itself (the Disappearance), then closed again and everyone had to go on as before, though things remained unstable – behaviour, certainly, remained unstable but so also perhaps did physical reality, as will be seen when we come to Gilcrest's healing powers.

In *The Leftovers* the arbitrariness and incoherence of the disaster is simply asserted; it's a given. In many contemporary disasters those who are or might well be responsible are unreachable or hidden and will probably never be got at. There's no chance of finding those responsible for the 'toxic airborne event' in Don DeLillo's *White Noise* (1985), for instance, as the name it has been allotted already suggests. The Disappearance in *The Leftovers* is a stunningly effective action that lacks an agent to whom it can be assigned. As they say, 'deal with it': our helplessness in the face of the big abstractions that tend to be as close as we get to labelling an agent of disaster or of radical change – History, Nature, the Market, Terrorism – is inflated to the point of painful absurdity. There's no available abstraction here; even Chance is ineligible, because the event is so widespread.

There is no prospect of aestheticising the event, or imagining disaster and mass death as opening the way to a new dimension of reality or of the psyche, as in Ballard or Lessing. The possibility of renunciation, of going further into loss and refusal and deprivation, of finding freedom in acceptance, is explored, but only in the sinister and eventually malign form of the Guilty Remnant, an ascetic, death-haunted sect that has come into being in response to the disaster. The mass of survivors have to live in the same place and in much the same way as before: the material context, houses, shops, clothes, cars, jobs, schools, is exactly the same. They are not camped among the ruins; everything is as shiny and as dull as before. We don't have the huge destruction that in fictions of disaster may be exhilarating, may be traumatic, but is always expressive. The enjoyment that disaster fictions (and action movies) offer us, that of destroying buildings, cars, cities, is never on offer in *The Leftovers*. This pleasure is at its purest in the car chases of action movies: cars are crashed, wrecked, piled up, but there is no sign of their drivers; in the Disappearance the driver may have gone, snatched abruptly away, but the car is still there. In its ordinariness *The Leftovers* perhaps alludes to such Rapture movies as *A Thief in the Night* (1972) that depict the scene after the rapture as 'eerily dull', with the (taken) husband's 'shaver still buzzing in the sink' and so on (Beal 2018, 181–186 and 191).

Leaving, Leaving Behind, Staying On

The features of Mapleton are entirely typical:

> ... everything was right where it was supposed to be – the Safeway, Big Mike's Discount Shoes, Taco Bell, Walgreens, that ugly green tower looming over the Burger King, bristling with cell phone antennae and satellite dishes. (342)

Similarly the furnishings of the houses have a familiarity not far from staleness. This is the setting for the recovery that has to be attempted, the ordinary life that has to be resumed. There's no disdain or satire in the depiction of Mapleton and its people – the bar, the softball competition, the meeting of the town council, what's in the fridge, what's at the mall – but there's no excitement either. No equivalent to the ecstatic passages about supermarkets in DeLillo's *White Noise*. No equivalent to the feeling that the mass murder in Margaret Atwood's *Oryx and Crake* (2003) has at least swept away a vicious, deranged, trivial, exploitative version of modern society. The society of *The Leftovers* is not particularly vicious and anyway it's all still there, untouched, but somehow exposed in its ordinariness. Calamity might call up some sense of the spiritual, but there's no sign of that in this neighbourhood. People have to make do with whatever is to hand, and it doesn't look like much.

It seems at first that they do make do, with many mistakes and hesitations and wrong turns. We have the Disappearance, an intrusion into the routine of marital and family troubles and irritations – Nora's husband and children disappear when she is out of the room for a moment, getting kitchen paper to wipe up spilt apple juice (321). Gradually people struggle back to some sort of decent continuity and order. They find more mundane problems, secondary consequences to the catastrophe and work provisional solutions to these problems. The mode is that of classic realism: small touches from recognisable life that concentrate larger meanings (but not revelations, not epiphanies).

Further discussion requires some précis of the situations of the dramatis personae. The story centres on what is left of the household of Kevin, a retired businessman, mayor of the town, struggling to keep the community positive and at peace. His older son Tom has left, and his wife Laurie leaves in the course of the story. Tom becomes the disciple of a certain Wayne Gilcrest, who has the uncanny power to relieve people's pain with a hug, becomes a classic cult leader, and as cult leaders tend to do, exploits teenage girls. Tom hangs around the movement even after Gilcrest is exposed and arrested, and becomes attached to Christine, one of Gilcrest's 'wives', who is pregnant, needs Tom and shows no feeling for him. Tom will return to Mapleton at the end of the story, with Christine and Gilcrest's baby. Laurie joins the Guilty Remnant, and this requires that she completely cut herself off from her family; she falls in love with a fellow member, Meg, and we learn later that the directors of the Guilty Remnant have planned this for their own sinister purposes. Kevin, then, is left with Jill and Aimee, an odd trio. Jill is his and Laurie's daughter, a troubled teenager; Aimee is Jill's friend, lively, feckless, maybe a bad influence, and maybe with designs on Kevin, which Kevin is tending to respond to: the nuclear family in disarray.

Kevin also has an off and on again relationship with Nora, one of those who suffered a disappearance, and is still suffering. Kevin is uncertain about Aimee, unconfident with Nora; Jill is led or misled by Aimee, tempted to join the Guilty Remnant; Aimee is experimenting with her youthful attractiveness; Nora is uncertain about Kevin, who is after all a bit dull, and can't decide whether to stay in Mapleton. Everyone is incomplete and uncertain and has plenty to cope with: the global consequences of the Disappearance, and larger dimensions of politics and society, are off their radars, and even the more immediate emotional consequences of the Disappearance are hard for them to focus. Everyday life is both intense and limited.

Nora visits the mall with her sister to do Christmas shopping:

> Her heart was still racing when she stepped inside, her face hot with pride and embarrassment. She'd just forced herself to make a solo circuit of the big Christmas tree on the main level, where all the parents and kids were waiting to meet Santa Claus. (193)

Given her own lost children, it's an act of courage.

Ordinary customs are going to be what people live through. We see Jill, Aimee and Kevin making a Christmas together, opening presents, exclaiming over the ceremony, drawing it out. Much of their success depends on what is emerging in the previously feckless Aimee – vitality maturing into a feeling for what others need ('I've matured. I have a much higher tolerance for boredom' she says later (299)) – but all three of them pitch in (205–207). There's one gift left over, unopened – Jill has bought it for her absent mother. Kevin gets a chance to give it to Laurie. The sequence of actions here falls into a pattern – he gives her Jill's present, and later she, as instructed, gives him an envelope of divorce papers, as the Guilty Remnant are eager to get hold of Laurie's half of his considerable wealth. Jill's present to Laurie turns out to be a cigarette lighter; members of the Guilty Remnant are required to smoke all the time, as sign and proclamation that there is now no future. On the lighter Jill has written 'Don't Forget Me'. Laurie drops it down the drainage grating; the Guilty Remnant are forbidden emotional ties (223–224). The episode concentrates what is happening with Jill (a recovery, not least of a sense of humour) and, contrariwise, what is happening to Laurie. Jill, who is still growing up, an unhappy teenager, can use the customs of everyday life (Christmas presents) to say something sensitive and witty; her mother can't respond. The novel makes no comment on Laurie's action – after all she is at the same time recovering aliveness and love in her relationship with Meg.

There's a moment late in the novel where Nora feels that her relationship with Kevin has failed, meaning that she has been too deeply wounded by her losses to make anything of her life in Mapleton; so she decides to leave town, to take on a new name and, to symbolise this, to have her hair dyed blonde (309–311; 315). This last action is the reversal of Jill's cutting all her hair off earlier, when she was in the throes of pain and resentment at her mother and brother leaving. There are actions that signify, such as these by Jill and Nora, and there are patterns of contrast, supplied by the novelist, so that events now have overall coherence. These actions – giving gifts, conveying messages, changing your hairstyle – are ordinary ones, but also overlap with elements of traditional stories. They have an anthropological dimension.

As for Nora's plan to leave (we remember Nora in *A Doll's House*), it is abandoned at the very end of the novel, when she finds the infant that Tom has left behind so that he can follow after Christine. We know this is Christine and Gilcrest's baby, rejected by Christine because it wasn't the expected boy. It hasn't yet been given a name: that will be for Nora and Kevin to provide. (Christine refused to name it, or even touch it.) Leaving and leaving behind are worked through and come to replace the being-left-behind that the Disappearance so cruelly and weirdly brought about. In summary: Aimee sensibly leaves the Kevin–Jill ménage;[10] Tom leaves the baby behind; Nora decides not to leave Mapleton and Kevin; and we can add that Jill refuses the Guilty Remnant, which she is being groomed to join, and that Laurie leaves Mapleton for reasons that will throw a harsher light on what has unfolded. The involuntary leaving and leaving behind of the Disappearance are replaced with provisional,

---

[10] 'Jill felt an emptiness open inside of her as she lifted her arm, a sense that something vital was being subtracted from her life. It was always like that when somebody you cared about went away, even when you knew it was inevitable, and it probably wasn't your fault' (341).

voluntary action, so that life has meaning again, though the meaning of, for instance, Tom's leaving the baby behind might not be a particularly positive one for Tom.

We get to this point through careful realist attention to the struggles and slips of ordinary people, and the turning points are patterned in classic realist ways – by making us pay attention to ordinary gestures and actions (having your hair done, giving a witty Christmas present, visiting the mall). The inexplicable and almost unassimilable Left Behind brought about by the Disappearance is replaced by a calibrated set of leavings and leavings behind and staying puts – calibrated because each action says something about the trajectory of each of the main characters. Perrotta doesn't explain the Disappearance, and none of those involved had a choice as regards what happened when the Disappearance occurred. All we are told is that huge numbers were involved and there was no discernible pattern; Perrotta patterns the recovery, however, and all of those involved have to work at whatever recovery they succeed in achieving, or fail to achieve. Recovery is at the same time a small thing and a difficult thing.

The outcomes of their struggles and decisions are nuanced, and not simply positive. Tom's running away from reunion with his father and sister, and from parenting (in the form of Christine's baby) is not exactly positive, given that he is running towards Christine and there has been no evidence that she is interesting or even sensible as a person. (Is Tom interesting as a person? Yes; his chaste protection of Christine for the previous few months has made him interesting.) Aimee is wise to leave Kevin and Jill when she does (from a close encounter by the fridge she realises that sex with Kevin is not far off if she stays, and that would be a bad idea on several counts), but she is now working at the yoghurt place and sleeping with its sleazy proprietor.

It's hard to tell whether the drifting quality of the characters' lives is due to the dislocation brought about by the Disappearance, or is just what things can be like in contemporary America. Perrotta makes the answer uncertain. There's a sense that people survive partly because the empty things they spend their time doing become stale and even emptier, as with the sex game that Jill and, for a while, Aimee play at Dimitri's house. They exhaust them rather than rejecting them.

Much of the novel concerns the ironies and compromises of enmeshment, of being involved with someone whom you can't separate yourself from or much influence or think clearly about – friend (Jill with Aimee), patron (Gilcrest), father, daughter, daughter's friend, girlfriend, girlfriend's baby. The characters are confined to the life of family and community, and then find it a trap. It fits this condition of enmeshment that Nora discovers that her husband (taken in the Disappearance) was having an affair with Kylie, 'her kids' beloved teacher from Little Sprouts Academy' (136) and that Meg's place with her fiancé, whom she left to join the Guilty Remnant, was soon filled by one of their intended bridesmaids. Tom can't disentangle himself from Gilcrest's movement even though he has decided that Gilcrest is tainted, nor can he disentangle himself from Christine, though he can't clearly explain to himself what he is doing. He is present at the birth:

> Tom stayed with Christine throughout the nine-hour labor, holding her hand while she drifted in and out of a drug-induced delirium, cursing the father of her child so bitterly that even the delivery room nurses were impressed. (325)

Then Christine leaves him, and he leaves the baby in order to follow Christine. We will see that this enmeshment is brutally demonstrated with Laurie and her lover Meg in the Guilty Remnant, whereas most of the other characters stumble their way through to a prospect, at least, of happiness, leaving or staying as finally seems right to them.

Getting on OK with your father or your daughter, finding a new partner after loss or desertion, won't do anything for climate change or the maldistribution of wealth. Personal relations are not the same as social relations, as Agnes Heller points out, but plenty of people in our society (society without the Disappearance) fail at these unavoidable tasks of personal relationship, and they continue to be set, regardless of climate change and the maldistribution of wealth. *The Leftovers* thus returns to the domestic problems that preoccupied the characters in many of the postwar disaster novels discussed in chapter 3, but with a difference. Perrotta's choice of the Disappearance as the catastrophe in this novel sets everything at an uneasy tangent, as contrasted to the earlier novels, but, given that *The Leftovers* is a success, it is a reminder that there is more to the history of apocalyptic fiction than increasing innovation of form or extremity of response to catastrophe.

Perrotta doesn't say that our coping with those around us (what faces everyone except a hermit in our society, regardless of orientation or 'lifestyle')[11] takes so much of our energy and wisdom that we have none to spare for the condition of the planet, Syria, racism and so on and on. He is too discreet and attentive for that, but it is a possible inference. The beginning and the end of the novel – the intervention

---

[11] Perrotta deals with the hermit in the passage with Kevin's memories of Balzer, how he became strong in his absolute loneliness, 203–205.

of the Disappearance and the qualified recovery that the characters work through to – make a contrast of absurdity and meaning (pattern). A sceptical comment might be that the contrast is between something global, something that at least hints at a worldwide plight (while at the same time denying it meaning), and what then takes over, the unremittingly local and personal. To carry this issue further it is necessary to examine how much the Disappearance has changed in people's lives.

The Guilty Remnant

The Guilty Remnant is the most emphatic sign in the novel that the catastrophe of the Disappearance has changed life in fundamental ways. The idea behind the cult is that the end is now nigh and normal life should not be resumed; instead, it should be renounced, by the members of the cult, and impeded, by the members of the cult in their relations with the remaining townsfolk. So the members of the Guilty Remnant don't talk, wear only white, don't enjoy themselves in any way, eat boring food, eschew sex (with an exception to be noticed in a moment) and children (having left their own – there seems no possibility of bringing a child with you when you leave the world and enter the Guilty Remnant). They roam the town, snooping, refusing to communicate and trying to impede the enjoyments, public or secret, of the townsfolk. They become in fact a bit like zombies, walking dead, minimally alive, enemies, if in a minimal, ungrisly way, of those who are fully alive. Since those who are fully alive are struggling to come to terms with death and loss, it fits that the members of the Guilty Remnant are like the walking dead – the dead attacking the living. As will be seen in a moment, they are in fact attacking the community with their own deaths, disguised as martyrdoms at the hands of others.

That people of some intelligence and feeling do join cults is a fact, so one has to accept the plausibility of the Guilty Remnant.[12] It's still hard to fit Laurie into this. We can see why she might have decided to withdraw from life after the shock of the Disappearance: exhaustion, unwillingness to face the absence of Tom or to face Jill's adolescent problems. But there's been no evidence of any malignity or spite in her such as seems to be exhibited in the Guilty Remnant's snooping and stalking. She goes along with it (and worse) without thinking. It's

---

[12] The members of 'Heaven's Gate', some of them educated and successful people, lay down on their beds *with their passports*, to await transition to a higher sphere (Carrière 1999, 112).

another instance of Perrotta's refusal to presume to judge: some people mature (Aimee); some get lucky, sort of (Tom); some work hard and win through (Nora, Kevin); some deteriorate (Laurie).

Laurie's history as a member of the Guilty Remnant undergoes a number of twists. She becomes the mentor and 'Trainer' of a younger woman, Meg, then they become friends, then they fall in love. She leaves her daughter and husband to join this unpleasant cult and then, after she does so, she finds love, clearly more and different than what she had with her family. The authorities at Guilty Remnant tolerate the friendship of Laurie and Meg, though it is quite against the rules. In fact, they set Laurie and Meg up in a house that is separate from the compound where most members live in more spartan and much less private conditions: Laurie and Meg live cosily upstairs, and a gay couple have noisy sex downstairs. It looks as if they have somehow been granted a sponsored hideaway for their developing relationship.

Laurie is required to ask Kevin for a divorce, and clearly understands that the purpose is to get money for the Guilty Remnant (253–255). She delivers the divorce papers as Kevin arrives home after a failed date with Nora (291). She doesn't let herself think about her daughter whom she has abandoned and will now make somewhat poorer. She discards Jill's Christmas present. Meanwhile one of the downstairs tenants of Outpost no. 17 is murdered, and his partner disappears. Jill arrives home, having come across the corpse and reported it to the police, just after Laurie has left after delivering the divorce papers to Kevin. As in comedy, nothing happens as and when it should.

> 'Gus and Julian are heroes,' she ['the Director'] said in a firm and quiet voice. 'We need to honor their sacrifice.'
> 'Gus?' Meg said. 'Did he get killed too?'
> 'Gus is fine,' the Director said. 'He's a very brave man. We're taking very good care of him.' (306)

There had been several earlier murders, which Mapleton ascribed to the hostility brewing against the Guilty Remnant, that is, to unknown assassins from outside the cult. Now it turns out that the sect is making its own martyrs. Meg is to be next, murdered, with her consent, by Laurie. That's why they were allotted their cosy hideaway. Two same-sex couples who have found love within the cult (255–256), against its rules, are thus set up in comfort, and then scheduled for martyrdom. The sensational evil of the plan creeps up on us, in this novel of small gifts and commitments. Laurie can't go through with it, so Meg, stronger in the faith, or weaker in the head, shoots herself; and that's how Laurie leaves town, spirited away as planned by other members of the Guilty Remnant, though how far she is going to get is unclear. We last see her in the getaway car, wiping bits of Meg off her face and saying, *'Brave, brave Meg'* (351; Perrotta's italics). We understand the significance of ordinary gestures (for instance, Jill's Christmas gift) because the characters' lives resemble ours. Now, with Laurie's response to Meg's death we discover that this assumption is unreliable. It's like what happens when people tell you that they believe that Hillary Clinton committed murder (fill in some more recent weirdness for yourself, if this one seems dated).

The novel has gone from an image of power and meaninglessness (the Disappearance) to a recovery from grief and a modest, uneven recovery of love and kindness; but Perrotta has inserted this renewed nihilism, purposive in a perverse way, but of a darkness in striking contrast to the modest goings-on of the other characters. Kevin will succeed at this and fail at that; Aimee will start from here and end up there; Tom will return home, deposit a baby, and leave to look for Christine again; Nora will get a new hair colour (very nice) and plan to leave town ...; and Laurie will submit to a death cult and watch her new lover kill herself according to instructions. Everyday life is not what it seemed.

Yet the novel does not end there. Nora writes to Kevin, explaining why she has decided to leave town; she doesn't deliver the letter, because she comes across the baby that Tom has left behind, and reads *his* letter asking that it be taken care of.

> The baby in her arms was a complete stranger, the way they always are when we find them for the first time, before we give them their names and welcome them into our lives. (355)

(Nora had planned to change her own name after leaving town.)

Reading the last chapters of *The Leftovers*, we might recall letters undelivered or unread in *Middlemarch* and *Tess of the d'Urbervilles*: among the tropes of classic realism. (Laurie's divorce papers, delivered to Kevin, are probably invalid anyway.) But here the relevant association is with *The Winter's Tale*: 'Thou met'st with things dying, I with things new born' (III, 3, 112–113).[13]

The effect of death is the founding reality in *The Leftovers*; everything begins from the Disappearance. After the Disappearance, those left over have to go on living and we witness their small decisions and revivals,

---

[13] 'Who can tell what may be the effect of writing?' (Eliot 1994, 412). For letters read or unread see chapters 33 and 35; 41; 49 and 54; 52 and 53; 65; 82; 85 in *Middlemarch* and chapters XLVIII, LI–LIII in *Tess of the D'Urbervilles*.

or failures, in the everyday, which has been left untouched, at least materially. They arrive at an imperfect but real recovery, embodied in the new baby who will be cared for by Kevin and Nora, the most important of the survivors whom we have followed in Mapleton, tentative middle-aged lovers. What will happen next is a bit easier to imagine here than with Leontes and Hermione after their reunion. Ordinary life will resume, but shadowed by the departure from ordinary life of Laurie and by the void opened up in it by the Disappearance and the Guilty Remnant.

Death isn't final, and in many respects isn't real, in *Girlfriend in a Coma*. Apocalypse takes a biblical form – there is even an angel of the apocalypse to preside over and point the moral of catastrophe and recovery, though, as in *The Leftovers*, the powers behind apocalypse remain hidden.

Girlfriend in a Coma

> The problematic of posthistory is not the end of the world but the end of meaning.
>
> (Lutz Niethammer)

Girlfriend in a Coma (first published 1998) is set in the suburbs of Vancouver, and among a small group of friends, together in high school, still together in their thirties. We spend a great deal of time with them, as they exchange witticisms, swap partners and worry about the stagnation and meaninglessness of their lives. Their lives are those of young people in contemporary consumer society – in fact their lives are still those of young people when they are no longer teenagers but well into their thirties. Their lives are ordinary, typical, yet unstable in profound and uncanny ways. They sometimes respond to this blend of the ordinary and the weird by thinking seriously about themselves and the condition of their age, and sometimes respond to it by retreat into jokes, or drinking. The language of the novel draws on the pop culture that makes up the experience of the characters, and does so in often illuminating ways. Into this troubled but familiar – generic – suburban life and culture there comes a series of uncanny events and presences: a ghost, a girl in a coma for years (and giving birth to a daughter within this coma), her seemingly miraculous emergence from the coma and then the end of the world – staged, in fact, faked, as we learn from the ghost, precisely and only for the edification of this group of likeable but undistinguished suburban slackers: 'This could go well beyond *real*' as one of them comments on the night when Karen lapses into a coma (22).

We thus have unqualified ordinariness, even banality, disrupted by unqualified weirdness; Coupland presses both to extremity. The novel is hospitable to the kind of skewed logic and fantasy that until recently circulated mainly in sets of half-serious believers (contrails inscribe secret messages, the CIA staged 9/11), roping it into a narrative already saturated with fakery and simulation, as well as flippancy and intelligent scepticism. There is emphatic unheroic ordinariness everywhere on the scene, even in the sky ('the clouds like soaked dishrags squeezing out wet grey glop', 85), but this can open into the spectacular, without, however, losing its reliance on the familiar. Here, for instance, mixing associations from movies and from the news, a moment from the end of the world:

> [...] Without warning, the Esso station by the Westview overpass explodes like a jet at an air show – bodies like ventriloquist dolls puked into the sky as though in a cartoon or an action-adventure film. (187)

'We were meaningless' (10)

The world of Richard, Linus, Hamilton, Penny and Wendy is a narrow one, but crowded, or rather, cluttered. They are intelligent, but they don't appear to read books or go to any movies other than action movies or take much notice of people outside their own circle (fixed since high school). They cling to their own neighbourhood and their own city, Vancouver, though they accept that it is just like anywhere else.[14] They live in the suburbs, enclosed in themselves. Their world is the world of consumer society and pop culture. Any contemporary even vaguely aware of the world of brand names and pop culture will recognise every item, either as it is referred to by name, or generically; this both enables readers to get the point, and reminds them that their heads are just as full of dross as those of the characters. We have the procedures of realism – full detailing of everyday things, for instance – but not the effect of 'thereness' and plenitude that this can deliver, and the characters feel this as a lack, the more intensely because – in comparison to the world of *The Leftovers*, for instance – there are so many everyday things, there is so much to be named. Consumer abundance

---

[14] As they notice when three of them become location scouts for the movies, Vancouver can stand in for anywhere (87). Richard notices that they seem destined always to return to their 'quiet little neighborhood' (142).

is disenchanted and doesn't connote hope or desire or even newness. Things are no longer glossy, as they are in advertisements and in Pop Art. There's a lot of bingeing and a lot of mess.

The friends are individualised in that they differ from one another and have definite traits, but their culture is uniform, and, in a blurred way, with the edges all rubbed off, familiar. They haven't watched a single TV programme or listened to a single rock song that might strike the reader with a note of differentness. (The one younger member of the group is Karen and Richard's daughter Megan, born during Karen's coma; when Karen revives and Megan meets her for the first time, she wants to tell her about the Buzzcocks and Blondie (118): these are the markers of her generation.) They are cut off from the past by their isolation as a group, a cohort with common experiences, almost as absolutely as the characters in *The Leftovers* are marked by the Disappearance. History is names and things from your teenage years that you can remember with a touch of nostalgia. It's not that being of the same generation explains their place in history; being in a generation is the only history they have, and it is placeless. The problems and challenges of generation are in fact absent from *Girlfriend*, because when they occur they stem from the relationships and conflicts of generations, in the plural, and in *Girlfriend* there is only one generation on the scene, that of the central characters.

At school, society told them how to be popular; afterwards, they were on their own, tolerated or ignored, and confined, or secluded, in the everyday life of consumer society. They sometimes rail against 'the system', but it's a sign of how accommodating the wider society is of them, and they of it, that how Karen's years of medical care in her coma are paid for is never mentioned. Society supplies them with products, jobs (mostly mediocre), even excellent medical care, but neither restriction nor purpose. Parents are amiable if sometimes annoying presences ('neither heavy moralisers nor stringent disciplinarians', as Richard says of his; 30); they are not links with the past that produced the present.

As they see themselves, they have got older and become dissatisfied and snagged, without developing. About this predicament – being young beyond their time – they can be witty:

> 'Imagine you're a forty-year-old, Richard,' Hamilton said to me around this time, while working as a salesman at a Radio Shack in Lynn Valley, 'and suddenly someone comes up to you saying, "Hi, I'd like you to meet Kevin. Kevin is eighteen and will be making all your career decisions for you." [...] But that's what life is all about – some eighteen-year-old kid making your big decisions for you that stick for a lifetime.' He shuddered. (56)

Karen's years in coma, neither living nor dead, her body becoming wizened, figure as a caricature of the friends' snagged condition: 'Whatta disaster. I look like a praying mantis', she says when she abruptly revives (119).

Their uneasiness and unhappiness shows itself in flares of intense physicality. Richard is told that Karen (now deep in a coma) is pregnant, and he is the father:

> From the top of my skull, flames burned downward; once again, I felt my skin grow quills, my forehead antlers. My stomach jumped off a cliff and my legs became stone. (43)

The hyperbole suggests both shock and a desire to evade it by exaggerating it. And again: 'Linus's brain empties as though passing through a trapdoor in the floor' (116); 'An adrenaline fang bites the rear of his neck' (175). Strong feeling in *Girlfriend* is emphatically physical, as if in illustration of Fredric Jameson's formula for the post-modern: intensities rather than emotions (1991, 15–16). For a Halloween party, Hamilton goes as a 'leaker', that is, he is made up as the corpse of someone who lived and died alone and was not found until weeks after their death: a reminder of death in its most lonely and desolate modern form, a real-seeming image of the body at its most gross and disgusting (102–104). This appearance of the 'leaker', as something to impersonate at a party, can be connected to the contemporary unease, horror and fascination with the body, from zombie movies to forensic crime dramas on television. *Girlfriend in a Coma* is crowded with corpses that are at the same time disgusting, and fakes.[15] Death is everywhere and nowhere. Life in a society of brand names, items that seem to exist more as names than as material objects, is varied by binges and addictions and haunted by images of death.

A few moments after Karen is described as 'rasping, blinded, and pretzeled in a wheelchair', she evokes 'a world of gentle Pacific rains, down-filled jackets, bitter red wine in goatskins, and naïve charms' (74–75). The text and the characters know that this oscillation figures a radical instability (there is reference to 'Richard's sentimental blurts',

---

[15] Tim Beal (2018, 195–200) suggests that fascination with zombies has succeeded to the fascination with the violent and horrifying side of Apocalypse that was expressed in fundamentalist novels and movies about the aftermath of the Rapture. Behind both Rapture fictions and zombie fictions he sees unease about the notion of the resurrection of the dead that is made explicit in many images of the Last Judgement.

148). There can be moments of equilibrium, as with the scene in which Karen suddenly wakes from her coma and returns to life, and her daughter Megan and Richard join her for a sleep on her hospital bed, 'drifting along with Karen in their boat that will not tip' (123), but the underlying note is edgy instability, kept at bay, mostly, by brittle jokes and witty exaggerations.

It is in this context of the humdrum, unhappy and edgy that amazing things happen and Coupland takes on the challenge of making us believe in them. Karen goes into a coma and awakens 17 years later, fully alert, having experienced visions of an ominous future while she was in the coma; the ghost of one of their friends makes increasingly frequent appearances, and in the last part of the novel directs and changes their lives, speaking almost always, however, as the high school sports star he was when he died; the world ends and all humans on the planet except the main characters fall asleep, die and rot, to the accompaniment of a great deal of turmoil and mayhem. All this happens in the suburbs, to our five increasingly washed-up characters (joined by Megan) and all is expressed in the language of brand-name consumerism and by reference to the shared currency of pop culture.

Apocalypse and Replication

Apocalyptic novels often move from the mass death that cannot be depicted to an individual death whose 'normal' pain can be faced, or to a final, willed self-immolation; in contrast, *Girlfriend in a Coma* is saturated with images and facsimiles of death: corpses, fake and real; death in life, a ghost, falling asleep as dying. Death intrudes, invades, as with Karen's falling into coma, as with the end of the world that is staged and depicted in the novel, but it was already present everywhere, endlessly imaged, manufactured – in the life but non-life of images and photos; in the stories about life and death that Hamilton mentions, for instance, the phenomenon of the 'leaker'; in dressing as Death (a goth phase that Megan goes through; 120); and in the sense of lack, of stymied or buried life, that sometimes grips the characters, or surfaces for a moment:

> We had all awakened X number of years past our youth feeling sleazy and harsh. Choices still existed, but they were no longer infinite. Fun had become a scrim, concealing the hysteria that lay behind it. (78)

Richard recalls reading Arthur C. Clarke's *Childhood's End*:

> In it, the children of Earth conglomerate to form a master race that dreams together, that collectively moves planets. This made me wonder, what if the children of Earth instead fragmented, checked out, had their dreams erased and became vacant? What if instead of unity there was atomisation and amnesia and comas? (60)

Richard feels that this must be what Karen has glimpsed:

> She saw a picture, however fragmentary, that told her that tomorrow was not a place she wanted to visit – that the future was not a place in which to be. (60)[16]

Beneath the *umwelt* of brand names and pop culture, offered half-nostalgically and half-satirically, is a lack; it is figured in Richard's idea of *Childhood's End* flipped to its negative. Absence is figured in The Disappearance in *The Leftovers*, and, in its aftermath, people will get on with their lives as best they can; lack is pervasive in *Girlfriend in a Coma* – and so is fakery.

The novel literalises the 'scrim' of Richard's image (78). Hamilton and Linus get jobs as special effects make-up artists, always to do with death and violence: 'aliens, zombies, vampires, Mafia-shot corpses, humans in all states of decay, mummification, terror, and explosion'; 'a galore of bodies' (88). They even make a mock-up of the comatose Karen. Richard happens upon it when visiting his friends:

> I heard a thunk behind me and saw a dummy that I probably ought not to have seen: a plastic female body almost identical to Karen – bony, taut, skeletal, made of polyurethane foam, with long straight brown Orlon hair parted in the middle. (89)

Richard's account is precise: he meets his friends' grossness with a gingerly carefulness ('probably ought not to have seen', 'almost identical'). The

---

[16] When Karen revives from her coma and is asked how she finds things now, 'Her friends have become who they've become by default' (136); the difference between the world she left and the world she returned to is 'a lack' (213). Linus asks Richard what the difference between the afterlife and the future is: '"The difference," I said, "is that the afterworld is all about infinity; the future is only about changes on this world – fashion and machines and architecture." We were working on a TV movie about angels coming down to Earth to help housewives' (91).

moment is a loaded one, because it is not only Karen and their feelings about her death in life that he has stumbled across, but a confronting image of the work of the artist, moulding images from fears and disgusts. This is how we make art now, almost in spite of ourselves, working on 'cheesy movies of the week' (91). Coupland takes the culture of action movies, zombie movies and forensic dramas seriously enough to suggest a discontent and a desire behind the obsession with mutilated corpses and big explosions.

The novel proceeds to the end of the world, which answers to that desire and discontent, but will later be revealed as yet another, highly 'realistic' simulation. Everyone stops what they were doing and falls asleep forever, in a global version of Karen's fall into coma, leaving behind them the undestroyed clutter of suburban life. The end of the world is thorough and spectacular but still suburban and domestic:

> The end of the world as we know it. Just another brick in the wall. It sounds glamorous but it's not. It's dreary and quiet and the air always smells like there's a tire fire half a mile upwind. (4)

Coupland evokes emptiness and slow decay, but interweaves a few (here, not too many) topical touches:

> Cathedrals fall as readily as banks; car assembly lines as readily as supermarkets. [...] In cities the snow sits unplowed; jukeboxes sit silent; chalkboards stand forever unerased. Computer databases lie untapped while power cables float from aluminium towers like long thin hairs. (4)

This catastrophe is less a destruction than a ceasing, a stoppage ('unplowed', 'unerased', 'untapped'). Even the everyday disposal of things, on which we spend a lot of our time, for instance, erasing chalkboards, has ceased.

The setting is still suburban. The moment of the end finds Lois, Karen's always irritating mother, in the meat section of the supermarket. She climbs in with the steaks: 'She closes her eyes and goes home' (182). Everyone dies, except our five friends. There is some disorder, as with the exploding Esso station, but then a lyrical diminuendo, still with consumer society details: 'a Missouri railway car sidled off its track with millions of scratch'n'play lottery tickets spilled into an overflowing creek' (204). The world as it ends seems somehow shameful, without dignity, in its ordinariness, the signs of its mundane preoccupations. The friends resume their slacker lives, able to overindulge in the material bounty that the catastrophe has left behind, mostly intact. Karen renews her disillusioned criticisms of their emptiness, and they can't disagree; the teen ghost Jared appears more often, but is still as immature and jokey as formerly.

Then Jared reveals that the apocalypse was faked, a gigantic, indeed global, simulacrum. The end of the world as we know it, though detailed with great vigour and made to seem as real as any that might be read, or seen on screen, has been staged by unknown powers who might well be divine but are never revealed. They make use of Jared as their angelic messenger, though without giving him much more brain or dignity than he had when a high school student. The end was staged, he tells them, to teach them a lesson, which will convert them into fierce and dedicated prophets of change; at which point they are returned to the moment before the (faked) catastrophe. The world comes back to life.

All catastrophes in apocalyptic fiction are fictional, of course, and figure as challenges to the author's imaginative powers, but this time the end of the world was laid on for the five friends. They were apparently the only survivors, and apocalyptic fictions need survivors: *Girlfriend in a Coma* pulls the rug from under this narrative convention too, because the whole catastrophe centres on these ordinary people, not as survivors making a new life if they can, like, for instance, the random group of Americans gathered around Ish and Em in *Earth Abides*, but as pupils being taught a very elaborate lesson. This is no doubt very often our position as readers when an apocalyptic fiction is to be seen as a cautionary tale, a very bad future staged as a warning, and a critique of how we live now, but recognising this doesn't lessen the shock of Coupland's baring of the device here.

Girlfriend in a Coma is a startling intervention into the discourse of the apocalyptic novel in a time of blurred boundaries and instability. That the apocalyptic catastrophe in this case should be faked may be implausible (given, for instance, the novel's vagueness about the powers that are behind the fake) but it fits a world in which most things are mediated, many things are replicated (including death), and the boundary between life and non-life is crowded with ghosts, visions, the half-life of coma. It is too late for the reader to argue with Coupland's choice of this group of ordinary (but intelligent) slackers as the privileged recipients of the lesson the simulated catastrophe carries. Even the unease many a reader will feel with the fact that the role of heavenly messenger is given to Jared has to reckon with the acceptance that Coupland is everywhere bestowing on the mundane details of consumer society, the scratch'n'play lottery tickets, Lois crawling in among the steaks to fall into sleep.

Everyone has to deal with and live through the circumstances given them, 'the "thrownness" characteristic of human existence – the fact that we live in a particular time, loaded down with the contingencies of our own personal circumstances and the practices of the society to which we belong' (Callinicos 1995, 84, summarising Heidegger). Coupland details these circumstances as a thick and particular encrustation and atmosphere, thicker and more particular than, for instance, the circumstances of Marianne in *Heroes and Villains* or those of the narrator and Emily in *The Memoirs of a Survivor*. The more the characters are surrounded by this encrustation and atmosphere, the less autonomy they are likely to have. Hence the contrasting effect of liberation in Ballard when civilisation is reduced to a few ruins and the psyche is free to roam; hence Lessing's refusal to describe and name in *Planet 8*, which minimises the characters' connection to a material life they are going to shed. The characters in *Girlfriend* are confined to the suburban everyday of consumer society and pop culture (no politics or religion; no culture beyond generic pop culture). They struggle to express the wider and deeper discontent that they do in fact feel, but their culture doesn't give them much help. They are in thrall to their thrownness. Their actions lead nowhere and in fact don't have much in the way of intention behind them (they hook up and break up, they take jobs and leave them).

They need the strong stimulus of an outside force: not apocalypse as desired, but apocalypse as needed. Hence the end of the world and then the revelation that it was staged. It was staged, therefore it had an intention behind it, in contrast to, for instance, a catastrophic epidemic. Confined to the everyday and particular, the characters are out of contact with what has made their world. With the catastrophe and its simulation, a world-making and unmaking power becomes visible. But the gods (to call them that) are hidden and we only see their messenger, Jared. Jared is facetious, superficial, immature: the limitations of their world, doubled. On the one hand, this supernatural mechanism for the solution of their problem is plausible because it participates in the conditions of their world, which is already uncanny and simulacral, and because it keeps to their world's consumer culture ordinariness. On the other hand, in his speeches to the others, Jared as the angel of this version of apocalypse reaches for 'the universe', 'the world': 'The universe *wants* us to win', [Jared says], 'The universe makes sure we're winning even when we lose' (232). 'The universe' means very little here. Similarly, 'Human beings and the world are now the same thing' (266). This is Jared on how the world needs the humans who have wrecked it – a praiseworthy thought in itself, but 'the world' in this grand sense has not really figured in the novel.

For Coupland, developments and decisions in personal relationships are not really a means to resolution as they are in *The Leftovers*. His characters crave a general social or spiritual explanation for their emptiness and discontent. In *Everyday Life*, Agnes Heller distinguishes between particularity (living so as to advance one's own interests, solve practical problems and conform to what society expects) and individuality (acting on a wider view of society and humanity). The growth from particularity to individuality is too hard for the characters at the centre of *Girlfriend in a Coma*, though they do attempt it. The change and the wider view will have to come from outside, through the apocalyptic catastrophe. The end of the world comes as the solution to their predicament – or rather, the revelation that the end of the world was faked in order to teach them a lesson comes as the offered solution. The solution proposed is not a matter, as in Ballard, of individuals following their impulses towards immolation. It's a change of life, and an attempt to change society by preaching to it:

> You'll soon be seeing us walking down your street, our backs held proud, our eyes dilated with truth and power. (281)

And we'll run a mile, having encountered evangelical zeal before. This outcome does not convince, but Coupland's evocation of the return of the world ('the very world, which is the world/Of all of us'),[17] is on firmer ground:

> Across the globe hydro dams generate electricity and radio towers send powerful signals out into the heavens advertising Fiat Pandas and crème rinses. Golden lights oscillate wildly. Giant receiving dishes rotate and scour the universe for voices and miracles. And why shouldn't they? (280)

---

[17] Wordsworth 1979, *The Prelude* (1805), book X, lines 725–726.

Chapter 8

Apocalypse in the Contemporary World City
Don DeLillo and China Miéville

Don DeLillo's *Cosmopolis* (2003) and China Miéville's *Kraken* (2010) return apocalypse to the city. The city is the evil Babylon of traditional apocalypse, and the Vanity Fair that has to be traversed on the way to the Celestial City. The city is the source, with its crowds, of apocalyptic violence in the age of revolutions; and the site of the novel's engagement with modernity from Dickens to Joyce and to Pynchon.[1] It is mostly absent from many of the fictions discussed in earlier chapters – it is present only to be turned away from in *Memoirs* – but *Cosmopolis* and *Kraken* are immersed in the energies and complexities as well as the violence of the city. Apocalypse is under way, proliferating. It may be averted, hence borrowings from the adventure novel, a topic to be discussed below in connection with *Kraken*. It may also, however, be the prevailing condition of the city itself. The question is undecided. The crisis and destruction do not come from outside, as with the invasion that is a precipitant of apocalypse in many earlier novels. It is embedded in the conditions and perhaps also in the vitality of the city. To depict it is also to interpret it, not as a kind of puzzle or mystery as sometimes is the case in earlier apocalyptic fictions, but as imbricated with the diverse energies and destructive forces at work in the society itself. The latter is imagined as 'an independent organism', 'going its own way' (Williams 1985, 46), so that the characters are figments and representatives of this huge, hybrid organism. The form and style of these novels changes to catch this quality.

[1] For the city in the age of revolutions, see Carlyle, *The French Revolution* (1837); Dickens, *A Tale of Two Cities* (1859); and the apocalyptic burning of Paris by the Communards in Zola's *The Debacle* (1892). As regards modern literature and the energies of the city, see Berman 1988. Pynchon in recent works has followed his earlier imaginations of London and Los Angeles with novels set in New York and (again) Los Angeles (*Bleeding Edge* and *Inherent Vice*). The phenomenology of experience in the contemporary city is explored in Beaumont and Dart 2010.

The heterogeneity and density of contemporary urban life is layered, crammed, overloaded into *Cosmopolis* and *Kraken*, and the result is less a representation in the style of classic realism than an intense assemblage.[2] In these novels, to write a story about apocalypse, threatened, ongoing, perhaps averted, is to make a figure of the condition of society itself, a story in which the intensity and fast-moving novelty of the crisis can draw out fundamental aspects of the society. Society as it was before apocalypse arrived is itself the seed of what is now happening; more, it provides its energy.

In earlier novels, wholesale destruction and collapse often releases energies, as is the case in Ballard's apocalyptic trilogy, and in Carter's *Heroes and Villains* and Aldiss's *Barefoot in the Head*, but society as it was before the crisis arrived tends to figure as a norm – inadequate, complacent, inclined to denial, certainly – but not itself the source of the crisis. In Lessing's *The Memoirs of a Survivor*, the ill that is giving rise to social breakdown is general and social, and there is no sign that it has arrived from outside society, but in a gesture of disgust or dismay the Survivor refuses to analyse it. The novel turns inwards, to mysterious other spaces, and eventually to escape. In *On the Beach* the nuclear fallout that will wipe out humanity is the result of political miscalculations in many nations, but the people the novel actually looks at are all decent and good natured, and government is still trusted as the world comes to an end: political folly is widespread in the war that has taken place, but not elsewhere.

The condition of the city can be seen as unfinished business in the history of apocalyptic fiction since 1945. The postwar fictions of disaster that were discussed in chapter 2 tend to leave the city early in the story. The long English imagination of the country as natural and authentic is implicit if not spelt out. This tradition revived in the early twentieth century (Hawkins, 1986). The hold on the national imagination of the mighty nineteenth-century cities waned; authentic Englishness was to be found in the nostalgically imagined village. In postwar fictions of disaster the city is represented by a few images of coming ruin and desertion. Cities had struggled into order after the haphazard disorder and mess of their huge nineteenth-century expansion, and in the process the complexity of their organisation and infrastructure and their consequent

---

[2] There are analogies with the many overlapping movements in art discussed in Potts 2013: 'Alternative means, such as assembling representations of disparate phenomena that could not be encompassed within a spatially realistic or unified picture, often have proved more appropriate than naturalistic depiction for creating a richness and density of range of reference to the complex concatenation of realities in the world inhabited by the artist' (3).

vulnerability had been revealed. It was logical to think that apocalyptic disaster would bring collapse, though, in fact, the big European cities proved hard to bomb into collapse in the Second World War.

Apocalyptic novels of the 1960s and 1970s depict very different landscapes, but still take their novels away from the city. Ballard and sometimes Kavan depict a destruction that has rendered the cities ruins and thereby pushed them into the past (most vividly in Ballard's *The Drowned World*), and both set their stories in psychic landscapes that have in many cases been cleared of inhabitants, doing this the more vividly and disturbingly to reflect the protagonists' desires and perversities.[3] In *Heroes and Villains* Angela Carter gets her protagonist away from the remnants of modern civilisation (which in its post-apocalyptic form is no more than a village anyway) as quickly as possible, and the heart of the novel is in the depiction of the post-apocalyptic 'Barbarians' in the burgeoning, but hardly pastoral countryside. As we will see, *Kraken* brings natural life *into* the city, and gives it a role in the teeming life of the place and, indeed, in the plot, but it is in the unromantic form of rats, pigeons, insects, and it is as it were citified.

Cosmopolis and *Kraken* are set in the metropolis, the thronging central city. They are traditionally modern in their location in the street, as in Dickens or Baudelaire. Traffic is supposed to have pushed the people off the streets in the contemporary city:

> The great novelty of urban life, in fact, does not consist of having thrown the people into the street, but in having raked them up and shut them into offices and homes. It does not consist in having intensified the public dimension, but in having invented the private one.[4]

If so, the people repossess the streets in these novels, especially in *Cosmopolis*, where the street is invaded by demonstrators and rioters, is the scene of an old-fashioned market, and is taken over by a funeral procession and later a crowd of naked bodies. Both novels, for all their

---

[3] In his later novels of social disaster and violence, Ballard does engage with the city as the site of disorder and of violence; so it is in *Crash*, *High Rise*, *Concrete Island*, *Super-Cannes* and *Millennium People*, for instance. In the last two, however, this is the contemporary gated community, deliberately cut off from the rest of the city – and in *Super-Cannes*, preying on it.

[4] Franco Moretti, quoted in d'Eramo 2007, 174. *Cosmopolis* gives us images of the private life lived in public, notably in the scenes of Eric Packer in his limo. For a parallel, see Trotter 2010 on the phone box, for instance 210 on 'excess'.

violence, sense of threat and sense of continual sudden transformation, work with an ideal of the city as gathering the populace in all its (often dangerous) variety and bodiliness. The ideal of the ordered and rationally planned city, dominant in the 1950s and 1960s, is long dead by the time *Cosmopolis* and *Kraken* are published, its grave marked by Jane Jacobs's *The Death and Life of Great American Cities* (1961). The city – the metropolis as distinct from the post-industrial city – is now the site of intense but unstable energies and perhaps in that respect *Cosmopolis* and *Kraken* foreshadow the current situation in which the metropolis booms unhealthily and uneasily while the provinces seethe in neglect and resentment; but perhaps to suggest this is to speculate too far. The demonstrators in *Cosmopolis* are still urban (they throw rats, the most urban of animals, especially in New York). The provincial protestors of the *gilet jaune* movement and at Trump's rallies are in the future.

Apocalypse is traditionally an all-encompassing and determined unfolding. In the Apocalypse of John, there is an all-powerful director, the Son of Man, a hierarchy of powers, a sequence of events keyed to the opening of the seven seals, and, to that degree, ordered, and a final outcome that is unqualified – the end of the worldly city, the end of History, the arrival of New Jerusalem, inaugurating Eternity. *Cosmopolis* and *Kraken* offer a challenge to the notion that succeeds traditional apocalypse, one that is central to globalisation and thence to contemporary modernity. This is that that we are consigned to, or even that we ought to bring about, one global history and fate. The all-encompassing unity of apocalypse is put into conflict with the messy disunity of the contemporary city. The ongoing apocalyptic situation – the breakdown of order, the proliferating violence – itself involves an almost chaotic diversity. There is no single source or image of catastrophe. The city seems to be infected or convulsed everywhere with the acts and signs of apocalypse, but its fractious energy, if it is exacerbated by this disorder, also refuses the reductive powers of apocalypse. In *Cosmopolis*, Eric Packer is a person of huge power and selfishness, and is bringing about the apocalyptic collapse of the financial system, and yet he passes through the fractious unpredictable self-expressions of the city in a kind of ignorance, only momentarily affected by them. In *Kraken*'s punk London, apocalypse is so habitual that it has given rise to sects and connoisseurs, and the arrival of a 'real' apocalypse threatens this way of life as well as the very existence of the city. The quest to avert apocalypse uncovers and mobilises more and more of the weird practices and possibilities of the city's denizens (if 'denizen' is a name for one who is embedded in a place beyond what is the case for a mere inhabitant). Further, as the adventure plot that the novel adopts is loaded to the point of excess, it uncovers a series of ultimate villains attempting to bring about The End. In both *Cosmopolis* and *Kraken*, this conflict of diversity and totality suggests an interpretation of contemporary life, a suggestion as to where apocalypse comes from. In these novels, it comes from within the life of the city and not from outside or from nature, as an invasion or an epidemic does. In *Kraken* the threatened city reveals more powers and possibilities the more darkly it is threatened. In neither novel does apocalypse lead to revolution, as it did in the nineteenth-century narratives cited above (n.1), and as was the case in Miéville's earlier novels, *Iron Council* (where revolution is not thwarted, but suspended) and *The Scar* (where a popular uprising averts an apocalyptic end to the city).

Individuals and Monsters

Catastrophe generates the beasts it needs.
(China Miéville, *London's Overthrow*)

Depiction of monsters and the monstrous undergoes radical shifts in recent apocalyptic fiction. In *Kraken*, circumstances select Billy and his companions to try to avert catastrophe, and the catastrophe in turn proliferates villains who have uncanny powers, but also reveals and involves more and more of the alternative processes (customs, physics) of the novel's fantastic alternative London. In this process emphatic individuality passes from being embodied in comic urban types (such as the police officer Collingswood) to being embodied in grotesque villains of monstrous ruthlessness, as if it had been drained into a sump. Meanwhile our heroes, Dane and Billy and Marg, are notable for unsensational ordinariness. The plot revolves around 'the Kraken', actually the stolen corpse of a giant squid. The name recalls the apocalyptic monster of the deep, but the squid in the novel is a victim. The individual who transforms situations by heroic will and skill lives on in contemporary action movies and – deeper into fantasy – in superhero movies and comics, and these texts are discussed in the context of apocalypse in Paik 2010. Elsewhere in contemporary fiction the individual of extraordinary power tends to figure as a psychopath or sociopath; an appropriately extreme example is Bret Easton Ellis's Patrick Bateman in *American Psycho* (1991). It is significant that Bateman doesn't make sense as a personage in even a satirically exaggerated New York, but moves in a hallucinated world of his own. At another extreme is the presumed killer in Roberto Bolaño's *2666* (2004), horrifying in his exhaustively narrated crimes, but absent, never seen or caught, and maybe not a single person. Jeff

VanderMeer's *Dead Astronauts* (2019) reassesses and disseminates the whole spectrum of the monstrous.[5] None of the personae of the novel is simply human, many are monsters or infected with monstrosity, but almost all are victims as well as ogres or torturers. In a world suffering the extreme effects of catastrophe, human individuals hardly exist, and monstrosity is everywhere but hard to distinguish from victimhood.

Cosmopolis begins with an anti-hero, the immensely rich and fecklessly nihilistic Eric Packer, and for much of the novel a proliferating disorder swirls around him, while he is pushing the world's financial system towards meltdown, as if only this megalomania could figure as a response to the vastness and irrationality of the system itself. As the crowded day darkens towards his inevitable, and self-desired, death, however, the urban scene (a different, demotic New York, not the New York of the glass banking towers in which he has his power) throws up a series of countervailing individuals and groups, from the naked crowd photographed in the street to Brutha Fez the rap artist, dead but releasing life-enhancing vitality and diversity in the way he is mourned. The crisis has proliferated individual acts of self-assertion and violence,[6] as well as riots, demonstrations and financial disaster; the city, in turn, proliferates individuals and frames their distinctness, from Brutha Fez to Eric's driver and his barber, as well as finding space for mass events and customs, such as the crowd photograph, the funeral of Brutha Fez, the perennial street life of the Diamond District. Packer's huge selfishness is measured against the varied individualities that make up the city.

Cosmopolis[7]

When he died he would not end. The world would end. (6)

Everybody wants to own the end of the world.

(DeLillo, *Zero K*)

Cosmopolis is a novel about a man who brings about an apocalyptic financial crash, and passes through or sees on screen a series of other events suggestive of social breakdown and (not quite the same thing)

---

[5] VanderMeer's earlier novel *Borne* (2017) concentrates monstrosity in the single giant figure of the title.
[6] The man who incinerates himself during the riot (97–100); the man who pies Eric (143); the disaffected employee who eventually kills him.
[7] References are to Don DeLillo, *Cosmopolis*, London: Picador, 2003. Cosmopolis is Oswald Spengler's name for the petrified World City of modernity (Conrad 1999, 330).

of a culture split into fragments. It's set on a single day, his last, and follows him to his death, a kind of suicide (just as the financial crash he brings about is one that he intends, though it will ruin him). Parker's trajectory is clear and is that of a shedding, a renouncing and refusing. The arc of the novel as a whole is somewhat different, but it is Parker's story that first asks for attention. Early in the novel he interviews members of his staff (his chief of technology, his chief of finance, his chief of theory) and is examined by a staff doctor – all of this in his limousine. He proceeds to shed all these appurtenances of his business as a fabulously successful and rich asset manager. He doesn't listen to their warnings about the danger of his bet on the yen: in fact, he seems to have provoked the warnings in order to refuse to listen to them. He sheds his bodyguards: one goes off duty, one stays behind at a rave, and he kills the third and last, his head of security. He sheds his clothes, mostly in a series of random sexual encounters (with his art advisor/mistress, with one of his bodyguards, with his wife), but also in a series of passing moments of violence (an anti-capitalist riot, an incident in which he is pied by a famous maverick).

Finally, he parts from the driver of his limo and is alone, at the end of the novel and end of the day, face to face with the would-be assassin whom his head of security has called a 'credible threat'. He is stripped of identity and ready to become 'Male Z' in the morgue. DeLillo often structures his fictions around a contrast between a willed withdrawal or refusal on the part of his central character, on the one hand, and the overload and excess of contemporary society on the other: for instance, the central character's withdrawal and eventual self-mutilation in *Great Jones Street* (1973), Bill Grey's blockage and eventual anonymous death in Lebanon in *Mao II* (1991) and the narrator's withdrawal from the world of football and nuclear scenarios at the conclusion of *End Zone* (1972). Packer sheds with an impulsive capriciousness, as if he were a consumer still. He is an extreme case. Around the axis of Packer's downwards course, the novel builds a phantasmagoria of excess, an accumulation of violence and disorder speeded up so as to fit into – or overflow from – a single day.

We begin the day in Packer's huge apartment, then take to the street in his huge limousine; there are scenes of riot and mayhem, but scenes also of street life, of traditional marketing in contrast to Packer's currency manipulation, and of crowds that suggest an urban community. DeLillo varies a New York topos, the contrast of the gleaming, aspirational skyscrapers and the teeming, gritty life of the streets.[8] Here the

[8] Clarke 1988. De Lillo's *Underworld* (1998) includes rather than contrasts the worlds of the street and of high above the city; for the latter, see 379 and

high towers are abstract not aspiring – the next historical stage is the almost immaterial world of figures on screens, represented at one point as projected onto the tall bank buildings. In *Cosmopolis* the street is ambiguously both threatening (the masked, well-drilled demonstrators) and consoling (the perennial life of exchange, the diverse community at the funeral of Brutha Fez). The mediating term between skyscraper and street is Packer's limo, so long that it is a kind of horizontal skyscraper, and as ridiculously luxurious as his apartment. In a way DeLillo is borrowing not merely the form of the urban novel over the span of a day, as with *Ulysses*, but also its basis in pedestrian wandering, since the limo is mostly stopped or crawling in heavy traffic.[9] The time of Charteris's free running 'Man the Driver' in *Barefoot in the Head* is long past, and with it the associations of the car with freedom and mobility. Parker uses his limo as his office, even as a site for intimate medical examinations, but he has sex elsewhere, in anonymous surroundings. By the end of the novel the limo is battered and defaced. It disappears at nightfall into an underground garage.

Eric Packer's power is raw and direct. His apartment is huge, with a shark tank, a meditation room, a card parlour and so on: 'he felt contiguous with it' ... 'It had the kind of banality that reveals itself over time as being truly brutal' (8). When he feels like it, he is inquisitive and witty; when he doesn't, he is rude. He has staff but he has no links of experience or affection or shared custom with others. He embodies the affinities between the contemporary, post-national, globalised wealthy and the figure of the terrorist as alienated loner. He is a personage with distinct traits, attitudes, impulses, but he is less a character than an allegory for Capitalism itself. There's no one around against whom he can measure his power or his will, so it operates unchecked, and in sudden impulsive spurts.

One of the many sources of disturbance in the city on the day on which the novel takes place is the visit of President Milwood and his entourage, in his limo; this merely disrupts the traffic flow. As is often the case in recent apocalyptic narratives, government is absent or ineffectual. The threat of financial apocalypse makes its appearance as that of nuclear war seems to recede; *Cosmopolis* was published in 2003;

385; this part of the novel is, however, set in 1974. The contrast is at the centre of the action of Kim Stanley Robinson's post-apocalyptic *New York 2140* (2017).
[9] Nel 2008, 13–15 discusses allusions to Joyce, especially *Ulysses*. In *Cosmopolis* the contrast with *Ulysses* underlines the differences between modern and postmodern cities, but there are still continuities, survivals of a modern urban culture, and DeLillo gives them scope, as will be noted below.

the Crash arrived in 2008. By way of contrast in *Underworld*, 'The state controlled the means of apocalypse' (563), that is, the Bomb, which is at the centre of *Underworld*'s treatment of an earlier period. The Bomb belongs with what Zygmunt Bauman calls the heavy phase of capitalism, giant machines and factories, now succeeded by an elusive lightness, well exemplified by both the nature of Packer's wealth and his dissociated personal style.[10]

'But this isn't true anymore. It was true earlier in the day. But nothing that was true then is true now' (121). We learn a lot about Eric Packer: his impulses of arousal and approval (the occurrences he instantly likes, or finds satisfactory, or right in the sense of fitting); his sudden feelings of hatred; his habit of refusing to look at others, or alternatively of deciding to look at them; his way of expressing his feelings or impulses by way of a form of words that puts the feeling or impulse at a remove: 'do I want to...'; 'do we feel this...'; his irritation with ordinary language, because he feels it is out of keeping with the present, or rather with the future that should have taken possession of the present.

Feelings or impulses come to him, happen to him, are acknowledged, but at a remove, as data. They are often acted on, suddenly, wilfully, but then depart, having left nothing behind. After they are done or felt, he feels no sense that they belong to him, though I think he does feel a sense that they mean something about him – yet, if so, it is not something about which he draws conclusions. The only thing he wants with any persistence in the course of a day in which he entertains very many momentary impulses, sexual or murderous, is a haircut: 'He didn't know what he wanted. Then he knew. He wanted to get a haircut' (7).

Packer could be seen as a case, a specimen of some psychological twist or deficiency, such as Asperger's syndrome, which is sometimes ascribed to dot-com billionaires and hedge fund criminals.[11] The novel does not pursue this kind of analysis; instead, it connects his behaviour to aspects of capitalism – the financial system as the extremity and parody of capitalism or as a kind of cancer within it, feeding and expanding in

---

[10] Bauman 2012; see chapter 4, and also viii on how power is separated from politics.

[11] For example, Tom Hayes, the young banker who instigated the rigging of the London Inter-bank Offered Rate (LIBOR) during the financial crash of 2008; like Eric Packer, he was betting on the value of the yen. See *The Guardian Weekly*, 10 February 2017, 26–30. Packer also resembles the boy geniuses from earlier DeLillo novels, Billy Twillig in *Ratner's Star* (1976), or Heinrich in *White Noise* (1984), characters whose intelligence seems unrelated to experience or social life.

its own terms, which are not necessarily those of money and markets as they behave elsewhere.

This difference is established by the contrasting glimpses of markets in operation at a more perennial and material level – the diamond market, the street masseur and his customer (64, 83). The novel's New York is both the heart of the financial world of abstract capitalism, where money is alive as figures on a screen, and a place of vibrant material exchange, building, selling, physical work (for instance, the tall stories of the two ex-taxi drivers, now Eric's limo driver and his barber, concerning how hard they used to work as taxi drivers). There's no idealisation of this other New York; it's plainly a tough place to live; but the contrast is a sharp one.

DeLillo equips Packer with a huge selfishness and a huge power, based on the interdependence between his own enterprise and the financial system as a whole. He does what he does, gets away with his impulses and whims, from the number of times he has sex (four) to his killing of Torval, his chief of security; from his insistence on having a haircut to what he knows to be his insane and impossible-to-justify bet on the yen, into which he pours all he can borrow, and also his wife's large fortune that he has in effect stolen. This would be ludicrous in most versions of our world, including the other, earthier New York, which is made vividly present at some moments in this novel. It rides close to the ludicrous even in this novel: the immensity of his limo in which he conducts business, has his prostate probed, watches multiple screens and cameras, with its Carrara marble floor and precious art works; the way his apartment tower has two lifts, so he can run one of them with Satie playing in the background and at Satie pace; his having a theorist on his staff ('chief of theory': does she have a staff of subordinate theorists under her?); his passing desire to buy not merely a Rothko but the whole of the Rothko Chapel in Texas, though perhaps in this last he is sending himself up (27). What we fantasise about nowadays is action heroes and superheroes; what we get is the super-rich. Maybe you can be so ludicrously rich as to be beyond proportionality and so beyond parody; but the novel does provide Packer with a world that he fits into but that also tests him, a world at a tangent to ours but still detailed in recognisable ways.

Excess

'Too much engenders too much.'

(DeLillo, *Zero K*)

Cosmopolis crams into a single day riots, rats, killings including a couple of assassinations caught on film, copulations, crowds in half a dozen manifestations; the raw and gross, the tendency to aestheticise the raw and gross (and everything else); the impulsive and reckless, the self-aware and detached. It's a world that is boiling over with violence, with sudden eruptions, and with signs and demonstrations of the end, or perhaps the nullity, of capitalism. Packer fits into all this with his violence, his wilful destruction of his own fortune and of the financial system itself, and his sudden impulses, likings, hatreds, resentments, which pass across the stage and disappear, like a procession that passes down the street and is gone, or a demonstration that rages for a while and then just leaves debris on the street, broken glass and graffiti, items on the evening news. Packer's killing of Torval happens on the same day as the assassination (live on TV) of Arthur Rapp the head of the International Monetary Fund (IMF), and that of the Russian oligarch Nikolai Kaganovich, shot down outside his dacha, not to mention the self-incineration of the demonstrator, and Packer's own assassination, or execution, at the hands of his alter ego Benno Levin.[12] Packer is set in a scene and situation in which his own flares of impulse and violence have nothing to bounce off, no recoil; they have a kind of normality, while also making it plain that the word normality hardly applies any longer.[13]

These eruptions in the life of the city can be related to the conditions of dissociation that are constant with Eric Packer and these in turn to the novel's fragmented temporality. The most obvious is the inconsequentiality of Packer's indulgences in violence and in sex. The copulations

---

[12] These mediated assassinations, viewed on screens, have counterparts elsewhere in DeLillo's depiction of violence: in the funeral of Khomeini in *Mao II*, the Texas Highway murders in *Underworld*, and the screens depicting mass panic and massacre that decorate the corridors of the cryogenic complex in *Zero K* (2016). The fact that these events are mediated tends to intensify rather than lessen their horror. The assassinations in *Cosmopolis* blend with the plethora of other incidents to an effect of the grotesque.

[13] The self-immolation of the demonstrator is an exception (97–100). Packer cannot feel his usual hatred and satisfaction. The action has an authority that is hard to impeach; yet Packer is also immolating himself, in his very different way.

leave a smell on him that is detected by his wife when she in turn encounters him, but have no other consequences that we can see. Again, he could be said to build towards his murder of Torval, because his antagonism towards him grows in the course of the day, and we can see the murder as coming from somewhere and not merely impulsive; but, then again, the killing happens shortly after he watches the grand funeral procession of Brutha Fez, and weeps. The procession has a human and urban richness, but for all that he weeps at it, none of that richness has rubbed off on Packer. Shortly after killing Torval he participates in the episode of naked photography and then has sex (with his wife at last), and the episode of naked photography has a human richness also – after which he approaches his final rendezvous with Benno Levin – again, unaffected. The one experience means no more to him than the other, so none has meaning for him.

He abruptly chooses to make eye contact, or to refuse to (also said to be a symptom of Asperger's syndrome):[14]

> Shiner was waiting inside the car, his chief of technology, small and boy-faced. He did not look at Shiner anymore. He hadn't looked in three years. Once you'd looked, there was nothing else to know. (11)

And again:

> The driver held open the door. Eric did not look at the driver. There were times when he thought he might look at the driver. But he had not done this yet. (32)

And later in the novel: 'The driver stood at the rear, holding open the door. Eric did not enter immediately. He stopped and looked at the driver. He'd never done this before and it took him a while to see the man' (157). What Eric now sees is that the man has a strikingly distorted face, especially in one eye; he has scarcely existed before, now he manifests an excess of life, of history – he was a minister in the government of his own country, was tortured and so on.

Packer has a particular obsession with language. He keeps singling out words because he feels they do not fit the present time, as if the objects they stand for should no longer exist ('skyscraper' and 'hand device' (9); 'office' (15); 'handgun' (19); 'airport' (22); 'satchel' (42);

---

[14] It belongs also with the stereotype of the arrogant aristocrat. See, for instance, Dickens's *A Tale of Two Cities* (1859), Book the Second, chapter 7.

'stethoscope' (43); 'ATM' (54); 'ambulance' (67); 'cash register' (71); 'phone' (88), 'walkie-talkie' (102); 'computer' (104); 'vestibule' (182)). This irritated objection to the way in which words come to us from the past and things survive into the present from earlier times seems trivial, but it fits his condition of dissociation. Yet the rest of the novel suggests that the past cannot so readily be thought away. It persists in customs (the diamond market) and memories (the barber's, his driver's).

Vija Kinsky, his chief of theory, provides a gloss on this condition. It's a matter of the new situation of temporality itself, the changed relations of past, present and future:

> Because time is a corporate asset now. [...] The present is harder to find. It is being sucked out of the world to make way for the future of uncontrolled markets and huge investment potential. The future becomes insistent. (79; and Packer at 36)

She interprets the protesters in the light of this:

> This is a protest against the future. They want to hold off the future. They want to normalize it, keep it from overwhelming the present. (91)

Time is subtly deranged in *Cosmopolis*:

> The camera tracked a cop chasing a young man through the crowd, an image that seemed to exist at some drifting distance from the moment. (90)

Packer himself experiences a more dramatic dislocation. Incidents happen on camera a few seconds *before* they happen in (unfilmed) reality:

> The car stopped and moved and he realised queerly that he'd just placed his thumb on his chinline, a second or two after he'd seen it on-screen. (22)

In the midst of the demonstration:

> His own image caught his eye, live on the oval screen beneath the spycam. Some seconds passed. He saw himself recoil in shock. More time passed. He felt suspended, waiting. Then there was a detonation, loud and deep, near enough to consume all the information around him. He recoiled in shock. Everyone did. (93)

There's a dissonance between reality on screens and reality on the street. Packer had begun from the conviction that reality is now what happens on screens:

> It was shallow thinking to maintain that numbers and charts were the cold compression of unruly human energies [...] In fact data itself was soulful and glowing, a dynamic aspect of the life process. This was the eloquence of alphabets and numeric systems, now fully realized in electronic form, in the zero-oneness of the world, the digital imperative that defined every breath of the planet's living billions. (24)

The reality of what happens on screen is set in a different temporality ('zeptoseconds', 'yoctoseconds').

We have a candidate for Anti-Christ, that is, a figure outside ordinary morality and reason who can bring on massive destruction, one with the power and also the capriciousness of a deity, and also the isolation. We also have a breadth of destruction already under way on a single crowded day (riot, financial collapse, assassination, self-incineration, the slow suicide on which Packer himself is embarked). Yet the conditions for apocalypse as it usually unfolds are skewed, because time is not happening as it usually does, and this is both an aspect of the collapse and an aspect of the situation preceding it, because of the capture of reality by finance, by the data on the screens. The novel then seems to drive towards inexorable breakdown. After he has stripped himself of his wealth and all that goes with it – even his wallet – and met Benno Levin, Packer sees his own death, indeed his anonymous corpse in the morgue, on the screen that is a part of his super-capable watch (an exaggeration of the kind of watch that the rich are expected to carry). This is the most sensational of the time derangements we meet with in the novel. Apocalyptic fiction has depended on a temporal sequence that is liable to be frayed by the conditions of modern temporality – the immediacy and even simultaneity of events as transmitted by the media or electronically, the alternations of interruption, waiting, distraction and shock. *Cosmopolis* adjusts to these conditions by a crowding, layering and juxtaposing of events, and by registering the different temporalities that coexist in the contemporary city, for instance, the temporality of the global currency market and that of the traditional diamond market.[15] A further step is taken in the depiction of a post-apocalyptic world after

---

[15] On simultaneity, and on the imperatives of 24/7 availability, see Nowotny 1994; on 'the city's interruptive temporality', see Sayeau 2010, 282.

modernity and largely after humanity in *Dead Astronauts*; the inhabitants of this world exist in different presents, and those presents are in turn haunted by glimpses of memory.

Crowds in the City

'the endless inspired catastrophe of New York'
(DeLillo, *Underworld*)

The arc of the novel is more complex and qualified than the discussion so far suggests. *Cosmopolis* features a series of crowd events that change in their quality as the novel's day moves towards dusk and that Packer can do little more than witness. They include: the demonstration by people dressed as rats and throwing rats into the crowd, accompanied by riot, sabotage of the giant stock sticker screens on the imposing bank building, mobs throwing paint and urine at Packer's limo, multiple responses from police and emergency services, and the solitary act of self-incineration; by way of aftermath, the incident when Packer has a pie thrown in his face and gets to beat up the man who did it, who in turn is used to this treatment and undeterred in his vivid boasting ('This is famous Flying Pie. It is museum quality video for the ages. I quiche Sultan of fucking Brunei in his bath', 143); 'The Last Techno-Rave', packed bodies of the young ('the end of whatever it was the end of', 127); the funeral procession of Brutha Fez, the Moslem rap star and benign and beloved hero of the ghetto, the most expansive of these street scenes; and, finally, the scene of the mass of naked bodies lying in the street to be photographed.

The series moves from disorder (the riot/demonstration) to order (Brutha Fez's funeral, an orderly march past of urban heterogeneity), and from aggression (the riot/demonstration) to acceptance (the mass of naked bodies, lying obediently on the street). Each of the later scenes has about it a poignancy and stability, which Eric momentarily appreciates. Yet each – the funeral procession and the mass nakedness – also exists in a kind of enclave of its own, something magical perhaps, a surrealist *rencontre*, but not a break with the presentness, the abrupt arrival of the earlier scenes of mass disorder. Eric feels the poignancy and power of Brutha Fez's funeral; indeed, he runs through a whole gamut of emotions as he watches it: awe, envy, admiration, love, grief. He joins in the scene of mass nakedness, becoming one with the crowd, accepting that he need not know the purpose and context of the scene. (They are being filmed, but whether the story concerns a mass cult suicide or some other kind of disaster or something quite different, he cannot tell.)[16] These scenes suggest the potential of New York to produce new events, positive new forms of the social. Brutha Fez's funeral procession is not an agglomeration of agents and incidents like the demonstration/riot; it's an orderly assemblage of people who respected or loved him, though it is his death that brings them together in this order. But these new forms of the social don't count for Eric. During the funeral he imagines the likely aftermath of *his* death:

> Who would come to see him laid out? (An embalmed term in search of a matching cadaver.) Men he'd crushed, to nourish their rancor. Those he'd presumed to be wallpaper, to stand over him and gloat. He would be the powdered body in the mummy case, the one they'd all lived long enough to mock. (136)

He will choose an anonymous death, utterly different from Brutha Fez's funeral procession, which so moved him for a moment. Similarly, the episode of the naked street photograph only helps him to strip himself of more of his possessions.

So, Eric proceeds to the death that has been his one sustained desire in the welter of passing quickly forgotten impulses and emotions. (After his outbreak of weeping at the funeral we have this: 'He was tired of looking at screens. Plasma screens were not flat enough. They used to seem flat, now they did not' (140) – a caricature of the restlessness of the speeded-up world of consumption.)

The last third of the novel broadens to encompass a series of events (the funeral, the nakedness) and also conversations (that of Anthony and Ibrahim in the barber's shop – not a conversation in which Eric really takes part, however). These events and conversations sketch a new world, an aftermath to the collapse. In this aftermath simple things and feelings (mourning, nakedness, reminiscence) can have form and stability. They suggest these things for us, not for Eric, who has taken himself from being a man of power, a kind of Anti-Christ, to being an anonymous scapegoat, ready for an anonymous death. Perhaps the allegory has loaded Eric Packer with all this, trapped him in an existence in which time itself is deranged, and freed us from that existence. The funeral of Brutha Fez comes out of a history, out of the life that it sums up, sings and collages, and it thus dissents from the most radical of the ills that the rest of the novel traces, through its depiction of Eric but also

---

[16] The scene is a rendition of the practice of the photographer Spencer Tunnick, but Packer doesn't know this.

through many of the events that he witnesses, that is, the lack of history and the crammed incoherence of the present. This quality, in turn, is what makes the novel a kind of anti-apocalypse, an investigation of the incoherence of apocalypse in a world in which the narrative coherence of past, present and future is, if not lost, hard to find.

Kraken[17]

> You are now
> In London, that great sea, whose ebb and flow
> At once is deaf and loud, and on the shore
> Vomits its wrecks, and still looks for more.
> (P. B. Shelley, 'Letter to Maria Gisborne')

Kraken is much closer than *Cosmopolis* to being a utopian novel, imagining how the city can be a source of vitality that defeats apocalypse, ridiculing apocalypse as the project of weird villains, and undermining, in its fantasy, the determined cause-and-effect progress of narratives of apocalypse. In *Kraken*, Miéville elaborates a version of the city that occludes or wishes away the middle and upper classes that dominate a city like London economically and politically. The punk society of the novel's London is attractively gritty, but also utopian in that it represents in adventurous and dangerous form the liveliness and openness to new things and moralities of the city. (Miéville's pamphlet *London's Overthrow* (2012) also celebrates the gritty, local and unplanned, but casts a cold eye on the rich and super-rich and their power; see, for instance, 18–24.)

Both *Kraken* and *Cosmopolis* depict the street as the scene of vitality and exchange as well as danger and violence; in this, for all their grittiness, they tend to idealise. As was noted earlier, the emphasis of commentators on the contemporary city such as Mike Davis and Marco d'Eramo is on how space has become privatised in the contemporary city, and how the street has been given over to traffic.[18] In contrast,

---

[17] References are to China Miéville, *Kraken: An Anatomy*, London: Pan, 2010.
[18] d'Eramo 2007, esp. 174–176 on the street, and a series of books by Davis, including *City of Quartz* (1990) and *Dead Cities* (2002); we may, however, recall the earlier city of curfews and closed gates, Blake's chartered streets and chartered Thames, and more: urban history is more a matter of a fluctuating struggle over control and possession. In the contemporary city, contrast the omnipresence of closed-circuit television (CCTV), and the rise of street art (Haring, Basquiat, Banksy, graffiti).

Miéville imagines spaces continually and at times shockingly penetrated, pervaded, by Wati and his fellows, by Goss and Subby, by the Sea, by Jason Smyle: this many-sided imagination of pervasion and penetration is one of the main ways in which Mieville undermines the reality of the contemporary, privatised and demarcated city. (In contrast is Miéville's *The City and the City* (2009), the novel that came before *Kraken*, in which two cities coexist, each superimposed on the other, and the inhabitants of each go about their lives on condition that they don't notice the other. They can't really possess the spaces they live in.)

Kraken is a crowded novel, full of images, puns, jokes, spanning the ordinary and the banal and kitsch and also violence, horror and nastiness, drawing freely on science fiction, fantasy and the genre of adventure. The result is mixed and shifting. There are tensions between the novel's enthusiasm for the counter-cultural, grunge and esoteric magic, the alternative London that constitutes the novel's novum, and on the other hand its sympathy for the at first bewildered characters from a more ordinary London such as Billy and Marge.[19] Billy and Marge are caught up in the alternative London with its magic and its perils, and learn to improvise and act in it, thereby advancing both the adventure plot and the novel's project as an 'anatomy', a survey of an alternative world with different rules. The counter-cultural is in important ways the normality that prevails in the unfolding action, but the focal characters come from outside it. There are tensions, again, between the novel's depiction of magical transformations and communications, with behind them a physics and metaphysics that is hardly that of the science we know, and on the other hand the way the denouement vindicates Darwin and asserts (but with qualifications) that the giant squid at the centre of the plot is a specimen not a god. There are tensions between the embrace of the pulp adventure story in the dramatic search for the ultimate villain posing the ultimate threat,[20] and the novel's rich and complex affirmation of the diversity of life and the power of the ordinary – both ordinary things and ordinary people. It's no wonder that *Kraken* so enjoys paradoxes, and that one of its characters is driven to say that there should be a word for both 'and' and 'but':

---

[19] On alternative London, see Baker 2003 ('Secret City: Psychogeography and the End of London') and Luckhurst 2003 ('Occult London').

[20] Marge, very much an ordinary person: 'I've been given this job on the grounds that it may be the one thing that stops the *end of the world*' (446; italics in original). This is somewhere between a celebration and a parody of the pop culture notion of the hero averting the ultimate doom (for instance, 'Captain Marvel battles the Plot Against the Universe' (*Captain Marvel* 100)); but parody is often celebratory.

'Just you wait. That's not all. There's an "and". Or maybe I should say a "but". Isn't there some word that means both?' (113)

Miéville is an 'and and but' writer.

There is a lot to be sorted out, then; but *Kraken* makes an intelligent and ethically passionate contribution to the genre of apocalyptic fiction, so the task is worth it. The novel criticises apocalypse for its tendency to uniformity and finality, while also enjoying the diversity of apocalypsists. It celebrates and elaborates the diversity of aliveness, what resists uniformity, finality and the clear cut and definite. What is threatened with an ultimate end here is not the world we already know, but an alternative world bursting with new practices, possibilities, sects and life forms. The structure of normality disrupted by catastrophe that we find in, for instance, *The Day of the Triffids*, no longer serves. *Kraken* introduces and elaborates a new, fantastical physics and metaphysics – new physical possibilities, new life forms, a variety of erasures of boundaries between alive and dead, the inanimate and the animate, or animated. In this it is drawing on the resources of science fiction and fantasy, and, in keeping with this generic hybridity, the text is allusive, plays with the tropes and conventions of science fiction and fantasy, and is full of puns and verbal jokes and inventions.[21] It enters the dangerous disorder of the beginning of this century with the same exuberance as *Barefoot in the Head* enjoyed the 1960s.

There are sweeping dimensions and suggestions: the kraken, a dark immense entity in the depths of the sea, domain of the unlimited, makes an effective image of potential and imminence, even though the legend says that in waking and rising (in growing from imminent to manifest) it dies on the surface, and even though the purloined squid in the novel is both a version of the real thing, carrying some of its divine aura, and a helpless carcase, stolen, teleported, fought over.[22] Again, the universe is actively listening to what we say or do and is sometimes persuaded

---

[21] For instance, 'certain certainties' (205, T. S. Eliot), 'not braving but frowning' (236, Stevie Smith) and the layers of puns on bottle (container; slang for courage) and fiasco (flask; anti-climax) that link Billy and the squid's glass tank in the climax and anti-climax of the novel (460).

[22] *Kraken* can also be seen in relation to the fear of the sea and sea monsters that according to Cohn (1993) is an important aspect of early apocalyptic thinking: fear of the limitless. As often with Miéville, there is a reversal: heaven, saints and godhead are all in the depths (197, 271), and the sea comes to the rescue at one point (295–298). A vast creature of the deep (the avanc) figures in *The Scar*, but it is cruelly harnessed to human purposes – more like Botch in *Dead Astronauts* than Moby Dick or the Biblical Leviathan.

by it ('the universe had heard Billy and he had been persuasive', 461). (There is a parallel with the denouement of Greg Bear's *Blood Music*, 1985.) Yet for Miéville the magic potential of the alternative universe of the novel's London doesn't come from the esoteric or from ethereal forces or emanations but from transformations of the actual, from takings and mistakings that have the same basis, the same power to change, as puns, wordplay, mishearings. The basis of the newly invented physics and metaphysics to which we are introduced is verbal or visual puns, resemblances, correspondences; this in turn is echoed in the language of the novel, its enjoyment of puns, jokes, the scabrous, the vivid, the lyrical.[23] There is an emphasis on unexpected, improvised episodes of communication – communication as a kind of sympathetic magic in itself: with the sea (chapter 52); with Grisamentum, supposed to be dead, his corpse consumed by fire (securing his co-operation by threatening to piss into his ash; getting him to write rudimentary messages through a medium, 399–403); the way Billy's message to Marge about Leon's death is conveyed by a faulty street lamp blinking in what turns out to be Morse code (193).

There is no powerful authority in *Kraken*: no oppressive dictatorship as there is in Miéville's *Perdido Street Station* and *Iron Council*, no authority needing to be overthrown as in *The Scar*, and no constraining set of rules and taboos such as governs the relations of the two cities that share a single space in *The City and The City*. In *Kraken* even the police (the FSRC, Fundamentalist and Sect-Related Crime Unit, profane, informal and not very effective) are part of the alternative world they are supposed to investigate. As in cyberpunk novels, there is plenty of power, to be exploited or resisted, but not much in the way of government (London is 'absent a sovereign'; 170). Government would be part of a non-alternative London. The setting is a vast city; there is no thought of exile, expulsion from or escape from this city, however, nor is it imprisoning as are the cities in the Bas-Lag trilogy (*Perdido Street Station*, *The Scar* and *Iron Council*). Billy dismisses the notion of taking the fugitive squid north, away from the city (420). In earlier apocalyptic novels the survivors flee the city for the country; in *Kraken* nature has infiltrated the city, as, according to many accounts, it is more and more doing in actuality (for instance, Vaughan 2015). London is the scene of power, but power is centreless, inheres in ordinary objects as well as criminal monsters, and is for almost anyone to take up if they can; London is the scene of emergency, violence and viciousness but leaving it is not an option.

---

[23] For an example of the scabrous, see the entertaining exchange between Collingswood and Baron, 277; for Miéville in quieter, lyrical vein, 'As always when a quiet holed the city, a dog barked to fill it', 263.

Energies of the Everyday

Kraken plays with our habituation to the competition of proposed apocalypses, and also to an atmosphere of crisis and strain. The London of the novel is thronged with sects, each with their own visions of and desires for the end. These are not those that compete for attention and anxiety nowadays (nuclear, ecological, financial, antibiotic and what not). Terrorists ('Al Qaeda and the Al-Qaedalinos', 37) and the threat of global warming (71) are jokily dismissed. In elaborating *Kraken*'s sects, Miéville is riffing on mutants and gangs in comics, rather than referring directly to contemporary circumstances. The threats that figure in this world are religious, old-fashioned, a bit kooky:

> 'What about your apocalypse, then?' 'Well, the universe is a leaf on the time-tree, and come autumn it's going to shrivel and fall off into hell.' Murmurs of admiration. 'Ooh, nice one. My new lot say ants are going to eat the sun.' (38)

The passages in which the narrative steps back and evokes the general atmosphere of the city, the sense of imminence, are less playful, however:

> Another uneasy lurch of history. Impossible to describe, a stutter, a switch, a timeline two-by-foured onto another course that looked, smelt, sounded the same but did not feel it, not in its flesh. (338)

This catches the atmosphere of the Last Days. The crisis that afflicts the city and gives rise to this disturbance comes when all this habitual competition and more or less zany creativity is threatened, along with the lives of ordinary non-alternative Londoners. The threat is the coming of the wrong apocalypse, a kind of unapocalypse (to borrow one of Miéville's characteristic idioms – his novel for children is *Un Lun Dun*):

> 'And everything's going now.' [...] '*Everything's* going. Not just what's there. It's burning undone. The world's going with it, the sky, and the water, and the city. London's going. And it's going, and now it's always been gone. Everything.'
> 'That is *not* how it's supposed to go,' Dane whispered. (187)

And after? Nothing. Not a phoenix age, not a kingdom of ash, not a new Eden. This time, for the first time, in a way that no threatened end has ushered in before, there was no post-after. (256)

When this ultimate fire burns, we learn, the thing burnt is as if it had never been; no one remembers it; the fire burns memory, too: the firefighters forget what and where they had been called out to fight (384). This is serious, and Miéville devises a series of monomaniac villains working to this ultimate end, each hidden behind the others and then revealed: the Tattoo, Grisamentum, Vardy. But the effect is also comic, because the threat that is highlighted is to the habitual ways of diverse apocalypsists, now discovering to their dismay that they all sense the approach of, and all fear, the same, the one apocalypse. Further, the villains, for all their monomania, participate in the conditions of existence that govern this alternative London; these conditions will be detailed later.

It's typical of science fiction that it begins with the elaboration of a novum, a new set of conditions, possibly life forms. In most of the apocalyptic fictions discussed so far, the novum consists of the invader or change in nature that precipitates catastrophe – the Martians in *The War of the Worlds*, the Overlords in *Childhood's End*, the crystallisation in *The Crystal World*, the Ice Age in *Planet 8*. If the novum is strikingly different from our familiar world and is something that the text has worked to make fascinating and meaningful in its difference from the familiar, then the apocalyptic threat opens the way for a disturbed response on our part to the contrast between the richness of what is being invented for us and the threat that it will all come to an end. There's no room for the tedium of and the irritation with present conditions and unsolved problems that can provoke the desire to see the familiar contemporary world brought to an apocalyptic end. *Kraken*'s alternative London, interwoven with the London we already know but exceeding it in all sorts of ways, positively seethes with life forms, processes, possibilities. It is certainly dangerous, violent, criminal, but it is also endlessly diverse. As we begin to appreciate all this, we learn that it may all disappear.

Miéville sets these complexities in motion by drawing on the adventure story, in which the main characters do not simply witness the ongoing catastrophe but strive to avert it. In doing this they discover more of its threats and dimensions, but also elicit more of the vitality and powers of resistance of the city that is threatened.

Adventure stories usually involve heroes, a group of allies (companions); journeys in wild and dangerous places; and a crisis that presents a wide-reaching threat (Green 1991). In consequence of the crisis, we often have a cliff-hanger, or a series of them, a set of challenges of increasing and nerve-shredding dangerousness. Facing the threat can elicit heroism, while the narrative involves the reader intensely and even exhaustingly from moment to moment. These ingredients, or many of them, can appear in vigorous form even in stories whose view of adventure is ironical, as in Conrad's *Lord Jim* and *Nostromo*. Introducing aspects of adventure fiction into an apocalyptic narrative can involve an advantage – excitement, reader involvement – and a problem. The problem is that apocalypse is almost by definition outside the control of anyone caught up in it: the protagonist of an apocalyptic fiction typically witnesses or submits, unheroically. The witness reports and interprets but his or her action can have no effect on the ongoing disaster. Hence the alternative subset of fictions showing superheroes battling apocalyptic threats: not an option that Miéville takes up in *Kraken*, and one that he entertains only to dismiss in other works (for instance, the failures of Uther in *The Scar*, and the revelation of the identity of Toro in *Iron Council*).[24] Again, apocalypse is a determinate process, heading inexorably towards a future that is wholly transformed, while adventure fiction tends to dwell in the all-demanding present: 'All I thought was just the time I was in, just the present. There were plenty of times when I thought I didn't have a future at all', says Lyra, the heroine of Philip Pullman's *The Amber Spyglass* (2007, 517). Adventure fiction introduces a useful, challenging friction into apocalyptic fiction, because it concentrates so intensely on the present, as Lyra's reflection suggests, and because it values the individual and thereby sets the individual as a challenge to the global. Yet there are risks, because of the nature of apocalypse, and we can see a kind of tremor of these risks in some of the jokey devices that Miéville invents for his heroes to thwart the novel's villains.

'Porosity is the inexhaustible life of this city'
(Walter Benjamin on Naples)

Kraken is rooted in the affinities between comedy, the ordinary and diversity (the tendency of life forms to diverge, to compete; simply for there to be a lot of them), though the near overload of diversity here also figures the particular heterogeneity of contemporary experience. Almost all the novel's many effects of transformation, teleportation and communication are brought about in emphatically ordinary ways with mundane, indeed often banal or kitsch, things. A few examples: Wati

---

[24] Miéville is closer in repertoire and interests to the makers of the apocalyptic fictions that Paik discusses than the other authors discussed in *Apocalypse in Crisis*, and has written a comic himself (with artist Mateus Santolouco, *Dial H*, DC Comics, 2013); yet he is also sceptical of the superhero ethos.

the spirit from ancient Egypt, an ally of our heroes Billy and Dane, manifests in whatever small image or figurine is to hand, for instance a Bratz doll (177: 'I've been in worse'):

> Wati went into a tiny cosy plastic dashboard Virgin; to a cemetery and a headstone angel, seeing through birdlimed eyes. [...]
> He strobed through floors in doll figure carvedsoapdish rabbitsextoy antique relic... (218)

Ordinary objects play a powerful role: a phaser (that is, a toy from the world of *Star Trek*), a key that has got mislaid and wedged in the tar of the footpath (247), a flickering streetlamp, 'ridiculously bust and imperfect' (192). When Billy and Dane are hunted by almost all the criminals of the alternative London, who have been set in pursuit by both the Tattoo and Grisamentum, the novel's two contending crime lords, they are 'disguised by how unremarkable they are' (321). One of Miéville's best inventions among the cast of habitués of alternative London is Jason Styles, 'the proletarian chameleon' (234), a person who can go anywhere, into any office or workplace, for instance, because he is able to make everyone vaguely feel that they know him, that he's a workmate, though they've forgotten his name. As often in London Gothic, it's the scraps of waste land, forgotten dead-end streets, overlooked courtyards, that are the repositories of mystery or potential, and the scenes of the action:

> A space between concrete sweeps of flyovers. Where the world might end was turpe-industrial. Scree of rejectamenta. Workshops writing car epitaphs in rust, warehouses staffed in the day by tired teenagers, superstores and self-storage depots of bright colours and cartoon fonts amid bleaching trash. (357)

An important clue to the fate of the Giant Squid whose theft kicks off the action of the novel comes when Billy and Dane trace Simon, the man who teleported the squid out of the Natural History Museum; not only has Simon, an obsessive Star Trek fan, managed to actualise the teleportation that is a famous feature of the series, but Billy discovers he himself can use as a real weapon the toy phaser that Simon has collected. Fiction has teleported into reality. Late in the novel when Billy and his allies go up against the menacing not-alive not-dead Grisamentum, their most important weapon is a household cleaner, for reasons that are clear enough at the time (434): Grisamentum is manifesting (returning from the dead) as ink, 'the very writing on the wall' (402), and so is to be eliminated with bleach. Miéville takes some risks with all this, 'the kitsch of the norms' (247): see, for instance, the conversation about *'extreme* origami' (85). Exotic transformation depends on and revalues the unregarded, discarded waste of the city and of our lives – trivial things, dumb unsophisticated enthusiasms, games, toys, crappy songs and impulsive japes, such as Billy's drunken claim that he was the first ever test-tube baby.

Life – aliveness – itself is hard to define and confine in this novel. It's a world of slidings and blurred differences, not so much interdependences as overlappings and metamorphoses (imminence, oncoming, rising; also fading, waning, hinting). Money is not much mentioned in *Kraken*;[25] this absence might simply reflect the conventions of the adventure novel, in which the need to earn a living is suspended for the adventurers, but money is after all that which exchanges, transforms, infiltrates, leverages and makes something out of nothing in our world, so its absence may clear the way for the transformations and exchanges that proliferate in *Kraken*.

Just as money is largely absent, material things are never commodities. Things are said to remember what happened to them (76); things can serve as momentary sites of life, as when Wati moves between figurines and toys, or they can self-organise, bundling bits of stuff into improvised aliveness, purpose and motion, as the 'memory angels' do. The text is constantly making new nouns and verbs for states and processes: 'finishedness' (428), 'un-having-been-ness' (469), 'the mostly-unseen' (180), 'intent' ('Because if this *were*, if this did intend, if an event can intent, to be it, to be the end', 356); 'functions', such as memory, can have aliveness and take on purposes (191, 234, 420); abstractions and electronic entities can take on autonomous life: 'A clot of angry vectors, a verdigrislike stain on the air, an excitable parameter. [...] a group of angry subroutines' (199).

There is no absolute division between death and life. Grisamentum is in the process of coming back to life, via the ink of the squid and even of the writings about the squid or the Kraken, added to his ashes.

---

[25] We hear that Marge is risking relations with her usual employer, as she immerses herself in the alternative London (152); Canary Wharf, the late twentieth-century financial complex, which can be taken as standing for contemporary capitalism, is mentioned in passing: 'Canary Wharf had been born dying: that was the source of its unpleasant powers' (194). Miéville unloads on the place in *London's Overthrow*: 'every day a thuggish and hideous middle finger flipped glass-and-steel at the poor of London's East End, every night a Moloch's urinal dripping sallow light down on the Isle of Dogs' (72).

He utilises 'an interzone closer to life' (that is, closer than his apparent state of being dead); 'a threshold-life' (402). Dane comes back from the dead after being tortured to death – contrariwise, as Dane says, 'You can torture anything' (even a dead god; 175). The squid, dead and preserved in the huge glass tank of fluid at the Natural History Museum, stolen, teleported to a truck, to the embassy of the Sea, back to the museum, comes to twitching life, dies again in self-sacrifice to restore the Darwinian universe and defeat the novel's final villain: transpositions, transformations. This final villain, the one revealed after all the pre-emptions, fakes, false leads and supposedly climactic actually inconclusive battles, is Vardy, who has no moral character, or at least none that has any kind of manifestation comparable to the highly coloured nastiness of characters like Grisamentum and the Tattoo, the candidates for ultimate villainy at earlier stages in the narrative. He is less a culminating revelation than a dead end, the novel's way of eluding the adventure conventions it has used.

Spirit and matter interconnect. The way to spirit (that is, aliveness with more capacities than aliveness has in our world) is through matter, and often the grungiest of matter at that: familiars or golems may be made out of 'a hand-sized clot of mange and clumpy hair' (215), for instance; magicians and esoterics animate and give purpose to a flock of pigeons or a cloud of dead leaves. Borrowing terms from Elaine Scarry (1993, 43), we could say that Miéville's procedure is both counter-factual (the element of fantasy) and counter-fictional (the element of grunge and the ordinary). The makers of magic work by improvisation, the pasting together of bits and pieces. This is how the 'memory angel' that labours to protect Billy makes itself a body out of odds and sods of glass (262). When this body is broken in combat, and the creature's strength depleted (as according to the rules of video games) it cobbles together a smaller, weaker body (293). And even though the plot is largely concerned with keeping the missing squid from a bunch of criminals who are capable of reckless violence and torture, there is a sense in which the lines between good and evil are blurred, because both sides are united by a similar kind of manic energy, no one is really in control of the oncoming apocalypse and both sides have to become manipulators of the forces and factions of alternative London. Goss and Subby, among the nastiest and also most powerful figures in the book, seemingly able to turn up anywhere in history or in the present city, are also extreme examples of the unbounded body: they are a symbiote, Goss's heart is in Subby's body. London itself is imagined to have a body, with literal guts that can be probed for clues to the future by a 'Londonmancer' acting as a haruspex. Bits of London brick can be kneaded into food. But London 'itself' is a congeries of fractious districts, 'It wasn't one thing, for a start – though it also was' (183).

As regards the world we live in, natural life is endangered and threatened with extinction; the figures for Britain are particularly alarming (for instance, population of swifts down by half in 20 years, population of sparrows in London down 71 per cent in the last 40 years). The London of *Kraken*, an emphatically humanised, urbanised nature, but teeming with life forms of all kinds, offers a utopian compensation.

Against Singleness

> Any moment called *now* is always full of possibles. At times of excess might-bes, London sensitives occasionally had to lie down in the dark. (116)

How is this potential – all these 'might-bes' – made active, how is it realised? As Billy comes to understand, things can transform or communicate because of the power of proximity, or resemblance, or metaphor: 'the power of anything derived from its metaphoric potency'; 'a thing has power, moronically enough, because it's *a bit like* something else' (244). Hence, by way of a kind of pun, the connections among Billy's drunken boast that he was the first test-tube baby, the giant squid's tank (that is, the tank was as important as the awesome creature that it contained), and a fiasco, both a bathetic outcome and (in Italian) a flask (460). Similarly, Grisamentum is trying to return to life by way of ink, both the dissolved ink from the many texts about the Kraken that his henchmen have stolen, and the ink of the squid itself, which existed as a sign that he has now understood 'the very writing on the wall' (402). There's a connection, dangerous as well as positive, between aliveness (in its variety of relations of transformation and communication), power and meaning. 'The longer it's out there it's *meaning* more and more, and that means it's more and more powerful', says Dane of the missing squid, though, as we have just seen, this accumulating power is based on a mistake: no one has realised that the tank is the important thing, not the squid. The legend of the Kraken has distracted them, though in believing in it they have also given it power.

Attributing meaning to something gives it life, and power. Life and power are created by human attention and imagination, but, contrariwise, the universe is a presence, listening, able to be persuaded. 'You have to persuade the universe that things make sense a certain way' (98). This is what Darwin did, and what Dane does at the end when he defeats Grisamentum, and also defeats the last in the series of villains, Vardy, who plans to burn Darwin's notes from the Beagle expedition and thus burn Darwinism out of ever having held sway.[26] Truth has become so malleable in a society in flux that the only recourse is for the universe to take over and validate it, but then again any theory about the world is a bet that the world will – next time, so to speak – confirm its truth.

Kraken sets the potentials of the modes it draws upon, alludes to and parodies against the threat of apocalyptic singleness. It thereby presents an argument about what is ultimately threatening about apocalypse, that is, its contention that all will end, that only one thing will come to count and to determine the behaviour of the characters. In traditional apocalypse, this is the deity; in earlier secular apocalyptic fictions, this one thing is usually the necessity of surviving and rebuilding civilisation, an agenda that those spared cannot refuse to try to implement. In later, more radical re-imaginations of apocalypse, such as those by J. G. Ballard and Doris Lessing discussed above, it is the imperative to submit to the expanding, ineluctable power of the Sun, or the crystallisation that, beautiful as it is, is going to absorb the universe, or to the death that will encompass everything on the planet, to cite *The Drowned World*, *The Crystal World* and *The Making of the Representative for Planet 8*: the disaster or epidemic or systemic change that can destroy everything, as if all life has one throat that can be strangled, or as if life has multiple points of dependence, any one of which can be imagined to bring on an apocalypse, a widespread and proliferating destruction. The comic exuberance and inventiveness of *Kraken*; the fluidity and playfulness of its language, its invented life forms and the speculative physics and metaphysics that underpins them; the way crucial twists of the plot depend on mistakings; the way ordinary people and banal things figure: all this refuses the singularity of apocalypse. Behind all these inventions, in which Miéville exploits fantasy and comedy, is the diversity of the city, utopian in the sense that it is open to possibility and transformation as well as being gritty and messy. *Kraken* is a poem to London as it is and as it could be.

[26] The threat of destruction by fire (here, book burning) conforms to apocalyptic tradition: the fire next time. Umberto Eco quotes from Fernando Báez, *A Universal History of the Destruction of Books* (translated by Alfred MacAdam): 'When man destroys with fire, he plays God, master of the fire of life and death. And in this way he identifies with a purifying solar cult and with the great myth of destruction that almost always takes place through fire' (2012, 64). In *Kraken* water is benign: the Sea rescues Dane and Billy; paradise is below, in the depths of the ocean.

The threatened apocalypse in *Kraken*, the destruction of the world so that it would never have been, is itself multiple. As in many a thriller or crime novel, there is no one villain, and the shocks and twists of the plot come from the way in which first the Tattoo (with his horrible henchmen Goss and Subby), then Grisamentum, and finally Vardy, are revealed as the prime threat. This is not, however, a contradiction so much as another affirmation of the fluid conditions of existence in the world of the novel. Even those who intend to end it must work with those conditions. In addition Grisamentum and the Tattoo, at least, are instances of the prevailing weirdness and marginality: the Tattoo exists only as a tattoo on and in Paul's back, and Grisamentum manifests first as messages inked by his lover Byrne whom he uses as a medium, and then as the ink he has had his followers collect.[27] Paradoxically, it is the novel's heroes, Billy, Dane, Marge and Paul – who are going to thwart the villains and avert the destruction – who are ordinary humans, usually bewildered, learning to use their wits and sense, and, with the exception of Dane, strangers to the London of interminglings and transformations whose conditions the novel surveys as 'an Anatomy'. Our heroes do become agents in the alternative London: Billy realises he is the bottle-messiah and goes along with what is both a joke and a clue to his vital role; Paul murders the psychopathic Goss and Subby, an act that depends on his realising that they are a symbiote and Subby is the element with the heart, and he has the mouth of the Tattoo sewn up and its eyes covered; Marge spends the novel investigating the conditions and communicating with the denizens of the other London, and eventually hooks up with Paul and then Billy. The villains are spectacularly of the margins yet are working to bring everything to destructive singleness (and nothingness); the heroes belong to a more familiar and commonplace London yet learn to use the ways of the other London. The complicated relations of heroes and villains can be seen as Miéville's reconciliation of the contemporary fascination with the marginal and liminal, which he proliferates in his fiction, with his commitment to ordinary decency, to the need to struggle and cope with the limited amount that you know and see. In this respect *Kraken* contributes to the valuation of the everyday in the time of apocalypse that was discussed in *The Lathe of Heaven* and in chapter 7.

Yet – so it might be retorted here – after due attention is given to *Kraken*'s inventive and utopian aspects, isn't it still true that a single catastrophe, such as global warming threatens, might well ruin almost

---

[27] Characters named Byrne and Cole figure in the drama of the threatened destruction of the world by fire: more puns.

everything? The next chapter discusses the still more radical and much more bleak imagination of the post-human in VanderMeer's *Dead Astronauts*, and the less utopian imagination both of contemporary heterogenity and of a way past catastrophic climate change in Robinson's *Green Earth*.

Chapter 9

Beyond Apocalypse – Two Paths
Jeff VanderMeer and Kim Stanley Robinson

Apocalypse in Crisis has taken apocalyptic fiction to tell of catastrophe, an aftermath to catastrophe and a final stage, which is roughly equivalent to the New Jerusalem of traditional apocalypse, and involves variously settlement, transcendence, the appearance of new life. This narrative sequence, loose as it is (as the phrase 'roughly equivalent' betrays), traces how contemporary apocalyptic fiction has remained in touch with traditional apocalypse, at least to the degree that setting a given contemporary instance in the frame of this sequence helps us the better to understand its varying inventions and decisions. It is a sequence that suggests order (if it is not the more confident order once imposed by God's direction of the catastrophe) and recovery (if it is not the glowing consummation of the rule of the saints, or the New Jerusalem). But contemporary apocalyptic fiction is haunted by a spectre that denies even this consolation or mitigation. This dark spectre is Doom, catastrophe unqualified and without recovery, and it arises because history (the World Wars, the Holocaust – to reach no further than these) points emphatically to the possibility, and suggests that catastrophe is the work of humans, needing no supernatural or unnatural agents, no gods or monsters. Global heating has the same doom-laden effect on many observers because it can seem that it is too late to avert catastrophe. In addition, the enticements as well as the cultural sources of unqualified pessimism are many. Apocalyptic catastrophe simplifies, and we have discussed how this simplification is embraced by some recent fictions and resisted by others: the temptation is to go further, to all the way into the unqualified blackness of 'Doom, Doom, Doom' to quote D. H. Lawrence. And insofar as apocalyptic catastrophe in fiction is a way of coming to terms with the inevitability of death for all of us, as well as the possibility and the fact of mass death or destruction in history, there is a logic to staging death and destruction unqualified. Many apocalyptic fictions struggle to avert or mitigate this aspect of apocalyptic catastrophe, and there is evidence that this struggle has become more difficult. *On the Beach* could present unmitigated doom for humanity, if in somewhat sanitised form in that the text never shows the dead and sick of the radioactive fallout that is eliminating everybody, and yet can still focus on the decency and calm of those facing extinction. In *Planet 8* all life on the planet is snuffed out, but humans are imagined to make an existential jump into another dimension.

Jeff VanderMeer's *Dead Astronauts* is a recent novel of extreme catastrophe and its dark aftermath. There are almost no humans and there is nothing that can be called a society or civilisation. In general, after a catastrophe removes humans from Earth, the resultant desolation might be imagined as empty (bereft of life because there are no humans),[1] as burgeoning in recovery now that humans are removed, or as poisoned and wrecked by whatever they did that led to their departure. The last is the situation in *Dead Astronauts* (2019). It's a scene that is all the bleaker because it is crowded with the maimed and traumatised, monsters and ghosts, relics and explorers, scarcely any of them human, but most of them in some relation to the human. It is this vision that this recent, extreme, formally complex and experimental fiction elaborates and also explores, and it stands in *Apocalypse in Crisis* for one endpoint: an unsparing depiction of a post-apocalyptic world in which individuals are largely isolated in their separate beings and dominated by the past or entrapped in repetition, a world in which there is some but not much prospect of recovery or redemption, some but not very much agency, some but not very much prospect of co-operation. There is a constant undertone of anger and disgust in the writing; the novel has sympathy for the denizens of this wrecked world, even when they are monstrous, but none for those who wrecked it, and they are, by implication, ourselves.

Dead Astronauts is paired with Kim Stanley Robinson's *Green Earth*, a novel that takes the opposite path, working through and beyond apocalypse. *Green Earth* is a novel about climate change (to accept that term for the moment), the catastrophe that is beginning to unfold in our time. Change in the climate is somewhat more advanced in the world of the novel, so that it is even harder to deny, but still has the shape of an emergency, a crisis. *Green Earth* imagines how catastrophe might be averted; it takes us beyond apocalypse in that way. Crisis never culminates

---

[1] Jonathan Schell, at the end of the chapter entitled 'A Republic of Insects and Grass': 'But if these effects [associated with nuclear annihilation] should lead to human extinction, then all the complexity will give way to the utmost simplicity – the simplicity of nothingness' (1982, 96).

in global catastrophe. There is no post-apocalypse in which survivors struggle in the ruins of civilisation or face the traumas of loss or violence. The way is cleared for a broad exploration of the potential of contemporary civilisation to mitigate disaster and avert catastrophe, as well as an exploration of the impediments to realising that potential. In imagining how this might happen, it envisages – details, elaborates, explains – several spectacular, global projects, but also marshals the resources and energies of contemporary American society – science, democracy, the habits and enjoyments and stresses of free exchange, talk. It is inclusive and discursive where *Dead Astronauts* works by motifs and repetitions. Its characters are communicative where those in *Dead Astronauts* are imprisoned in their conditions and, sometimes, unable to say a certain word or complete a sentence. There are stretches of the text where the ongoing and oncoming crisis is on hold while we explore other possibilities and problems, those of the main character Frank Vanderwal, or those to do with Charlie Quibler's fears about the uncanny behaviour of his son Joe. Social and personal life refuses to submit to the all-encompassing demand of the crisis. As Henry James pronounced, relations are endless, and *Green Earth* is certainly interested both in plenitude and overload, and in secrecy and withholding: not endless, but richly ramified. The novel explores those vital depths of the self – the brain and the body – that the self is not always in contact with, and as well as dealing with possible advances in science and technology that might alleviate the effects of climate change, it looks at radical advances in medicine, and in political arrangements. It evokes not merely the American past as tradition and inspiration (Roosevelt, Lincoln, Emerson, Thoreau), but the human past as speculated by sociobiology, and the 'paleo' that contemporary humans can be imagined to touch and relive. Sometimes these apparent tangents of theme and speculation can be seen to complete a circle, so that, for instance, the reflections on humans as adapted by evolution for life in groups complete the treatment of the life of science as one of exchange and discussion (and committee meetings). *Green Earth* can seem a grab-bag of Robinson's interests and fascinations, but when discussion turns to the novel in detail, its underlying structure of contrasts and relations will be delineated. As the novel's scope stretches, intriguing tensions emerge between its depiction of humans as sociable and its investigations of the individual as alone.

Dead Astronauts approaches questions of identity and of the power of the past very differently, conveying an elemental sense of the beginnings of awareness and memory in a world so shaped by violence, exploitation and sadism that any extension of awareness or imaging of memory is both an achievement and unstable.

Dead Astronauts[2]

Dead Astronauts presents a world in the aftermath of catastrophe, a dark post-human world in which nature is maimed, and the inhabitants are haunted by pasts of abuse and cruelty, or trapped in repetition. The conditions of this world, much more than any unfolding of narrative, are at the centre of the novel. These conditions are unstable, because the world (the novum) is maimed, but they can be mapped; as is said in VanderMeer's *Acceptance* (2014, 189), 'Patterns could suffice as purpose.'

Dead Astronauts is dark, difficult and angry. The text sometimes draws on types of story that the reader can recognise: the fairy tale or folk tale (talking animals, mistreated children: the blue fox, Charlie X); the story of an expedition or team of adventurers in the wilderness (chapter 2, 'The Three');[3] the contemporary subset of stories about abused children, where the trauma of abuse necessitates an oblique narration (Charlie X; Sarah). In each case the extremity of the situation pulls the story type off its conventional bases, as if it had been subjected to high pressure.

The condition of aftermath means that *Dead Astronauts* has affinities with novels set in an after-death limbo in which the characters are neither fully dead nor fully alive, and time halts, or circles – *Lincoln in the Bardo* (George Saunders, 2017), *Solar Bones* (Mike McCormack, 2016), *The Following Story* (Cees Nooteboom, 1991), *The Third Policeman* (Flann O'Brien, 1967): 'Alive but not. Dead but not' (*Dead Astronauts*, 158); 'Neither alive nor quite yet dead' (309); stuck in 'areas of temporal contamination' (84), and haunted by the past: 'Perhaps all the answers lay in the past, or maybe time did not move as we thought it did', as the blue fox speculates (306). This orientation towards the past points away from science fiction and towards the fiction of horror, and *Dead Astronauts* is full of monsters and hauntings; but the orientation towards the past is qualified, as in the limbo novels just mentioned, by the lack of a defined past, present and future,[4] and by the way the monsters are also victims.

---

[2] References are to Jeff VanderMeer, *Dead Astronauts*, London; Fourth Estate, 2019.

[3] This story type shapes *Annihilation*, the first of VanderMeer's 'Southern Reach' trilogy (2014), in the form of an expedition of selected scientists into uncanny and dangerous territory, and it figures also in *Acceptance*, the third. In each case matters go even more terribly wrong than is usual in this kind of story.

[4] The blue fox speculates for a moment about the three astronauts: 'Once upon a time, I spoke to three dead astronauts. Past, present, future? All so proud, so determined. All so doomed' (307).

The dramatis personae are at once strongly differentiated, and constantly shifting, transformed, blended. None is exactly human, and several are animal; all share a degree of consciousness; and all have been injured or mistreated. There is a continuum of consciousness from, say, Botch to the blue fox, with the humans and human-like personages (Grayson and Sarah in the first category, Chen and Moss in the second) by no means at the top: a spectrum more than a hierarchy. *Dead Astronauts* is populated by personages maimed, monstrous and singular in various degrees. They all bear a mark of difference, but they cannot be stigmatised. Stigmatising – 'the creation of spoiled identity' – doesn't happen in this world.[5] There is no society of the similar to stigmatise the different, and in this the novel expresses the contemporary abhorrence of stigmatising and its valuation of inclusion.

The text unfolds in overlapping but separate sections, experimental, not consecutive, shifting in place and in temporal location ('moments stacked atop one another so there was no difference, no difference at all', 236). Chapters 1 to 5 probably happen before chapter 6, though it is better to say that they circle in memory and intimation around a place (the burning shed) and a person (Sarah) that comes into clearer view in chapter 6. Most chapters give their close attention to one of the personages. There is no central character or central action – the conditions of the post-apocalyptic world don't allow for either. Chapters 1 to 6 seem to establish Sarah (who probably becomes Moss) as central, only for Sarah/Moss to recede from view (after all Moss has died at the end of chapter 1) and be replaced by the blue fox. The result of this complex shifting organisation is this breadth of attention, a sustained inwards look at these sometimes violent and mostly injured personages. On the other hand, the convenience of a central character or even group of characters (as in *Girlfriend in a Coma*) is that it is easier to define where the novel ends up; with *Dead Astronauts*, you find yourself producing a very different picture when you focus on, for instance, Sarah as against Charlie X, or Moss as against the blue fox, and the ramifications of this will be explored later in this discussion.

There are back-stories, memories and hauntings, but no collective past emerges, and the text recalls no time at which catastrophe took a particular shape such as invasion or epidemic. There are prospects of endings, though not of an End, and these endings are sometimes associated with release or escape, even when they involve death, or because they involve death (269; 314), though the personages of the novel have already experienced drastic endings, erasures and curtailments,

---

[5] Porter 2002, 62, drawing on Erving Goffman.

so an ending might amount to a repetition. The situation is such as to spawn blockages and dead ends (for instance, 201). There are blends of love and pain, victim and monster, freedom and death. We encounter images and states of repetition (endless 'versions' in the case of the Three, for instance) and of entrapment in a state or memory: the condition of Sarah for a while and of Charlie forever; what could be called the arrested development of Botch, which gains some memory and awareness, and has a history that we can assemble, but is confined to its pool/lair – immobility corresponding in Botch's case to entrapment, qualifying Botch's power as a predator, a kind of ogre.

The weight of the past is often light in apocalyptic fiction, because the catastrophe has destroyed so much that the survivors are cut off from it. If the past makes an appearance, it does so in glimpses (in *Ice*, for instance), or in enclaves (the rooms in which the Survivor witnesses scenes from Emily's childhood in *Memoirs*). In *Dead Astronauts* the weight of the past is crushing, or the past is present, or repeating ('What's the present but a version of the past?' (197); 'The past always waited. To wound, to rend, to tear' (91); 'Demons would come from the future to infect the past' (180)).[6]

The catastrophe was, and continues to be, a breaking and impairment, so that neither a clear diagnosis nor a clear history is likely to emerge. *Dead Astronauts* seems to *collect* wrongs and perversions and mutilations: the abuse and suffering of children; corporate indifference and facelessness (human institutions are figured by 'the Company and the City', both defunct); alienation from and manipulation of nature; waste, in the botched and discarded products of biotech; pollution; homelessness; torture and cruelty. It's not easy to see what might underlie all this; a generalisation such as that humans have got fundamentally out of tune with nature might serve. The biblical myth of the Fall, which has a similar generality, at least has behind it a story and a series of decisions to account for what has gone wrong with nature. *Dead Astronauts* presents inordinate catastrophe, but this catastrophe is not of a kind that can be underpinned by a story such as that of the Fall, or by an event such as an invasion or epidemic, or even a definable general predicament such as global heating. Does the novel structure nonetheless its scene of catastrophe so as bring forth light and shade, point and emphasis?

The discussion that follows doesn't attempt even a précis of the novel's complications of content and form: a mere list opens out into a

---

[6] The last quotation here is from one of the passages in chapter 6 that records Sarah's memories and is printed feint, except for 'Demons', which is in bold.

consideration of implications and contrasts. One implication is that the strand of the text concerned with child abuse (of Charlie X; of Sarah) and the strand of the text concerned with cruel and botched biotechnology point together to a perversion of reproduction. Another is that the condition of aftermath is making for new and shifting kinds of being as well as blockage and repetition. One contrast that can be staged by looking at the novel's personages is between Sarah and Charlie X; another this that between the blue fox and Moss. Sarah and Charlie X are both victims of abuse; the blue fox and Moss offer contrasting images of passionate resistance to exploitation; and to complicate matters further, there are suggestions in the text that Sarah and Moss are the one personage.

The dramatis personae of *Dead Astronauts* are varied; none is conventionally human, that is, human as are the characters in the other novels treated in *Apocalypse in Crisis*; all have human features – awareness, consciousness, inner life. Collectively, they are best described as abhuman. Each is given a section of text that varies in form (in sentence structure, typography, layout on the page, kind of narrative). This variation of form is often expressive in a literal way: when a character's awareness falters or baulks, he can't complete a sentence or can't say a word (Charlie X); when consciousness fades, the font goes feint (Botch; Sarah); when there is something a character can't face, this appears in bold, like a rock the stream of awareness eddies round (Sarah); when a character is gripped by bitter memories, this condition takes the form of exact repetition, and can last for pages (the blue fox).

Persons of the novel: the Three, Chen, Moss and Grayson engaged in a mission to penetrate the derelict precincts of the Company – of these Grayson is the novel's possible human, though she dies repeatedly;[7] Charlie X, now a wraithlike figure, powerless, haunted, but in his boyhood a biotech genius, maker or modifier of many of the other personages, but also victim of abuse at his father's hands; the blue fox, once victim of biotech torture to equip it for space travel, now transformed, powerful, elusive; Botch, a monster that lives in the holding tank beside the Company's installation and devours the creatures discarded from the Company's biotech program; the Duck with a Broken Wing, one of Charlie X's products, actually metallic, powerful; Sarah, a homeless girl with a traumatic past, living on the outskirts of

---

[7] See her exchange with the blue fox:
   'Do you have a plan that includes the human?'
   'It includes people. Are you a person?'
   'Once, I was several.' (117)

a polluted city, and encountering both the Duck with a Broken Wing and a salamander.

Almost all of these personages have several identities, either at the same time or in succession, and very often they are possessed by others, either as a prisoner, or by way of a programme or a voice inside them. (Hence by contrast the blue fox's celebration of 'the joy of living without interference'; 293–299.)[8] Chen encounters and fights his exact double, perhaps an event to be understood as the meeting of two selves from two temporalities, and at the moment of his death (in the version of a repeated mission that is recounted in the text) transforms into a brilliant spawn of tiny salamanders; Moss, a loving companion to Chen and Grayson, is also moss; Botch is in some pasts also Behemoth and Leviathan; the Duck is also, in violent manifestations, 'the dark bird': as duck, she is the favoured creation and pet of the child Charlie, and later an enigmatic observer of the Three; as dark bird she is violent, monstrous, given to impulses of slaughter. Sarah eventually moves from her setting outside the city and beside the salamander's river into the desolate dry world that the rest of the personages mainly pass through; in her chapter she is an unnamed 'you' until at the very end she can name herself, 'Sarah'. She perhaps becomes Moss whose being is double, as Moss and moss. Charlie X was once both victim (of his father's abuse) and figure of power (he moulded Chen, Moss, the duck and the blue fox); now he scarcely has any life. Charlie X varies between 'I' and 'the son'. The blue fox is both victim of repeated torture and figure of prophetic denunciation and power. These multiple identities and these changes figure a world in fragments, but also in most cases figure power, either lost or emerging: 'diagrams of creatures that look like autopsies or recipes' (170).[9] Power, like other qualities, such as aloneness, figures however as an attribute, a fate, more than something that can be willed. The duck has power in the same way as it has a broken wing. This condition of the novel's personages can be related to the fact that they are all monsters in different ways ('What was a person but someone who turned monstrous, anyway?' thinks Moss (85)). Something – the regime of the City and the Company – has wrecked the world and then left the scene, or lives on only in the dangerous places the Three

---

[8] Interference can be an aspect of transmission, as with interference on the radio; this is Saul's predicament near the end of *Acceptance* (2014c, 324): 'Unable to escape the sensation of interference and transmittal, a communication pressing in on the edges of his brain.'

[9] This is what Sarah deciphers as she reads Charlie X's journal, which has come into her possession.

have to venture into in the first part of the novel. New identities and powers have emerged, but tend to fluctuate and also to be stymied; the personages of the transformed world often have formidable powers but remain separate, 'alone': their encounters may be brutal or salvific but they are passing.

Identity is open and permeable. Sometimes this is to painful effect; sometimes it issues in revelation or rescue. The blue fox, the most powerful personage in *Dead Astronauts*, communicates telepathically. It speaks sometimes in the first-person singular and sometimes in the first-person plural, in the first and second of the passages of exact repetition that recount how the blue fox as individual and as foxes in general was tortured (251–257, 270–277); this merging with others, in this case his species, is fluctuant, however. Chen, Moss and Grayson form a loving intimacy so close that they seem to become one body, but the first long episode of the novel sees the dissolution of their unity. Both the dark bird and Charlie X are in effect possessed and programmed by Charlie's sadistic father (244, 231). Sarah is haunted by memories of her impulsive and sometimes insane mother and her mother's lovers: these memories form one of the alternating subsections of the part of the novel that gives her story, and they are dominated by **demons** (in bold) that she cannot face or define. She encounters a salamander that rescues her, enters her mind, changes her blood, makes her safe for a while and gives her an experience of the benignity and fertility of nature. Moss joins part of herself (a part that is literally moss) to Botch and this, growing on the creature's back, is lost to Moss herself but bestows the beginnings of memory and self-awareness on Botch, but also 'memories' of the burning shed that is otherwise part of Sarah's past.

It can be seen, then, that the conditions of the novel's world make for change and thence potential as well as instability. The question of whether this potential is realised will be discussed later, but the intense horror and cruelty of the world of the novel, and the anger behind the writing, needs to be emphasised. Charlie X as child is the victim of his father's unrelenting sadism (for instance, 232–233), which involves among much else the eradication of even the memory of his mother, and as biotech genius he is the maker or moulder of a proliferation of misshapen and grotesque creatures. Botch gains memory and displays some compunction in its predation, but its violent past has gained it a network of scars and one huge white eye, and mostly we see it voraciously devouring the misshapen creatures the Company sends its way, Charlie's failures: 'The mighty jaws lined with diseased and glistening yellow teeth that spread illness as well as lacerations' (65). Chen, Moss and Grayson, for all their loving intimacy, are defeated in their mission to penetrate the Company, and each of them dies, Grayson at the very end of *Dead Astronauts*. If this 'mission' of the Three is also a 'version' (as with a computer program or video game), and is therefore a repetition, and they have died before in other versions ('and already they were dying again', 9), this apparent outcome is not exactly an end anyway. Sarah is rescued and transformed by the salamander, and faces her demons and in particular the meaning of the burning shed at the heart of her past, but she is injured by the dark bird, and her role at the end of the novel is to console Grayson in her death. As The Duck with a Broken Wing, this misshapen but powerful product of Charlie X's haunts the early part of the text in enigmatic fashion (the Three can't know whether she will be ally or enemy from one 'version' to another); altered into 'the dark bird' in the later parts of the novel she is programmed by 'murder control' to slaughter, and is trapped into this program. The blue fox, the most powerful and elusive of the novel's personages, recounts how it was endlessly tortured, its revival from death a kind of mockery because it was followed by another death. This part of the blue fox's account simply consists of 'They killed me. They brought me back', repeated for five pages; it ends with the single line 'One time I escaped', and indeed the blue fox as it slips in and out of the text seems unquenchable and unkillable.

It was noted above that the novel draws on fairy tales of mistreated children, deepening them into the horror of abuse, in the stories of Charlie X and Sarah, and suggesting how this past abuse can only be faced obliquely, for instance in the image of the burning shed in Sarah's case, and in the memory of Charlie's special room that his father destroyed. (The burning shed has threads of connection with several of the novel's personages: these connections are discussed below.) Here, parents are sadistic (Charlie's father) or demonically destructive (Sarah's mother and probably the stepfather who abused her). Natural parenting is the site of trauma; artificial production (biotechnology) proliferates but it gives rise to distortions and monsters that are dumped into the holding pond ('a convenient hell or purgatory, full of dying life', 34), and is associated with the wrecked and polluted landscapes of the novel; generation is only seen as productive when it happens without copulation, with moss and with the salamander.[10] That which is made by biotechnology is misshapen and monstrous but what humans otherwise make (furniture, for instance) repels the blue

---

[10] The third of the blue fox's passages of repetition does celebrate the joy of natural life, including 'The joy of mating and raising children' (293). This happened, however, in some unlocated past.

fox as dead and poisonous (288: stink of pesticides, toxic cleaners, cancer, bellies full of plastic). Charlie X, who is a victim and a wraith without power when he is glimpsed in the novel, has been at the heart of the Company's cruel and wasteful biotechnology, producing many grotesques that are discarded (though there are suggestions that they should be and sometimes are spared), and shaping the lives of Chen, Moss, the blue fox and Botch.

Charlie X thus draws together the offence against nature that is child abuse and the interference with nature that is biotechnology; yet as seen in the novel he has no power, indeed is barely alive, and his father, who had such power over him, is an even more shadowy presence, one whose motives it would be futile to investigate. Here the novel draws on the Frankenstein tradition of males sidelining females, taking over generation and making a mess of it. Charlie X can't remember his mother at all, and his monstrous father is responsible for this erasure. ('X' signifies erasure, as well as ten, this number being associated with the Company in the novel's elaborate numerology.) Charlie's agency, and that of his father, is powerful in that their actions have huge effect; indeed, the monstrous, the mutilated or scarred or distorted, is almost everywhere in the text. On the other hand, they are not agents at all; their actions stem from dark impulses and compulsions that can't be seen as decisions, and the Charlie X whom we meet in the novel is powerless, a ghost and mutilated as well (by his father). Here we approach an aspect of the novel as aftermath, the scene of the novel as the playing out of forces and routines determined long before, the personages of the novel as in many ways marked, visited with qualities that seem to have been prescribed to make them what they are, though as was noted they shift and fluctuate. Hence the insensate predation of Botch and the dark bird – as if compelled by nature, or as if programmed. This is not the whole story, however, as will be seen when we turn to the other victim of abuse, Sarah, and to Moss, the figure in the novel in sharpest contrast to the blue fox.

Moss is one of the novel's most daring inventions. Moss presents as a person, indeed a loving and calming one, but is also in some way moss, and immortal or capable of many existences, though she has gone by the time we get to the end of the novel, the death of Grayson. She stands for love, care, sacrifice. Sacrifice often comes up in the novel in contexts of pain and sadism (for instance, with Charlie X's father, and even with the blue fox, 'Love must be cruel' (120)); this is true of Moss's altruism too, but in a milder, purer form. Moss, a modest unspectacular substance of almost imperceptible growth, dependent on what it grows on, would seem as far as possible among living things from the violence of predation, and also from consciousness, awareness, although Moss the personage, the one who binds the Three in loving amity, is presented as empathetic and self-aware (aware of her limits and her fate, for instance; 72). The most sustained incident involving Moss is that in which she communicates with Botch by growing on its back, becoming part of it and affecting it with the beginnings of self-awareness. The result for Moss is that she simply loses the part of herself that became moss on Botch's back: a kind of sacrifice. The person of Moss as wise and loving, and the connotations of moss as growing harmlessly and persistently, both work positively in this novel of violence and monstrousness. The image of Moss unwinding the scars from Botch's body, for instance, is a haunting one (67). On the other hand, Moss/moss is such a strange creature that it is probably no accident that she is not given all that much to do in the text as a whole. Her presence fades after the second chapter, and harsher, more tortured figures become more prominent. She is associated with tidal pools (in contrast to Botch's lair, the holding pond). A tidal pool is a place of quiet fertility in the ecotone between land and sea, but we don't come across an actual tidal pool until the very end of the novel, where one is the site of Grayson's death, that is, her release from the repetitions of life and death. In this scene it is Sarah who substitutes for the now departed Moss and cradles the dying astronaut.[11]

Similar to Moss in being a figure of benign generosity is the salamander that rescues and transforms Sarah. The salamander has unity of being, and seems to appear and remove itself from the scene at its own will; it is big, sinuous, riverine (adding to the novel's set of images of liquidity, in a context mostly of dry desolation), and associated with colour in the night, mostly red and pink. (Moss is associated with green.) It insinuates a strange language into Sarah, but is mostly non-verbal. In all these ways it is further into the natural and further away from the human than the somewhat awkwardly divided Moss/moss, and at the end of its appearance in the novel it spawns – generation without sex, as far as we can see – a phenomenon at the outer edge of the novel's usually grim presentation of parenting as abuse and biotechnology as exploitative:

> The limbs and torso fall like living red sand into the river, taken by the swirls. Until there is only the head and the eyes that stare

[11] The tidal pool as image of undisturbed fecundity and of peaceful seclusion features also in VanderMeer's Southern Reach trilogy, especially in *Annihilation* and *Acceptance*, the first and third novels.

at you, until the erosion of self takes them too, and it all crumbles into the water and the river is awash with motes of life.

Such joy in the sight. (200)

Dead Astronauts arrives repeatedly at moments of anti-climax and even bathos, and this is particularly true of the passages that imagine kindness and fertility as distinct from predation and aggression. Sarah reaches recognition of her past and is transformed by the salamander, then largely fades from the novel, as does the salamander – though spectacularly. The salamander has protected Sarah with pink vomit ('The salamander throws up all over you.' [...] A light pink liquid', 189). The Duck with a Broken Wing is a metallic monster, and becomes the dark bird, but it is a duck, and ducks have a homely image. Modern humans, when encountered late in the novel in the blue fox's narrative, seem feeble and ignorant, only, though they are responsible for the exploitation and destruction elsewhere associated with the more abstract Company and City. They don't seem to be commensurate with the harm humanity has wrought. These effects of bathos and anti-climax can be connected to the novel's refusal or postponement of conclusions. Endings have already happened – Sarah's recovery of her name and recognition of her past is recognition of the burning shed of her primal crime, 'a building that burned and never turned to ash' – or they can now only happen as repetitions: 'Nothing left to do. Nothing you can do. For what could you do. This has all already happened' (201; just after the joyful dissolution of the salamander).[12]

The blue fox is a very different creature from Moss and the salamander, elusive, taunting and aggressive, embittered and expatiating. As was suggested above, the novel's imagination of humans' destructive relation to nature takes the form of a sustained diatribe in the passages given to the blue fox. The blue fox compels attention because it has been the victim of vicious and almost interminable mistreatment at the hands of humans (and so have foxes as a species), and has survived this to emerge as powerful and elusive, appearing now here, now there. Many of the novel's personages are haunted by repetition, for instance the Three who are compelled to repeat their mission; or they are chained to their past, for instance Charlie X; or they are emotionally or literally chained to a place, or more precisely a site, as Botch is literally confined to the holding pond and Sarah is emotionally chained to the burning

---

[12] This burning shed is remembered by Botch as if Botch had come to share Sarah's memory (215). The image may also allude to the bush that burned and was not consumed by which Jehovah manifested.

shed, at least until the end of the chapter that centres on her. It might seem that repetition is intensified almost to madness in the blue fox's case, but that the fox survives and escapes, to roam free. The effect of the fox's later speeches and story-tellings is, however, of a narrowing, a return to the same condemnation with more and more anger and 'never-ending bile' (as the fox puts it, 290) and less and less chance of moving beyond it.

In addition, the indictment is indiscriminate. In the last parts of the novel the fox's teasing wit is replaced by hectoring, and by lurid stories of violent revenge on humans, and disgusted but also sneering images of how horrible humans are, with their cancer and plastics. This is the point in the novel when the impression that it is collecting wrongs and evils is strongest. While reading the parts of the novel that centre on the fox, we *can* call to mind various practices in our world – the fur trade; torture and misuse of animals for experiments; hunting of foxes; sending a dog into space to die there; administering torture so that the victim almost dies, then bringing it back to life to torture it again – but these wrongs and evils are simple examples of cruelty. They are not connected with the novel's imagination of reproduction gone wrong, its linkage of destructive parents and brutal biotechnology as part of the one syndrome. It is a fox speaking of course, and it is entitled to its own emphasis, but it's hard to see the blue fox's recounting of how humans have killed foxes as reflecting anything other than cruelty (270–275 gives 28 ways in which humans killed foxes, repeated ten times). The sense of motiveless sadism is present elsewhere, it is true, for instance, in Charlie X's father, but the passage about the killing of foxes can lead the reader, in reaction, to recall that the presence of foxes in human culture is actually varied and complex – admiration of the urban fox, fictions from Roald Dahl's *Fantastic Mr Fox* to Ted Hughes's 'The Thought-Fox', to give only modern examples. Here the situation of aftermath, in which so much is lost or forgotten or irrelevant, produces a narrowing and a stridency, and this in a text in which so much is inescapably embodied and made present so that one can't object to it as one can to an idea or an argument.

Yet, as was noted, in *Dead Astronauts* attention is distributed and there is no central character or story; there is a strong contrast between the blue fox, and Moss or the salamander. Beside and in some contrast to Charlie X we can put Sarah, the other victim of abuse. The parent whose memory haunts Sarah is her mother not her father, and her mother is unstable and troubled by religious delusions and compulsions, not simply sadistic as was Charlie's father. Sarah is alive not a wraith, and she has a definite situation, a homeless girl trying to make do, living under a bridge beside a polluted river. As this is the part of the novel with the most stable topography, so also it has the clearest storyline. Sarah finds a journal, learns to decipher some of it and comes to write in it, and she encounters and is magically rescued by a salamander, the most benign of the powerful creatures in the novel – 'a monster, yet not monstrous' (178). Her chapter is written in two alternating forms – one of them traces her haunted past, the other her life under the bridge and encounters with the salamander. Both come to a point of closure: the first strand when she can recall the moment of the burning shed, when her mother tricked her into incinerating her stepfather, and, having done this, can name herself, Sarah; the second when the salamander rescues her from the dark bird and itself magically spawns, a life-affirming image of generous reproduction in nature.[13] Charlie X's story, like much else in *Dead Astronauts*, is one of blockage: the equivalent in his story of the burning shed in Sarah's is the room in which he kept his deformed creations as pets, which was destroyed by his father; but Sarah's story has issue and involves healing, and agency (she writes in the journal that she has found, which was formerly Charlie X's).

This interpretation of Sarah's place in the text can be taken further, as Nina Allen does when she refers to 'Moss, whose name was once Sarah'.[14] The burning shed is key to Sarah's story; Moss emerges from the burning shed (18). At the very end of the novel Grayson has Sarah to console her in her dying when she was expecting Moss (317) – though here Sarah seems to see herself as a separate person from Moss. There are hints on 205 and 243 that could suggest the change from Sarah to Moss, by way of Charlie's work to make Moss (59). The text takes care to connect the burning shed not only to Sarah and to Moss, however, but also to Botch (126), the blue fox (146), Charlie X (136) and the salamander (178, 201). Rather than taking hold of one strand of connection, that between Sarah and Moss, it is better to see the image of the burning shed as part of a network, suggesting glimpses of a common consciousness, though not quite a shared consciousness. The novel seems to invite the reader to connect images of experience such as the burning shed laterally, to realise the conditions of this world, rather than to try to recover a sequence across time that might connect, for instance, Sarah and Moss in a narrative. The burning shed can suggest the vitality of flame, fire within (19), the flame-like red of the salamander, but it is connected to a primal crime, Sarah's burning

---

[13] The parts of Sarah's story are numbered to count down from 7 to 1 and then 0, and this reinforces the effect of closure.
[14] In a review in *The Guardian*, 16 January 2020.

of her stepfather, and more generally to the past violence that haunts or was perpetrated by most of the novel's personages. In contrast is the other recurring image, that of the tidal pool, with its network of connections predominantly to Moss, but also to Sarah (the forest as like a tidal pool, 196; her stepfather told her of tidal pools, 193), and to Botch ('the tidal pools that must be holding ponds', 153).

Dead Astronauts has behind it and through it an angry disillusionment: humans have failed, they have wrecked the world. We can take that as given, and proceed to ask what might follow, given that whatever it is will have been shaped by wreckage and will be lived in conditions of aftermath – what kinds of creature will succeed humans, and in what conditions of being. This is a radical question, broader than a question such as what might happen next. The novel provides a range of answers to this question. All of them participate in the human in their qualities of awareness and memory but virtually none of them are human. All are extreme; all depart from expectations governing identity – the distinctness and yet similarity of individual beings. They merge, overlap, are possessed, interfered with, become double or triple – yet are also fundamentally alone most of the time. There is marked variation, between, for instance, Moss and the blue fox, or between Charlie X and Sarah. There are possibilities in this dissemination of identity, as well as exploitation; there are developments and releases; there are glimpses of Edenic enclaves, places of fecundity that have not the oppressive, imprisoning quality of most places in the novel's world.[15] But these possibilities and developments are usually transient or lost, or come to anti-climax or a dead end. Violence and predation persist; memories – even those of the elusive and resourceful fox – tend to be haunted or embittered.

Apocalyptic fiction imagines death on a large scale, and often, as if in response to this, imagines also individual death, and this latter happens as well in *Dead Astronauts*, as with the death of Grayson on the last pages of the novel.

Death is so prevalent in apocalyptic fiction that apocalyptic fiction is often provoked to imagine the possibility of new life. The world of aftermath presented by *Dead Astronauts* is conditioned and confined, as

---

[15] For instance, Charlie X's 'magical garden' (172), his haven for discarded biotechnological creatures, which was destroyed by his father – this one an anti-Eden, like the garden of deadly flowers in Hawthorne's 'Rapaccini's Daughter'; the Eden that the blue fox finds in his journeys (266: 'a vast plateau of wildflowers'; 306); the moment of stillness and perception shared by the dark bird and the shapeshifter (237); but the most important of these is pushed into the remembered past, the joyful life of the foxes (recounted by the blue fox in the third of his passages of repetition, 293ff.).

if by iron bands, by what has become of birth and of death. It is this conditioning and confinement that limits the potential of the possibilities, developments and glimpses of Eden that the novel does imagine. In *Dead Astronauts*, the making of new life is compromised in multiple ways: by the abuse of human parenting; by the exploitation and the distortion of organic life that prevails in biotechnology; and by the way most personages in the novel live in violence or as victims of violence, and live in the past or in repetition. The coming of death is also compromised; death has lost its quality as ending. Death is re-experienced; it is expected but not final, because it ends merely the current 'version' of life. The nadir in this context is the blue fox's memory, 'They killed me. They brought me back' (251–255, repeated exactly); the two processes are so locked together that they might as well be one, and what in earlier imaginations has been a miracle (resurrection) is now a torture.[16] Freedom is longed for but identified with death, as a release. Birth, when it happens, for instance with the spawning of the salamander, is also death, dissolution. Most of the novel's personages experience neither death nor new life, but existence in a perpetual shifting present, populated by memories, often of trauma – as if they haunt where they are rather than live in it as the scene of possibility.

Dead Astronauts thus marks a point beyond which fiction of catastrophe can hardly go. Catastrophe, and particularly ecocide, so haunts the contemporary imagination that *Dead Astronauts* had to be written, the point had to be reached. The rest of this chapter examines a novel that is in drastic contrast to *Dead Astronauts* and to most of the other novels discussed in part 3 of *Apocalypse in Crisis*. *Green Earth* refuses to treat catastrophe as already past, and plunges into imagining and detailing the resources of modern society that might be energised to avert its worst consequences.

Green Earth[17]

The setting of *Green Earth* is a *slow*, unfolding crisis, punctuated, however, by 'abrupt climate change', episodes of dramatic shifts in the weather,

---

[16] This cancelling of birth by death and death by birth is perhaps prompted by contemporary torture (for example, the prisoner who was waterboarded 139 times by the Central Intelligence Agency (CIA) was almost killed, and brought back).

[17] References are to *Green Earth: The Science in the Capital Trilogy*, London: Harper, 2015; *Green Earth* is a revision of a trilogy of novels originally

floods, intense cold, inundation of an island near Bangladesh. There are lots of crises and changes in the characters' personal lives, and a good deal of violence. It would not be productive to force *Green Earth* into the grand narrative of traditional apocalypse – thorough-going disaster followed by redemption – even given the appearance of a secular Messiah in the person of President Phil Chase, who implements measures of radical change such as can only be dreamt about in our time, sensible as they are. To fit *Green Earth* into this redemptive framework would be to overlook the immense amount of practical thinking involved and explicit in the novel, and also to overlook the complex ramifications of the story of its central character, Frank Vanderwal. These aspects of the novel will be discussed later; meanwhile we can acknowledge that the novel does borrow conventional story patterns, those of the thriller and the love story, indeed the romance, in the Shakespearean sense of the term. These conventional story patterns are, however, embedded in a complex architecture of contrasts: communicative transparency as against withholding and secrecy, epiphanies as against lapses, singleness as against sociability, thinking as against doing, the bureaucratic as against the paleolithic, the American and the globalised, living in nature as against manipulating and changing nature. This architecture of contrasts will receive further discussion below.[18]

An effect of stories of apocalyptic catastrophe is that events funnel towards the End, towards global, unstoppable disaster, and this entails an exclusion of other stories and possibilities. This is the imperative of emergency, of the state of exception, which exerts powerful authority in contemporary society. *Green Earth* resists this. It has a strong and broad discursive element: it exploits science fiction's willingness to embark on explicit discussion, to talk about ideas, problems and processes. In part this is just realism: the novel is about scientists and scientists talk and think about ideas, problems and processes. *Cosmopolis* and *Kraken* put power and action in the streets; in *Green Earth* institutions and organisations, with their practices and their arrays of signifiers (acronyms, for instance), have to be dealt with, or manipulated.[19] So we have, for instance, an extended depiction of the meeting of a grants committee,

published separately as *Forty Signs of Rain* (2004), *Fifty Degrees Below* ((2005) and *Sixty Days and Counting* (2007).

[18] See also Palmer 2011.

[19] There is a comment on the novel's valuation of sociability below. It is worth recalling the contemporary American context, the dangers of political and also social polarisation, visible in the isolation of citizens into intolerant groups, resistant to compromise, dialogue and even social contact, with, behind this, arguably, the phenomena of isolation that Robert Putnam

with the technical language as well as the manoeuvres and calculations laid out for us (92–101). Other meetings tend to be mentioned rather than narrated, but there are dozens of them. (These, often tedious, practices of liberal democracy are apt to be very rapidly discarded in apocalyptic fictions.) The novel does count the cost of making policy and working for change in this way, through committees, meetings, a forest of acronyms, competing and turf-conscious bureaucratic entities. There are several scenes in which one of the main characters, Charlie Quibler, explodes in angry denunciation of the self-serving denialism and parochialism he is encountering. By way of strong contrast, *Green Earth* also investigates the 'paleolithic', going off the grid, living in a treehouse: the absolute opposite of the bureaucratic-social. There is an episode (212–217) in which Frank rappels into his boss's office by night, using his mountaineering skills, to retrieve a letter of resignation that he regrets having sent: the active outdoors brought indoors to the National Science Foundation building (he fails to get the letter, but she ignores it anyway). Charlie's outbursts are invigorating, and Frank's pursuit of autonomy and self-sufficiency in the woods answers to what the novel presents as an intense, physical need to be in nature, to connect with the elemental in nature, the body and the historical and the deep past, but *Green Earth* leaves us in no doubt that what is required for change and improvement is self-restraint, patience and a kind of drudgery. The confronting move that founds *Dead Astronauts* is to write off humans' relations with nature as all loss and destruction. 'Do you ever wonder what it would be like not to live in the world of humans?' asks one character (*Dead Astronauts*, 249). Humans have gone but the world they wrecked is the world the novel's personages have to live in. *Green Earth* sets change and improvement in a very broad context of questions: how do humans belong in nature, how are they part of nature, how much do they know and control their own natures – but it asserts that what is needed in the prevailing crisis is for humans to use science and technology – and money – to change and manipulate nature.

These qualities of self-restraint and patience are undramatic, and have as counterpart the slow, and to that degree undramatic, unfolding of the crisis, which Robinson is adapting his novel to express. The crisis intrudes, and that is dramatic, but the rhythm and pace of the novel is that of shifting patterns of day-to-day work, one preoccupation or field of study succeeding another as a character responds to phases as well as jolts of the crisis, but also to other events and relationships.

    analysed in *Bowling Alone* (2000). See the lucid discussion in Diamond 2019, 340–355.

The novel's appeal is to the reader's curiosity, to his or her appetite for observing, describing, reading, arguing; for learning things about the world, including what humans have made of it by theorising, speculating, experimenting, and also getting out into it and walking or running or climbing. In a way, this is the return of the novel as 'baggy monster', ambitious to take on any kind of topic or variety of person and social situation.[20] The reader is at times left breathless by the number of topics, personalities and experiences in which one is invited to participate. Of course, there has to be, and there is, a structure and a drama to the novel; it is not really a grab-bag of interests and topics, a kind of commonplace book. But it is in this aspect that *Green Earth* most clearly breaks with that funnelling effect of inexorability that was nominated earlier as an aspect of many – and many of the best – apocalyptic narratives. If climate change is having and will have a radical effect on the planet and on modern civilisation (not climate change but *'everything change'*, says one of the characters; 644), then the mind and spirit has to meet this radical effect with a drastic broadening of view and scope.[21] Commenting on the formula 'other things being equal', Eric Hobsbawm (1997, 42) reminds us of 'the real world in which other things are never equal or negligible' – and there are so many other things in *Green Earth*. The novel attempts something like a total view, but also acknowledges the strains and dangers of this inclusiveness: excess, overload, a range of problems that induces 'an awe so great that it resembled apathy' (699), dark forces of surveillance that aim for their own, sinister, 'Total Information Awareness' (365).

It is as if things can only enter the novel as they are experienced and used, and this tilts it towards the local and away from the global, a move that was discussed above as a possible limitation to *The Leftovers* and *Girlfriend in a Coma*. Frank acquires a neolithic hand axe – he buys it on the net – then he uses it – he throws it at his antagonist, Edward Cooper (673). The act is a declaration of open hostility against the secretive Cooper; a piece of archaic technology used against the man who controls refined and insidious technology of surveillance; and an intrusion of the deep past into the modern city. Characters sometimes feel the apocalyptic resonances of what is going on, but this is given us as a local matter and as it happens to specific people; it is not portentous:

[20] The utopian novel is an 'absurd hybrid', Robinson 2011, 13.
[21] Contrast the approach of *Green Earth* with, for instance, Margaret Atwood's 'Time Capsule Found on the Dead Planet': Earth's history from beginning to end in five paragraphs (2011, 191–193).

A strong smell of mud and rotting vegetation evoked the tropics, or Atlantis after the flood. Yes, he was feeling a bit apocalyptic. He was in the end time of something, there was no denying it. (289)

Or consider this: 'Green buds on a wet black bough' – it varies Pound's imagist poem – but the passage continues: 'life coming back to the forest. It could not have been more beautiful. No moment in a Mediterranean climate could ever match this moment of impossible green' (600). The poetic observation is not left to stand alone; it happens to Frank, is followed by his reflections on it, and recalls the way his friends on the West Coast (where he used to live) disdain the climate of the East Coast.

Science and Politics

'You're suggesting we have to save the world so science can proceed?'
'Yes, if you want to put it that way.' (228)

The values and procedures of science are at the heart of the grand projects that are implemented to alleviate the effects of climate change in *Green Earth*, and even the transformation that comes over politics in the final volume of the novel is stimulated by the political actions of scientists in the earlier volumes. If we fear that science has lost its autonomy and become tied to corporate research and development, or wonder whether denial of the science of climate change comes from annoyance at science reasserting its autonomy, then *Green Earth* is a story of science re-finding and exploiting its autonomy.

Science depends on exchange, discussion and collaboration, and so it values openness ('A secret scientific method? Was not that a contradiction in terms?' (27)). Scientists contribute to an enterprise extending into the future:

> A cosmic history read out of signs so subtle and mathematical that only the effort of a huge trans-temporal group of powerful minds could ever have teased it out; but then those who came later could be given the whole story, with its unexplored edges there to take off into. This was the human project, this was science, this was what science was. This was what life was. (188; and see 396)[22]

---

[22] The quotation above is Frank's thought; Anna Quibler draws a contrast between 'all the hysterical operatics of "history"' and 'the ongoing irregular

The echo of science-fictional tropes of wise aliens, for instance the Overlords in *Childhood's End* ('a huge trans-temporal group of powerful minds') is surely deliberate, and corrective. The wisdom is ours, or there is none.

Not that this practice is uncomplicated: the entanglement of science and money does in fact involve secrecy (68); the business of fixing on priorities and dispensing awards requires people-management, and sometimes Machiavellian calculation (100–101; 364).[23] The novel continually shuttles between ideal and real, but as regards science the diverse thinking of almost all its characters is based on scientific reasoning. It is the idiom of the novel.[24]

Politics is not presented in the same way. There's an area of light, represented by Phil Chase, who becomes President and implements the measures the scientists have set in train, and an area of darkness represented by Edward Cooper, Frank's antagonist, who operates in secrecy and stands for an opposition that sees no need to justify or explain itself and is therefore outside the world of discussion and open exchange in which almost all the other characters live. The distinct values of politics receive less attention.[25]

The story, then, centres around a group of scientists (with women particularly prominent – Diane Chang, Anna Quibler) who manage to gain support and finance for a series of spectacular projects to alter the seemingly inexorable and cascading effects of changes in the climate: resalinating the ocean from a giant fleet of converted oil tankers to get the Gulf Stream flowing again; pumping the Antarctic ice melt into depressions in the deserts or the desertified areas of the world; genetically

---

pulse of good work, often, since the seventeenth century, supported by science' (635).

[23] Elsewhere in his fiction Robinson can show scientists as reckless (Sax in *Red Mars*, 1993), prejudiced against ordinary workers (the central character, known as X, suffers this in *Antarctica*, 1997), scarred by corruption and chicanery (Dennis the engineer in *The Gold Coast*, 1988).

[24] Science is bureaucratic; it works through systems and institutions; but it is also based on small groups who test and trust the expertise and honesty of their colleagues. See Shapin 1994, 414–415: 'So one story about the modern condition points to anonymity and system-trust in abstract capacities, while the other identifies persisting patterns of traditional familiarity and trust in known persons' (415). And see above, 205, on the contemporary conditions of truth, trust and mistrust.

[25] Contrast Robinson's later, and bleaker, imagination of how the globe might avert climate disaster, *The Ministry For the Future* (2020). Action is global, but the narrative keeps returning to Mary Murphy, ex-politician and United Nations official.

engineering lichen that takes up CO_2, and inducing it to settle on the conifer forests of north Eurasia on a vast scale (this last happens without much attention to the open and democratic procedures of the other scientists).[26] These are ambitious interventions in nature, a nature already irrevocably altered by human action. The emphasis is not on the waste and self-indulgence of contemporary society, the need to change lives and habits, restrain, renounce, which often figures in ecological critiques and proposals. A contemporary ecologist would probably be horrified by the air miles that the characters rack up in taking us to view various emergencies and unfolding projects. Instead, the emphasis is on the abundant resources of contemporary society, and on mobilising organisations and collectives that can in turn apply these resources to new purposes: respectively, advanced science and its organisations; the financial muscle of the reinsurance industry; and the US Corps of Engineers. These are projects as sweeping as those that figure in or underpin science fiction (for instance, Robinson's trilogy on the terraforming of Mars), and as sweeping and transformative as those that made industrial and then electronic civilisation – and also led to climate change. All this may seem utopian, and it is; this is a topic that will be discussed later.

The localism that is often put forward as the antidote to our present wastefulness and its dangerous effects is present not in the projects that come about in the course of the novel, but in the way they are worked on and in their day-to-day context. These utopian outcomes are made plausible because they are worked on in meetings, committees, 'a whole sheaf of lists' (532),[27] and endless discussions and exchanges. Problems are analysed and progress is step by step; then there are breakthroughs and abrupt shifts to a broader level of organisation and effort. The procedure involves the striking of a balance: attention to daily work and experience has to establish the plausibility and thence the possibility of big changes that are seen as depending on the realism of science as collective work, as day-to-day analysis and exploration. Yet the utopian impulse is by no means rationed: we hear of the insertion of biogenetically altered

---

[26] Pages 960–961 give the reservations of other scientists in the face of this 'reckless' project.

[27] Lists and dot point passages are one of the novel's ways of suggesting the complex abundance and at times overload of information and possibility that has to be drawn upon and coped with: see also 373 (all the different terms for what is happening and what might be done); 692 (a list of current problems that ends with the feedback loop caused by the 'cumulative impact' of all the problems); 775 (a list of New Deals); 415 (a list of acronyms for relevant organisations); 496–499 (Chase's election 'contract', a utopian wish-list); 517 (Frank's 'to do' list); 922 (a list of 24 US intelligence agencies).

material into the cells of the body to counteract lesions of the sort that Frank has suffered; there is the election of Phil Chase, amiable, eloquent, popular, 'the world's senator' become the world's as well as America's President (we are given his speech at his inauguration); among much else, he manages to get investment redirected to end unemployment and make private sector wages more able to be lived on. (This last is a possibility that has been glimpsed in the course of responses to the coronavirus pandemic.) Behind this, as it can easily seem, fantasy, is again the novel's sense of a plenitude of social resources and energies, a society humming with energies, avocations, curiosity that might be released and mobilised. It's a reassertion of the energies and potentials of the modern, though, as we will see, underpinned by the past, the archaic, and threatened by areas of darkness, lapses, blanks. The utopian process, that is, the process of improvement and alleviation that seems utopian because it hasn't started in the contemporary world, if it were to start, could not stop, but would have to continue and proliferate, and *Green Earth* embraces this imperative.

Yet the local can serve as refuge from global problems and threats, as well as serving to set them in a manageable framework of analysis and step-by-step process. Globally, the world faces the sixth extinction, vast loss of species; locally, the animals of the Washington Zoo have to be released into the woods when flood threatens, and the result is an abundance of wildlife, to be observed and encountered by Frank and others – the simiang to whose hootings he responds; the doe he encounters, 'a female of another species'; tigers; an aurochs, 'a creature from the cave paintings, sprung live into their world' (458). None of these species is native to America: they are involuntarily introduced, and the way they survive and flourish makes an oblique comment on the United States as a multi-cultural society, as well as reversing, in imagination, the global depletion of species. At this local level, and in the lives of characters such as Frank Vanderwal, the novel qualifies its emphasis on grand projects that intervene in nature. At this level, nature is not a thing to be manipulated but 'the birth place of new meanings'.[28]

But how does the change start? *Green Earth* is not set in our contemporary world, though it is very close to it. In the world of the novel, for instance, Washington itself is flooded, making denial or obfuscation of the problem of climate change rather more difficult. Later Washington is severely frozen:

---

[28] Bowie 1998, 138: 'If nature is merely to be used it ceases to be a living resource that can be the birthplace of new meanings'. (An issue also with *Dead Astronauts*.)

'Everyone knows now that the problem is real. This isn't like the flood; this could happen three or four times every winter. Abrupt climate change is real, no one can deny it, and it's a big problem. Things are a mess!' (570)

The positive, practical and very ambitious action that comes to be undertaken is being undertaken after the catastrophe has begun, in response to its fierce teaching. The ground is prepared for the election of Phil Chase: an idealised figure, cheerful, folksy, eloquent, bold, a man who *enjoys* the politician's work of meeting people, including potential donors (4,200 events in each of his terms as senator: another example of proliferation become excess; 154). Not only might his election be needed, but also the fact that he survives an attempted assassination and returns to the fray bolder and more radical, seizing the moment. So, if he is an idealised figure, a figment of wish fulfilment, the novel suggests that radical change might need that kind of person, distinctly American in all kinds of ways, but very unlike most contemporary politicians; a kind of Lincoln redivivus, this time surviving an assassination attempt (a visit to the Lincoln Memorial makes the connection; 321–324). So the novel is suggesting that changes that can seem utopian are needed, and that they might in effect need all these emergencies and contingencies to become possible. The utopian requires a measure of the dystopian. People have to become 'desperate' (588). If immediate and inescapable emergencies had not occurred, and on the very doorstep of government, huge projects of alleviation would not have been implemented; if they had not been implemented, prospects would have been even more bleak. Without Phil Chase, and possibly without his having survived an assassination attempt, the necessary political skill and intelligence would have been lacking. Utopia involves the exertion of reason, a lot of work and contingency.

The emergency is not a dire one. The novel is in fact more interested in the experience of happiness and joy than in the experience of desperation. The Washington flood is exciting; it leads to the release of the animals from the zoo and after that to the activity of tracking and observing them, and sheltering them during the worst of the cold snap. The phenomena of emergency and alleviation are often greeted with festivity.[29] Crisis brings people together in mutual effort (237–241; 266); when shortages issue in hoarding, the psychology and economics of this

---

[29] See 281 ('the festival mood' at the flood); 451 (*'The most beautiful regatta in the history of the world convened that year on Midsummer Day at the North Pole'*); 565 (a 'Carnivale' on the ice in Washington).

become an object of study, aroused analytical curiosity (568, 638, 766 and 785). Looters are glimpsed at one point (265), but the activities of 'fregans' and scavengers (925), and the routines of the homeless with whom Frank makes friends, are given much more attention. It seems at times as if Robinson has made a list of the commonly imagined responses to catastrophe (looting, hoarding, social breakdown) and decided to downplay them. In this respect *Green Earth* is systematically anti-apocalyptic.

Slow climate change affects the oceans; abrupt climate change causes flooding and extreme storms, but the novel enjoys water – boats out exploring the flood, kayaking, surfing, the sound of rain on a tent:

> The rain pounded down with its plastic drumming noise, like the shower you hear in the morning when your partner gets up – a susurrus or patter, riding on the liquid roar of the forest and the clatter of the creek below. (411)

President Chase's tactic is to 'flood' the Congress with proposals (997).

Darker Notes

Green Earth is the scene of continual contrast, which often takes the form of conflict between oppositions that are both valuable. It is by means of this dynamic that the novel extends and also controls its scope, and also by this means that it darkens the picture of optimism and energy that is conveyed by its conspectus of the power of science, the effectiveness of co-operation and the plenitude of resources and energies of contemporary American society. These contrasts are multiple and shifting:

- Centred on America – there are excursions into the heroic American past – Lincoln, F. D. Roosevelt – and into the tradition of imagination of nature in America – Frederic Church, Thoreau, Emerson), yet reaching out to the globe (and emphasising multicultural America – Hispanic, Chinese).[30]

---

[30] See the scenes at the Lincoln Memorial (321–323) and the Roosevelt monument (1028); Phil Chase on the US and the world (454); readings from Emerson (505, 552, 761), Thoreau (697, 877 878); a Frederic Church exhibition (731, 846–847); the important roles played by Diane Chang and

BEYOND APOCALYPSE 321

- Ranging from the high bureaucratic and political – plans, meetings, calculations – to the paleolithic, through Frank's speculations and observations when he ventures into the woods and lives for a time in a treehouse.[31]

- Calibrating the necessities of sociality as against individual aloneness: discussion, conviviality, mutual help in disaster, the evolutionary advantages of fitting into a group, as against the singularity of subjective experience and the degree to which the depths of the self and of others are hidden from the individual.[32]

- In close relation to the contrasts of sociality and aloneness, a contrast between exchange and withholding, the communicable and the incommunicable.

- A range of positions and actions in and on nature: being part of nature, being – and playing – in nature, but also caring for nature, and also manipulating and altering nature.

The best way of exploring all this material is to look at the passages through the novel of two characters, Charlie Quibler and Frank Vanderwal. Each is closely connected to the unfolding attempts to alleviate the effects of climate change, Charlie as a presidential advisor and Frank as a scientist; each is on hand to witness public events and emergencies; but each also has an intense personal history that asserts itself apart from the collective action. Each participates in the enterprises and successes that constitute the novel's detailed riposte to apocalyptic gloom and doom, but the personal history of each swerves towards uncertainty and uncontrol. The result is to qualify the novel's optimism,

---

by Edgardo. The excursions into the American past are for inspiration and counsel; there is not much on the historical origins of the current crisis.

[31] Remarks about primates, 11, 85, 313; remarks about the savannah, 13, 56, 60, 104; living in a tree, 295, 341, 542; Frank's stone axe, 376–377; Frank is like Alpine Man, 514; stalking Cooper, and throwing the axe, 670–675.

[32] Getting along with the group as adaptive, 173, 502; 'moods in a group', 104; lots of meditations on the mutual life of couples, for instance, 440–441, 488–489, 617, 773, 885; 'The sound of three thousand voices all talking at once in a big enclosed space was perhaps the most beautiful music of all' (Edgardo at the tango concert, 862); 'a healthy sufficiency of human society', 984; 'Thirteen thousand human beings, all thankful at once', 911; and see note 29 above on festivities.

especially if one interprets the story of Frank (at least) as a kind of microcosm of the macrocosmic collective action; in this movement uncertainties and limits that were overcome in the macrocosm assert themselves at times dismayingly in the microcosm.

Charlie's wife Anna works full-time and he juggles (on the phone, mostly) his work as advisor to Senator Chase with caring for the infant Joe. Joe is challenging – obstreperous, unpredictable, exhausting – and it is contact with Joe that pulls Charlie into the world of physical being and activity that Frank more deliberately seeks out in the woods. Charlie is a success; he wins acceptance from the mothers at childcare; he 'has it all' (721). Eventually he is able to return to work with (now-President) Chase while Joe adjusts to life at a crèche. Meanwhile, however, Joe begins to act strangely – alarming moods, sudden changes – indeed he begins to seem strange, as if not quite of the same species. The Quibler family are involved with Tibetan refugees from Khembalung, and Charlie in his distress begins to imagine that Joe has somehow become an avatar of the Panchen Lama; he gets his Tibetan friends to arrange a kind of exorcism, and then a re-exorcism when the first seemed to have produced a too subdued Joe out of the previous wild and ungovernable Joe. The crisis diminuendos: the Tibetans suggest that they were in fact exorcising Charlie of his fears and suspicions, not Joe, and we are left with the episode as simply underlining how children have depths that are sometimes uncanny and incommunicable.

Frank Vanderwal's history is more complex. He is the novel's main point-of-view character, and his private speculations, experiments and troubles attract much of the novel's attention. He is lonely, yearning for a partner, fascinated by the life of couples, and by what makes women attractive. A series of delays and changes of mind leave him homeless, and he takes to the woods. This stimulates his habits of speculation, based often on sociobiology, centring on the archaic heritage and the adaptability of human nature, and humans in and part of nature – prompted by his encounters with the animals released into the woods from the zoo. Meanwhile, active as well as speculative, he builds a treehouse and experiments with a paleolithic way of life. So far, this carries the novel's buoyancy and omnivorousness into new territory, and sets up a contrast between the collective action that is working to control and alter nature, and Frank's lone, and secret, absorption in nature and contact with wild creatures, chiefly the simiang (a species of baboon), whose morning chorus of hootings he joins, and whose life as couples he observes; but the focus tightens and darkens.

Frank has had an exciting erotic encounter with a woman in a stuck elevator, and this becomes his love affair with Caroline, conducted under extreme difficulty as a matter of hurried assignations, because Caroline is married to and threatened by Edward Cooper. Cooper heads a 'black' agency, and disposes of resources of violence and, more particularly, surveillance. He stands as the malign counterpart of the scientists and Phil Chase, working in the dark, yet able to track and surveil his targets. Caroline and Frank become aware that Cooper's organisation is planning to tamper with the presidential election; this is eventually thwarted by a rival, enlightened group headed by Edgardo, whom Frank has contacted. These manoeuvres remain offstage, dark doings left dark in a novel the style of which is usually explanatory and forthcoming. What we actually see of Frank's contest with Cooper is more a matter of thwarting the latter's control over Caroline.

In the course of this contest Frank is beaten up in a brawl, suffering a hard to define brain injury. This puts the darkness within Frank, in a way that has similarities to Charlie's anxieties about Joe's strangeness. Frank becomes indecisive, subject to bewilderment and self-mistrust. Earlier, in his inquisitive way, he explored the differences between deliberate, thought-out action and the instinctive capabilities of the body; now he feels out of contact with his own mind, and his will wavers. We see his trouble most vividly when he is hiking with friends in the Sierras, and is observed by his friend Charlie.[33] His disturbance never goes beyond a certain point, and for all his hesitations he succeeds in rescuing Caroline and (through Edgardo) thwarting Cooper, but this part of the novel intensifies the strand of lapse, uncertainty, blankness or darkness. Sometimes instances of this strand are more positive, epiphanies rather than lapses: encounters with Caroline, with a jaguar, glimpses of a mysterious female kayaker. We are then led back to Frank's interest in what makes joy or bliss and his reading of, for instance, Emerson on this topic.

The novel ends on a note of achievement and hope, as regards the alleviation of the consequences of climate change, and the achievements of President Chase, and also as regards the lives of individual characters whose story, by the end, shifts into the mode of romance. Not only do Caroline and Frank come together, in the daylight as it were, after their life of snatched meetings and separations, but Caroline is pregnant. This echoes the trope of the appearance of new life at the end of an apocalyptic novel, but has extra salience here because of Charlie's previous troubles with young Joe. In addition, Phil Chase is marrying Diane Chang, the figure in the novel who sums up what a scientist bureaucrat needs if

---

[33] A situation that Robinson explored in 'Ridge Running', a story dated 1975/1977/1983, reprinted in *The Planet on the Table*, 1986.

she is to achieve something in the jungle of committees and funds and rivalries – that is, Diane is the counterpart in the world of science politics of Phil Chase in the world of electoral and presidential politics; and a couple of minor characters, Roy and Andrea, are also marrying. All this comes about when the Tibetans celebrate a reconciliation with China brought about by American help with a Chinese ecocrisis, and when a trio of our characters have just found out that their Tibetan friend Drepung is actually the Panchen Lama, escaped from Chinese imprisonment and living incognito in Washington, DC. This pile of blessings has the Shakespearean quality: as many marriages as possible, for marriages are signs of new life (reinforced by Caroline's pregnancy), as much reconciliation as possible, a moment of celebration by the assembled cast list, before we end the play.

Works Cited

Abrams, M. H. 1984. 'Apocalypse: Theme and Variations', *The Apocalypse in English Renaissance Thought and Literature*, edited by C. A. Patrides and Joseph Wittreich, Manchester: Manchester University Press, 342–368.
Ahrends, Jorn. 2009. 'How to Save the Unsaved World? Transforming the Self in *The Matrix, The Terminator,* and *12 Monkeys*', *Media and the Apocalypse*, edited by Kylo-Patrick R. Hart and Annette M. Holba, New York: Peter Lang, 53–65.
Aldiss, Brian W. 1964. *Greybeard*, London: Faber.
— 1969. *Barefoot in the Head: A European Fantasia*, London: Faber.
— 1989. *Forgotten Life*, London: Mandarin.
Aldiss, Brian W. with David Wingrove. 1986. *Trillion Year Spree*, London: Gollancz.
Alexievich, Svetlana. 2016. *Chernobyl Prayer: A Chronicle of the Future*, translated by Anna Gunin and Arch Tait, London: Penguin.
Allen, Nina. 2020. Review of *Dead Astronauts*, *The Guardian*, 16 January.
Amis, Martin. 2003. *Einstein's Monsters*, London: Vintage (1987).
Anderson, Perry. 1992. 'The Ends of History', *A Zone of Engagement*, London: Verso, 279–375.
Ariès, Philippe. 1981. *The Hour of Our Death*, translated by Helen Weaver, London: Allen Lane.
Atwood, Margaret. 2008. *Payback*, Toronto: Anansi.
— 2011. 'Time Capsule Found on the Dead Planet', *I'm With the Bears: Stories from a Damaged Planet*, edited by Mark Martin, London: Verso, 191–193.
Auden, W. H. 1966. 'The Bonfires', *Collected Shorter Poems 1927–1957*, London: Faber, 39.
Baker, Phil. 2003. 'Secret City: Psychogeography and the End of London', *London Punk to Blair*, edited by Joe Kerr and Andrew Gibson, London: Reaktion, 323–333.
Ballard, J. G. 1962. *The Drowned World*, New York: Berkley Medallion.
— 1966a. 'The Illuminated Man', *The Terminal Beach*, Harmondsworth: Penguin, 75–106 (1964).
— 1966b. *The Crystal World*, London: Jonathan Cape.

— 1966c. 'The Terminal Beach', *The Terminal Beach*, Harmondsworth: Penguin, 136–157 (1964).
— 1967. *The Wind from Nowhere*, Harmondsworth: Penguin (1962).
— 1978. *The Drought*, London: Granada (1965).
— 1991. *The Kindness of Women*, London: HarperCollins.
— 1996. 'The Visual World', *A User's Guide to the Millennium*, London: HarperCollins, 92–93.
Banks, Iain M. 1988. *Consider Phlebas*, London: Futura (1987).
Banville, John. 2019. 'Of Terrorists, Tourists, and Robert Frost', *The New York Review of Books*, 26 September, 60–61.
Barnes, Julian. 1984. *Flaubert's Parrot*, London: Jonathan Cape.
Barthes, Roland. 1980. *New Critical Essays*, translated by Richard Howard, New York: Hill & Wang.
Bauman, Zygmunt. 2012. *Liquid Modernity*, London: Polity.
— and Carlo Bordoni. 2014. *State of Crisis*, London: Polity.
Baxter, Jeannette. 2009. *J. G. Ballard's Surrealist Imagination*, Farnham, Surrey: Ashgate.
Beal, Timothy. 2018. *The Book of Revelation: A Biography*, Princeton and Oxford: Princeton University Press.
Beaumont, Matthew and Gregory Dart, editors. 2010. *Restless Cities*, London and New York: Verso.
Beckett, Andy. 2009. *When the Lights Went Out: Britain in the Seventies*, London: Faber.
Berman, Marshall. 1988. *All That is Solid Melts into Air: The Experience of Modernity*, New York: Penguin.
Bertelsen, Eve. 1988. 'Who is it Who Says "I"?: The Persona of a Doris Lessing Interview', *Doris Lessing: The Alchemy of Survival*, edited by Carey Kaplan and Ellen Cronan Rose, Athens, Ohio: Ohio University Press, 169–187.
Best, Geoffrey. 1980. *Humanity in Warfare*, New York: Columbia University Press.
Binns, Amy. 2019. *Hidden Wyndham: Life, Love, Letters*, n.p.: Grace Judson Press.
Biro, Matthew. 2013. *Anselm Kiefer*, London: Phaidon.
Biswell, Andrew. 2006. *The Real Life of Anthony Burgess*, London: Picador.
Blake, William. 1979. *Milton: A Poem by William Blake*, edited by Kay Parkhurst Easson and Roger R. Easson, London: Thames and Hudson (c.1804).
Bolaño, Roberto. 2009. *2666*, translated by Natasha Wimmer, London: Picador (2004).
Bowie, Andrew. 1998. 'Critiques of Culture', *The Cambridge Companion to Modern German Culture*, edited by Eva Kolinsky and Wilfried Van Der Will, Cambridge: Cambridge University Press, 132–152.
Bowie, David. 1972. *The Rise and Fall of Ziggy Stardust and the Spiders from Mars*.

Boyer, Paul. 1996. 'Exotic Resonances: Hiroshima in American Memory', *Hiroshima in History and Memory*, edited by Michael J. Hogan, Cambridge: Cambridge University Press, 143-167.
Boyle, Nicholas. 2008. *German Literature: A Very Short Introduction*, Cambridge: Cambridge University Press.
Brigg, Peter. 1994. 'J. G. Ballard: Time out of Mind', *Extrapolation*, vol. 35, no. 1, 43-59.
Burgess, Anthony. 1972. *Oedipus the King* (translation of Sophocles' play). Minneapolis: University of Minnesota Press.
— 1982. *The End of the World News: An Entertainment*, London: Hutchinson.
— 1990. *You've Had Your Time*, London: Heinemann.
— 2019. *Puma*, edited and introduced by Paul Wake, Manchester: Manchester University Press (1976).
Burrow, John W. 1966. *Evolution and Society: A Study in Victorian Social Theory*, Cambridge: Cambridge University Press.
Byatt, A. S. 2011. *Ragnarök: The End of the Gods*, Melbourne: Text.
Byron, George Gordon, Lord. 1970. 'Heaven and Earth: A Mystery', *Byron: Poetical Works*, edited by Frederick Page, corrected by John Jump, Oxford: Oxford University Press, 545-559 (1821).
Callinicos, Alex. 1995. *Theories and Narratives: Reflections on the Philosophy of History*, Durham, NC: Duke University Press.
Carpenter, Mary Wilson and George P. Landow. 1984. 'Ambiguous Revelations: The Apocalypse in Victorian Literature', *The Apocalypse in Thought and Literature*, edited by C. A. Patrides and Joseph Wittreich, Manchester: Manchester University Press, 299-322.
Carrière, Jean-Claude. 1999. 'Answering the Sphinx', *Conversations about the End of Time*, produced and edited by Catherine David, translated by Ian MacLean and Roger Pearson, London: Allen Lane, 95-170.
Carter, Angela. 1969. *Heroes and Villains*, London: Heinemann.
Chadwick, Owen. 1975. *The Secularization of the European Mind in the Nineteenth Century*, Cambridge: Cambridge University Press.
Christopher, John. 2009. *The Death of Grass*, with an introduction by Robert Macfarlane, London: Penguin Classics (1956).
Clarke, Arthur C. 1973. *Childhood's End*, New York: Ballantine (1953).
Clarke, Graham. 1988. 'A "Sublime and Atrocious" Spectacle: New York and the Iconography of Manhattan Island', *The American City: Literary and Cultural Perspectives*, edited by Graham Clarke, London: Vision Press, 36-61.
Clarke, I. F. 1970. *Voices Prophesying War 1763-1984*, London: Panther.
Clute, John and John Grant, editors. 1999. *The Encyclopedia of Fantasy*, London: Orbit.
Clute, John and Peter Nicholls, editors. 1993. *The Science Fiction Encyclopedia*, London: Orbit.
Cohn, Norman. 1993. *Cosmos, Chaos and the World to Come: The Ancient Roots of Apocalyptic Faith*, New Haven and London: Yale University Press.

Conrad, Joseph. 1973. *Heart of Darkness*, Harmondsworth: Penguin (1902).
— 1963. *Nostromo: A Tale of the Seaboard*, Harmondsworth: Penguin (1904).
Conrad, Peter. 1999. *Modern Times, Modern Places*, London: Thames & Hudson.
Corra, Bruno. 2015. *Sam Dunn is Dead*, translated and introduced by John Walker, illustrated by Rosa Rosà, London: Atlas (1915).
Coupland, Douglas. 2004. *Girlfriend in a Coma*, London: HarperPerennial (1998).
— 2009. *Generation A*, London: William Heinemann.
Cunningham, Valentine. 2002. 'Shaping Modern British Fiction: The Forms of the Content, and the Contents of the Form', *On Modern British Fiction*, edited by Zachary Leader, Oxford: Oxford University Press, 149–180.
DeLillo, Don. 1986. *End Zone*, London: Penguin (1972).
— 1998. *Underworld*, London: Picador (1997).
— 2003. *Cosmopolis*, London: Picador.
— 2007. *Falling Man*, London: Picador.
— 2017. *Zero K*, London: Picador (2016).
Delumeau, Jean. 1995. *History of Paradise*, translated by Matthew O'Connell, New York: Continuum.
d'Eramo, Marco. 2007. 'Bunkering in Paradise (or, Do Oldsters Dream of Electric Golf Carts?)', *Evil Paradises*, edited by Mike Davis and Daniel Bertrand Monk, New York and London: The New Press, 171–188.
Diamond, Jared. 2005. *Collapse: How Societies Choose to Fail or Survive*, London: Penguin.
— 2019. *Upheaval: How Nations Cope with Crisis and Change*, London: Allen Lane.
Dickens, Charles. 1985. *A Tale of Two Cities*, edited by George Woodcock, London: Penguin (1859).
Disch, Thomas M. 2000. *The Genocides*, New York: Vintage (1965).
Douglas, Jack D. 1970. 'Understanding Everyday Life', *Understanding Everyday Life: Toward the Reconstruction of Sociological Knowledge*, edited by Jack D. Douglas, Chicago: Aldine, 3–44.
Doyle, William. 1999. *The Origins of the French Revolution*, Oxford: Oxford University Press.
Draine, Betsy. 1983. *Substance Under Pressure: Artistic Coherence and Evolving Form in the Novels of Doris Lessing*, Madison, WI: University of Wisconsin Press.
Draper, Michael. 1987. *H. G. Wells*, London: Macmillan.
Eco, Umberto. 1984. *The Name of the Rose*, translated by William Weaver, London: Picador (1980).
— 1987. 'On the Crisis of the Crisis of Reason', *Travels in Hyperreality*, translated by William Weaver, London: Picador (1980).
— 2012. *Inventing the Enemy*, translated by Richard Dixon, London: Harvill Secker.

Eliot, George. 1994. *Middlemarch*, edited by Rosemary Ashton, London: Penguin (1871–2).
Enzensberger, Hans Magnus. 1982. 'Two Notes on the End of the World', *Critical Essays*, edited by Reinhold Grimm and Bruce Armstrong, New York: Continuum, 233–241.
Farrell, John P. 1980. *Revolution as Tragedy: The Dilemma of the Moderate from Scott to Arnold*, Ithaca and London: Cornell University Press.
Flahaut, François. 2003. *Malice*, London: Verso.
Forster, Leonard, editor. 1957. *The Penguin Book of German Verse*, Harmondsworth: Penguin.
Friedländer, Saul. 1985. 'Themes of Decline and End in the Nineteenth-Century Western Imagination', translated by Susan Rubin Suleiman, *Visions of Apocalypse: End or Rebirth?*, edited by Saul Friedländer, Gerald Holton, Leo Marx and Eugene Skolnikoff, New York and London: Holmes & Meier, 61–83.
Fritzsche Peter. 2005. *Stranded in the Present: Modern Time and the Melancholy of History*, Cambridge, MA and London: Harvard University Press.
Funkenstein, Amos. 1985. 'A Schedule for the End of the World: The Origins and Persistence of the Apocalyptic Mentality', *Visions of Apocalypse: End or Rebirth?*, edited by Saul Friedländer, Gerald Holton, Leo Marx and Eugene Skolnikoff, New York and London: Holmes & Meier, 44–60.
Fussell, Paul. 1975. *The Great War and Modern Memory*, London and Oxford: Oxford University Press.
— 1989. *Wartime*, New York: Oxford University Press.
Galbreath, Robert. 1983. 'Ambiguous Apocalypse: Transcendental Versions of the End', *The End of the World*, edited by Eric S. Rabkin, Martin H. Greenberg and Joseph D. Olander, Carbondale and Edwardsville, Southern Illinois University Press, 53–72.
Gasiorek, Andrzej. 2005. *J. G. Ballard*, Manchester and New York: Manchester University Press.
Golding, William. 1958. *Lord of the Flies*, London: Faber.
Gordon, Edmund. 2016. *The Invention of Angela Carter: A Biography*, London: Chatto & Windus.
Green, Martin. 1991. *Seven Types of Adventure Tale: The Etiology of a Major Genre*, University Park: Pennsylvania State University Press.
Hale, Terry. 1994. *The Automatic Muse: Surrealist Novels by Robert Desnos, Georges Limbour, Michel Leiris, and Benjamin Péret*, translated by Terry Hale and Iain Willis, introduced by Terry Hale, London: Atlas.
Hardy, Thomas. 1978. *Tess of the D'Urbervilles: A Pure Woman*, introduced by A. Alvarez, edited by David Skilton, Harmondsworth: Penguin (1891).
Harrison, E. L. 1990. 'Divine Action in *Aeneid* Book 2', *Oxford Readings in Virgil's Aeneid*, edited by S. J. Harrison, Oxford: Oxford University Press, 46–59.
Harrison, J. F. C. 1979. *The Second Coming: Popular Millenarianism 1780–1850*, New Brunswick, NJ: Rutgers University Press.

Hawkins, Alan. 1986. 'The Discovery of Rural England', *Englishness: Politics and Culture 1880–1920*, edited by Robert Colls and Philip Dodd, London: Croom Helm, 62–88.
Hazareesingh, Sudhir. 2015. *How the French Think*, New York: Basic Books.
Heller, Agnes. 1984. *Everyday Life*, translated by G. L. Campbell, London: Routledge and Kegan Paul (1970).
Hilton, Boyd. 2006. *A Mad, Bad, & Dangerous People? England 1783–1846*, Oxford: Clarendon Press.
Hobsbawm, E. J. 1997. 'Looking Forward: History and the Future', *On History*, London: Weidenfeld & Nicholson, 37–55.
Huxley, Aldous. 1994. *The Doors of Perception* and *Heaven and Hell*, with a foreword by J. G. Ballard, London: Flamingo (1954 and 1956).
Jackson, Rosemary. 1981. *Fantasy: The Literature of Subversion*, London and New York: Methuen.
James, Edward. 2005. 'Arthur C. Clarke', *A Companion to Science Fiction*, edited by David Seed, Oxford: Blackwell, 431–440.
James, P. D. 1994. *The Children of Men*, London: Penguin (1992).
Jameson, Fredric. 1991. *Postmodernism or, The Cultural Logic of Late Capitalism*, London: Verso.
— 2002. *A Singular Modernity: Essay on the Ontology of the Present*, London and New York: Verso.
Jay, Martin. 1998. 'Songs of Experience: Reflections on the Debate over Alltagsgeschichte', *Cultural Semantics: Keywords of Our Time*, London: The Athlone Press, 37–46.
— 2005. *Songs of Experience: Modern American and European Variations on a Universal Theme*, Berkeley and Los Angeles: University of California Press.
Johnstone, Christopher. 1974. *John Martin*, London: Academy Editions.
Jones, Colin. 2003. *The Great Nation: France from Louis XIV to Napoleon*, London: Penguin.
Joyce, James. 1960. *Ulysses*, London: The Bodley Head (1922).
Judt, Tony. 2005. *Postwar: A History of Europe Since 1945*, New York: Penguin Press.
— 2015. 'The New World Order', *When the Facts Change: Essays 1995–2010*, edited and introduced by Jennifer Homans, London: Penguin, 234–251.
Kavan, Anna. 1967. *Ice*, New York: Norton.
Keller, Catherine and Mary-Jane Robinson, editors. 2017. *Entangled Worlds: Religion, Science and New Materialism*, New York: Fordham University Press.
Kermode, Frank. 1985. 'Apocalypse and the Modern', *Visions of Apocalypse: End or Rebirth?*, edited by Saul Friedländer, Gerald Holton, Leo Marx and Eugene Skolnikoff, New York and London: Holmes & Meier, 84–106.
— 2000. *The Sense of an Ending: Studies in the Theory of Fiction*, with an Epilogue from 1999, New York: Oxford University Press (1967).
Kershaw, Ian. 2016. *To Hell and Back: Europe 1914–1949*, London: Penguin.
Ketterer, David. 1976. 'The Apocalyptic Imagination, Science Fiction, and American Literature', *Science Fiction: A Collection of Critical Essays*, edited by Mark Rose, Englewood Cliffs, NJ: Prentice-Hall, 147–155.

Klein, Carole. 2000. *Doris Lessing: A Biography*, London: Duckworth.
Koerner, Joseph Leo. 2008. *The Reformation of the Image*, Chicago: University of Chicago Press (2004).
Koselleck, Reinhart. 1988. *Critique and Crisis: Enlightenment and the Pathogenesis of Modern Society*, Oxford, New York and Hamburg: Berg (1959).
Kubin, Alfred. 1973. *The Other Side*, illustrated by the author, translated by Denver Lindley, Harmondsworth: Penguin (1909).
Lassner, Phyllis. 2011. 'Olivia Manning', *Resurgent Adventures with Britannia*, edited by Wm. Roger Louis, London: I. B. Tauris, 121–132.
Lawrence, D. H. 1961. 'Studies in Classic American Literature', *Selected Literary Criticism*, London: Mercury, 295–407 (1924).
Le Guin, Ursula. 1989a. '*Shikasta*', *Dancing at the Edge of the World*, New York: Harper & Row, 249–252 (1979).
— 1989b. '*The Sentimental Agents*', *Dancing at the Edge of the World*, New York: Harper & Row, 276–278 (1983).
— 1997. *The Lathe of Heaven*, New York: Avon Books (1971).
Leithem, Jonathan. 2002. *Amnesia Moon*, London: Faber (1995).
Leonard, John. 1986. 'The Spacing Out of Doris Lessing', *Critical Essays on Doris Lessing*, edited by Claire Sprague and Virginia Tiger, Boston: G. K. Hall & Co., 204–209.
Lessing, Doris. 1973. *The Summer Before the Dark*, New York: Alfred A. Knopf.
— 1974. *The Memoirs of a Survivor*, London: The Octagon Press.
— 1983. *The Making of the Representative for Planet 8 (Canopus in Argos – Archives)*, London: Grafton (Collins) (1982).
Lippy, Charles H. 1982. 'Waiting for the End: The Social Context of American Apocalyptic Religion', *The Apocalyptic Vision in America: Interdisciplinary Essays on Myth and Culture*, edited and introduced by Lois Parkinson Zamora, Bowling Green, Ohio: Bowling Green University Popular Press, 37–63.
Luckhurst, Roger. 2003. 'Occult London', *London Punk to Blair*, edited by Joe Kerr and Andrew Gibson, London: Reaktion, 334–340.
Lundberg, Christian. 2009. 'The Pleasure of Sadism: A Reading of the Left Behind Series', *Media and the Apocalypse*, edited by Kylo-Patrick R. Hart and Annette M. Holba, New York: Peter Lang, 97–128.
Maalouf, Amin. 1993. *The First Century After Beatrice*, translated by Dorothy S. Blair, London: Abacus (1992).
McCarthy, Cormac. 1989. *Blood Meridian or The Evening Redness in the West*, London: Picador (1985).
— 2007. *The Road*, London: Picador (2006).
McCarthy, Patrick A. 1997. 'Allusions in Ballard's *The Drowned World*', *Science Fiction Studies* 72, volume 24, 302–310.
MacCulloch, Diarmaid. 2004. *Reformation: Europe's House Divided 1490–1700*, London: Penguin.
— 2017. *All Things Made New*, London: Penguin.

McGinn, Bernard. 1984. 'Early Apocalypticism: The Ongoing Debate', *The Apocalypse in English Renaissance Thought and Literature*, edited by C. A. Patrides and Joseph Wittreich, Manchester: Manchester University Press, 2–39.

MacNeice, Louis. 2016. 'Aubade', *Collected Poems*, London: Faber and Faber, 28 (1934).

Manne, Robert. 2016. 'The Mind of the Islamic State: An Ideology of Savagery', *The Monthly*, June, 26–39.

Mannheim, Karl. 1952. *Essays on the Sociology of Knowledge*, edited by Paul Kecskemeti, London: RKP.

Marwick, Arthur. 1998. *The Sixties: Cultural Revolution in Britain, France, Italy, and the United States, c.1958–c.1974*, Oxford: Oxford University Press.

Melville, Herman. 1961. *Moby Dick, or The Whale*, New York; Signet (1851).

Midgley, Mary. 1985. *Evolution as a Religion: Strange Hopes and Stranger Fears*, London and New York: Methuen.

Miéville, China. 2010. *Kraken: An Anatomy*, London: Pan.

— 2012. *London's Overthrow*, London: Westbourne Press.

— 2017. *October: The Story of the Russian Revolution*, London: Verso.

Moorcock, Michael. 1993. *The Dancers at the End of Time*, London: Millennium.

Neithammer, Lutz, in collaboration with Dirk van Laak. 1992. *Posthistoire: Has History Come to an End*, translated by Patrick Camiller, London and New York: Verso.

Nel, Philip. 2008. 'DeLillo and Modernism', *The Cambridge Companion to Don DeLillo*, edited by John N. Duvall, Cambridge: Cambridge University Press, 13–26.

Noon, Jeff. 2003. *Falling out of Cars*, London: Black Swan (2002).

Nowotny, Helga. 1994. *Time: The Modern and Postmodern Experience*, translated by Neville Plaice, Cambridge: Polity Press (1989).

Orlando, Francesco. 2006. *Obsolete Objects in the Literary Imagination: Ruins, Relics, Rarities, Rubbish, Uninhabited Places*, translated by Gabriel Pihas and Daniel Seidel, with the collaboration of Alessandra Grego, New Haven and London: Yale University Press (1994).

Osnos, Evan. 2017. 'Survival of the Richest', *The New Yorker*, 30 January, 36–45.

Overy, Richard. 2009. *The Twilight Years: The Paradox of Britain Between the Wars*, New York: Viking.

— 2013. *The Bombers and the Bombed: Allied Air War over Europe, 1940–1945*, London: Penguin.

Paik, Peter Y. 2010. *From Utopia to Apocalypse: Science Fiction and the Politics of Catastrophe*, Minneapolis and London: University of Minnesota Press.

Palmer, Christopher. 2011. 'Free Exchange and Dark Secrecy in the Capital', *Changing the Climate: Utopia, Dystopia and Catastrophe*, edited by Andrew Milner, Simon Sellars and Verity Burgmann, Melbourne: Arena Publications, 45–56.

Park, Tim. 2015. 'Dante: Hell and Back', *A Literary Tour of Italy*, Richmond, Surrey: Alma Books, 5–23.

Parrinder, Patrick. 1995. *Shadows of the Future: H. G. Wells, Science Fiction and Prophecy*, Liverpool: Liverpool University Press.

— 2002. 'The Ruined Futures of British Science Fiction', *On Modern British Fiction*, edited by Zachary Leader, Oxford: Oxford University Press, 209–233.

Parry, Richard Lloyd. 2017. *Ghosts of the Tsunami*, London: Vintage.

Perrotta, Tom. 2012. *The Leftovers*, London: Fourth Estate (2011).

Pope, Alexander. 1967. *Windsor Forest, Poems of Landscape and the Night*, edited by Charles Peake, London: Edward Arnold (1713).

Porter, Roy. 2002. *Madness: A Brief History*, Oxford: Oxford University Press.

Potts, Alex. 2013. *Experiments in Modern Realism*, New Haven and London: Yale University Press.

Pullman, Philip. 2007. *The Amber Spyglass*, London: Scholastic (2000).

Rabkin, Eric S. 1979. *Arthur C. Clarke*, Mercer Island, WA: Starmont House.

Rabkin, Eric S., Martin H. Greenberg and Joseph D. Olander, editors. 1983. *The End of the World*. Carbondale and Edwardsville: Southern Illinois University Press.

Roberts, Adam. 2006. *Science Fiction*, London and New York: Routledge.

Robinson, Kim Stanley. 1984. *The Wild Shore*, New York: Ace.

— 1986. 'Ridge Running', *The Planet on the Table*, London: Futura, 64–82 (1975/1977/1983).

— 2011. 'Remarks on Utopia in the Age of Climate Change', *Changing the Climate: Utopia, Dystopia and Catastrophe*, edited by Andrew Milner, Simon Sellars and Verity Burgmann, Melbourne: Arena Publications, 8–21.

— 2015. *Green Earth: The Science in the Capital Trilogy*, London: Harper.

Roitman, Janet. 'Crisis and Contradiction', www.politicalconcepts.org/issue/crisis, published winter 2012.

Rose, Mark. 1981. *Alien Encounters: Anatomy of Science Fiction*, Cambridge, MA: Harvard University Press.

Rosen, Elizabeth. 2008. *Apocalyptic Transformation: Apocalypse and the Postmodern Imagination*, Lanham, MD: Lexington Books.

Rossi, Umberto. 1994. 'Images from the Disaster Area: An Apocalyptic Reading of Urban Landscapes in Ballard's *The Drowned World* and *Hello America*', *Science Fiction Studies*, vol. 62, no. 21, part 1, 81–97.

Rozario, Kevin. 2007. *The Culture of Calamity: Disaster and the Making of Modern America*, Chicago and London: University of Chicago Press.

Runciman, David. 2018. *How Democracy Ends*, London: Profile Books.

Sage, Lorna. 1988. 'Lessing and Atopia', *Doris Lessing: The Alchemy of Survival*, edited by Carey Kaplan and Ellen Cronan Rose, Athens, Ohio: Ohio University Press, 159–168.

Saramago, José. 2008. *Death at Intervals*, translated by Margaret Jull Costa, London: Harvill Secker (2005).

Sayeau, Michael. 2010. 'Waiting', *Restless Cities*, edited by Matthew Beaumont and Gregory Dart, London and New York: Verso.

Scarry, Elaine. 1999. *Dreaming by the Book*, New York: Farrar, Straus, Giroux.

Scheffler, Samuel H. 2013. *Death and the Afterlife*, Oxford: Oxford University Press.
Scheidel, Walter. 2017. *The Great Leveller: Violence and the History of Inequality from the Stone Age to the 21*st *Century*, New York Princeton University Press.
Schell, Jonathan. 1982. *The Fate of the Earth*, London: Picador.
Schmidt, Arno. 1995. *Nobodaddy's Children*, translated by John E. Woods, Champaign and London: Dalkey Archive Press (1963).
Schulman, Audrey. 2018. *Theory of Bastards*, New York: Europa Editions.
Scott, James C. 1998. *Seeing Like a State: How Certain Schemes to Improve the Human Condition Have Failed*, New Haven and London: Yale University Press.
Sebald, W. G. 1999. *The Rings of Saturn*, translated by Michael Hulse, London: Harvill Press (1995).
— 2005a. 'Between History and Natural History: On the Literary Description of Total Destruction', *Campo Santo*, edited by Sven Meyer and translated by Anthea Bell, London: Hamish Hamilton, 68–101.
— 2005b. 'Constructs of Mourning: Gunter Grass and Wolfgang Hildesheimer', *Campo Santo*, edited by Sven Meyer and translated by Anthea Bell, London: Hamish Hamilton, 102–129 (1983).
Shapin, Steven. 1994. *A Social History of Truth: Civility and Science in Seventeenth-Century England*, Chicago and London: University of Chicago Press.
Shriver, Lionel. 2016. *The Mandibles: A Family, 2029–2047*, London: The Borough Press.
Shute, Nevil. 1957. *On the Beach*, London: Heinemann.
Sinclair, Iain. 2010. 'Sickening', *Restless Cities*, edited by Matthew Beaumont and Gregory Dart, London and New York: Verso, 257–276.
Slusser, George E. 1987. 'Metamorphoses of the Dragon', *Aliens: The Anthropology of Science Fiction*, edited by George E. Slusser and Eric S. Rabkin, Carbondale and Edwardsville: Southern Illinois University Press, 43–66.
Snyder, Timothy. 2011. *Bloodlands: Europe between Hitler and Stalin*, London: Vintage.
Sontag, Susan. 1976. 'The Imagination of Disaster', *Science Fiction: A Collection of Critical Essays*, edited by Mark Rose, Englewood Cliffs, NJ: Prentice-Hall, 116–131 (1966).
Sophocles. 1972. *Sophocles: Oedipus the King*, translated and adapted by Anthony Burgess, with comments by Anthony Burgess, Michael Langham and Stanley Silverman, Minneapolis: University of Minnesota Press (c.429–420 BCE).
Spinrad, Norman. 1990. 'The Strange Case of J. G. Ballard', *Science Fiction in the Real World*, Carbondale and Edwardsville: Southern Illinois University Press, 182–197.
Stableford, Brian. 1983. 'Man-Made Catastrophes', *The End of the World*, edited by Eric S. Rabkin, Martin H. Greenberg and Joseph D. Olander, Carbondale and Edwardsville: Southern Illinois University Press, 97–138.

Stewart, George R. 1972. *Earth Abides*, Greenwich, CT: Fawcett (1949).
Tate, Andrew. 2017. *Apocalyptic Fiction*, London: Bloomsbury.
Taylor, A. J. P. 1967. 'Up from Utopia: How Two Generations Survived Their Wars', *Europe: Grandeur and Decline*, London: Penguin, 328–336.
Trotter, David. 2010. 'Phoning', *Restless Cities*, edited by Matthew Beaumont and Gregory Dart, London and New York: Verso, 193–211.
Tuveson, Ernest L. 1984. 'The Millenarian Structure of *The Communist Manifesto*', *The Apocalypse in English Renaissance Thought and Literature*, edited by C. A. Patrides and Joseph Wittreich, Manchester: Manchester University Press, 323–341.
VanderMeer, Jeff. 2014a. *Annihilation*, London: Fourth Estate.
— 2014b. *Authority*, London: Fourth Estate.
— 2014c. *Acceptance*, London: Fourth Estate.
— 2019. *Dead Astronauts*, London: Fourth Estate.
Vaughan, Adam. 2015. 'Urban Wildlife: When Animals Go Wild in the City', https://www.theguardian.com/environment/2015/mar/08/urban-wildlife-animals-in-city (published 8 March).
Vergo, Peter. 1977. *The Blue Rider*, Oxford: Phaidon.
von Kleist, Heinrich. 1974. 'The Earthquake in Chile', translated by Nigel Reeves, *The Penguin Book of German Short Stories*, edited by F. J. Lamport, Harmondsworth: Penguin, 43–57 (1807).
Walker, Jeanne Murray. 1988. 'Memory and Culture within the Individual: The Breakdown of Social Exchange in *The Memoirs of a Survivor*', *Doris Lessing: The Alchemy of Survival*, edited by Carey Kaplan and Ellen Cronan Rose, Athens, Ohio: Ohio University Press, 93–114.
Walker, J. Samuel. 1996. 'History, Collective Memory, and the Decision to use the Bomb', *Hiroshima in History and Memory*, edited by Michael J. Hogan, Cambridge: Cambridge University Press, 187–199.
Watkins, Susan. 2010. *Doris Lessing*, Manchester and New York: Manchester University Press.
Watson, Ian. 1992. 'Le Guin's *Lathe of Heaven* and the Role of Dick: The False Reality as Mediator', *On Philip K. Dick: 40 Articles from Science-Fiction Studies*, Terre-Haute and Greencastle: SF-TH Inc., 63–72.
Watson, Peter. 2010. *The German Genius*, New York: Harper Perennial.
Waugh, Evelyn. 1941. *Put Out More Flags*, Boston: Little, Brown and Company.
Wells, H. G. 1975. *The War of the Worlds*, London: Pan (1898).
— 1988. *The World Set Free*, London: Hogarth Press (1914).
Williams, Raymond. 1985. *The Country and the City*, London: Hogarth Press.
Wittreich, Joseph. 1984. '"Image of that Horror": The Apocalypse in *King Lear*', *The Apocalypse in English Renaissance Thought and Literature*, edited by C. A. Patrides and Joseph Wittreich, Manchester: Manchester University Press, 175–206.
Wolfe, Gary K. 1983. 'The Remaking of Zero: Beginning at the End', *The End of the World*, edited by Eric S. Rabkin, Martin H. Greenberg and Joseph D. Olander, Carbondale and Edwardsville, Southern Illinois University Press, 1–19.

Wordsworth, William. 1979. *The Prelude 1799, 1805, 1850*, edited by Jonathan Wordsworth, M. H. Abrams and Stephen Gill, New York and London: Norton.
Wyndham, John. 1955. *The Kraken Wakes*, Harmondsworth: Penguin (1953).
— 2014. *The Day of the Triffids*, London: Penguin Essentials (1951).
Zamora, Lois Parkinson. 1982. 'The Myth of Apocalypse and the American Literary Imagination', *The Apocalyptic Vision in America: Interdisciplinary Essays on Myth and Culture*, edited and introduced by Lois Parkinson Zamora, Bowling Green, Ohio: Bowling Green University Popular Press, 97–138.

Index

Page references in bold indicate the main discussion of a novel

1960s 58, 78, 119–120, 139, 157–158, 164, 166, 172, 174–175, 202
1970s 119, 121, 158, 174, 182, 204

Abrams, M. H. 61–63
Adam 17, 40, 138, 139, 142, 151n27
Adam and Eve 170–171, 87–88, 166, 213
adventure stories 286–287
The Aeneid 15n21
Aldiss, Brian
   in Burma and Sumatra 121–122
   Barefoot in the Head **158–165**
   Greybeard 11, 78, 89, 106, 116
   other works 78, 122, 158
Alexievich, Svetlana 240n1
allusion
   in Aldiss 162–163
   in Ballard 131–133, 135n8, 139n11
   see also Shakespeare
Amis, Martin 13, 33
Anderson, Perry 52
Andreas-Salomé, Lou 228
Anti-Christ 28, 34, 48, 49, 64, 234, 278
apocalypse

definition of 2, 295
fundamentalist 4, 6–7
habituation to 3, 6, 11, 203–206, 224–225, 230, 239–240, 268
hegemony of 20, 74, 203, 209–210, 240, 268, 292–293, 312
as release 13, 30, 38, 128, 131, 169, 172, 179, 219, 225–226
secularized 4–5, 7, 17–18
traditional 2–3, 4, 11, 15–18, 34, 61, 64, 69, 140, 158, 268
Apocalypse Now 10n13
Ariès, Philippe 245n8
Asperger's syndrome 273
Atwood, Margaret 30, 31–32
   Oryx and Crake 38, 43, 106, 116, 247, 314n21
Auden, W. H. 175
Augustine 7

Ballard, J. G. 20, 32, 78, 129, 182n12, 267n3
   in China 121–122
   short stories 13–14, 129, 133
   The Crystal World **143–154**
   The Drought **129–134**
   The Drowned World 30, **134–142**

337

'The Illuminated Man' 143n14, 148n25
The Wind from Nowhere 83–84, 99n17, 130, 119n1
Balmer, Edwin 220, 223
Balzac, Honoré 217
Banks, Iain M. 31, 47–48, 114n27, 205, 207
Barthes, Roland 183
Baudelaire, Charles 267
Beal, Tim 258
Bear, Greg 284
the Beatles 230, 237
Bester, Alfred 124
birth 42–44, 60n1, 106
   in Burgess 227–229
   in Perrotta 47, 249–251, 254–255
   in Robinson 323
   in VanderMeer 301, 304–305, 310–311
Blake, William 7, 60–61, 62, 125n8
Blondie 257
Bolaño, Roberto 269
Böll, Heinrich 210
Bowie, David 165
Burgess, Anthony
   The End of the World News **219–229**
   Puma 220–221
Burroughs, Edgar Rice 231
the Buzzcocks 257
Byatt, A. S. 5, 204
Byron, George Gordon Lord 60, 125n8, 135n9

Callinicos, Alex 263
canonical texts 23
Carlyle, Thomas 61
carnival 132, 136, 139–141, 144, 319
Carrière, Jean-Claude 15n21, 243
Carter, Angela 177
   in Japan 122
   Heroes and Villains **165–172**
   other works 169, 170
catastrophe 34, 128, 242
   image of 35–40, 205–206
   qualities of
   in Ballard 130, 137–138
   in Coupland 261–264
   in Kavan 175–176
   in Lessing 182
      Memoirs 186–189
      Planet 8 189–190
   in Miéville 285–286
   in Perotta 244–246
   in Robinson 314–315, 317–320
   in Shute 102–103
   in VanderMeer 300
   in Wells 66–69
   in Wyndham 97–98
Catch-22 217
Celan, Paul 77
Cherry-Garrard, Apsley 198
children, abuse of 298, 302–304
   anxieties about 42, 104, 116–117, 188, 322
   see also birth
Christopher, John, *The Death of Grass* 35, 41, 84, 101n18, 117–118
Churchill, Winston S. 231
city 28, 46, 75, 98–99, 135, 265–269
   see also country and city
Clapton, Eric 164
Clarke, Arthur C.
   Childhood's End **107–116**
   2001 105n21
Clarke, I. F. 80n33
climate change 11–12, 29, 81 251, 293, 295, 296, 300
Cohn, Norman 15n20, 64n9
Coleridge, S. T., *The Rime of the Ancient Mariner* 130n6, 132
colonialism 49, 73, 113, 115, 123, 146, 193–194
   see also post-imperial subjects
Conrad, Joseph, *Heart of Darkness* 10n13, 63–65, 125n8, 146–148

INDEX

the contemporary, definition of 3
Cooper, James Fenimore 215, 217
country and city 20, 24, 38, 80–82, 117, 266–267
    in Coupland 241
    in Kavan 178
    in Miéville 284
    in Wyndham 99–100, 103
    see also nature
Corra, Bruno, *Sam Dunn is Dead* 77
Coupland, Douglas
    Generation A 204–205
    Girlfriend in a Coma, 27, 242–243, **255–264**
Covid-19 2, 204, 205, 318
crisis 1–12, 28, 42, 131, 176, 186, 203, 225, 270, 286, 296–297, 311, 313
Cunningham, Valentine 242

Dahl, Roald 308
Daniel, the Book of 16
Davis, Mike 281
death 34, 40–48, 295
    in Ballard 134, 142, 150
    in Burgess 225n14, 227
    in Carter 170–172
    in Coupland 27, 205, 259–261
    in DeLillo 28, 278–280
    in Kavan 178–179
    in Le Guin 235, 238
    in Lessing 189–190, 202
    Planet 8 198–199
    in Miéville 289–290
    in Perrotta 245–246, 252–254
    in Shute 104–106
    in Stewart 95–96
    in VanderMeer 298–299, 310–311
    in Wells 68, 74–75
    in Wyndham 100–101
The Decameron 240n1
deities *see* the sacred
de la Motte Fouqué, Friedrich 212, 216

DeLillo, Don
    Cosmopolis 32, **270–281**
    End Zone 204
    Falling Man 12, 244
    Underworld 273
    White Noise 246, 247
    Zero K 31, 271, 275
d'Eramo, Marco 281
Diamond, Jared 52n40
Dick, Philip K. 124, 245
Dickens, Charles 267
    A Tale of Two Cities 10, 60, 265, 276n14
Disch, Thomas M., *The Genocides* 87n7, 165n10
Dix, Otto 76
A Doll's House 249
doom 8, 28, 102, 210, 295–296
Dracula 63–65
Draine, Betsy 183, 189n22
Dr Jekyll and Mr Hyde 63–64

Eden 135–136, 138, 184n14, 285, 310, 311
Egan, Greg 144n15, 223
Eliot, George 61n3, 254
Eliot, T. S. 79, 184n14
    The Waste Land 29, 76, 283n21
Ellis, Brett Easton 269
Ensor, James 163
everyday life 36, 44, 47, 62–63, 206–207, 210, 239–264
    in Le Guin 232n19, 234
    in Miéville 287–289
    in Shute 102–104
    in Stewart 94
    in Wells 67–75
    in Wyndham 98
    see also the local
evolution 108–110, 297

Falstaff 211
fire and flood, imagery of 60–61, 68–69, 100, 292n26
First World War 76–77, 194
Frankenstein 63–65, 305

Freud, Sigmund 220, 222, 224–225, 228
Friedländer, Saul 63–65
Fukuyama, Francis 51–52
Funkenstein, Amos 15
Furet, François 9

Gasiorek, Andrzej 148
Goethe, Johann Wolfgang von 212n3, 217
Golding, William *Lord of the Flies* 21, 140n13, 188
Goncharova, Natalya 77
the gothic 36, 63, 165, 288
Grass, Günter 210, 218
grief 190, 198, 243, 245

Hawthorne, Nathaniel 310n15
Heidegger, Martin 263
Heinlein, Robert A. 162
Heller, Agnes 239, 242, 264
history 9, 12–14, 16, 35, 96, 246
   in Schmidt 216–219
Hobsbawm, Eric 314
the Holocaust 22, 28, 33, 34n32, 77, 110–111, 219
Hopkins, Gerard Manley 221
Hughes, Ted 308
The Hunger Games 67
Husserl, Edmund 245
Huxley, Aldous 144

invasion 8, 11, 18, 27, 30, 36, 66, 99, 107, 143, 187, 235
Invasion of the Body-Snatchers 66
Isherwood, Christopher 90
Ishi 89–90

Jacobs, Jane 268
Jacobson, Howard 33, 180n8
James, P. D., *The Children of Men* 11, 43, 116, 80n32
Jameson, Fredric 78, 258
Jones, Colin 9
Jones, Ernest 222

Joyce, James 31, 33, 78, 79, 91n9, 205, 265, 272
Jung, C. G. 137–138
Jünger, Ernst 32n31, 72

Katanga 147
Kavan, Anna, *Ice* 32, 173–174, **175–181**
Kermode, Frank 13, 15, 16, 34, 67–68
Ketterer, David 19
Klein, Carole 185n15
von Kleist, Heinrich 59–60
Koerner, Joseph L. 5n4
Koselleck, Reinhart 9n11
Kubin, Alfred 77

language, qualities of 13, 125–126
   in Aldiss 160, 162–164
   in Ballard 131–132, 146–148, 150–154
   in Burgess 221, 223, 228
   in DeLillo 276–277
   in Lessing 174, 182
     Memoirs 186
     Planet 8 195–197
   in Miéville 289
   in Schmidt 215–216
   in Shute 105
   see also allusion; proper names
Lawrence, D. H. 7, 59, 181
Lear 191
Le Guin, Ursula K.
   on Lessing 191n23, 195n27
   The Lathe of Heaven 207, **229–238**
Leithem, Jonathan 33
Lessing, Doris
   in Africa 122
   The Diaries of Jane Somers 182
   The Four-Gated City 117
   The Making of the Representative for Planet 8 173–175, **189–199**
   The Memoirs of a Survivor **181–189**
   Shikasta, 193

The Sirian Experiments 193, 198
The Summer Before the Dark 182, 186
Lewis, C. S. 149
Lincoln, Abraham 319
the local
  in Burgess 225
  in Robinson 317–318
  in Schmidt 211, 217
  in Stewart 86
  in Wells 67–71
  see also everyday life
Lundberg, Christian 6n7

Maalouf, Amin 11
McCarthy, Cormac
  Blood Meridian 31, 49
  The Road 10, 29, 37, 106, 156, 244
McGinn, Bernard 15
MacNeice, Louis 83
Mann, Thomas 181
Mannheim, Karl 202
Marc, Franz 77
Martin, John 11n15, 60
Marwick, Arthur 157n1, 174n1
Marx, Karl 61
Medea 191
Meidner, Ludwig 76
Metropolis 29
Midgley, Mary 110
Miéville, China
  Bas-Lag trilogy 9, 205, 269, 284, 287
  The City and the City 282, 284
  Kraken **281–293**
  London's Overthrow 289n25
  October 9
  Un Lun Dun 285
millenarian thinking 7, 8, 61
Miller, Walter M. 223
Moby Dick 37, 59, 63–65, 283
modernism and anti-modernism 57–59, 76–78
monsters 16, 35–34, 63–67, 269–270, 283n22, 302

Moorcock, Michael 123n6
Moretti, Franco 267n4
Murdoch, Iris 242

Nabokov, Vladimir 132
names *see* proper names
narrative form 206, 173
  in Ballard 136, 155
  in Burgess 220–222
  in Clarke 113–115
  in Kavan 179–180
  in Lessing
    Memoirs 183–189
    Planet 8 192
  in Stewart 86–89, 91
  in VanderMeer 299–311
  in Wells 69–73
nature 20, 80–82
  in Ballard 127–128, 134–135, 143–145
  in Carter 169–170
  in Clarke 112–113
  in DeLillo 268, 279
  in Le Guin 235
  in Miéville 267
  in Robinson 20, 82, 313, 317, 321
  in Schulman 20, 82
  in Stewart 92–93
  in VanderMeer 300, 307
  in Wells 73
  in Wyndham 96–100
  see also country and city
New Jerusalem 2, 4, 34, 111, 138, 144, 151, 158, 163, 164, 199, 202, 209, 295
'New Wave' science fiction 123–124, 164
New Worlds magazine 123, 160
Nietzsche, Friedrich 64
Noon, Jeff *Falling Out of Cars* 31, 158, 164, 205
Nooteboom, Cees 298
Nowotny, Helga 31
nuclear war 85, 102–103, 212, 219, 229, 272–273, 296n1

O'Brien, Flann 298
Oedipus 228–229
Orlando, Francesco 124, 127n1, 150n26, 243n7
Orwell, George 79, 80n32, 230
Overy, Richard 14, 79n30

Paik, Peter Y. 43, 50–53, 206
Park, Tim 6
Parrinder, Patrick 79–81, 169n12
Parry, Richard Lloyd 12, 140n12
Pater, Walter 153
Perrotta, Tom, *The Leftovers* **242–255**
The Picture of Dorian Gray 63
Poe, Edgar Allan 178, 213
post-histoire 32
post-imperial subjects 25–26, 121–123, 126
Pound, Ezra 315
power 48–53
  in Clarke 107–108
  in DeLillo 272–274
  in Le Guin 235, 237
  in Miéville 284
  in Stewart 89
  in VanderMeer 207, 302
proper names
  in Ballard 147
  in Carter 172
  in Kavan 176
  in Le Guin 230
  in Lessing 196
prophets 17, 49, 159–160
Pullman, Philip 287
Pynchon, Thomas 66, 161, 265

Rabkin, Eric S. 5, 21
race 89–90, 92, 95, 234
Rapture, the 7, 241, 244, 246
realism 5, 32, 59, 221, 239, 246, 250, 254, 312
Revelation of St John 11–12
  see also apocalypse: traditional
revolution 9, 51–52, 61, 157, 220
Roberts, Adam 73

Robinson Crusoe 214
Robinson, Kim Stanley 19, 30, 87n6, 82
  Green Earth 19, 20, 82, **311–324**
  The Ministry for the Future 316n25
  New York 2140 273n28
  The Wild Shore 87n6
Rose, Mark 140
Rousseau, Henri 126, 169n12
ruins, 99n17, 243
Runciman, David 206
Russell, Conrad 9

the sacred 17–18, 39
  in Ballard 137–138
  in Clarke 114–115
  in Coupland 241, 262–263
  in Le Guin 238
  in Lessing
    Planet 8 191
  in Miéville 282–283
  in Perrotta 241, 244–245
  in Stewart 87, 89
  in Wells 69
  see also Eden; transcendence
Sandler, Adam 244
Saramago, José 189
Satie, Erik 274
Saunders, George 298
Scarry, Elaine 290
Scheffler, Samuel H. 106
Schell, Jonathan 296n1
Schmidt, Arno
  'the good German' 218–219
  Nobodaddy's Children **211–219**
Schulman, Audrey, *Theory of Bastards* 20, 47, 82
science and scientists 58, 79–82, 205, 209
  in Ballard 138
  in Clarke 111, 114–116
  in Le Guin 231–235, 238
  in Robinson 19, 79–82, 297, 315–317
  in VanderMeer 301–305

INDEX

science fiction 5, 18–23, 58–59, 63, 79–82, 204, 209, 220, 286
   Ballard and 123–124, 129, 133
   Burgess and 221, 223
   Le Guin and 230–231, 236–237
   Wells and 68
Scott, James C. 79
Scott, Robert Falcon 194, 199
Sebald, W. G. 22, 128, 218
Second World War 22, 57, 83–85, 101n19, 210, 212, 214, 217–218, 220
Shakespeare, William
   allusions to 132, 163, 168, 213, 254, 324
   see also Falstaff; Lear
Shelley, P. B. 60
Shriver, Lionel 11n15, 19
Shute, Nevil, *On the Beach* **102–106**
Sinclair, Iain 11
Snyder, Timothy 14
Spengler, Oswald 270n1
Spinrad, Norman 123n7, 162
Stableford, Brian 21
Stewart, George R., *Earth Abides* 30, **86–96**
subjectivity, qualities of
   in Aldiss 161–162, 121
   in Ballard 132–134, 148–150
   in Carter 167–169, 171–172
   in Coupland 255–259, 263
   in DeLillo 270–276
   in Kavan 176–181
   in Le Guin 229, 232–235, 237
   in Lessing
      Memoirs 186
      Planet 8 195
   in Schmidt 212–216
   in Shute 104–105
   in VanderMeer 296, 301–304, 308–310
   in Wells 70, 72
the sublime 18, 20, 27
suburbs 241, 255–256, 261
Sufism 175, 192, 194
superheroes 50–53, 287n24

Tanguy, Yves 126
Tate, Andrew 10, 67
Taylor, A. J. P. 84
technology 38–39, 97, 303–305
temporality 4, 29–34
   in Aldiss 162
   in Ballard 132, 145
   in DeLillo 277–281
   in Le Guin 231–232
   in Lessing 186
   in Stewart 92
   in VanderMeer 299–300
Tennyson, Alfred Lord 168
Tess of the D'Urbervilles 254
A Thief in the Night 246
Todorov, Tzvetan 177
transcendence 44–45, 53, 67, 202
   in Clarke 107–109
   in Ballard 17
   in Lessing 184
      Memoirs 189
      Planet 8 198
Trotsky, Leon 220, 222, 224, 228
truth 205–206, 292
Tunnick, Spencer 280n16

Urquhart, Thomas 221
the utopian
   in Clarke 108
   in Robinson 317–319

VanderMeer, Jeff
   Borne 270n5
   Dead Astronauts 4, 29, 40, **298–311**
   Southern Reach trilogy 144n15, 298n3, 306n11
Van Vogt, A. E. 162
Vonnegut, Kurt 130n5

Wagar, W. Warren 21
Wallace, Edgar 147
Watkins, Susan 122, 182, 189, 190n21, 193n26
Waugh, Evelyn 83
Wells, H. G.

'The Door in the Wall' 151n27, 184n14
'The Star' 220, 223
The War of the Worlds 18, 24, **65–75**
The World Set Free 41n34, 75n22, 113n26
West, Nathanael 96n14, 72
White, Patrick 166
Wieland, Christoph Martin 217
Williams, Raymond 29
Wilson, Edward 198
Wolfe, Gary K. 15, 21, 37n33, 88
Wordsworth, William 62, 264
Wylie, Philip 220, 223
Wyndham, John
   The Day of the Triffids **96–101**
   The Kraken Wakes 71n19, 81

Zamyatin, Yevgeny 79
Zola, Emile 22, 265n1